About the Editor

Nicolás Kanellos is founding publisher of the noted Hispanic literary journal *The Americas Review* (formerly *Revista Chicano-Riqueña*) and of the nation's oldest and most esteemed Hispanic publishing house, Arte Público Press. He has been professor of Hispanic literature at the University of Houston since 1980. In 1994 Dr. Kanellos was appointed by President Clinton to the council for the National Endowment for the Humanities (NEH).

Kanellos's four-volume reference book *Handbook of Hispanic Cultures in the United States* has received two awards, the American Library Association Denali Press Award for best reference work and outstanding reference work of 1994 by *Choice*. His work *The Hispanic-American Almanac* won a Reference and Adult Services Division (RASD) Award for Outstanding Reference Source of the Year from the American Library Association in 1993. Dr. Kanellos is also the director of a major national research project, Recovering the Hispanic Literary Heritage of the United States, a ten-year program to identify, preserve, study, and make accessible tens of thousands of literary documents from the colonial period to 1960.

Dr. Kanellos has been honored with numerous awards for his publishing achievements, including the 1996 Annual Hispanic Publication Award, the 1995 Annual PREMIO Award, and the 1995 Annual Achievement in Publishing Award from the National Hispanic Academy of Media Arts and Sciences.

Also from Visible Ink Press:

Latinas! Women of Achievement

"When I was growing up female and Puerto Rican in New York City, I would have thought any dream or ambition possible in my future had I been able to read about the talented Latinas in this outstanding collection of biographies." —from the foreword by writer and illustrator Nicholasa Mohr

Celebrating the accomplishments of 70 prominent Hispanic women in the Unites States, this collection of biographical profiles represents all fields of endeavor—from astronaut Ellen Ochoa to zoologist Maxine Baca Zinn.

Diane Telgen and Jim Kamp • 7¼" x 9¼" • paperback • 405 pages• 70 photos • in print • ISBN 0-7876-0883-1

Hispanic Almanac
From Columbus to Corporate America

"Documents Hispanic achievements over the ages, from politics to business to art." —*Evansville Courier*

Take an intriguing look at the people, places, and events that shape Hispanic America. Includes hundreds of profiles of entertainers, artists, athletes, and other major figures, from Ponce de León to Henry Cisneros, plus thoughtful discussion of current issues and topics.

Nicolás Kanellos • 7¼" x 9¼" • paperback • 644 pages • 200 photos and line drawings • in print • 0-7876-0030-X

The
Hispanic Literary Companion

The
Hispanic Literary Companion

edited by Nicolás Kanellos

VISIBLE
INK

DETROIT • NEW YORK • TORONTO • LONDON

The Hispanic Literary Companion

edited by Nicolás Kanellos

Copyright © 1997 Visible Ink Press™

Visible Ink Press is a trademark of Gale Research

Most Visible Ink Press™ books are available at special quantity discounts when purchased in bulk by corporations, organizations, or groups. Customized printings, special imprints, messages, and excerpts can be produced to meet your needs. For more information, contact Special Markets Manager, Gale Research Inc., 835 Penobscot Bldg., Detroit, MI 48226. Or call 1-800-776-6265.

Art Director: Pamela A. E. Galbreath
Permissions: Diane Cooper

Library of Congress Cataloging-in-Publication Data

The Hispanic literary companion / edited by Nicolás Kanellos
    p. cm.
Includes bibliographical references and index.
ISBN 0-7876-1014-3 (alk. paper)
    1. American literature–Hispanic American authors. 2. American literature–Hispanic American authors–Bio-bibliography. 3. American literature–20th century–Bio-bibliography. 4. Hispanic Americans in literature–Bibliography. 5. Authors, American–20th century–Biography. 6. Hispanic Americans–Literary collections.

I. Kanellos, Nicolás

PS508.H57H566   1996
810.9'868–dc20
[B]

96-24810
CIP

For the great crew at Arte Público Press
and, as always, for my loving wife Cris
and my much-adored son Miguel.

Contents

Enigmatic writer of the early Chicano Movement who converted his life into the material of literature. His search for identity and his desire to re-create himself were inspiration to Chicano authors and the community.

■ Perla Is a Pig

Fiction writer who creates penetrating psychological narratives, which are based on her rise from abject poverty in Puerto Rico to the highest realms of academia in the U.S. and abroad. Noted for her lyrical, rhapsodic style and minute attention to detail.

■ Chupacabras, The Goat Sucker

Author of the prize-winning novel, *Bless Me, Ultima,* he sees his role in literature as that of the shaman: his task as a storyteller is to heal and re-establish balance and harmony.

■ Bless Me, Ultima

Although she has published only two books, which are the result of some twenty-five years of work, Cervantes's poems are so finely crafted and insightful that they are chosen to be reprinted in anthologies and textbooks more often than the works of any other Hispanic woman writer.

- ■ Pleiades from the Cables of Genocide
- ■ Refugee Ship

The leading Chicano mystery writer is also a poet and essayist, and is one of the most fully bilingual Hispanic writers in history.

- ■ Eulogy for a Brown Angel
- ■ A Mystery Novel

This Mexican-American writer has brought mystery and adventure into the framework of multicultural children's literature.

- ■ The Girl from Playa Blanca

The most important female writer to come out of the Nuyorican group of writers, she is also a performance poet whose works have deep roots in community life and popular culture. She poses eloquent and passionate queries into the themes of feminism, machismo, racism, and biculturalism.

- ■ Amor negro
- ■ Transference
- ■ Anonymous Apartheid

Part of the vanguard of Cuban American literature, he has made the transition from the literature of exile to a literature that is very much of the culture and social conditions of Cubans in the United States.

- ■ Holy Radishes!

The first Cuban American woman to achieve mainstream success as a novelist, she had been a successful journalist before she quit that life to write *Dreaming in Cuban*.

- ■ Inés in the Kitchen

way to organize students, communities, and labor unions around a cause.

■ Bernabé

The Chicana poet who has most sensitively portrayed and celebrated working-class culture. She is also one of the leading exponents of bilingual code-switching in poetry, which for her is as natural as conversation at the kitchen table.

■ was fun running 'round descalza
■ ser conforme

Through his novel of immigration, *Macho!,* he brought Chicano literature to the widest audience of the American reading public. Today he is known by English- and Spanish-reading audiences alike for his *Rain of Gold/Lluvia de oro.*

■ Death of an Assassin

One of Hispanic literature's most distinguished craftspersons of short fiction, she began her writing career when she was the literary editor of the avant-garde Chicano magazine *ChismeArte.*

■ The Moths

Cuban American writer whose novels and stories based on Hispanic life in the United States were published by some of the most respected publishing houses in the country.

■ The Guns in the Closet

Introduction

Since before the United States was even founded, Hispanics have imagined themselves through literature and have provided a record of their culture in North America. And within the United States, Hispanics have written and published their works since the early days of the Republic. From the mid-19th-century on, Hispanics have written in English as well as Spanish. The literary heritage is continuous and unbroken, expressed in two languages, and representative of the diverse ethnic and racial bases (Cuban, Mexican, Puerto Rican, Spanish, etc.; Afro-Caribbean, Native American, mestizo) that make up the Hispanic communities in the various regions of the United States.

Despite this centuries-old Hispanic literary legacy, the flood of novels, memoirs, poems, short stories, and essays that have appeared in the English language during the last two decades came as a surprise to many in academia and the world of publishing: "Are not Hispanics a largely illiterate population?", they mused. "Are they not too entrapped by the culture of poverty and/or the demands of blue-collar labor to devote themselves to artistic higher pursuits and values? If they do have literature, is it not to be found in their popular songs and superstitions, their folklore? And wouldn't it be articulated only in Spanish or some bastardized Spanglish?" The answer is: Hispanic tradition in the United States has never been an illiterate one; it has never been bereft of writers, readers, newspapers, publishing houses, literary critics, intellectuals, or any other mediators of culture—-high and low. The answer is also: Yes, the working-class population predominates among Hispanics, and, proudly we state that working-class people have both oral and written traditions in the United States. And even when the children of the Hispanic working class obtain an advanced education and "refinement," for the most part, they continue to see themselves as products of the working class and they continue to develop a literature that is true to their roots.

This is the United States of America, and Hispanics have proven themselves to be among the most ardent believers in the promises of freedom and democracy. They believe in the right of children of all social classes to an education and, consequently, the right of all classes to be respected culturally and linguistically—and they have always believed in their right to publish their ideas and their art. The democratic vision has called for the creation of a democratic literature; such is the Hispanic literary legacy and practice in the United States.

In a more stratified society, such as that of Spain, the development of literature can be seen following two parallel paths, which, on occasion, intersect and nourish each other: the culto (cultured or lettered) and the popular (folk literature, popular culture). Some of the most important works in the history of Spanish and Spanish American literature gained their vigor and dynamism by crossing the class boundaries that are inherent to the division between high and low culture: Don Quijote, the picaresque novels, the plays of Lope de Vega, the ballads of Federico García Lorca, the novels of the Mexican Revolution, and the poems of Gabriela Mistral, Nicolás Guillén, and Palés Matos.

The literature in English, Spanish, and combinations of both languages that emerged from the Chicano and Puerto Rican civil rights struggles in the 1960s and 1970s was unanimously oriented toward the empowerment of the working class, and was expressed through a vernacular bilingualism derived from the popular culture of farm workers, factory workers, and service employees. Writers emerged whose sole cause was to provide spiritual and cultural motivation for the sociopolitical movement. They were largely unaware of written antecedents; their art was learned through example from community bards, folklore, and popular culture. The role of the poet in society was then regarded as high shaman, synthesizer of tradition, and spirituality. Their craft was to be found in the performance, in the ability to communicate and inspire through recitation and dramatization of the written word. The writers who went on to achieve a college education and conscientiously continue a written tradition also identified with this oral art and respected its place in community life—they saw themselves as part of that working-class community and it was their desire that their works return to the community. Writers who benefitted from advanced schooling but who nevertheless sought to perpetuate through their works the language of everyday life, the values of the Hispanic family, and the struggle for social justice include Tomás Rivera, Angela de Hoyos, Lucha Corpi, Rudolfo Anaya, Evangelina Vigil-Piñón, and Floyd Salas. There were the others who did not have access to advanced education, but who were nevertheless sophisticated analysts and writers, highly experimental innovators of language, style, and perspective, who fought for the dignity of the urban poor and the farm workers, and even for the "underclass" and the extremely marginalized. These writers were Victor Hernández Cruz, Tato Laviera, Jose Yglesias, Miguel Piñero, Nicholasa Mohr, Ricardo Sánchez, Sandra María Esteves, Piri Thomas, Ofelia Dumas Lachtman, and Luis Omar Salinas. Then there were the satirists—middle-class and educated, but identifying nevertheless with the working class—who salvaged the traditional humor, vernacular speech, and customs of a people in cultural transition so that they could ask the deep questions about life and death, about the community and the individual: Oscar Zeta Acosta, Rolando Hinojosa, Alba Ambert, Lionel García, Max Martínez, and Roberto Fernández.

Due largely to the struggles and achievements of the Civil Rights Movement and the writers who broke into print as its literary co-conspirators, more and more Latinos had access to college and the means of producing a published literature in English. In the 1970s, ethnic studies, bilingual education, and women's studies programs reformed the structure of academia and created a place for the study of Hispanic literature of the United States. For the first time, Hispanic and non-Hispanic students could study a formally acknowledged body of literature and knowledge that was seen as part of American culture. In this newly democratized university, the Hispanic student could envision her- or himself as a writer, an artistic interpreter of her or his people. By the beginning of the 1980s, a new generation of college-educated writers made itself known, and some even had masters degrees in creative writing in hand. This contingency of writers, whose sensibilities had been distilled in academia, also included the children of Cuban refugees, such as Carolina Hospital and Gustavo Pérez-Firmat, and within another decade was joined by the children of the Central American refugees. They inscribed themselves on the published page precisely at the time when literary publishing was also opening up to women as writers and intellectuals. It was again surprising that Hispanic culture would also provide so many free and aggressive female voices capable of holding their own in the national culture wars: Judith Ortiz Cofer, Pat Mora, Lorna Dee Cervantes, Graciela Limón, and many others.

But these were unmeltable ethnics: they were still Hispanics, their material was still their community. Miraculously, many of them still could write in either English or Spanish, although most favored the language of their formal education (English). It was this generation, very much aware of the business of writing, of the industry's networks, and of the norms of language, metaphor, and craft protected by the academy, that was able to break into commercial and intellectual circles and cause a stir. These writers included Sandra Cisneros, Gary Soto, Cristina García, Judith Ortiz Cofer, Oscar Hijuelos, Virgil Suárez, Helena María Viramontes—all products of creative writing programs, who were able to lead Latinos in the largest proportion ever onto the canonical pages of The New York

Times Book Review and into the Norton anthologies of American literature. They inscribed forever the Hispanic communities presence on the hallowed lists of Pulitzer Prizes, National Endowment for the Arts, and the MacArthur Fellowships. While the younger group continued to gain respect and broaden the canon, the earlier generation, nevertheless, continued to make inroads into popular culture and to re-image Hispanics as part of the daily life of the national culture: Movies were made of Tomás Rivera's and Luis Valdez's works; Victor Villaseñor proved that masses of working-class Hispanics would buy 500-page tomes in English and Spanish; Hispanics of all ages filled theaters to see the works of Dolores Prida performed in Spanish; and working-class cultural emblems, such as *pachucos* (social rebels and bandits like Gregorio Cortez and the Cisco Kid) and legends of wailing women (La Llorona) still had the power to reach deep into the Hispanic psyche.

So here, then, is a compendium of the polished and the popular, of the passionate and the pensive, the challenging and the celebratory produced over the last two decades by the largest consort of Hispanic creators of literature in the English language. While the authors may differ in background and ethnicity, you will see how remarkably consistent they are about language and culture and the importance of literature in creating and preserving identity and for making our national ideals real for all of the peoples of the United States.

Acknowledgements

Many, many thanks to my wonderful editor Becky Nelson and to my friend Chris Nasso, both at Gale Research.

—*Nicolás Kanellos*
Houston, Texas, July 1996

Credits

The editors wish to thank the holders of the literary excerpts and photographs in this column and the permissions managers of the many publishing companies and photograph sources assisting us in securing reprint rights. We are also grateful to the staffs of the Detroit Public Library, the Library of Congress, the University of Detroit, Wayne State University, and the University of Michigan libraries for making their resources available to us. Following is a list of the copyright holders who have granted us permission to reprint material in this volume. Every effort has been made to trace copyright but if omissions have been made, please let us know.

Copyright excerpts in The Hispanic Literary Companion were reprinted from the following books:

Acosta, Oscar Zeta. From "Perla is a Pig," in *The Uncollected Works of Oscar Zeta Acosta,* edited by Ilan Stavans. Arte Público Press, 1996. Houston: Arte Público Press—University of Houston © 1996. Reprinted by permission of the publisher.

Ambert, Alba. From "Chupacabras, The Goat Sucker," in *The Eighth Continent*. Arte Público Press, 1997. Houston: Arte Público Press—University of Houston © 1997. All rights reserved. Reprinted by permission of the publisher.

Anaya, Rudolfo A. From *Bless Me, Ultima.* © 1972 by Rudolfo A. Anaya. Published by Warner Books, Inc., New York. Originally published by TQS Publications. Reprinted by permission of the author and Susan Bergholz Literary Services, New York. All rights reserved.

Salinas, Luis Omar. From *The Sadness of Days: Selected and New Poems.* Arte Público Press, 1987. Copyright © 1987 by Luis Omar Salinas. Reprinted by permission of the publisher.

Sánchez, Richardo. From *Selected Poems.* Arte Público Press, 1985. Copyright © 1985 Ricardo Sánchez. All rights reserved. Reprinted by permission of the publisher.

Suárez, Virgil. From *Little Havana Blues.* Edited by Virgil Suárez and Delia Poey. Arte Público Press, 1997. Reprinted by permission of the publisher.

Thomas, Piri. From *Stories from El Barrio.* Arte Público Press, 1997 (reprint). Reprinted by permission of the publisher.

Valdez, Luis. From "Bernabé," in *Luis Valdez—Early Works: Actos, Bernabe and Pensamiento Serpentino.* Edited by Luis Valdez and El Teatro Campesino. Arte Público Press, 1990. Copyright © 1971 by Luis Valdez for El Teatro Campesino. Reprinted by permission of the publisher.

Vigil-Piñon, Evangelina. From *Thirty an' Seen a Lot.* Arte Público Press, 1985. Copyright © 1985 by Evangelina Vigil-Piñon. All rights reserved. Reprinted by permission of the publisher.

Villaseñor, Victor. From *Walking Stars: Stories of Magic and Power.* Piñata Books, 1994. Copyright © 1994 by Victor Villaseñor. Reprinted by permission of the publisher. (Also appears on front cover)

Viramontes, Helena María. From *The Moths and Other Stories.* Arte Público Press, 1995. Copyright © 1985 by Helena María Viramontes. All rights reserved. Reprinted by permission of the publisher.

Yglesias, Jose. From *The Guns in the Closet.* Arte Público Press, 1996. Reprinted by permission of the publisher.

Copyright excerpts in The Hispanic Literary Companion were reprinted from the following periodicals:

The Americas Review, v. XVII, Spring, 1989. Copyright © 1989; v. XX, Fall-Winter, 1992. Copyright © 1992; v. XXI, Fall-Winter, 1993. Copyright © 1993 The Americas Review. All reprinted by permission of the publisher.—*Prairie Schooner,* v. 63, Fall, 1989. © 1989 by University of Nebraska Press. Reprinted from Prairie Schooner by permission of the University of Nebraska Press.

Photographs appearing in The Hispanic Literary Companion were received from the following sources:

AP/Wide World, p. 95; Archive photos, p. 335; Arte Público Press, pp. 3, 24, 45, 51, 66, 77, 84, 101, 113, 130, 140, 144, 149, 155, 168, 207, 231, 239, 247, 266, 285, 294, 310, 315, 324, 329, 360, 369, 385, 391; Jerry Bauer, p. 120; Cynthia Farah, p. 41; Pat Mora, p. 225.

Oscar Zeta Acosta

Oscar Zeta Acosta converted his life into the material of literature and in so doing became the most enigmatic writer of the early Chicano Movement. His search for identity and his desire to re-create himself were inspiration to Chicano authors and the community at the same time that his real-life activism as a lawyer furthered the cause of social justice. However, Acosta neither took himself nor his literature seriously enough; he was a picaresque character caught up in the drug and counter cultures, involvements that may help explain his mysterious disappearance during a trip to Mazatlán, Mexico, in 1974. No word has been heard from him since, even though his books have been reprinted and have gone on to become successes.

Acosta was born in El Paso, Texas, and raised in a small rural town in the San Joaquin Valley of California. He graduated from high school in Los Angeles and served four years in the Air Force. Upon discharge, he moved to San Francisco where he spent years studying law in night school while he worked as a copy boy on a San Francisco newspaper during the day. In 1966, he passed the California State Bar exam and went on to work in a legal aid clinic in Oakland. He soon became disenchanted and moved to Los Angeles, where he became a member of the Con Safos literary group, which published the magazine in which his writings first appeared. It was through Con Safos that he became one of the first writers to develop a

Chicano aesthetic in literature, and went on to establish some of the perspectives and style that later became common, especially among that first group of socially committed Chicano authors: identification with the working classes, a biting humor, an interest in promoting ethnic identity, rejection of the established order.

During this time Acosta continued his social activism and became the lead attorney in a number of landmark cases, including *Castro v. Superior Court of Los Angeles,* in which he successfully protected the right to free speech of teachers involved in the Los Angeles school walkouts, and *Carlos Montez et al v. the Superior Court of Los Angeles County,* in which Acosta argued that Spanish-surnamed individuals had been systematically excluded from serving on juries.

In 1970, Acosta published "Perla Is a Pig," which analyzes how people of Mexican ancestry discriminate against each other because of skin color and the refusal to conform. For Acosta, his own dark skin color and Native American ancestry and features had been a stigma and, like many racial minority writers of the time, he strove to create a pride in the non-white, non-European heritage. The central character in "Perla Is a Pig" is Huero (literally "white"), whose physiological difference and iconoclasm eventually lead to his banishment from the community.

Acosta's two books, *Autobiography of a Brown Buffalo* and *Revolt of the Cockroach People,* represent two parts of a fanciful autobiography of the author in which contemporary events and people are the setting for a picaresque, satirical romp of the "Brown Buffalo" alter-ego of Acosta in his tongue-in-cheek sallies to fight for the rights of Chicanos. In reality, the books represent a journey of self-discovery, where the main character seeks to establish his ethnic, cultural, and psychological identity. *The Autobiography of a Brown Buffalo* charts how this confused main character, addicted to drugs and alcohol and psychotherapy, becomes a committed Chicano activist. In *The Revolt of the Cockroach People,* the ethnic pride and activism that "Brown Buffalo" achieved at the end of the *Autobiography* becomes the basis for his involvement in the political upheavals occurring in Los Angeles during the early 1970s. Here the Chicano lawyer Buffalo Zeta Brown raises a series of challenges to the courts, the schools, and the church. Acosta takes the reader into the midst of guerrilla-movement politics in Los Angeles, describing the plotting of bombings and political demonstrations. In addition to being an engrossing adventure novel, *The Revolt of the Cockroach People* is the Chicano novel that has best and most closely captured the spirit and detail of the militant phase of the Chicano Movement.

For all of his ability and insight, and for all of his irreverence, Acosta became a model to Chicano writers who sought to balance their aesthetics with their social commitment; but he also represented that uniquely Chicano/Mexican propensity for self-deprecation and for not taking oneself too seriously.

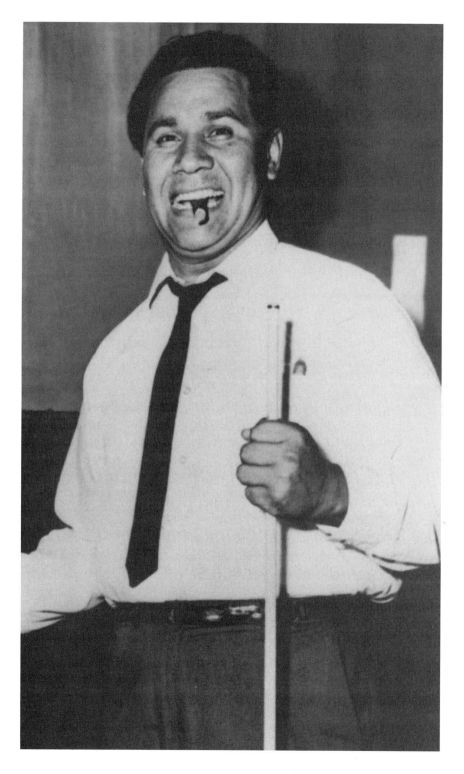

Oscar Zeta Acosta

Personal Stats

Lawyer and writer—during the early Chicano Movement. **Born:** April 8, 1935, in El Paso, Texas. **Education:** After graduating from law school, he was admitted to the California Bar in 1966. **Career:** Lawyer, legal aid clinic, Oakland, 1966–?; late 1960s–1974, became a writer and political activist.

Perla Is a Pig

"Perla is a Pig" (unpublished), Arte Público Press

Part I

He was an old man who peddled corn in the Mexican barrio and he had gone five days now without a sale because the rumor had spread that he urinated in his cornfield.

On the evening of this fifth day he slowly pushed his orange cart to the pig's pen to dispose of the freshly cut corn. Those which had become yellow, he fed to the black sow.

"It is the same, Perla," the old man whispered in his native Spanish. "Our misfortune is your joy. Or so it seems." The fat, black pig grunted as it crushed the tender corn ears. "So eat and grow fatter. We'll have you when you're ready."

He chuckled and playfully threw one of the ears at the pig. Then he rolled the cart behind the one room adobe shack and went to the water pump. He could see no one from there, for in the spring he had planted the tiny kernels of corn in circular furrows surrounding the shack, the pig's pen and his outhouse. Now it was summer and the green stalks were higher than a man's head.

He removed his eye-patch that hid a purple socket, which he rubbed as though he were scrubbing an elbow, to clean the phlegmy, white particles that caked there during the day. He washed only his face. He did not trouble to roll up his sleeves and so his cuffs were always brown and wrinkled, as were his other garments. He dried his face with his shirt tails, then with his hands still wet, he flattened his few thin strands of yellow hair.

He went into the outhouse to complete his toiletry. He laughed to himself of the new rumor as he urinated.

He took some corn and picked green squash growing alongside the plum tree next to the shack to prepare the meal for the guest he was expecting within the hour.

The corn had not yet cooked when the old man heard his guest's whistle. "I'm in here, Nico. Come on in," he responded.

Nico, the business invitee, was about half the old man's size. He wore a Levi jacket, Levi pants, and Lama boots. His brilliant black hair was immaculate. He wore a long mustachio, as did the Mexican cowboys in Texas from whom he had learned all there was to know of manhood. This same little man had also learned from his mother that no gentleman should be out in the streets without a pencil, a pad of paper, a comb and, at the very least, fifty cents on his person.

He entered and said, "Ah, here you are, eh? I thought you might be out pissing." He giggled the shrill laugh of a dirty boy.

"Excuse my bad manners, but I'm at the stove now," the old man explained. "Sit down, Nico. Take all that weight off your feet."

Nicolás hung his nose over the boiling pots. "No meat, Huero?" he asked the old man whom they called *el Huero*, because of his light skin, green eye and yellow hair.

"Sorry, but she's not ready yet."

"Ah, what luck. When my mother told me you said it was urgent, I thought, or at least I had hoped that you were ready to stick the knife in its throat."

"In her neck," the old man corrected.

"In its neck, in its throat, what does it matter? So long as we can get to it. I saw it when I came in. He's going to be beautiful, he'll bring in a lot."

"She is beautiful, Nico . . . Why don't you sit down.?"

"Can I help?"

"No, just rest yourself."

"I thought you might want me to help set the table. I don't mind, Huero. Shall I get the wine glasses?"

"No, we won't need them. I thought we might drink some goats' milk. It's nice and fresh," the old man said, smiling.

"Goats' milk? Yes, it's nice. My mother serves it every night. Says it's supposed to be good for your liver."

"I know, you've told me. That's why I thought you might like it."

The little cowboy waited a moment. "I wouldn't mind trying some of your wine though, Huero," he suggested.

"Wine? But, Nico, what would your mother say? She'd smell it, you know."

"That is of no consequence, Huero! . . . besides I can stop at Lodi's and get some sweets on the way home."

The old man turned and faced Nicolás. "Well, if you want. But don't tell the old lady. She's mad at me as it is. Like all the others, she wouldn't buy my corn today because of this new rumor. It's up to you."

"Jesus, hombre! I'm fifty-five! You think I worry about her?"

"Well, I don't know, Nico. She's what? Seventy-five?"

"I don't know. I suppose."

"I don't mind, Nico. You're the one living with her."

"So what? Come on, *viejo,* don't play games with me . . . I have to stop at Lodi's any-way. She wants some of that Mexican chocolate."

The two men ate the meal and drank the wine. They did not speak of the business for which the cowboy had come. When they finished, they sat outside and watched the orange, purple sun silently disappear somewhere behind the brown foothills surrounding their valley of San Joaquín. They sat on huge logs smoking slowly. The mosquitoes from the cornfield picked at the little cowboy. He constantly swung at them and cursed them. Huero, the older man, made no such motions. Even if one were to rest on his eyeless socket, he did not bother it.

"Well, Nico, we'd better start on the business," the old man said suddenly, throwing the cigarette at the water pump.

"Business! What business?" Nicolás asked with surprise.

"Don't come at me with foolishness, Nico. You know it well."

"If you have some, well go ahead, but I don't know what you have in mind," the little cowboy said innocently.

"Then why are you here?" Huero said impatiently. "Are you here only to eat and drink?"

"My mother only said you wanted me for dinner as a guest."

"Guest? Ah, what a guest! . . . You know, Nico, sometimes you are like a pimp."

"A pimp? A pimp! Huero, you slander me."

"Quiet yourself, I say it without malice. What I mean is, you try to hide your business, your true business, I mean."

"Business? That I am a pimp? You know, Huero, sometimes I seriously believe you're los-ing it. Maybe what they said was true . . . maybe you did lose your eye from syphilis."

"Don't start, Nico."

"Well, I don't know, Huero. How should I know? How does anyone know anything?"

"Let it alone, *viejo!*" the old man of one eye warned.

"But the little cowboy would not let it alone. "God only knows, *viejo,* but I should know. I who am your friend. Your counselor. Your business agent. Of a truth, if anyone should know, if any-one should know how you lost your eye, it should be me. But you are stubborn, you don't know who your true friends are."

"Look, Nico, we haven't time for that. This new rumor is serious. I've not sold one *elote* all week."

"But it might be important to this case," Nicolás reasoned. "Perhaps the original rumor has not died down. Perhaps it is a recurrence of the same thing."

"It is not the same thing, you jackass! I tell you this is new gossip, a new rumor. Forget the others. I tell you I've not sold all week. You know corn must be sold within a day or two lest it rot."

"Huero, you are using too many vile names. I cannot concentrate when you are rude to me."

"He's gone and started another one on me, Nico. I know it is he. And you know the children need their corn."

"Who?"

"Ay, but look at what a mosquito you are? Who? Who else but the fat Spaniard, you runt!"

"Lodi? Lodi Ulloa?"

"And he's using the same tricks. He has no morals, that *español!* To use one's children to spread evil gossip shows poor education. To gain a business advantage one should not have to lie. He is poorly educated, that one is."

"Huero, if you have something to tell me, why do you hide it? I know nothing of any rumor. I know only of the ones I helped you with in the past."

"But why do you play the part of the cat with this mouse? If indeed you do not know, then why did you ask me if I was pissing in the cornfield when you first entered?"

"Well, that is a natural thing, Huero. Surely you know that."

"You think I don't know what you're doing? You think I am such a fool?" The old man brought out another cigarette. He lit it carefully, deliberately. He inhaled evenly and waited for the words to come to him; for now the bargaining had begun. His words came firmly: "So you know nothing of this new rumor, is that it, Nico? You have no knowledge of the pissing in the cornfield, of the condition of sales. You are here only as a guest."

"The counselor cowboy arose and stepped on the stub of his cigarette with the heel of his boot. "*Viejo,* I'm merely here sitting, smoking, and listening to the talk of a man whom it seems to me has a problem, and who is talking like a mad one . . . A man, I should remind you, who claims to be a *Mejicano,* though he has blond hair and one green eye."

"Ay, dios, save me from this imbecile! I tell you we have work to do, we have plans to make, arrangements and terms of the agreement to decide . . . And if my color is different from the others, of what concern is that now?"

Nicolás scratched his ear. "How should I know? I remember some years back there was talk you were a gringo."

The old man did not speak now. He saw Nicolás pull at his ear with his thumb and fore-finger. He watched him as he stared at the ground and occasionally at the sky which was now black and dotted with pinpoints of white and orange.

Nicolás paced the ground before the old man. Now and then he would stop and look directly into the old man's face. Now that the counselor cowboy was at work, the old man did not interfere. "Shall I tell you the details?" Nicolás finally asked.

"You know you have charge in the matter."

"With the thing about your being a gringo . . . sst! Nothing. A word here, a suggestion in the right ear . . . nothing! A child could have thought that one . . . That was the first rumor, no?"

"As I recall. And this is harder?"

"A gringo! Eh, it was so simple I've forgotten how I did it."

"You made me paint the Mexican flag on the cart."

"Ah, *sí* A flag . . . sst! A child could have done that one." The cowboy pulled up his slight shoulders. "But you shouldn't have taken it off. Who knows, if you had left it on, and it wasn't that bad looking, maybe you wouldn't be facing this now."

"It looked like a child's drawing," the old man said simply.

"What's that to you. It served its purpose. They thought you were a gringo, because of your color. They would not let you drink in peace at the cantina . . ."

"And so you had me paint a flag on my peddler's cart to prove I am a *Mejicano*."

"Yes, if that's what it took, why not? They no longer bother you at the cantina with their questions, do they? I don't know, Huero, you bring these things on yourself."

"That's of no consequence now, Nico. Let's get on with it."

"No? But that's your problem. You concern yourself only with your own ways, with the things of today. You are like a mule, each day you must learn what you were taught the day before. You do not see the continuity of things."

"Don't start again, Nico," the old man pleaded.

"No, you are stubborn! You surround yourself too much with yourself thinking that by so doing you are hiding from others. But you are only calling attention to yourself."

"How's that?"

Nicolás stopped his pacing. Looking down at the corn peddler like a judge from his bench, he said, "Like this corn. Look at it!" He pointed to the circular furrows.

"What's the matter?"

"Well, look. *Jesús y María,* what a man you are! Who ever heard of a round field?"

"It helps the land. It rotates the soil, Nico."

"What a help! Don't you come at me with this foolishness. I know why you did this. And as you can see, everyone else knows."

"What? How's that?"

"To help the land! What nonsense. Who ever saw a round field of corn? It is clear to me, Huero. You did it to hide them. Do you think we are such fools? Even to the children it is clear."

"Hide? But what have I to hide?"

"Well, what else but the pig. And perhaps your plums. There is nothing else. Unless it was to hide your laziness. So that you could piss outside your house without being detected."

"I hide nothing, you *idiota*!" Huero exclaimed.

"But look at yourself. I try to help you. I give you counsel. You do well with my instructions at the beginning, but then as soon as you are doing well then you refuse to abide by my directions. Either you forget or you are a fool. When will you learn?" The cowboy shook his head and sucked at his teeth.

"I should have left that flag painted on my cart? What for? They took that, a child's drawing, as evidence of my *raza*? Anyway, I choose not to go to the cantina anymore?"

"Yes, and now you come to me for help again."

"Yes, but I know I will not always need the counsel of a spider. God will forgive me this weakness . . . but as I have said, this is a different matter."

"That is where you are a fool or a child. Can you not see it? Are you really such a *pendejo*?"

The old man pondered. "You really think this is the same thing?"

"It is for the same reasons," Nicolás said, tossing an obvious rule of law to the wind.

Huero tugged at the cigarette and nodded at the sky. He inhaled the warm breeze and fixed his gaze on Venus. "And the syphilis? That came after the gringo thing. Was that also part of it?"

Now the little cowboy from Texas was in his glory. "Exactly. Look . . . First it was the gringo. They would not give you the drinks, right? So you painted a flag. It was a simple idea, true, but it was good, and it worked . . . Then you removed it. And then what happened? Then they started the rumor of the syphilis; that you lost your eye because of syphilis."

"Well, it wasn't clear. It was sin, I think."

"Sin, syphilis, they are one and the same."

The teacher continued without interest in the obvious past. "Look, dumb one. Pay attention. Sin, syphilis, what does it matter what they think. The reason behind the acceptance of a rumor hardly matters. What matters is that you cure them."

"I went to church as you suggested."

"Yes, you went to the mass . . . One time."

"I couldn't do it, Nico. I went the one time to show them where my religious thoughts were. I didn't mind that one time to prove to them, but to continue . . . Besides, the padre was a gringo, an Italian, they say."

"Sometimes I think you do have syphilis, Huero. It has spoiled your brain like a squash that has rotted from the frost . . . Can't you see it was not for religion that I sent you there? It was to dispel the suggestion of sin."

"You believe that, Nicholas?"

"No, of course not. I am merely a counselor giving argument."

"I can't see it," the old man said, scratching his socket.

"Sure, look, it is very simple. If you had continued to go, if you had gone but a month and waited for the padre to hear of your sins. If you would have had the padre bless you in front of all the people . . . sst! You think Lodi would have dared start another rumor after that? Not even an español would be so stupid!"

The old man laughed fully. He slapped the ground and nodded slowly, saying, "*Ay, qué cabrón,* what a bastard you are! You have such crazy notions."

"It is not a thing to laugh at. You refused to carry out my instruction, you refused to go get blessed and so now what? Now you have to wear that patch over your eye, that is what. But that is not all, and this is what you still do not see . . . This thing of the passing is the same thing."

"I guess I'm too old."

"Then listen. You've worn that patch for three years now. And the people have forgotten about the syphilis. But the patch was your idea, it was certainly not one of mine. I am like a surgeon. I cut away the roots. With that patch you merely delayed this new one. You merely hid the sin. Now Lodi has seen fit to start another one because you have been selling too well in the past few years . . . so there you have it. Listen to my counsel and you will be cured once and for all."

The crickets lessened their clicking and the frogs took up their place. Mosquitoes hummed and buzzed while the fireflies occasionally lit the night air. Now there was a suggestion of a moon, as the Mexican cowboy issued his judgment. The counselor paced before the old man. He smoked and sighed now and again. "I have it! I have found it!" Nicolás burst suddenly. "Ho, ho, there we have it, *viejo*!" he shouted to the old man.

"Has the wine gone to your head, Nico?" asked the old man, thinking that perhaps Nicolás was drunk.

"Si, Nico! Nicolás Bordona! Old Nico has done it again. Go and get us some wine, old man," the cowboy ordered.

"Sit down and tell me. Calm yourself before your heart falls to your feet," said the old man.

"No, give me some wine first!" Nicolás paraded before the peddler, like a proud bantam rooster after the battle. "Bah! who has need of wine when his head is full like mine?"

"Have you a good plan, a big one?" asked the old man.

"Good? You say good? *Ay, ay, ay*! Don't use such small words."

"Well, tell me. What clown do I play this time, doctor?"

"Sst! Clown? I'm not a beginner anymore, old man. My ideas have grown with me. I remember before I used to need the quiet of my home, a certain solitude, before they came to me . . . Clown? No more."

"Well, hurry and say it, Nico," the old man was impatient with the cowboy's crowing.

"Yes, I'm growing big in my old age. You should see what ideas I have. Before, the thing of the flag: of the church, they were nothing. Sst! *Nada*, not a thing. A child, an idiot could have worked those up. But this one? I'm telling you, Huero, right from up there."

"You're telling me nothing, Nico."

"Nothing, I tell you," he continued without paying heed to the old man. "In those earlier years it was nothing . . ."

"For the love of God, Nico, say it and be done with it!"

With that the counselor returned to earth from his exaltation and began to unfold his plan before the peddler of corn who had gone five days without a sale because of the rumor in the Mexican *barrio* that said he urinated in his round cornfield. "Here you have it," began the cowboy. "This plan must dispel, once and for all, all the bad feelings of these people, these Mexicans of superstition. This plan must wipe out from their minds the idea that you are different, or that you are unclean. These are the things that tell the people that you are not one of us, and it is for these reasons that they accept the rumors about you. It is a universal occurrence that people will believe what they want to believe according to their feelings of the person in question; and these people, perhaps because they are but poor Mexicans, these people will believe any malicious gossip about you until you can show them . . ."

The old man interrupted, "Nico, please. I have no need for speeches."

"Just tell me what I must do, *por favor*."

"I see. Here, I will show you . . . You see, the people, including the children, they believe you have planted your round rows of corn to hide something. To hide what? you may ask. Well, that I do not know, but again you stand apart, again you show your difference and thus again you give them cause for suspicion. Maybe they think you have something special, your pig, your plums, who knows? But I do know that it is because of that that they find it so easy to accept the accusation of this pissing."

"Nico! Jesus, hombre, speak! Say something!"

"Yes, yes. You are without learning. You have no love of philosophy in you."

"It is not philosophy I seek from you, worm. Nor these devious words of yours. I only want to know what I must do to sell my corn. Now will you counsel me or shall I seek out another?"

The counselor sighed deeply and shook his head more in pity than in disgust at the old man of such little knowledge, and then he said, "You will give your plums to the children."

"Give my plums?"

"Yes. To get them, and this is why I like this plan, to get them to spread, as it were, a rumor come from you. In a word, to get them on your side."

The old man turned his one eye up toward the little cowboy. *Surely the wine has gone to this one's head,* the old man thought. *For I ask him to sell my corn and he tells me to give away my plums.*

The gnarled, black-trunked tree blossomed violet each Spring and when the sun assaulted the hot fields in July the boys from the *barrio* crept through the tall green, yellow stalks and stole away the old man's plums. He knew of their entrance, he saw them run through the field, their pockets laden with the purple fruit. He heard them giggle their fear away, but he never once in all those years prevented their taking, without asking, the gorgeous, tender fruit, sweet to the dry mouths of brown-baked Mexican boys.

"Give them my plums, eh? To get them on my side?"

"Yes, that is the first part. I will go and tell them that you have decided to give away your plums. Then, and this is where the plan intrigues me. Then I will go and see Lodi and compliment him on his good meat."

"His meat?"

"Yes, his meat. I will tell him he has the best meat in the entire valley . . . And then, and then, ho, ho, ho . . . and then I will tell him that others have said the same thing."

The old man scratched at his eyeless socket. "That he has good meat, the best in the valley."

"Yes, and then . . . but this is good! Then I will, ever so slowly, suggest to him that if I were he I'd raise the price. *It is worth it, Lodi, I shall say. Not only is it the best, but it saves us a trip to Riverbank; and above all, we do not have to deal with the gringos.* I can do such a thing, you know, Huero. You know I have a way with words. Si, Lodi, were it not for you we would have to buy from those fucking gringos. And then, Huero, as you shall see, and then he will in fact raise the price of his meat. And it would not surprise me if he raises all his prices, for I will blow up his head 'til it is like a pumpkin, you'll see."

The old man nodded in amazement. He could barely speak. "I see, he'll raise the price of his meat, that's it?"

"Sure. And then all you have to do is sell yours for about ten cents cheaper."

The old man shook his face and scratched at his head. He spoke quietly, "Nico, I am not selling meat! I'm trying to sell my corn."

"Well, sell meat, dumb one."

"But it is you who are the dumb one. I have no meat to sell."

"And the pig?"

"Perla? She is not ready yet."

"Ready? Why not? The animal looks good and ready to me."

Huero looked toward the pig's pen. "Then I am not ready, frog!"

"We must truly come from different countries, Huero. I cannot understand how it is your head works. Here I've arrived at a solution, what appears to me to be the ultimate solution to your problem. A plan that will not only help you sell your pig and your corn but most important it will endear you to these people. For as even you can see, when the women learn from their sons that you are a generous man given to kindness, they will think well of you. When you tell the children that you planted the round field to keep away the dust from the roads to protect your beautiful animal so that she would be clean, how can they not think well of you? . . . And then when these same women learn that the *español,* that fat one who is not a *Mejicano,* when they hear that he has raised all his prices . . . Can't you see it? There you are, a kind man selling clean pork at bargain prices on Sunday afternoon in front of the church . . . Jesus, hombre, it is a beauty!"

"What? What's this of the church? And this thing about the dust not getting on Perla, what is that? So again you would have me play the clown and tell more lies. Again you would have me fight one lie with another one."

"So what? What is that to you? Look, you fool, you'll sell cheaper, true, but you'll sell it all in one day, or in two at the most while the story circulates. It'll mean less work and then next week you can go back to your corn. By then that story will be dead . . . It is simple. You kill the pig tomorrow. You give the boys the plums and tell them the story. Sunday you take the pig to the church at twelve noon. I'll leave as they're saying the last prayers and when the women start coming out I'll tell them you're selling Perla for much less than what Lodi sells for. You watch, you'll sell all the pig before the sun has set."

The old man sat quietly. He looked to the moon. He nodded his head slowly as the blood rose to his head. He clenched his fists and shouted at the little Texan, "Jesus Christ! I must be as dumb as my pig. Why do I ask you to counsel me? Why must I always turn to the spiders and the mosquitoes for assistance? . . . All I want to do is sell my corn and be left in peace. If I don't sell it, the worms will have it. It is too late to have it dried for cornmeal; I've given it too much water for that. And even if the worms don't get to it the sun will take up the sweetness . . . And you will have me slaughter Perla when she is not ready . . . God, but I am surely a fool!"

The old man was explaining these things for himself, because he knew now that he had already committed himself to the plan by simply having asked the little man to counsel him. But he wanted, for a later time, to have this seeming rebellion as a comfort. He knew this would be his only outburst. Now he was but a soldier offering his distaste for war, knowing all along he would concede to his general.

He arose and went into his shack. He soon returned with two glasses full of wine. They drank slowly while the old man finished the examination of his conscience.

When he spoke again his voice was soft and without emotion. I'll fix the pig and be at the church at noon. Take some corn on your way out. It is still fresh, I cut it only yesterday."

Nicolás had seen the old man like this before, so he did not speak further on the matter. He took only an armful of the green elotes. His fee was all the corn he desired throughout the season.

Part II

The old man had begun the fires under two large tin tubs filled with water. He honed at a long knife with a stone he had found at the river, while his pig snorted and grunted unaware and oblivious.

The line of boys came noisily through the dense field of green, yellow, brown stalks of seven, eight, nine feet. They walked single file, all barefooted and in short-sleeved shirts or in none at all. They wore patched pants or swimming trunks. All were brown like earth, all had black eyes or brown hair too long or too short. Fifteen Mexican boys coming for their plums. They ceased their hornet's nest buzzing as they carefully approached the old man.

One came forward. "Well, here we are . . ." He hesitated. "Uh, Huero?"

The old man continued to sharpen the knife. "¿Sí muchachos? ¿Qué es?"

The brown boy looked at his own mud-caked feet. "Well, Nico, Nicolás Bordona, he said . . . He said we could have the, some plums."

"Oh, sí, muchachos." The old man hesitated, for he was unaccustomed to dealing with the children. "Take them. There they are."

"They have asked me to speak for them," the boy said.,

"No, we didn't!" One of the boys standing in file broke away. "You said we should let you talk, but I want to say it for myself."

"Well, speak," the old man said.

"Senor Huero. We, I want to thank you for the plums . . . And I am sorry I told those lies about you. But I had to. My father says it is for my own good. He made me."

"You're one of the Ulloa boys?"

"Sí, senor. But I didn't believe the story."

"It's all right. One has to obey his father. It is that way."

"I know. My mother said so too. But aren't you mad at me?"

"No, son. I am not angry with you. If a father tells his son to lie, then he must lie. Sometimes one must lie of necessity."

The boys murmured "See?" one reminded the others.

"I said it too," the shortest one called in.

"Huero," another said, "Huero, I'm sorry I called you a . . . *el ciego.* I was just kidding."

"Eh, what does it matter? I wish I were blind. For all the good my one eye does me, I might as well be blind."

"You can see, can't you?"

"Some things. But if I were totally blind then the government would pay me. They give you money if you cannot see anything."

"Huero?" Another one called in. "Huero, I stole a piece of sugar cane once when you weren't looking."

"Ah, what's a piece of sugar cane?"

"Me, too, 'ere," the shortest one squealed. "Oh, no, it was a tomato, I think."

The others laughed at him and the old man smiled.

"One time you gave me too much change," another said, "and I kept it. I'm sorry."

Each one in his turn confessed his sin before the old man. He laughed or smiled and tried to offer consolation. But he was running out of absolutions. Although he had been amongst these children for seven years this was the first time they had come to him. The plan, the counselor's scheme, kept twisting within him. He looked at his sow and he saw the water giving up the steam. He ran his finger along the knife's edge. He used his eyeless socket to advantage. When he did not want others to see him he turned that void toward the speaker. When people told stories, or made attempts at a laughing matter he wished not to hear, he would turn away from them. No one truly expected a man with one eye to have all his wits, or to be completely competent in his perception and therefore no one called this rudeness to his attention.

So now as the boys looked upon him without their accustomed rudeness, the scheme raced through him. He turned away from them because he did not like to look upon people when they could measure his emotion. He looked at his plum tree and at his pig. He exhaled deeply, resignedly and decisively. "Look, *muchachos,* did not Nico tell you you could have the plums? Have I not said, take them? Well, take them, they are yours . . . Not just now, but whenever you want them. This year and the next. They are yours. It will be your tree."

"Always?" one asked.

"Yes. It is yours . . .but there is just one condition. You must do me just one favor in exchange . . .You must not tell anyone about this . . .You must keep this a secret between us. Not even the girls. Because, well . . . the more people know, the fewer plums it will be for you." He smiled and saw it was not so difficult to speak to them. He saw clearly that they were but little boys with dirty bare feet and that all he wanted was to peddle his corn."

"Huero, you say always? With your permission, may I ask, Are you going away?"

"Don't you like the plums, Huero?" another asked. "Do they make you sick? My mother says if you eat too many you'll get sick."

"No, I'm not going away. Not now, at least."

"But you are going away? You say not now?"

"Well, everyone goes away someday, you know."

The short one chirped in, "You mean to die? My dog died. My father said he was going away. I know he just died."This shortest one, a little bit of a boy, he was not the age of the others. He had merely come with his older brother to the feast.

"Boys, why don't you just take the plums."

"Are you very sick?"

"No, not very sick," the old man answered.

"My dog had a sickness. His eye was all red, and white, too. It was ugly. He had blood in it. Is that what you have, 'ero?" the little one asked.

The others boys turned to him and with their eyes and their faces they tried to warn him, to silence him. Their embarrassment compelled them to turn away from the old man with one eye.

"Well, in a way it is my eye, *hijo*."

"Oh, I am sorry, 'ero. I'm very sorry you have the leprosy."

"Shut up, Paquito," his brother yelled.

"Why? I am sorry. And I know about it. The sisters told me about leprosy in catechism. It's like whatTeto, my dog, that's what he had. He had it too. Isn't that what you have, 'ero?"

The old man chuckled. "I don't know, Paquito. Maybe I'll die of that, like your dog. His name wasTeto, eh?"

"Sí. I called him that for my uncle Hector. And the sister said he just went away too. But I know he just died of the leprosy."

"I see. Well, look, boys, you've thanked me for the plums. I say you are welcome. Now take them, they are yours.They are ripe now."

The boys did not wait.They leaped to the tree and pulled at the branches. The purple tender balls came off with a touch. They ate as they picked more to stuff in their pockets. They yelled and pushed and buzzed and filled their mouths with the fruit. It was not a big tree. Shortly it was clean of the fruit. With their mouths purple and their pockets wet, they left down the path through which they had entered.

The old man stirred the flames more. "Bueno, Perla it is your time. I would have waited . . .but you have eaten well, have you not?"

What a pearl! he thought to himself as he drove the knife into her neck. He drained her blood, he sliced her skin, he burnt and scraped the bristles. He pulled the intestines. He preserved the brain and eyes. He cut cleanly the meat from the fat.

Huero worked late into the night under a lamp beside the now thinned plum tree.

Part III

It was Sunday morning in the *barrio*. The old, wrinkled burnt-skinned Mexican women, covered with black shawls, gathered at the entrance to the wooden building. The church steeple was crowned with a bleeding Christ and housed a hornet's nest.

The children in stiff bright clothes held back their laughter. They carried black or red or white missals. The men in tight, white starched collars and pin-striped black or brown suits smoked quickly before the mass began.

"Have you heard about the old man?" a woman asked several others.

The others came closer. "*Sí, que lástima,* what a pity."

"El Huero, you mean?"

"My boy told me. It is sad."

"I wonder if we shouldn't send the men to inquire."

"I don't know, we might be intruding. I don't want to be a *metich*."

"Yes, but, Rosa, when it is a thing like this . . ."

"But with him? It is different. He does not join us."

"Well it is a shame. But I could not buy his corn after what was said. My man would have thrown it to the trash."

"I know. It is the same with me. Mine would have cracked a plate over my head . . . Still, he does have a heart. Like my boy said—he's a little sick this morning, I guess he ate too many . . ."

"Isn't that a coincidence? Manuelito is sick, too. You say yours ate too many? What's that?"

"The plums. You know, Paquito said the old man gave them some plums."

"Your boys are sick? You say Huero gave them . . ."

"*Sí,* Paquito said all the boys went there . . ."

"All the boys. Elisa, what are you saying? Don't you know, didn't your boy tell you? My boy, Oscar, he told me that Huero had some bad illness. He's sick too. He's got stomach trouble."

"Wait a minute. Paquito . . . but he's just a baby, he said the old man had what his dog died of. He said the old man told him he was dying of leprosy. But surely, that is just a baby talking."

"Leprosy!"

"Now wait, just wait. My boy, Oscar, he never lies, he is a good honest boy; now he said, and he is no baby . . ."

"Well, what is it, Rosa?"

"He did say the old man was sick, of a disease . . . You say leprosy? But he said it might just be a rumor . . ."

"*Jesús y María*! If they all went there, as you say . . . and he has leprosy . . . and now they are sick . . . *Dios mío!*"

Several of them crossed themselves. Two of them, without another word, turned and ran home. The others talked faster and louder and gathered momentum in their gesticulations. They called the men into their discussions.

The men laughed at them and called them chirinoleras. The men told their women to leave the old man alone. The men in their tight clothes returned to finish their cigarettes, for the priest had arrived.

The women continued in their anxiety. They quoted scripture to one another. One suggested it was not communicable. Another said it was the mark of Cain. They carried their grief into the church and prayed with the priest for all the sick.

But it was all too late. For the rumor had spread during the mass. During the collection, the rumor went round from one to the other, from pew to pew, that the old man had leprosy. The evidence was overwhelming, beyond a reasonable doubt. The Huero had leprosy as was proven by the illness of all the children who had eaten too many plums.

While the congregation recited their *Hail Marys,* the little cowboy slipped out to meet the old man who had rolled his cart near the entrance to the church.

"What's this about your illness?" The counselor wore a black suit and a green tie four inches wide.

"My illness? I am well."

"I don't get it all. I got here a little late. Mother wanted some fresh milk before I left. Look, here they come!" He spun around and hurried to the door to meet the women. But they would not stop to talk as was their custom. They only touched the priest's hand. They hurried away holding tightly to their children. They wanted to find a doctor. Some wanted to go to the older women, the very old and wiser women would counsel them in times of distress, the viejitas who found wild mint and red spinach among the peach trees for the illnesses of the children.

The women had no time for the politeness of the counselor who bid them seek out the old man's pork at bargain prices. Nicolás went from one to another pleading with them to look at the meat. They paid him no heed.

One of the women walked up to the old man standing by his cart, and the old man said, "*Ah, buenos días, señoras.* I have nice fresh meat, thirty cents to the pound. The skins are crisp and the blood is red."

"Huero, I don't come here to buy. I must know, this is a serious thing. Did my son, Paquito, did he go to your house yesterday?"

The old arranged the meat in the cart of two unnecessarily large wheels, one painted black and the other white. The cart itself was painted orange. "Paquito? Well, what did he tell you?"

"That doesn't matter, Huero. He is just a boy. But I must know for certain. Did he?"

"Don't ask me. I know nothing of your son."

Nicolás came to his defense. "Ladies, perhaps what you should do is buy some of these *chicharrones* for your children. You know how they like them."

"You stay out of this, Nicolás Bordona. This is very serious. We have to know. Huero, we know, you are sick and we know some of the boys went to your house yesterday. We have to know which ones."

"I am sick? What is this of my being sick?" he asked the excited women who eyed the pork meat with the eye of the bargain hunter.

"*Si, viejo,* we know of it. It is out and we've got to know which boys were exposed. Now tell us!"

"Señor Huero, please, this is a serious thing. Even though the *padrecito* just told me it is not catching, still we should know. I'm sorry if she is rude, but we are all concerned," a younger one apologized.

"I'm not being rude, Carmen. But leprosy is a bad thing, don't you know?"

"Leprosy?" the old man asked. "I have leprosy?"

They all fixed their gaze upon him. "Well, do you deny it?"

The old man touched his eye patch. "Where did you hear that one?"

"From the . . . the boys told us. I think it was Rosa's boy, Paquito, and Elisa's boy, Oscar, he said you told them."

The old man smiled and remembered. He looked at the meat in the cart and he remembered the confessions he had heard the previous day. He saw again the boys scampering through the plum tree and he chuckled when he thought of Paquito's dog, Teto. With a twinkle in his eye he said, "I don't know, ladies. How would I know what I have. I have not talked to a doctor since I was but a child. How should I know for certain if I have leprosy . . . for that matter who can say he does not have it."

The women stared at him and looked with nervous eyes at one another. They tightened their shawls about them and some clutched a the missal or rosary they held in their hands.

"Well, we know, at least the father told Carmen that it is not catching . . . But you are right, who knows."

"Maybe it's just a coincidence that they're all sick," Carmen said.

"Or a warning," Rosa said as she hurried away.

Nicolás said, "But ladies, how about this beautiful meat?"

"The meat? . . . No, I think Ill wait."

"But it's fresh, and it is much less than at Lodi's," he wailed.

"No Nico . . . I don't think my man would want me to buy just now. Maybe we'd better wait until tomorrow, after we see a doctor or talk to the *viejitas,* they should know."

Nicolás tried the last remaining worshippers. But their decision was the same. They would wait until the following day. If their sons were only sick from too many plums . . .perhaps they would reconsider.

So now I am a leper, the old man chuckled to himself as he covered the meat in the cart with a white cloth.

"How do you do it, Huero? Of all my clients how is it that you bring me the most hardships?"

"It is over with, Nico."

"But you can bring me some problems, can't you? You cannot keep my counsel. You must always play the part of the clown."

"Leave it be, Nico. It is done."

"No, wait, *viejo.* This was a business matter. You were to take my advice for a price."

"You can have your corn, hyena. You can have all that enormous belly of yours will hold. But away with you and your advice!"

"I don't know, Huero. First a gringo, then syphilis, then the pissing . . . Now leprosy . . . But why did you not deny it? Why did you let them know that is what it is. Are you such a *pendejo?*"

"What are you saying, frog face?"

"Ah, well, never you mind, old man. I'll come up with another plan. You'll see. We'll sell your pig yet."

"Pig? But it is you who are the *pendejó.* This is not a pig This is but pork meat, can't you see that? . . . Perla is a pig!"

For the first time the counselor took notice of the old man's seriousness. The little cowboy's eyes fluttered and he bit at his mustachio. "Huero, you are disappointed because the plan did not work. But then you should not have said anything about this leprosy. You should have denied it. You should not have let them know you have it, or whatever it is . . . So that is what it is. I thought, for years I had known you'd lost that eye from something strange and mysterious."

Huero pushed his cart away. The counselor followed after him and tried to stop him. The old man pushed his hand away angrily. He mumbled curses at the cowboy. Nico placed himself in front of the cart.

"Jesus, hombre, but you are loco. Cabrón, but you are weak in the head," Nico shouted.

"Loco? Yes, Nico, that I am. I am weak in the head. But as it goes, *He who has no head had better have good feet.* So get away from me before I run over you!"

Nicolás stepped away from the cart. "Jesus, but now you are like a wild one caged too long without water."

The old man advanced toward the little cowboy from Texas. "Nico, you know they say if a leper rubs his sore on sweet skin it will harden and fall off like cold wax. Want me to try it on you?"

Nicolás jumped back. "God, but now you've really gone off."

Huero laughed fully. His whole body trembled with delight as he watched the frightened little man scampering away with short steps like a busy field mouse.

The old man returned to his hut surrounded by circular furrows of tall corn stalks. He had planted it that way because he had read in a magazine that it did the soil good.

The Mexican peddler of corn hummed an old song as he dug a grave behind the plum tree. The grave was large enough for the coffin, which was the cart, stuffed with the meat of the pig that had once been his Perla.

He knew then, that he too, like Paquito's dog, would have to leave the Mexican *barrio* of Riverbank.

Writings

Novels: *The Autobiography of a Brown Buffalo,* Straight Arrow, 1972. *The Revolt of the Cockroach People,* Straight Arrow, 1973. **Collected Works:** *The Uncollected Works of Oscar Zeta Acosta,* edited by Ilan Stavans, Arte Público Press, 1996. **Short Stories:** "Perla Is a Pig," in *Con Safos* 2/5 (1970). "Tres Cartas de Zeta," in *Con Safos* 2/6 (1970). "The Autobiography of a Brown Buffalo," *Con Safos* 2/7 (1971).

Alba Ambert

In her works of fiction, Alba Ambert creates penetrating psychological narratives, which are based on her rise from abject poverty in Puerto Rico to the highest realms of academia in the United States and abroad. A poet and scholarly writer as well, Ambert combines a lyric, rhapsodic style with a minute attention to detail.

Born and raised in a San Juan slum, Ambert was a "scholarship child" who, through force of will, determination, and extraordinary intelligence, pulled herself out of adversity to not only make something of herself but to contribute greatly to humanity. She followed a circuitous route to become a barrio teacher in Boston, and later a successful creative writer. Her path out of poverty began at the University of Puerto Rico, where she earned her B.A. in philosophy, graduating with distinction in 1974. She went on to graduate study at Harvard University where she earned M.A. and Ed.D. degrees in psycholinguistics in 1975 and 1980, respectively. It was during her graduate work that Ambert became a bilingual teacher, concentrating on teaching curriculum writing and theory to special-education students. Some of this experience and study is reflected in the scholarly works she has written.

In 1986 Ambert traveled to Athens, Greece, to teach and conduct research at Lesley College, and later Athens College. During her early days in Europe (where she still resides), Ambert also returned her attention to creative writing, something she had been interested in since childhood. The result of her work was the publication of her poetry in Europe and in the United States. In 1987 she published *Porque hay silencio*, a highly autobiographical novel charting the protagonist's psychological struggle to resolve her previous life of poverty with her present life as a highly successful woman of letters. The book proved to be a milestone for Ambert: It was awarded the Literature Prize of the Institute for Puerto Rican Literature. Ambert subsequently re-wrote the novel in English (titled *A Perfect Silence),* which also received rave reviews and won the Carey McWilliams Award, a highly regarded multicultural book prize.

The *San Francisco Chronicle* reviewed the novel:

> Using lyrical and evocative language to make the pain bearable, this compelling novel by poet Alba Ambert tells a story of overwhelming anguish. *A Perfect Silence* is a tribute to women who break away from age-old patterns of destruction . . . . *A Perfect Silence,* through its portrayal of the acts and scars of mistreatment, presents a powerful story of a young woman who heals from a defiled youth.

Her childhood demons expurgated in the passionate story of *A Perfect Silence,* Ambert went on to publish *The Eighth Continent,* a collection of stories demonstrating the cool detachment of modern life. These tales deal with everything from underground revolutionary groups to contemporary folk legends, as in "Chupacabras" (The Incredible Story of the Ingenious Doña Fermina Beltrán, Her Obsession with North American Television Talk Shows and The Unexpected Fate That Resulted from Her Passion for Orchids), which is included in this anthology.

Though she is a recent entry into the contemporary Latino literary movement, Ambert promises to become one of its major voices.

> "A Perfect Silence *is a tribute to women who break away from age-old patterns of destruction."*
>
> **San Francisco Chronicle**

Personal Stats

Puerto Rican writer, educator. Born: October 10, 1946, in San Juan, Puerto Rico. *Education:* B.A. in Philosophy, Magna Cum Laude, University of Puerto Rico, 1974; M.A. in Psycholinguistics, Harvard University, 1975; Ed.D. in Psycholinguistics, Harvard University, 1980. *Career:* Bilingual teacher, curriculum writer, Boston Public Schools, 1975–78; bilingual teacher, Belmont Public Schools, 1978–79; Director and professor, Bilingual Special Education Program, 1980–84; Visiting professor, Department of Linguistics, M.I.T., 1984–85; Visiting professor, Lesley College, Athens, Greece, 1986–87; Senior research scholar, Athens College, Athens, Greece, 1985–93; Senior research scholar, Richmond College, London, 1993 to present. *Awards/Honors:* Literature Prize, Instituto de Literatura Puertorriqueña, 1990, for *Porque hay silencio*; Carey McWilliams Award, Multicultural Review for outstanding scholarly or literary publication, for *A Perfect Silence*, 1996. *Memberships:* PEN, Writers' Union, Amnesty International, National Association for Bilingual Education. *Address:* Richmond College, Queens Road, Richmond, Surrey TW 10 6JP, England

Chupacabras, The Goat Sucker

(The Incredible Story of the Ingenious Doña Fermina Beltrán, Her Obsession with North American Television Talk Shows and The Unexpected Fate That Resulted from Her Passion for Orchids.)

from *The Eighth Continent,* Arte Público Press, 1997

Fermina rocked steadily in her mahogany chair and stared at the TV set that one of her four daughters, Mariluz, had given her for Mother's Day after the one Fermina brought from New York, when she and her late husband Neftalí moved to Puerto Rico, conked out. The commercial break over, Geraldo's deep voice filled the living room. Fermina canted forward, feet firmly planted on her Spanish tiled floor, rocking chair gliders tipped to the ceiling. She turned her good ear toward the TV and distractedly petted one of her five cats: the sleek, slate-gray Cervantes, who napped placidly on her lap.

In today's show about sexual addiction, a young blonde, quite ordinary looking, Fermina judged, described her multiple trysts with strangers in shopping mall parking lots where she would pick up her more than willing partners. Every single day the blonde needed a fix. She'd had sex with hundreds of anonymous men, she said. Oh, no, the young woman shrieked when Geraldo asked, my husband doesn't know. He will now, Fermina chortled. Greta, the part Persian, part who-knows-what, looked up at Fermina with eyes like slits, from her favorite spot on the sofa where she spent half her life, removed from the other cats, sleeping.

Earlier in the day Oprah had interviewed transsexuals, both male and female. Fermina had a hard time keeping track of who had been what because the men who had operations to become women then fell in love with other women and the women who became men, went on to fall in love with other men.

"Virgen María Santísima! They supposed to be gay?" Fermina asked the TV and shook her head not understanding this conundrum at all. "Maybe they really are what they were and that makes them not-gay, huh? That's what I think!" she informed Oprah in no uncertain terms. In her excitement, she rocked back crunching poor Ewok's fat tail with the chair glider.

" *Ay,* I'm sorry, Eee-goo-ah." Mariluz's son had named the cat and Fermina could hardly pronounce his name. Grunting, she picked up the 12-pound cat, gave him a few rubs under the chin and poured some milk in his saucer. As soon as she sat down again, Cervantes had homed into her lap.

Fermina hated it when someone on a show was shouting at someone else, usually something juicy, and time ran out and the station started running the credits. Fermina couldn't catch what the blonde nymphomaniac was shouting to a member of the audience. Frustrated, she zapped the TV off with her remote. While Cervantes kneaded on her cushioned belly, Fermina shook her head thinking about the difficulties of intercourse in shopping mall parking lots. What do they do with all those arms and legs? she asked herself and thought of her late husband Neftalí, may he rest in peace. He never demanded too much from her in that department. All he wanted was some coochie, coochie once in a while. But when he had a little too much Palo Viejo while he watched Iris Chacón on TV, he'd always get frisky and it took him forever to finish. But she didn't mind even when she knew it was Iris Chacón's formidable buttocks that were pinned to his mind.

Neftalí was a good hard-working man, who always provided for her and their daughters. His face was rugged like a mountain surface, but he was a gentle soul. Just as he turned sixty, and after all the daughters had finished university, they bought the long-dreamed for *finquita,* a little farm, and settled in Barrio Esperanza, Canóvanas. They were glad to be away from cold, dreary New York. Even though two of their girls stayed behind. But Mariluz, the chemical engineer, and Graciela, the general practitioner, came to Puerto Rico with them once they finished their studies.

Mariluz was now divorced with teenage twins—a boy and a girl—and worked at a pharmaceutical in Carolina. Fermina was always lighting candles to a framed picture of Saint Anthony that she kept upside down on her dresser to guarantee a new husband for Mariluz. Graciela, thank her lucky stars, was okay. She married a surgeon and they both worked at the Fajardo Municipal Hospital and had private practices in the city. But after five years of marriage, they still hadn't given Fermina more grandchildren.

While Neftalí farmed, Fermina took care of the house and tended to her pride and joy: the lushest, most lavish, sumptuous, fragrant orchid garden Canóvanas had ever seen. Neftalí built a shed behind the kitchen where Fermina repaired whenever she could to commune with her little darlings. In the shed she made sure they could bathe in the necessary light, yet be protected from the inclement tropical sun. Every morning before breakfast, Fermina inspected the clusters of richly hued petals. She loved the colors, their satiny sheen brighter than any jewel. Amethyst, fuchsia, lavender, crimson, indigo, golden yellow, dazzling white. She fingered the soft petals gently. If she closed her eyes she could identify each plant by the texture of its leaves and petals. They were feathery or waxy or leathery or ruffled at the edges like elegant gowns. Delicate aromas rose with the humidity as she watered the spongy bark compost or moss where the orchids thrived. She loved the graceful symmetry of each flower, the way the lip nodded daintily toward the roots, like a nostalgic trumpet. Some resembled little ears, others fiddles or horns. They reminded her of tiny, defenseless animals, like all the cats she had picked up over the years.

The only troubles that marred Fermina's life in those days, and which continued to this very day, were don Jacinto's goats. Don Jacinto, the irascible owner of the *finca* adjoining theirs, allowed his goats to wander into neighboring parcels of land where they chomped up everything in their path. Sometimes Fermina would be watering her delicate lady slippers when the unmistakable stench of old goat would make her nose screw up in disgust.

"*¡Fo, qué peste*! She'd run out pinching her nose with one hand and shooing the goats with the watering can in the other. "What a stink these *cabras* make, *por Dios!*"

She had tried everything to make don Jacinto take responsibility for the goings on of his *cabras*. She even reported him to the Humane Society. Surely, allowing goats to dine on orchids consisted of the most brutal cruelty. Why, some of the orchids could be poisonous. Couldn't they? Or at least cause serious intestinal problems. But no. They wouldn't take her complaints seriously. "Lady, we got people torturing horses around here. Starving and beating them to death. We know don Jacinto and he takes good care of his goats." (Everyone knew everyone in the small town. Unfortunately.) "What do you want from us?" Neftalí, who didn't want to cause any trouble, he was that kind of man, put up a fence between the two properties and sealed it with chicken wire. The goats always managed to jump over the fence, though. They could really leap those sons-of, of, old goat.

Other than the trouble with don Jacinto's goats, Fermina had been happy in their retirement. She was finally living like a lady of leisure. In New York, Neftalí had been a repairman for the telephone company. He made good money and was frugal. They bought a small brick house in

Queens and educated their daughters at state universities. Fermina cleaned houses in more affluent neighborhoods. With her earnings Fermina bought fabrics to sew her own and her daughters dresses and helped with other household expenses.

Neftalí would not waste a penny. He never had a beer with his fellow workers at quitting time nor did he ever buy an unexpected gift for Fermina. Graciela used to say that he was tighter than a scared mollusk. Whatever that was. But Fermina thought he was more like a clam. Small, but muscular, all he needed were his three meals a day, not counting snacks at ten and three, to be happy.

The years took the edge off Neftalí's frugality. Or at least that's what Fermina thought after they sold everything they owned in New York and acquired their farm and she developed a passion for orchids. Neftalí bought a car, built her orchid shed and seemed more relaxed about money. He started saying that they could not take their money to the grave, so they might as well enjoy it. But then, when she least expected it, his overabundant frugal genes acted up again.

One fateful day, Neftalí, who had started to institute some stringent economic measures in the *finca,* decided to artificially inseminate one of his cows himself. When he shoved an arm sheathed in a long plastic glove into the cow's private parts—all the way to the elbow—the cow did not take kindly to this defilement and kicked Neftalí so hard, he was last seen alive soaring through the air, right arm sticking up and smeared with a reddish viscous substance Fermina could not identify at the time. Poor Neftalí, may his soul rest in peace, landed with a thud, head first, into a pile of cement blocks he had purchased to build a kitchen extension. The cow didn't even get pregnant. At least not due to Neftalí's efforts.

"Ay, Neftalí, *mijo,* if you could only see how fat the cow is now." Fermina looked up to the ceiling while Cervantes continued kneading—he was a championship kneader—.

"Got her a young bull from a neighbor and he did the job real easy. It don't cost so much either. Been calving ever since. I wish you had not been so thrifty. It always got you in trouble. Remember that time, *mi corazón,* when to save some *pesitos* you . . .

Her thoughts were crushed by her daughter Graciela, who snuck up behind her.

"Still talking to Papá, eh Mami?"

Fermina started and Cervantes sprang on top of the TV set, hackles up like the frond of a pineapple.

"*Ave María purísima, muchacha,* one of these days you give me a heart attack!" "Look what you done!" Fermina spread out her shaking hands for Graciela's inspection.

"Sorry, Mami." Graciela plunked down on the sofa, picked up the remote and started channel surfing. Something Fermina hated.

"Don't get carried away, Graciela. Mahreelee Cagan is on soon."

"Who?"

"Mahreelee, Mahreelee."

"Yeah, I got that, but did you say her last name was *cagan,* to shit? In the plural?"

"What a strange name, *verdad?* I'd change it if I was her. Imagine, everybody thinking her family was named after, you know, something so filthy."

"It's probably pronounced Kagan in English, you know, with the broad *a?*" "Whatever." Fermina waved both hands in front of her face. She was nettled by any perceived criticism of her talk show idols.

Graciela made a face.

"What's the matter?" Fermina asked angrily. "Your mouth full of live fire ants or something?"

"Sorry, Mami." Graciela attempted to mollify her mother with a big kiss.

"Don't you see the shows, *mija?* They so educational. You don't know how much I learn from these shows," Fermina said, appeased.

"Such as?"

"Oh, a lotta things. Like the other day, Salee Rafael had a show about men who treat women like slaves. Can you believe in this day and age that sort of thing going on? There was this man who makes his wife clean his behind after he go to the, you know, the *servicio."*

"You mean a guy makes his wife wipe his ass? And she does it? You call that educational?"

Fermina rolled her eyes up to the ceiling beams made of ausubo wood and thought to herself: *How can this woman go to medical school and not know nothing about nothing?*

Her head bobbed and nodded.

"I learned that some men think that that's what a woman is for."

"You hadn't noticed this before?" Graciela shook her head. "Sometimes I wish you would take up calligraphy or go to the malls or something."

"Not those malls, *mija!!* You don't want to know what goes on in those places."

"Don't tell me. I'll pass on that one."

"Okay with me if you don't wanna learn about life. And you a doctor and all. Well, I'll get you a little coffee before you go to the hospital."

Fermina got up and with a slight limp that favored her left leg headed for the kitchen.

Graciela followed her to the kitchen and frowned. "Did you hurt yourself, Ma?"

"No, *mija.* So how's everything at the hospital?"

"Don't change the subject. What have you been up to now? Tell me the truth." Graciela's eyes narrowed with suspicion.

Fermina wouldn't look at her. Graciela took this to be a bad sign.

"Well, you know, I borrowed this tape from Mariluz's girl. She want to be a model, you know?" Fermina limped around the kitchen bustling and clattering pots and pans.

"What's all the fuss, Ma? All you gotta do is turn on the espresso machine I gave you and put some milk in the microwave." Graciela took charge and prepared the coffee herself. "So, what kind of tape is this you borrowed? God, this is like pulling teeth!"

"Exercise, you know, for fitness." Fermina mumbled.

"Since when have you been interested in that sort of thing? I can't believe it, my own mother prancing to the tune of an exercise video tape!" Graciela paused and stared at her mother in horror.

"Wait a minute. Ma, are you by any chance, uh, how can I put this delicately, in love?" Graciela turned up her nose so high you would think she was assailed by a putrid smell.

"What, you crazy?" It was Fermina's turn to be horrified. "I almost sixty-five years old, look at this head full of gray hair," she plunged her chin into her chest to show Graciela, "and with a pack a grandchildren. None from you, by the way. I gotta foot in the grave already, what do I want with an old man?"

Graciela, much relieved, could afford to joke. "How about a *gallito*, a young rooster?"

"That all I need, someone after my Social Security check. No, thank you."

"So why the fitness craze all of a sudden?"

"Okay, I tell you, but don't blab it to Eduardo or anyone else, okay? I'm too old to be my son-in-law's laughing stock." Fermina sipped some of the strong coffee that she took *puya*, black and with no sugar.

"I still wanna be on a talk show. I know I promised you girls that I wouldn't try again." She dipped a cube of cheddar cheese in her coffee.

"Ma, what am I gonna do with you? You already tried to train those cats to do tricks, unsuccessfully I might add. You attempted to start the first psychic telephone service in Puerto Rico and got into trouble with the Treasury Department. Then, you wanted to be the first anoretic senior citizen in history, but couldn't give up pork. Or that cheese you shouldn't be eating." Fermina looked up at her daughter guiltily. But Graciela continued. "Next thing, you'll try to establish a religious cult."

"Hey, good idea."

"Forget I said that."

"But listen, Graciela, anyone can be famous today. All you need is do something strange, like that man who had his peepee pierced on Jeree Espringel " Fermina pointed at an indistinct spot below her belly.

"Oh, my God, Ma, that's sick."

"Yeah, yeah, but they have stupid things too. Like a little kid who collect toothpaste. It was sooo boring. *Imagínate,* I snored all through the show. But I got a idea. If I become a senior fitness queen, you know, at my age, that's something else, *verdad?* So maybe I can get on Rolonda or Montel Güiliam and show the whole United States that an old Puerto Rican woman can do exercises and look, you know, good. I'll be famous."

Graciela rolled her eyes up and sighed. "Ma, you gotta stop watching TV all day. Ever since Pa died that's all you do."

"Don't say that. You know I got other things to do, like take care of all these cats and my orchids."

Graciela glanced at her watch and got up. "Ma, I'm on duty in half an hour, so I gotta go. But I'm really worried about you. Do you want to see someone about your little problem?"

"What problem you talking about?"

"You seem to be addicted to television, Ma." Graciela said.

"Addiction? Like some drug? On the Oprah show there were some real addicts. Like the man who got addicted to those nicotine patches he bought to stop smoking and had his arms all full of them all the time."

"Okay, Ma. We'll talk about this later. By the way, did you catch the news conference that Güiche gave last night."

"The mayor? Why waste my time. That man got nothing to say. And he got such a nice name, José Luis Santos. It's so disrespectful to let people call him by that silly nickname he got when he was just a boy."

"It was about the *chupacabras.*"

"Did they find him? I hope so," Fermina said with conviction, "because I'm afraid that thing is going to kill one my cats any day now. You don't know how much I worry."

"It hasn't attacked cats yet, Ma. Just rabbits and dogs. And, of course, remember that the first victims were goats who had all their blood sucked out."

"Too bad it didn't suck on don Jacinto's goats." Fermina said sadly.

"Well, you won't believe what Güiche said. Listen to this. Our mayor actually announced, on television, that the *chupacabras* isn't an animal. It's an alien from outer space. Not only that, but he organized an expedition to track it down. Can you believe it?"

"Don't look at me, I didn't vote for him."

■ ■ ■

After Graciela left, Fermina had half an hour to tend to her orchids before the Maury Povitch Show. Maybe she should do her weight lifting too. She didn't know whether she could keep up with this exercise business, though. It was tough. Then the lady on the exercise video said, quite emphatically, cut out the fat!! And Fermina knew she could not live without the pork with crackling that she loved to roast every Sunday. Or the stewed eggplants with lots of garlic, dripping in olive oil. Or plantain fritters stuffed with crabmeat, for that matter. No, this plan wasn't going to work for her.

She limped to the orchid shed, mumbling to her cats, the orchids and herself.

"My *florecitas* need me now. Shoo, Teehee, out of my way. One of these days you gonna make me trip and break my neck." Fermina said to the small cat whose fur was white as coconut meat.

Humming lightly, she snipped a dead leaf here and sprayed a dry plant there. "How're my pretty girls? Oh, my darlings need a little water and some food, don't you, my *preciosas?*"

She moved the plants that did not take well to a full day of sun toward the shaded corners of the shed to join those that needed to be well protected. Fermina bent down to move a large pot. She groaned and straightened up rubbing the small of her back. As the flash of pain hit her coccyx, an idea struck her. Eagerly, she turned to Teehee.

"I got it! What if I grow the biggest, most beautiful, most fragrant orchids in the world. Can't let those damn flies fertilize them, though, they stink up all the flowers. Only bees. And I make the bees feed on my thyme bushes somehow and then I try to find a fertilizer that make them grow and grow like doña Marta's banana plants. She told me herself she was using this hormone to make her plants grow and they so big. Humongous, like my grandson say. You'll see *gatita linda,* I'll be on Rolonda or Oprah or Charlee Pérez. And I don't have to do those stupid exercises. It was after those *malditos* sit-ups this morning that I feel like someone ground my bones like pepper in a great big *pilón."*

Fermina looked down at Teehee who had a rear paw stuck up in the air and was vigorously licking her behind.

"Is that what you think of my idea, *gata?"*

Fermina harrumphed and dashed into the house to check the living room clock which was just then pinging the hour. When she clicked on the TV, Maury Povitch was giving a prize to a man who had the worse luck of any other contestant. The man who won a trip to the Bahamas, all expenses paid, told the audience of his fishing accident. He jumped into a river to retrieve a fishing pole not knowing that a signpost had been thrown and hidden in the weeds. He jumped right on the signpost and the piece of wood stuck between his legs. He saw blood gushing all over the place and when he touched the spot where the blood was coming from, he realized his testicles had fallen off. They sewed them back in, but he couldn't have sex now.

"*Ave María Purísima,"* Fermina said out loud as she put her hands to her head. "Can't complain about my luck, let me tell you," she addressed Ewok who just happened to stop in front of the television to lick his front paw and then proceeded to groom his face.

"When you come right down to it," she continued while Ewok blinked in her direction and yawned, "I had a good life with my Neftalí, may he rest in peace. My daughters are good to me and always help me out whenever I need it, I have beautiful grandchildren, but I don't know when that Graciela's gonna give me some before I die. Then I have my orchids and you sweeties. Come here, Eeee- goo-ah," Fermina patted her lap and Ewok swooped into it and gave her a vigorous knead.

"*Ay,* don't dig your claws into my thigh like that!"

■ ■ ■

It was a quiet evening. Graciela was busy at the hospital and called to say she wouldn't be stopping by and Mariluz, who lived way out in San Juan, only visited on weekends. Fermina was sorry there were no talk shows on in the evening, but then she needed some time to figure out how she could grow the most impressive orchids. Maybe if she grafted an orchid plant into an orange tree, while feeding them those super duper hormones doña Marta had. She could call the hybrid *chinorqui.* She liked that. It had a nice ring to it. She could just imagine the fragrance of an orchid fertilized by a thyme-fed bee and combined with orange blossoms. It was sure to be heavenly. She had to talk to doña Marta tomorrow, *a primera hora,* to get her advice. She had to brace herself, she thought, because doña Marta talked and talked and she always made Fermina feel really tired. But, doña Marta knew more than anyone, even don Jacinto, about plant hormones.

"Frankly," Fermina muttered to herself, "I think she feeds those hormones to her son. He's bigger than a refrigerator. And where did that come from? Doña Marta is tiny like a *coquí* and her husband's smaller than a cumin seed."

With these reflections, Fermina filled a skillet with pork chops. "Am I glad I don't have to do that fitness business anymore. One day was enough for me!"

Just as she was turning a pork chop with a long two-tined fork, Fermina heard a loud bang in the orchid shed. Fork in hand, she stepped over the cats who were hungrily collected around the stove, even Bruno, the nervous one was there. She tiptoed to the door and very quietly stepped into the dark shed. The noise came from the potting area. At first, she heard a sound like crumpled paper tossed by the wind against a wall. Then she could hear the metallic clatter of gardening tools and buckets. For a moment, Fermina thought it was an earthquake. But then, through the slant of light coming from the kitchen, she saw a short, stubby tail. She reared up her head as though someone had poured vinegar up her nose when she realized that, mingled with the sweet scent of her orchids, there was the unmistakable stench of male goat in rut. As she crept to the potting table, she caught sight of mangled flowers and bruised leaves on the ground. To Fermina's horror, the goat was poking a basket of tiny seedlings and munching at the contents contentedly.

"You son of an old goat, you," Fermina seethed. Blinded by an unexpected fury, she jumped, fork in hand, toward the animal. Too startled to leap out of harm's way, Fermina's way, that is, the goat stood, transfixed with fear, for a split second before reacting. Long enough for Fermina to poke him in the neck with her sturdy cooking fork.

The goat bucked wildly and when it flung its head back, disengaged his neck from the fork. He stumbled out of the shed, leaving a trail of broken pots, torn petals and strewn dirt in his wake. Fermina clutched her bloodied fork like a trident and hurled invectives at the beast.

"You devil, you demon, look what you've done. And that don Jacinto who smells like an old goat himself! Wish I could get my hands on that fool right now."

She flicked on the light switch and gently picked up her saplings.

"My little sweeties. Destroyed. Completely." She held the tiny crumbled plants in her palm and pressed them to her chest. Her face set angrily.

"I hope the damn goat is dead. Where's that good-for-nothing *chupacabras* when you need him? I tell you, Cervantes, what is this world coming to when they let ugly, filthy goats trample on the most beautiful, the most delicate flowers in the world. There is no justice in this world. No justice at all."

■ ■ ■

That evening don Jacinto, inevitably, paid Fermina a visit. Fermina would have loved to pierce his neck with a fork too, but she had to be civil. Too bad.

Don Jacinto's permanent scowl was deeper, darker, when he entered the living room. Fermina turned off the TV and bid him to sit down.

"May I get you some coffee or maybe a glass of lemonade, don Jacinto."

He looked at the chair before sitting down, as though expecting nettles to have been placed there for his discomfort.

"One of my billy goats was hurt," he charged into the discussion like a bull in a ring, without preamble. "Did you see anyone around here who may have committed such a despicable act?"

His attitude struck Fermina as very impolite. He could have at least inquired about her health, her family, talked about the weather, and then settled into this business with the goat.

"And how is doña Martina?" She was determined to display some common courtesy even though the injured party in this business was certainly her.

"The billy goat, that's what I want to talk about. I'm a busy man, so don't waste my time. My goat was stabbed," he stated curtly.

"Is he dead?" Fermina asked hopefully.

"Injured. Two vampire wounds in the neck. Whoever did this had fangs, I'm sure of it." His eyebrows almost touched his hairline.

"Well, I've told you a million times that your goats are always jumping into my *finca,* destroying my beautiful orchids. Why don't you keep those smelly goats in your own property where they belong?"

"Give me a break! Those flowers of yours aren't worth my goats' *caca!*"

"*Perdón.* Pardon me?"

"Listen, doña Fermina, I'm a reasonable man."

Fermina snorted.

Don Jacinto's dark bushy eyebrows came together and he dropped his voice.

"Was it by any chance you who inflicted the wounds on my billy goat? If so, you pay me the vet expenses, promise you'll never hurt one of my animals again, and I won't report you. Don't forget, the mayor is my son's best friend and *compadre.* If I report you, Güiche's office is involved and it could become a big scandal. Now, is that what you want?"

"How dare you come into my own home and accuse me of something like that?" Fermina threw her head back. "I want you to get out of my house this minute!"

"You crazy old woman. You belong in the looney bin."

"*Viejo sinvergüenza,*" Fermina cried after don Jacinto stalked off. "I bet he's on his way to the police right now. Or worse, running with his tail between his legs to that stupid mayor we have. May his tongue fall off before he starts spreading tales about me through the whole town. Maybe I'll be lucky and the mayor's out hunting the *chupacabras* tonight."

Fermina was too upset to watch her favorite soap opera or even call her daughters. She burned with rage and rocked vigorously in her chair while she mumbled to herself.

"Shouldn't have let my anger blind me like that. The poor goat. I hope he's okay. But, what am I going to do if the police come looking for me? I gotta make something up, some kind of tale. I hope nobody saw me. *Ay, Virgen María,* help me come up with a good story to save my skin. That *viejo* don Jacinto is capable of suing me for all I got. I could lose the farm. Everything. What can I do, what can I possibly do?" Fermina addressed all the cats who were lying about the living room, except for Bruno who, when don Jacinto stomped into the house, had scurried away to hide uttering squeals of distress.

Fermina was not surprised when she heard the rap on her screen door. She peeked through the curtains and saw the two young policemen. She recognized them right away. Pablito Sánchez and Chucho Jiménez. Neftalí used to thwack them with a switch when the boys played hookey and came into their *finca* to steal *quenepas,* the plentiful Spanish-limes that grow all over their property. Now, they were grown men and here they are, Fermina thought, ready to cart me off to jail. I told Neftalí he shouldn't go after those kids. Those were just boyish pranks. Oh, well, I better open the door and face the music. With this uncomfortable thought, Fermina opened the screen door.

"*¿Cómo está*? How are you, doña Fermina?" Chucho inquired politely as he and Pablito came in. Fermina shooed Greta so the young men could occupy the sofa. After some preliminary conversation about the weather, their families and the state of the crops, Pablito cleared his throat.

"Sorry to bother you at this time of night, doña Fermina, but the mayor's office called us."

"Would you like some *cafecito, mijos*? Fermina interrupted.

"No, *gracias*," Pablito continued while Chucho bent down to pet Teehee who, not knowing this was inappropriate behavior toward an upholder of the law, had been purring and rubbing against his leg.

"So, what can I do for you?"

"A goat belonging to don Jacinto was stabbed this evening," Pablo said. "He filed a complaint against you. He seems to think you may have had something to do with the incident."

"No, *mijo,* I was cooking for all these cats. You don't know how much they eat. And all they want is meat with rice and beans. Just like people. Then, I had my dinner too, we all eat together, you know, and then, let me see," Fermina searched for inspiration in the ceiling beams, "I watched television—the eight o'clock soap opera was on. And now, my goodness, look at the time it is, I was getting ready to go to bed. I gotta lot a things to do tomorrow. Before the first rooster crows, I gotta get up, *imagínense.*"

Chucho straightened up. "Doña Fermina, did you see or hear anything suspicious while you were cooking, or having dinner, or watching television?"

Ay Dios mío, these kids were interrogating her. Her, Fermina Beltrán, who had lived a blameless life. That her head full of gray hairs should have to bear this shame. And all because of that *viejo* don Jacinto. Forget about a law suit, he wanted her in jail, that's what the old goat wanted.

"To tell you the truth, I did see something." Fermina paused for effect and to collect her scattered thoughts. "I was cooking when I saw one of don Jacinto's goats in my orchid shed. So I just went out with my cooking fork still in my hand. You see, I was turning a pork chop just then with one eye on the skillet and the other on those cats, they're such grubbos, especially that Eee-goo-ah, he's perfectly capable of jumping into the pan to snatch one of the pork chops. Anyway, where was I? Oh, yes. I stamped on the floor and shooed the goat away. Then," Fermina paused to let some breath out and inhale again, "suddenly I saw this flash of light, red light, yes, that was it, red light, maybe it had a little blue in it too, and and this thing, this this big flying thing came down from the heavens, like like a ball of fire and and the next thing I knew the ball of fire was on the poor goat. The goat was running like the devil who just saw the cross, but the thing was kind of stuck to his neck."

Fermina reached for her own neck while she searched in the policemen's expressions to see what effect her startling revelation had had on them. Pablito and Chucho looked at each other and did not say a word. Fermina, in her nervousness, decided to plunge ahead. She had never lied like this before, but it was easy, she thought. In fact, the more she lied, the easier it got, especially if she talked fast.

"So there I am, *imagínense,* worried about the poor goat, *bendito,* but I had to run into the house because I could smell the pork chops burning." Fermina stared at the policemen pie-eyed, trying to look as innocent as the Virgen María. She nodded a few times and then shook her head to express the amazement her experience had instilled in her.

■ ■ ■

"Um, doña Fermina, why didn't you inform this to don Jacinto when he came to see you?" Chucho asked.

"That a very good question, young man! You boys are so smart, I'm so happy you turned out okay after playing hookey so much, remember, *mijitos?*"

The minute she said that, Fermina clamped her mouth shut. *Caramba,* shouldn't have mentioned that, she thought, after Neftalí clobbered them so soundly.

"I'm sorry my late husband, may he rest in peace, went after you, you know, because of the *quenepas,* but he was a nervous man and sometimes his temper got the best of him."

"That was a long time ago, doña Fermina, don't worry about that," Pablito said. "But could you answer the question, please?"

"What question was that, *mijito?*"

"Why didn't you inform don Jacinto about this fireball or whatever it was."

Fermina crossed her arms over her chest angrily. "That *maleducado* dared to come into my very own home and insult me. In my very own home. *¡Qué falta de respeto!* How disrespectful! He takes advantage of me because I'm just an old widow, who has no one to defend her. I don't even have any sons. Your mothers are lucky to have you two. Look at you, so handsome in those uniforms. Your mothers must be very very proud."

Fermina, who loved her daughters fiercely and never cared to have sons at all, pretended to wipe an errant tear with her thumb.

"Calm down, doña Fermina," Chucho said. "Your statement is very important. You know the mayor is collecting information on *chupacabras* sightings. He thinks it's an extraterrestrial being. Didn't you see him on television making the announcement? Maybe that's what you saw, the *chupacabras,*" he added.

"*Sí, sí, eso mismo,* that's it!" Fermina replied enthusiastically. This was turning out better than she thought. "The *chupacabras,* imagine that."

"Last night, the *chupacabras* struck again," Pablito said. It mutilated two sheep down in El Tuque."

"Did it suck all their blood out?" Fermina might as well find out as much as she could about this *chupacabras*.

"We don't have the details right now. But we do know that don Jacinto's goat was injured. We checked him out ourselves. Lucky for him that the goat's still alive. It was a close call."

"Oh, yes, that was lucky," Fermina said without enthusiasm.

"We won't bother you anymore tonight, but tomorrow morning we'll pick you up at around nine to take you to the station. Then we can fill out a complete report of the sighting. For the mayor's office, you understand. Is that convenient for you, doña Fermina?" Pablito said politely as he and Chucho got up to leave.

"You gonna arrest me? I didn't do nothing." Fermina's heart sank when she thought they had caught on to her lies. She shot a desperate glance at the telephone. She had to call Mariluz and Graciela.

Chucho patted Fermina on the shoulder. "No, doña Fermina, we'll explain everything to don Jacinto right now. Don't worry, no one will arrest you. We just need a report for the mayor. He's a friend of don Jacinto's family, you see." And he winked at Fermina.

News of the *chupacabras* sighting by Fermina Beltrán spread like wild fire through the island. From San Juan to Ponce to Mayagüez, reporters from newspapers, radio stations and even TV rushed to Barrio Esperanza in Canóvanas to interview Fermina. Her photograph, sitting in her rocking chair and surrounded by all her cats (except Bruno, who terrified of all the people stomping through the house, quivered under the bed), appeared in *El Nuevo Día* and *The San Juan Star*.

In the midst of a press conference held at Güiche's office, Graciela elbowed her way through the throng and pulled Fermina to the side.

"Ma, let me get you an appointment with a psychiatrist."

"You think I'm crazy?" Fermina whispered and grabbed Graciela's arm. "Come to the house, so I can tell you what happened."

Over several cups of coffee and lots of cubed cheddar cheese, Fermina recounted the story of her imminent arrest and destitution at the merciless hands of the hideous don Jacinto. Just as Fermina was about to ask Graciela's advice on what to do with this mess, the phone rang.

"The phone always rings when you busy," Fermina muttered.

"Hello, who is it calling?" Fermina had an uneasy alliance with the phone. "Yes, I am Fermina Beltrán, *a sus órdenes*. Who? Is this true? I cannot believe it!! Yes, I can go there. Anytime you want. Okay, whatever you say. Thank you, thank you, *señor* Geraldo."

With a smile, broader than the side of her house, Fermina hung up the phone.

Writings

Novel: *Porque hay silencio,* Ediciones Tres Tiempos (Buenos Aires), 1987; Editorial Edil (Puerto Rico), 1988. *A Perfect Silence*, Arte Público Press, 1996. *The Eighth Continent*, Arte Público Press, 1997. **Poetry:** *Gotas sobre el columpio*, Florian, 1980. *The Fifth Sun*, Cactus Publishing (Athens), 1989. ***Scholarly Books (selected works):*** *Bilingual Education: A Sourcebook* (co-authored with Sara Meléndez), Teachers College Press, Columbia University, 1987. *Bilingual Education and English as a Second Language*, Garland, 1988; 1991. *Puerto Rican Children on the Mainland An Interdisciplinary Perspective* (co-authored with María Alvarez), Garland, 1991.

Rudolfo Anaya

Rudolfo Anaya is a believer in and promoter of a return to pre-Colombian literature and thought through the reflowering of Aztec civilization in Aztlán, the mythic homeland of the Aztecs, which corresponds to the five states of today's Southwest. He sees his role in literature as that of the shaman: his task as a storyteller is to heal and re-establish balance and harmony. These ideas are present throughout his works, but are most successfully represented in his prize-winning novel, Bless Me, Ultima, *in which the indigenous folk-healer Ultima works to re-establish harmony and social order in the life of the Mares family and to bring psychological well-being to Antonio, the protagonist who is struggling to understand the roles of Good and Evil in life.*

Anaya was born on October 30, 1937, in the village of Pastura, New Mexico, in surroundings similar to those celebrated in *Bless Me, Ultima,* his famous (and his first) novel about growing up in the rural culture of New Mexico. He attended public schools in Santa Rosa and Albuquerque and earned both his B.A. (1963) and his M.A. (1968) in English from the University of New Mexico. In 1972 he also earned an M.A. in guidance and counseling from the same university. From 1963 to 1970 he taught in the public schools, but in 1974 he became a member of the English Department of the University of New Mexico. With the success of his writing career, Anaya rose to become the head of the Creative Writing program at the University of New Mexico. Among his many awards are an honorary doctorate from the

University of Albuquerque; the New Mexico Governor's Award for Excellence; the President's National Salute to American Poets and Writers in 1980; and the national prize for Chicano literature, Premio Quinto Sol, in 1972 for his first novel, *Bless Me, Ultima.* Anaya is also a fellow of the National Endowment for the Arts and the Kellogg Foundations under whose auspices he has been able to travel to China and other countries for study.

In *Ultima,* as in most of his works, Anaya is concerned with instinct and intuition as guides to man's understanding the universe. As he himself has stated, "Each of us is neither all good nor all bad, we share the human emotions. A writer is no different from the vast swarm of mankind, only in us, something is heightened, that vibration of creativity forces us to [move] closer into the lives of our brothers and sisters." Anaya grounds these intuitive guides in plots, characters, and symbols drawn directly from New Mexican Hispanic culture. In *Ultima,* the protagonist Antonio must find his place in society by choosing between the indigenous farming and the Spanish ranching heritages of his family; he must also decide between a religious or a secular path to knowledge. Antonio's journey is a mystic quest through real dangers and puzzling dreams. His mentor throughout is Ultima, the wise, old faith-healer, who is possibly a witch.

Largely based on the popularity of *Ultima,* Anaya has been recognized with the City of Los Angeles Award (1977), the New Mexico Governor's Award for Excellence and Achievement in Literature (1980), and a fellowship from The National Endowment for the Arts.

Ultima and most of Anaya's other works were first published by university and small Chicano presses. In 1995, Warner Books recognized the value of his works and began re-publishing his corpus of novels, including his latest, *Albuquerque* (1994), a generational novel about the development of New Mexico.

"Each of us is neither all good nor all bad, we share the human emotions. A writer is no different from the vast swarm of mankind, only in us, something is heightened . . ."

—Rudolfo Anaya

Personal Stats

Chicano novelist and short story writer, teacher. **Born:** October 30, 1937, in Pastura, New Mexico. *Education:* Attended Browning Business School, 1956–58; B.A. (1963), M.A. in English (1968), and M.A. in Guidance and Counseling (1972) from the University of New Mexico. *Career:* English teacher, Albuquerque public schools, 1963–72; counselor, University of Albuquerque, 1972–74; professor, English Department, University of New Mexico, 1974–94. *Memberships:* PEN, Before Columbus Foundation Board. *Awards/honors:* Premio Quinto Sol, 1972; National Endowment for the Arts Fellowship, 1980; New Mexico Governor's Award, 1980; President's Salute to American Poets and Writers, 1980; Kellogg Foundation Fellowship, 1983–86. *Address:* c/o Susan Bergholz Agency, 17 W. 10th Street, #5, New York, NY 10011

from Bless Me, Ultima
a novel

from chapter one of *Bless Me, Ultima,* TQS Publications, 1991, pp. 1–12

Uno

Ultima came to stay with us the summer I was almost seven. When she came the beauty of the llano unfolded before my eyes, and the gurgling waters of the river sang to the hum of the turning earth. The magical time of childhood stood still, and the pulse of the living earth pressed its mystery into my living blood. She took my hand, and the silent, magic powers she possessed made beauty from the raw, sun-baked llano, the green river valley, and the blue bowl which was the white sun's home. My bare feet felt the throbbing earth and my body trembled with excitement. Time stood still, and it shared with me all that had been, and all that was to come. . . .

Let me begin at the beginning. I do not mean the beginning that was in my dreams and the stories they whispered to me about my birth, and the people of my father and mother, and my three brothers—but the beginning that came with Ultima.

The attic of our home was partitioned into two small rooms. My sisters, Deborah and Theresa, slept in one and I slept in the small cubicle by the door. The wooden steps creaked down into a small hallway that led into the kitchen. From the top of the stairs I had a vantage point into the heart of our home, my mother's kitchen. From there I was to see the terrified face of Chávez when he brought the terrible news of the murder of the sheriff; I was to see the rebellion of my brothers against my father; and many times late at night I was to see Ultima returning from the llano where she gathered the herbs that can be harvested only in the light of the full moon by the careful hands of a curandera.

That night I lay very quietly in my bed, and I heard my father and mother speak of Ultima.

"Está sola," my father said, "ye no queda gente en el pueblito de Las Pasturas—"

He spoke in Spanish, and the village he mentioned was his home. My father had been a vaquero all his life, a calling as ancient as the coming of the Spaniard to Nuevo Méjico. Even after the big rancheros and the tejanos came and fenced the beautiful llano, he and those like him continued to work there, I guess because only in that wide expanse of land and sky could they feel the freedom their spirits needed.

"¡Qué lástima," my mother answered, and I knew her nimble fingers worked the pattern on the doily she crocheted for the big chair in the sala.

I heard her sigh, and she must have shuddered too when she thought of Ultima living alone in the loneliness of the wide llano. My mother was not a woman of the llano, she was the daughter of a farmer. She could not see beauty in the llano and she could not understand the coarse men who lived half their lifetimes on horseback. After I was born in Las Pasturas she persuaded my father to leave the llano and bring her family to the town of Guadalupe where she said there would be opportunity and school for us. The move lowered my father in the esteem of his compadres, the other vaqueros of the llano who clung tenaciously to their way of life and freedom. There was no room to keep animals in town so my father had to sell his small herd, but he would not sell his horse so he gave it to a good friend, Benito Campos. But Campos could not keep the animal penned up because somehow the horse was very close to the spirit of the man, and so the horse was allowed to roam free and no vaquero on that llano would throw a lazo on that horse. It was as if someone had died, and they turned their gaze from the spirit that walked the earth.

Writings

Novels: *Bless Me, Ultima,* Tonatiuh International, 1972. *Heart of Aztlán,* Editorial Justa, 1976. *Tortuga,* Editorial Justa, 1979. *The Legend of La Llorona,* Tonatiuh/Quinto Sol International, 1984. *The Farolitos of Christmas* (a children's book), New Mexico Magazine, 1987. *Lord of the Dawn: The Legend of Quetzalcoatl,* University of New Mexico Press, 1987. *Albuquerque,* Warner Books, 1994. **Short Stories:** *The Silence of the Llano,* Tonatiuh/Quinto Sol International, 1982. **Epic Poem:** *The Adventures of Juan Chicaspatas* (epic poem), Arte Público Press, 1985. **Plays:** *The Season of La Llorona* (1979). *Who Killed Don Jose?* (1987). *The Farolitos of Christmas* (1987). **Nonfiction:** *A Chicano in China,* University of New Mexico Press, 1986.

Lorna Dee Cervantes

Lorna Dee Cervantes may well be the most celebrated Hispanic poet in the United States. Although she has published only two books, which are the result of some twenty-five years of work, Cervantes's poems are so finely crafted and insightful that they are chosen to be reprinted in anthologies and textbooks more often than the works of any other Hispanic woman writer.

Of Mexican and Amerindian ancestry, Cervantes was born into a very poor family in the Mission District of San Francisco, California. She discovered the world of books at an early age. When she was only five years old, her parents separated and she moved with her mother and brother to San Jose to live with her grandmother. Cervantes began writing poetry when she was six; poems she wrote when she was fourteen were published in a magazine after she had established her career as a writer. In 1990, Cervantes left her Ph.D. studies in philosophy and aesthetics at the University of California, Santa Cruz, before finishing her dissertation. She went on to teach creative writing at the University of Colorado in Boulder.

Cervantes's early career as a poet achieved recognition in 1974 when her work was published in *Revista Chicano-Riqueña*. She was one of the first Chicana poets to be published and she quickly assumed leadership in the literary movement by founding and editing a literary magazine, *Mango*, out of San Jose. Her work was circulated throughout the Chicano literary community and soon began to appear in anthologies and textbooks nationwide. Many of these early poems, which deal with identity and roots, became part of *Emplumada* (Plumed, 1981), Cervantes's first collection of poems, published by the prestigious University of Pittsburgh Press Poetry Series. The book's popularity has made it the best-selling title in the Pitt series. *Emplumada* as a whole presents a young woman coming of age and discovering the gap between hopes and desires and what life eventually offers in reality. The predominant themes include culture conflict, oppression of women and minorities, and alienation from one's roots. Cervantes uses highly lyric language and yet her poetry is direct and powerful, which makes her work distinctive.

Cervantes's second book, *From the Cables of Genocide: Poems of Love and Hunger*, is the work of a mature poet dealing with the great themes of life— death, social conflict, and poverty. *From the Cables of Genocide* was awarded the Paterson Poetry Prize and the Latin American Writers Institute Award for 1992. Native American poet Joy Harjo has said of *Cables*, "Lorna Dee Cervantes is a daredevil braving the cables of genocide. We are transfixed as she juggles rage, cruelties, passion. There is no net. Seven generations uphold the trick of survival. No one is alone in this amazing act of love . . . I have waited impatiently for this poetry." Jessica Hagedorn's evaluation concludes, "Her work is refreshing and deceptively simple, reflecting love of language and its music. She manages all this without sacrificing the humor, power, and complexity of themes she explores as a female, Latina-American, lover, intellectual, and writer."

> *"Lorna Dee Cervantes is a daredevil braving the cables of genocide. We are transfixed as she juggles rage, cruelties, passion. . . . I have waited impatiently for this poetry."*
>
> **Native American poet Joy Harjo**

Personal Stats

Mexican and Amerindian poet, professor. **Born:** August 6, 1954, in San Francisco, California. ***Education:*** B.A. in Creative Writing, San Jose State University; graduate study at University of California, Santa Cruz. ***Career:*** Assistant professor of creative writing, University of Colorado, Boulder, 1990 to present. ***Memberships:*** PEN-Oakland. ***Awards/Honors:*** National Endowment for the Arts Fellowship, 1978; Paterson Poetry Prize for *From the Cables of Genocide*, 1992; Latin American Writers Institute Award, New York, for *From the Cables of Genocide*, 1992; Visiting Faculty Fellowship, Mexican American Studies Program, University of Houston, 1994-95. ***Address:*** English Department, University of Colorado, Boulder, CO 80302

Pleiades from the Cables of Genocide

"Pleiades from the Cables of Genocide," from the collection, *From the Cables of Genocide: Poems on Love and Hunger,* Arte Público Press, 1991, pp. 43–45

for my grandmother and against the budgets of '89

Tonight I view seven sisters
As I've never seen them before, brilliant

In their dumb beauty, pockmarked
In the vacant lot of no end winter
Blight. Seven sisters, as they were before,
Naked in a shroud of white linen, scented angels
Of the barrio, hanging around for another smoke,
A breath of what comes next, the aborted nest.
I'll drink to that, says my mother within. Her mother
Scattered tales of legendary ways when earth
Was a child and satellites were a thing of the
Heart. Maybe I could tell her this. I saw them
Tonight, seven Hail Marys, unstringing;
                    viewed Saturn
Through a singular telescope. Oh wonder
Of pillaged swans! oh breathless geometry
Of setting! You are radiant in your black light
Height, humming as you are in my memory.
Nights as inked as these, breathless
From something that comes from nothing.
Cold hearts, warm hands in your scuffed
Up pockets. I know the shoes those ladies wear,
Only one pair, and pointedly out of fashion
And flared-ass breaking at the toes, at the point
Of despair. Those dog gone shoes. No repair
For those hearts and angles, minus of meals, that
Flap through the seasons, best in summer, smelling
Of sneakers and coconuts, armpits steaming
With the load of the fording boys who garnish
Their quarters: the gun on every corner,
A chamber of laughter as the skag
Appears—glossed, sky white and sunset
Blush, an incandescence giving out, giving up
On their tests, on their grades, on their sky
Blue books, on the good of what's right. A star,
A lucky number that fails all, fails math, fails
Street smarts, dumb gym class, fails to jump
Through the broken hoop, and the ring
Of their lives wounds the neck not their
Arterial finger. Seven sisters, I knew then.
Well. I remember the only constellation
My grandmother could point out with the punch

Of a heart. My grandma's amber stone
Of a face uplifts to the clarity of an eaglet's
Eye—or the vision of an águila
Whose mate has succumbed, and she uplifts
Into heaven, into their stolen hemispheres.
        It is true.
When she surrenders he will linger by her leaving,
Bringing bits of food in switchblade talons, mice
For the Constitution, fresh squirrel for her wings
The length of a mortal. He will die there, beside
Her, belonging, nudging the body into the snowed
Eternal tide of his hunger. Hunters will find them
Thus, huddled under their blankets of aspen
Leaves. Extinct. And if she lives who knows what
Eye can see her paused between ages and forgotten
Stories of old ways and the new way
Of ripping apart. They are huddled, ever squaring
With the division of destiny. You can find them
In the stars, with a match, a flaring of failure,
That spark in the heart that goes out with impression,
That thumb at the swallow's restless beating.
And you will look up, really to give up, ready
To sail through your own departure. I know.
My grandmother told me, countless times, it was all
She knew to recite to her daughter of daughters,
Her Persephone of the pen.
        The Seven Sisters
Would smoke in the sky in their silly shoes
And endless waiting around doing nothing,
Nothing to do but scuff up the Big Bang with salt
And recite strange stories of epiphanies of light,
Claim canons, cannons and horses, and the strange
Men in their boots in patterns of Nazis and Negroes.
I count them now in the sky on my abacus of spun duck
Lineage, a poison gas. There, I remind me, is the nation
Of peace: seven exiles with their deed of trust
Signed over through gunfire of attorney.
        She rides
Now through the Reagan Ranch her mothers owned.
I know this—we go back to what we have loved

And lost. She lingers, riding in her pied pinto gauchos,
In her hat of many colors and her spurs, her silver
Spurs. She does not kick the horse. She goes
Wherever it wants. It guides her to places where
The angry never eat, where birds are spirits
Of dead resumed for another plot or the crumb
Of knowledge, that haven of the never to get.
And she is forever looking to the bare innocence
Of sky, remembering, dead now, hammered as she is
Into her grave of stolen home. She is singing
The stories of Calafia ways and means, of the nacre
Of extinct oysters and the abalone I engrave
With her leftover files. She knows the words
To the song now, what her grandmother sang
Of how they lit to this earth from the fire
Of fusion, on the touchstones of love tribes. *Mira,*
She said, *This is where you come from.* The power
                    peace
Of worthless sky that unfolds me—now—in its greedy
Reading: Weeder of Wreckage, Historian of the Native
Who says: *It happened. That's all. It just happened*
And runs on.

The Chumash who inhabited the Santa Barbara coast may have believed that they descended to earth from the Pleiades, also known as The Seven Sisters.

The Seven Sisters also refers to the seven big oil companies.

Refugee Ship

"Refugee Ship," from *A Decade of Hispanic Literature,* Arte Público Press—University of Houston, 1982, p. 558

Like wet cornstarch, I slide
past my grandmother's eyes. Bible
at her side, she removes her glasses.
The pudding thickens.
Mama raised me without language,
I'm orphaned from my Spanish name.
The words are foreign, stumbling
on my tongue. I see in the mirror

my reflection: bronzed skin, black hair.
I feel I am a captive
aboard the refugee ship.
The ship that will never dock.
El barco que nunca atraca.[1]

[1] *El barco que nunca atraca (el bahr'koh keh non'kah ah-trah'kah): The ship that never docks.*

Writings

Poetry Books: *Emplumada*, University of Pittsburgh Press, 1981. *From the Cables of Genocide: Poems of Love and Hunger*, Arte Público Press, 1991. **Poems:** In *Mango, Revista Chicano-Riqueña/The Americas Review, De Colores, The Norton Anthology of American Literature* and numerous other magazines, anthologies and textbooks. **Other:** Editor/Publisher, *Mango,* a literary review in the 1970s. Co-Editor, *Red Dirt* (University of Colorado literary magazine).

Lucha Corpi

Lucha Corpi is the leading Chicano mystery writer, but she is also a poet and essayist, and is one of the most fully bilingual Hispanic writers in history. Corpi has written her detective novels in English, but for her short fiction and for her poetry, she relies on the language of her childhood and early education.

Born in the small tropical village of Jáltipan, Veracruz, Mexico, in 1945, Corpi married young and moved with her husband to Berkeley, California, when he began his studies at the University of California. At the time of their emotional divorce in 1970, Corpi too was a student at the university and was heavily involved in the Free Speech Movement and the Chicano Civil Rights Movement. Corpi has remained politically active since, which is evident in much of her creative writing. She eventually earned both a B.A. and an M.A. in comparative literature and since 1977 has been a tenured teacher in the Oakland Public Schools Neighborhood Centers Programs, where she specializes in adult education. She is also a founding member of the cultural center, Aztlán Cultural, which later merged with a center for writers, Centro Chicano de Escritores.

During the 1970s, Corpi began publishing Spanish poetry in small magazines; it is a poetry luxuriant and sensual and reminiscent of her tropical upbringing. In 1976, a group of her poems, along with those of two other poets, were issued in book form in *Fireflight: Three Latin American Poets.* By 1980 Corpi's collected poems were published in her first book, *Palabras de mediodía/Noon Words,* along with their translations by Catherine Rodríguez-Nieto. In 1990, Corpi published a third collection, *Variaciones sobre una tempestad/Variation on a Storm,* again with translations of her poems by Rodríguez-Nieto.

In the early 1980s, Corpi made the transition to prose and to writing in English with the publication of various short stories in magazines. In 1984, she published her first novel, *Delia's Song,* based on her involvement in the Chicano Movement and campus politics at the University of California. *Delia's Song* is one of the very few novels that deal with that historical period which is so important in the making of the modern Chicano.

It was not until 1992 that Corpi's writing career took another turn with her creation of an ongoing series of detective novels. In *Eulogy for a Brown Angel,* Corpi introduced the astute Chicana detective, Gloria Damasco, who unravels the mysterious assassination of a young boy during the Los Angeles protest activities during the 1970 Chicano Moratorium against the Vietnam War. Described as a feminist detective novel, *Eulogy* is fast-paced, suspenseful, and packed with an assortment of interesting characters. Her feminist protagonist, Gloria Damasco, is somewhat of a clairvoyant who is able to use more than reason and logic in solving a puzzling crime. *Eulogy* was awarded the PEN Oakland Josephine Miles award and the Multicultural Publishers Exchange Best Book of Fiction award. In 1995, Gloria Damasco returned in *Cactus Blood,* a mystery set against the background of the United Farm Workers Movement in California.

Cactus Blood opens with a flashback to the 1970s when a young woman was raped, then exposed to pesticide contamination. Five men and two women saved her and helped her put her life back together. Sixteen years later, one of the men who helped her is found dead, and two others have disappeared. Gloria Damasco's investigation into their disappearance begins with the 1973 United Farm Workers Strike and Boycott in the San Joaquín Valley and continues to an old Native American ghost dancing site in the Valley of the Moon. Historic settings, California panoramas, and Hispanic culture give texture to this suspenseful search for a ritualistic assassin.

Lucha Corpi's bilingual artistry has manifested itself differently from other writers who either use Spanish-English code-switching or create two, separate versions of their works (one in Spanish, the other in English). Throughout the body of her highly symbolic, intimate poetry and in her short fiction for children, Corpi uses the language of her early upbringing and education in Mexico—Spanish. Her prose fiction, on the other hand, is written in the language of her professional life and education in California—English.

Of her novelistic writing, Corpi has said, "I write in English because my dreams are—literally—expressed in that language. Also, I write about the political struggle I have witnessed and have shared with so many Chicanos during my life in California."

J. Madison Davis, president of the North American Branch of the International Association of Crime Writers said of Corpi, "There are many more Americas than the dominant media would have us believe. The community in which Lucha Corpi's detective, Gloria Damasco, lives in has roots going back centuries and Corpi paints it as she portrays Gloria—in all its vivid and vital complexity."

Personal Stats

Chicana teacher, mystery writer, poet, essayist. **Born:** April 13, 1945, in Jáltipan, Veracruz, Mexico. **Education:** B.A. and M.A. in Comparative Literature, University of California—Berkeley, 1975 and 1979, respectively. **Career:** Teacher, Oakland Public Schools, 1973 to present. **Memberships:** PEN Oakland, International Association of Crime Writers, Centro Chicano de Escritores. **Awards/Honors:** San Jose Studies Award for Poetry, 1978; National Endowment for the Arts Fellowship in Poetry, 1979; *Palabra Nueva* Award (First Place) Prize for short fiction, 1983; University of California Irvine Chicano Literary Prize for Short Fiction, 1984; PEN Oakland Josephine Miles Award, 1992; Multicultural Publishers Exchange Award for Best Book of Fiction, 1992. **Address:** c/o Arte Público Press, University of Houston, Houston, TX 77204-2090

Eulogy for a Brown Angel
A Mystery Novel

Chapters One, Two, and Three of *Eulogy for a Brown Angel,* Arte Público Press, 1992, pp. 17–22, 23–28, 29–33

One
City of Angels

Luisa and I found the child lying on his side in a fetal position. He was about four years old, with curly, soft brown hair falling over his forehead, and partly covering his brows and long lashes. Small, round and still showing those tiny dimples that baby fat forms around the joints, his left hand rested on his head. He was wearing a Mickey Mouse watch on his wrist, marking 3:39 in the afternoon. Four minutes ahead of mine. His right arm partly covered his face, pulling his T-shirt up over the roundness of an over-sized liver. A soft, sleeping, brown cherub, so like my daughter Tania, probably napping back home at that very moment.

As the image of my daughter asleep in her bed surfaced so did the suspicion that something was very wrong. How could a child be asleep on a sidewalk off Whittier Boulevard in East Los Angeles? Had he gotten separated from his parents during the disturbance, then cried himself to sleep amid the popping and hissing of exploding gas canisters a few hundred feet away from us?

For two hours, we had been hearing the screams and cries of adults and children as they ran from the gas and the shattering of store windows. There seemed to be no end in sight to the violence.

It was August 29, 1970, a warm, sunny Saturday that would be remembered as the National Chicano Moratorium, one of the most violent days in the history of California. Young and old, militant and conservative, Chicano and Mexican-American, grandchild and grandparent, Spanish-speaking and English-speaking, *vato loco* and college teacher, man and woman, all 20,000 of us had marched down Whittier Boulevard in the heart of the barrio. From as far north, west and east as Alaska, Hawaii and Florida, respectively, we had come to protest U.S. intervention in Southeast Asia and the induction of hundreds of young Chicanos into the armed forces. Laguna Park had been our gathering spot.

With our baskets of food, and our children, our poets, musicians, leaders and heroes, we had come to celebrate our culture and reaffirm our rights to freedom of expression and peaceful assembly as Americans of Mexican descent.

In our idealism, Luisa and I, and others like us, hoped then that the police would appreciate our efforts to keep the demonstration peaceful and would help us maintain order with dignity. Surely, we thought, they would realize that we would not needlessly risk the lives of our very old and our very young. How foolish we had been. When a few of the marchers became disorderly, they were subdued by police officers in a brutal manner. People gathered around them and protested the officers' use of undue restraint. A bystander threw a bottle at the police, and five hundred officers armed with riot equipment marched against us. Our day in the sun turned into the bloody riot we were now running from.

I looked at the child again, at the unnatural stillness of that small body bathed in the afternoon sunlight, then felt Luisa's hand on my arm, pulling me away from him. Freeing myself I walked over to the child, hoping all the while that he was asleep or perhaps only slightly injured.

As I bent over, reaching out with a trembling hand to shake him, I became aware of the strong smell of excrement coming from him. Automatically, I pulled up the leg of his shorts and looked in. He was soiled, but not enough to account for such a strong smell. A fly swooped down and landed on his right arm, then another. Resisting the desire to fan them away from him, I watched as they raced over and under his elbow to his mouth, and with a trembling hand I lifted his arm. I was shaking violently by the time I saw the human excrement in his mouth.

I don't know that I understood entirely then what I had just uncovered, but when I realized that the child was dead and his body so defiled, I felt a jolt moving from my chest to the back of my neck, then to my stomach. With my eyes closed I felt my way to the wall. No sooner did I reach it than a burning wave of horror and impotent anger shoot up from my stomach and out of my mouth. My body went limp and I fell down in my own vomit, my eyes wide open. For an instant, I felt that I was looking down at the child, at Luisa and at myself from a place up above while the action below me rushed, like an old film, over a screen.

I felt I was floating over the rooftops. In the distance, clouds of teargas rose and mingled with the smoke of a dozen fires burning out of control. The fumes quickly overtook the crowds who then rushed onto the nearest streets that fanned out from Whittier Boulevard.

Two older people were hosing the teargas off the faces of passersby, among them several eighth-grade students and their teachers who were running towards a school bus. Two teenagers helped a third one, whose leg was bleeding profusely. Over their shoulders or cradled in their arms, some parents carried their children who had been overpowered by the gas fumes.

Policemen and sheriff's deputies armed with riot equipment marched against the crowds, using their batons to strike anyone who crossed their path or dared to strike back. Then they cuffed and filed them into the paddywagons.

Downtown, brown and black men gazed on the world through the reeky mist of alcohol, while beyond, in Beverly Hills, people gracefully slid in and out of stores on Rodeo Drive, then into chauffeured Roll Royces, Mercedes or Cadillacs. They headed down palm-lined streets towards their mansions, where their dark-skinned domestic staff tended to their every need.

On the horizon, a thin blue layer of haze marked the place where the Pacific Ocean, indifferent to the affairs of men, had met the land indefatigably every instant of every day since time immemorial.

I looked down at myself. There I was—all one hundred five pounds, five feet-four inches of me—lying fragile next to the dead boy, my dark skin glistening with sweat. How did I get up here? I wondered.

Luisa had her hands on my shoulders and was shouting my name again and again. Despite my desire to stay where I was, I began to descend and suddenly, I was holding on to her hands. I looked into her worried eyes and struggled to stand up.

Surely at least an hour had passed, I thought, as I collected myself and looked again at the dead boy with a coolheadedness that surprised me. I glanced at my watch: 3:45.

"Let's find a phone," I said.

"A phone? My God. Let's get out of here! You just scared the hell out of me. You looked dead, too." Luisa was pulling me by the arm. "There's nothing we can do for him." Her voice trembled and she cleared her throat, pretending to be tough, although I knew she was as affected by the death of the boy as I was. "They're getting closer. Listen," she warned.

I shook my head. "We're too far out of the way. They won't come here. At any rate, I can't just leave him here. You go on. I'll meet you at your house later."

Luisa began to walk away, then changed her mind and faced me. "Okay," she said, in resignation. She pointed in the direction opposite the Boulevard. "My friends Reyna y Joel Galeano live about two blocks from here. Remember I introduced you to them outside the *La Causa Chicana* newspaper yesterday? Joel is a freelance reporter." I nodded and Luisa added, "I'm sure you can call from their house. Go to the corner and turn right, go another two blocks, then left. It's the only blue house, the second one on your right. Number 3345, I think. I'll wait for you here."

"What if they're not home?" I asked.

"I'm sure Reyna is home. She told me she wasn't going to the march. She says she's terrified of crowds. Go on," Luisa commanded. "I'll watch over him." I turned in the direction she was pointing.

As soon as I rang the bell at the blue house, Reyna Galeano looked out the window; recognizing me, she opened the door. Joel was on the phone in the breakfast nook, and seemed to be dictating a news report.

"Joel just came in, too," Reyna told me, as she invited me to wait in the living room. "Rubén Salazar is hurt. He may even be dead. We don't know for sure." There were tears in her eyes.

"Who is Rubén Salazar?" I asked.

"He's a reporter for the *L.A. Times.* We just saw him yesterday. Joel talked to him about taking photos of the march for the paper."

"Oh yeah, now I know who he is. He also works for one of the Spanish-speaking TV stations here in L.A., doesn't he?" I sat down and looked at Reyna. "What happened to him?"

"We don't exactly know, but he was probably shot. At the Silver Dollar Cafe, where La Verne Street dead ends—oh, my God! I didn't mean to put it that way. Joel just came in and he's trying to get the facts."

"That's only a few blocks from here," I murmured. My legs itched and I started to scratch as I quickly considered and dismissed any possible connection between the shooting of Rubén Salazar and the death of the child. "We just found a little boy a couple of blocks from here," I said to Reyna. "He's dead. I came to call the police."

"You found a dead boy on the street?" Reyna looked incredulously at me. "I'm so glad our kids Mario and Vida are at my mother's in Santa Monica. We figured it was better not to have the children around today. From what you're saying, we were right."

Before I could answer Reyna's quick questions, I saw that Joel had finished with the phone, and I rushed to pick it up. "Sorry, don't mean to be rude but I need to call the police," I explained, then added, "I don't know if you remember me. I'm a friend of Luisa's."

"I remember you." He looked concerned. "Is it about Rubén Salazar?"

"No. I just found out about him from Reyna."

"I really don't think you should be calling the pigs. We're almost sure one of them shot Rubén."

"This isn't about him," I interrupted. "It's about a little boy Luisa and I just found." I wasn't making sense, yet I knew that groping for words and getting the sequence of events right was going to take too long. Joel raised his eyebrows but he didn't question me further. He sat at the table and began to go over his notes.

I dialed "information," then hesitated. Should I call the homicide division? I was very sure I had found a murder victim, but I dialed the general information number anyway.

Since I was rambling on about finding a little boy dead on the sidewalk in the vicinity of Whittier Boulevard, I kept getting transferred from one section to another of the L.A.P.D. I had been reluctant to mention the excrement in the child's mouth, afraid that I would not be taken seriously. "Somebody listen, please," I pleaded into the static at the other end of the line when I was put on hold once more.

Aware that Joel was giving me an "I-told-you-so" look, I tried avoiding his gaze and turned my attention to the photos and certificates on the wall in front of me. I could see he'd won a couple of awards for photos he'd taken in Viet Nam. I studied a photo of Joel in fatigues with other Marines until a voice came on the phone.

"This is Matthew Kenyon. I understand you have a matter for homicide?" Too late to worry now about having called the police. Joel frowned, shook his head, then left the kitchen.

"A child was murdered this afternoon, I tell you. I found him on the street with *shit* in his mouth. I mean that literally. *Shit!*" I said impatiently to this Matthew Kenyon, no doubt an old cop with a desk job, feeling sorry for himself for not being out there where he could get some action. Immediately, I felt ashamed for blurting out such a crude description of a child whose death had so profoundly disturbed me.

Ironically, it was the crudeness of my remark that made Matthew Kenyon take notice of what I had to say. As I found out soon thereafter Kenyon was a middle-aged detective in the homicide division who had purposely, I suspected after meeting him, not participated in the assault on the demonstrators at Laguna Park.

"What's your name?" he asked me. I hesitated. A Spanish surname always meant a delay of at least an hour in emergencies. He seemed to guess the reason for my hesitation and added, "All right. Just give me your first name."

"Okay," I answered, "my name is Gloria. Gloria Damasco."

"That's good, Gloria." There was no hint of pleasure or displeasure in his voice. "Are you related to the dead boy?"

"No. I just found him." I was losing patience.

"Yes. Now, tell me. Where exactly did you find the boy?"

"On Marigold Street, corner with Marguerite, a few blocks from Whittier Boulevard."

"Are you there now?"

"No. But I can meet you there."

"I'll be there in ten minutes. But I want you to do me a favor. Go back to the place where you found the boy and make sure no one touches him or anything around him."

As I put the receiver on the hook, I realized that somewhere in that city named after Our Lady of the Angels of Porciúncula, a killer roamed the streets or waited at home for news, the knowledge of his crime still fresh in his consciousness.

Two
Insidious Disease

Little Michael David Cisneros had been identified by his mother and father, Lillian and Michael Cisneros, about six hours after Luisa and I found him. His maternal grandmother, Otilia Juárez, who had reported him missing at 2:45 that afternoon, claimed that he'd been taken from the porch of her house on Alma Avenue, about three blocks from Laguna Park.

We had found him less than two miles from Otilia Juárez's house, approximately the length of the area swept by the police during the riot as they forced the crowd from the park back towards Atlantic Park where the march had originated.

Joel had insisted on going back with me to that spot. Michael David's body was there, still with no more company than Luisa and the flies. I knelt down to fan them away so that Joel could take pictures of the scene. He didn't seem to have the same reaction I'd had when I first looked at the body, but his hands shook as he snapped photo after photo.

Luisa assured me that nothing had been disturbed. No one had passed by, for the area was quite isolated. A building rose to a height of about three floors on the side of the street where we stood. It was one of those windowless low-budget plaster fortresses where unwanted memories are stored and sometimes forgotten. Across the street, a number of small neighborhood stores had been closed because of the disturbance. Even under ordinary circumstances this was an out-of-the-way street, a good ten blocks from the main thoroughfare.

Suddenly I saw a Chicano teenager standing at the corner, smoking a cigarette and glancing furtively in our direction. He was wearing a red bandanna, folded twice and tied around his head, a black leather vest, no shirt, and black pants. Just then, he turned around and I noticed that a skull with a halo above it and the word "Santos" were painted on the back of his vest. He seemed no older than eighteen, most likely a "home boy," a member of a youth gang. What was he doing there, I wondered. Luisa told us she'd seen him cross that intersection twice since she'd been there. It was obvious the young man didn't seem disturbed by our surveillance and, after a few minutes, he began to walk in our direction. Luisa instinctively retreated behind me, and I, behind Joel. Finding himself suddenly cast in the role of defender, Joel put his camera in its case and began searching his pockets for something to use as a weapon.

Two years before, after a couple of attempted rapes of students at Cal State Hayward, Luisa and I had taken a self-defense course for women and, as a reward for our good performance, we had received a small container of mace, a permit to carry it, and a whistle. I reached for the whistle and Luisa grabbed the mace from her purse. Seeing our weapons, Joel gave a sigh of relief. Then he frowned as though he recognized the young man.

"Is this guy someone you know?" I asked Joel. He shook his head.

With a slow stride, young man approached, then stopped a few feet away from us.

"Soy Mando," he said and looked straight at Joel, but his eyes took in everything between the wall and the opposite sidewalk. He threw a quick glance at the body, then at me. *"El chavalito este. ¿Es tuyo?"*

"No," I replied, "it's not my child." This Mando was much younger than he'd seemed from a distance, not quite fifteen. Not a bad young man either, I sensed, and relaxed a little.

"The dude who brought the *chavalito* here dropped this." Mando handed me a folded newspaper clipping which had turned yellow and was already showing signs of wear at the creases. No doubt it had been kept for a long time in a wallet.

My heart beat wildly and my hands shook as I reached for the clipping. Almost automatically, I closed my eyes. I suddenly sensed the presence of a man. I saw his shadow, then a small house surrounded by tall trees. Somewhere in the area children were laughing. The scene passed and I felt nauseous, but I managed to overcome the desire to vomit. Still I had to hold on to Luisa.

My strange behavior disconcerted her, but Mando didn't pay any heed to it. Perhaps he had witnessed stranger things, seen a lot of pain or wanton cruelty in his short life. I doubted there was much left in this world that would shake him, except perhaps the death of the child. Why had he decided to give *us* the clipping? And why did I trust him? Instinctively I felt he had nothing to do with the death of the child.

"Did you see the person who did this? Can you tell us what he looked like?" Joel took a small memo pad and pencil from his shirt pocket, flipping for a blank page. Like my husband, who was also left-handed, Joel held the memo pad in the hollow of his right hand, across his chest.

"I didn't see nothing. Understand? *Nada.*" Mando looked at Joel's hand, put his palms out, and took a couple of steps back.

"How do we know it wasn't you who killed this *chicanito?*" There was a double edge of contempt and defiance in Joel's voice, which surprised both Luisa and me.

Mando stood his ground across from us. His eyes moved rapidly from Joel's face to his torso and arms, locking on the camera hanging from his neck. A wry smile began to form on Mando's lips. He spat on the ground, wiped his mouth with the back of his hand. "Later, *vato,*" he said, waving a finger at Joel.

"*Cuando quieras,*" Joel answered back, accepting the challenge. "Any time," he repeated.

Irritated with their childish confrontation, Luisa commanded, "Stop it! Both of you!" She looked at Joel, then added, "A child is dead. That's why we're here."

Joel's face flushed with anger, but he remained quiet. Mando turned slightly to the left, cocking his head. The only noise was the distant clattering of the waning riot. Mando moved close to me and whispered in my ear, "The dude—the one who brought the *chavalito?* He wasn't a member of the Santos. I know 'cause he was wearing a wig. *Era gabacho.* He had a scar, a *media luna,* a half-moon on his right arm."

Looking over his right shoulder, Mando began moving swiftly down the street, every muscle in his body ready for either attack or defense. I was fascinated, yet sad. A mother would be crying for him sooner than later, I thought. Not many gang members live long enough to bury their mothers.

"I'll see if I can get some more information from him," Joel said. He ran off in pursuit of Mando, who was already turning the corner when Matthew Kenyon's unmarked car stopped with a screech beside us.

Why is it that cops and tough men, young or old, have to brake or start up a car with a screech, I wondered. Do they think they are establishing turf, like moose or sea elephants?

I looked towards the corner. How had Mando known the cops were on their way? I had a feeling I would never have a chance to ask him

So I gave my full attention to Kenyon. He was a lanky man, six feet tall, with very short red hair already graying and a pallid, freckled face. Everything seems to be fading in this man, I thought, as I focused on his Roman nose, his only feature that seemed atypical.

With Kenyon was another man who answered to the name of Todd, obviously from the crime lab since he was already marking the place where the body lay. A third man, driving a car marked with the seal of the Los Angeles County Coroner's Office, pulled up behind Kenyon's car. He, too, got out and began to examine the body.

Before questioning us, Kenyon helped Todd cordon off the area. Actually, he hardly paid any attention to us at all until Todd referred to the vomit on the sidewalk and I claimed it as mine.

"Ah, yes. Gloria Damasco?" Kenyon said. It amazed me that anyone besides Marlon Brando and Humphrey Bogart could speak without moving his upper lip in the slightest. True, it is easier to do that in English than in Spanish, because of the closeness in quality of English vowels; but Kenyon's case, next to Brando's and Bogie's, was definitely one for the books. He had soulful, expressive eyes, and perhaps because of that I expected his voice to reveal much more emotion.

"Yes," I said, "I'm Gloria Damasco."

I asked Luisa for the clipping Mando had given us and was about to hand it to Kenyon when I was seized by the same kind of fear I had felt when I had tried to take it from Mando earlier. Again, I saw the house, but this time I saw the word "park" carved into a board next to it. In my haste to get rid of the clipping before I became nauseated again, I threw it at the policeman. "Here. I think the murderer might have dropped this."

"So much for fingerprints," Todd muttered, shaking his head.

"I told you not to disturb anything." Despite his perfectly controlled tone, Kenyon's eyes showed anger, but I didn't care since I was more preoccupied with the realization that I was experiencing something out of the ordinary every time I touched that clipping. Perhaps it was only the product of what my grandmother called my "impressionable mind," her term for an imagination that could easily develop a morbid curiosity for the forbidden or the dark side of nature. Even a liking for death. These possibilities distressed me.

I must have looked pretty distraught because Kenyon invited Luisa and me to wait in his car. Since he had already taken note of our names and addresses perhaps he simply wanted us out of the way until he had time to question us, I thought.

We got into the back seat and I lowered the window so I could hear what Todd and the Coroner were telling Kenyon, who was now putting Michael David's body on a stretcher and covering him with a cloth. "Well, Dr. D., was he strangled?"

Dr. D., whose full name, according to his tag, was Donald Dewey, nodded, then shook his head, making the detective raise an eyebrow. "Whoever did this wanted to be extra sure the boy would die. So the boy was drugged. I'm almost sure. This is all preliminary, you know. I'll have more for you in the morning."

"That soon?" Kenyon smiled. "They're putting the others in the deep freeze, huh?" He flipped the pages in his notebook and read aloud: "Rubén Salazar, Angel Díaz and Lynn Ward."

"Looks that way." Dr. Dewey picked up his equipment and headed towards the coroner's wagon. "Just buying time, I suppose. They got themselves into a real jug of *jalapeño* this time." I wondered if "they" referred to the police or to the demonstrators. Dr. Dewey came back after putting everything in the vehicle, then called Kenyon aside.

Trying not to be too conspicuous, I stuck my head out the window but I could hear only fragments of the conversation since both men were speaking in a low voice. " . . . Second opinion. You never know. You'll have to tell them . . . soon." Dr. Dewey patted Kenyon on the shoulder.

"Maybe Joel was right," I concluded. "Maybe it was a mistake to call the cops."

"Someone was going to do it anyway," Luisa said in a reassuring tone.

Todd and Kenyon picked up the stretcher and headed towards the wagon.

"Before I forget," Kenyon said to the coroner. "Will you find out as much as you can about the fecal matter?"

"Try my best," Dr. Dewey answered. "Need about two weeks though." He shook his head. "Real backlog and two lab boys just went on vacation." Kenyon nodded and waved at the coroner.

I made the sign of the cross, closed my eyes and said a silent prayer for the dead child. My eyes were burning inside my lids. I opened them again and looked at my watch. It was now 5:15. The sun was still beating down on the streets and the sirens of ambulances and patrol cars were still wailing in the distance.

I had aged years in just a few hours. By sundown, I would be as old as Mando.

For Rubén Salazar, Angel Gilberto Díaz, and Lynn Ward there was no going home, and the horror that would make the living toss and turn for many nights was of little consequence to them now. They were lying on autopsy slabs, side by side, waiting for their bodies to be opened and drained of blood, their insides emptied, then studied and tested to determine the exact cause of death.

In time, perhaps someone would admit to the *real* cause of what happened that day. But perhaps we already knew the name of the insidious disease that had claimed three, perhaps four, more lives that late August afternoon.

More than ever before, I wanted to go home, to hold my daughter and seek the comfort of Darío's arms. But the spirit of the dead child had taken hold of me. I would no longer be able to go about my life without feeling his presence in me.

Three
Optical Illusions

Night finally came, restoring peace of a sort to that bloody Saturday. It let those wounded in flesh as well as spirit go home and begin the healing process.

It was about eleven o'clock when we got to Luisa's apartment. Until two months ago, she had lived in Oakland but once she received notification of admittance as a graduate student to U.C.L.A., she had moved to Los Angeles, wanting to get settled before classes began.

Joel had been kind enough to pick us up outside the L.A.P.D., where we'd spent the last five hours as reluctant guests of Matthew Kenyon.

The evening mist had moved inland from the ocean. By the time we left, the mist was already condensing enough to release its moisture at the slightest contact with a cold wind. I welcomed it.

Something over which I didn't seem to have any control was working in me or around me. I sensed it the moment we walked out of the police department into the wet evening. A glimmer, a smattering of a presence, of someone out there, waiting for me, raised the hair on my arms.

It did not fill me with fear or horror. The rational part of me told me this sensation had to be simply the manifestation of an overloaded nervous system. We were carrying a layer of dry sweat, teargas and dust on us like a second skin and our souls were burdened with the sediment of the frustration and anger that results from a confrontation with violence.

Luisa and I each showered as soon as we arrived at her apartment. She was so tired she did not eat dinner, and she went to bed immediately. As a matter of fact, neither of us had had any food since that morning. My stomach, like my mouth, felt raw.

I'd answered every question Kenyon had asked about our activities during the Moratorium. Luisa and I had reviewed every detail related to our discovery of little Michael's body and the brief conversation with Mando. Joel had not been able to catch up with Mando, so we had no information about how he'd discovered the murdered child.

During the interrogation, I didn't have an inkling about what Kenyon was considering. I had sensed, however, that he'd been caught between two possibilities. Either I'd been telling him the truth and this Mando of the Santos gang really existed. Or I had been hiding something because I really knew who the murderer was but was protecting him or her. Either way, Kenyon had advised me to stay in town for two or three days in case he needed to talk to me again or to identify Mando if they caught up with him.

I drank a tall glass of cold milk while I called Darío in Oakland, to let him know I was all right. He was a resident physician at Merritt Hospital, and his shift was over at nine in the evening on Saturdays. By now, he would have picked up Tania at my mother's, and my daughter would have been in bed for hours.

"She wants Mommy to come home with the Bugs Bunny you promised her," Darío told me. I sensed from his voice that he had already heard about the disturbance at the Moratorium and had been very worried, but didn't reproach me for not calling earlier.

I shrank from the prospect of having to go over everything again. Fortunately, the late evening news had featured parts of the riot and the death of Rubén Salazar, and I only talked to Darío briefly about the march. Then I told him about my discovering the child's body and relayed Kenyon's request that I stay in town for a few days. Before hanging up, I promised him I'd be at my job interview at the speech clinic at Herrick Hospital on Thursday. Yes, I would call collect every night, and yes, I would take care of myself. I purposely didn't mention any of my "flying" experiences. I suppose I felt embarrassed since I had always sought rational explanations for anything that happened to me, using intuition to support reason rather than the other way around.

After a long day of dragging around a psyche gone amuck, with only rage and fear as ballast, I now felt I was drifting into what I could only describe as neurotic lucidity. Sitting up in the darkness, unable to go to sleep, I had a sense that I was looking at two sides of myself as if on a photographic negative—the lighter areas being "reality"; the darker shades of colors, even perhaps the absence of color, being optical illusions.

A similar illusion had been at work in Mando's description of the person who had carried little Michael's body to the street, where we'd found him. Thinking it over, I concluded that whoever had moved the body had been purposefully dressed like the Santos.

Mando must have had his reasons for waiting around, perhaps knowing I would be back, preferably before the police arrived. It occurred to me then that Mando had probably spotted the individual wearing a Santos vest, and had followed that person to the place where we had found little Michael. He must have managed to get close enough to notice the scar and the man's wig. It stood to reason then that he also knew the color of the man's eyes, his build and height. But how had Mando managed to see so much without being seen himself? Was it safe to assume that the man with the wig—assuming that Mando was right and the Santos' impersonator was a man —was also little Michael's killer? Yes, I told myself, It was one and the same. My own certainty scared me.

Perhaps Mando and the rest of the Santos were looking at that very moment for the individual who'd impersonated one of them. Perhaps, for Mando that was all that mattered—his and the gang's honor. Yet, Mando could obviously have gone after the Santos' impersonator, he could even have killed him, but had not. No doubt he hadn't acquired a taste for death. So instead, Mando stopped to check on little Michael. Like me he must have gone through the shock of discovering the excrement in the child's mouth, then waited for someone else to find the body. He must have picked up the newspaper clipping and, hoping for a clue to the killer's identity, must have read it.

I realized this train of thought might be leading me on to yet another deception. I had to believe that Mando hadn't lost all sensitivity, that he had experienced the same horror I had at the sight of the shit in little Michael's mouth.

In the meantime, the killer had probably sought the anonymity offered by the disorder and confusion of the riot. My intuition (and I would use that word very carefully from that day forward) told me that this was no ordinary killer. It couldn't be a kidnapping gone awry, as Luisa had suggested, because kidnappers would have kept the body until they had collected the ransom. No. This murderer must have had access to the kind of information he needed to formulate his plan and then execute it

Kenyon had told Luisa and me that the boy's parents, Michael and Lillian Cisneros, lived in the San Francisco Bay Area, and that they'd come to L.A. specifically to attend the Moratorium march. Since little Michael had been taken from his grandmother's house, his abductor had to know both her address and the surrounding area. That person also had to be aware of the route chosen for the march, and maybe even the size of the police force that would be used to confront the marchers.

Joel had told me he suspected a policeman had killed little Michael. At that point, with such little evidence, almost anything was possible however, a particular detail nagged me. The killer had planted the excrement in Michael David's mouth. Was it his own private joke, perhaps, or his calling card? And if so, for whom was it intended? What was his reason for killing a child? Obviously I didn't have all the information I needed to walk this through my mind, but perhaps Mando could give me a fuller description of the murderer and clarify some other details for me.

I felt revulsion and anger rising up in me once more and closed my eyes. To my surprise I heard the laughter of children again, then I saw tall pine trees, a few picnic tables and a house. A wooden sign with "park" written on it was visible a hundred feet away. If only I could get closer to the sign and see the rest of it, I would know which park I was looking at, I thought. I began moving but not towards the sign. Instead, I climbed up a small hill towards an area where the children were playing, and I could hear their laughter and chatter getting closer. Then an older man's loud voice began calling for Michael. Now, I could see the little boy's back. He was standing next to a Spanish pine in the yard of a house, but this was definitely not the house in or near the park.

When the scene faded, I opened my eyes. Surely there was a connection between the clipping and this array of images triggered in my imagination every time I thought about the clipping. What was the significance of its contents, I wondered as I turned on the light and got up to get my purse?

I pulled out the copy of the clipping I had requested from Kenyon. Someone had scribbled *January 10, 1947* at the top of the article. The name of the newspaper didn't appear anywhere, but the information in the article referred to a Cecilia Castro-Biddle. The woman was claiming to be a descendant of the Peralta family, who under Spanish and then Mexican rule had owned a land grant the size of five large cities across the bay from San Francisco.

Luisa had laughed when we first had looked at the clipping, for it was clear that the writer had had an ax to grind with Mrs. Castro-Biddle for claiming a link to the historically important Peralta family and was trying to put her in her place.

I hadn't a clue as to how the content of the newspaper clipping related to the murder of little Michael Cisneros, I decided, then went back to bed.

I closed my eyes and began to fall asleep. I wanted to pray but all I could say was: "God, may it all have been a nightmare." Then, on some subconscious second thought, I added: "But if it wasn't, let me find the solution to this puzzle. Point the way."

Laughing at the ambivalence of my prayer, I felt myself rising again, joined by a silver thread to a little boy who watched in fascination as our shared umbilical cord wound around the Spanish pine between us.

Writings

Novels: Delia's Song, Arte Público Press, 1989. *Eulogy for a Brown Angel,* Arte Público Press, 1992. *Cactus Blood,* Arte Público Press, 1995. **Poetry Books:** *Fireflight: Three Latin American Poets,* Oyes Press, 1976. *Palabras de mediodía/Noon Words,* Fuego de Aztlán Press, 1980. *Variaciones sobre una tempestad/Variations on a Storm,* Third Woman Press, 1990. **Poetry and Short Stories:** In *The Americas Review, Fuego de Aztlán, Third Woman, Palabra Nueva,* and many others.

Ofelia Dumas Lachtman

Ofelia Dumas Lachtman has brought mystery and adventure into the framework of multicultural children's writing. Her picture books and young-adult novels present—within the framework of Mexican American family life—puzzles for young people to solve.

Born on July 9, 1919, in Los Angeles of Mexican immigrant parents, Ofelia Dumas Lachtman attended Los Angeles city schools and received an A.A. degree from Los Angeles City College in 1939, but suspended her plans to study further when she married and moved to Riverside, California. There, she raised two children while developing a writing career in her spare time. She had been writing since childhood, and, in fact, her first work was published in an anthology of children's poetry when she was only twelve years old. Little did she know then that as an adult she would become a successful writer for young people. During World War II, Dumas Lachtman worked as a stenographer. Later, after her children were grown and had left home, she became a group worker and eventually rose to the position of executive director of the Los Angeles-Beverly Hills YWCA. She retired from that position in 1974, and devoted herself full-time to writing. In addition to her books, she has published personal interest stories and short fiction in major city dailies and magazines throughout the country.

Dumas Lachtman's first young adult novel, *Campfire Dreams*, was published in 1987 by Harlequin, and was eventually translated into French, German, and Polish. *Campfire Dreams* is the story of a camp counselor who believes she has found her biological mother and does not know how to break the news to her adoptive mother, whom she loves very much. Despite the success of *Campfire Dreams*, Dumas Lachtman was not able to find another publisher until her agent placed her works with Arte Público Press in the mid-1990s. Thereafter, Dumas Lachtman's productivity seemed boundless, as she completed many books including a novel for adults, *A Shell for Angela* (1995), which explores the consequences of rejecting one's heritage. The novel charts a well-to-do Mexican American woman's past and her journey to Mexico to solve the mystery of her father's deportation from the United States and his subsequent murder. But the journey becomes more than just a quest to solve a mystery—it becomes one of finding roots and identity.

Dumas Lachtman is the author of two children's picture books, *Pepita Talks Twice* (1995) and *Lupita y La Paloma* (1997). The first tells the story of a girl who decides to give up speaking Spanish because she always has to say things twice; that is, she is always asked by her relatives, neighbors, and even her teacher to translate from one language to the other—a linguistic and cultural dilemma that many Hispanic children experience. The second picture book is an adventure story about a girl who successfully thwarts the theft of a valuable piñata from her parents' restaurant. This work, like Dumas Lachtman's others, highlights the inventiveness and genius of young girls.

Initiative, courage, and resourcefulness also win the day in Dumas Lachtman's most important book to date, *The Girl from Playa Blanca* (1996), which received critical acclaim and won the Benjamin Franklin Award for Young Adult Literature. The adventure follows a teenager and her little brother from their Mexican seaside village to Los Angeles in search of their father, who has disappeared while working in the U.S. The young protagonist unravels the mystery behind a major crime and not only succeeds in finding her father in the metropolis, but also falls in love along the way.

Dumas Lachtman's most recent work is a novel for middle readers, *Leticia's Secret* (1997), which sensitively—and in the context of the Hispanic family—deals with the subject of death. Leticia is a terminally ill pre-teen whose family members attempt to keep her illness a secret. Leticia's cousin and close friend, on the other hand, sees Leticia's secret as a mystery to unravel. *Leticia's Secret* is a book that can help pre-teens and teens deal with death and grief, topics that are deftly, even poetically, handled by Dumas Lachtman.

Death and grief are topics that Dumas Lachtman handles deftly, even poetically.

Personal Stats

Mexican American writer—children's and young adult fiction. **Born:** July 9, 1919, in Los Angeles. **Education:** A.A., Los Angeles City College, 1939. **Career:** Director of Teenage Programming, Centinela Valley YWCA, 1965-68; Director, Los Angeles-Beverly Hills YWCA, 1968-74. **Memberships:** PEN, The Society of

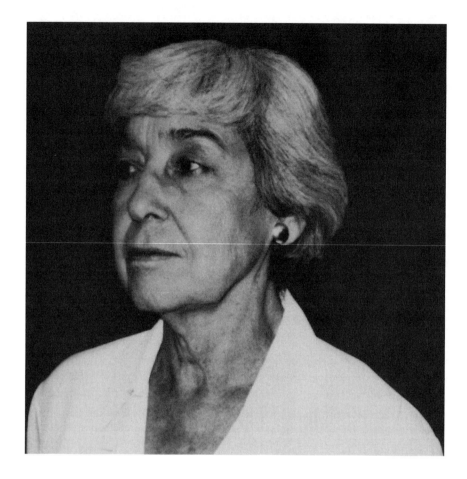

Children's Book Writers and Sisters in Crime. **Awards/Honors:** Stepping Stones Award for Children's Multicultural Literature for *Pepita Talks Twice/Pepita habla dos veces,* 1995; Benjamin Franklin Award for Young Adult Literature, Publishers Marketing Association, 1996, for *The Girl from Playa Blanca*. **Address:** c/o Arte Público Press, University of Houston, Houston, TX 77204-2090

The Girl from Playa Blanca

Chapter One and Chapter Two of *The Girl from Playa Blanca,* Piñata Books, 1995, pp. 7–11, 12–21

Chapter One

She had made it this far. Nothing could change that. María Elena Vargas straightened up in the seat behind the bus driver and stared at the distant yellow lights flashing in the after-midnight blackness. This must be it, she thought, and a little tremor of fear chilled her. This must be the immigration checkpoint I heard about on the border in Tijuana. So, if nothing goes wrong here, we'll soon be in Los Angeles and on Emerald Avenue—and I'll be talking with my father.

Her fingers tightened on a thick bundle of letters on her lap. She had been saving them since she was a child and her parents had left her with her aunt in Mexico while they worked in Los Angeles. They hadn't ignored her. Every week they sent letters. Every month they sent money. And several times a year they came to see her. After her mother died, her father kept on sending letters and money. And when she went to work for Doctor Flores, the money continued to come for her brother Carlos. But five months ago all of that had stopped.

She glanced again at the lights on the highway ahead. She had made it this far, and no matter what happened here, she would not go back to Playa Blanca. Her aunt's words still stung. "You should be married by now, Elena. In a home of your own. But no. You've chosen to be an old maid!" Old maid? At seventeen? Elena swung her hair over her shoulder and shrugged. She hadn't argued. She hadn't even been angry. But then her aunt flung the final barb. "As for your father," she had said, "it seems that he's forsaken you."

Now on the seat beside hers, seven-year-old Carlos grunted and turned. "Look, Elena," he said somberly, "this trip is getting longer and longer. Are we there yet?"

A ghost of a grin twitched Elena's lips. "No," she whispered. "Go back to sleep."

Stretching uncomfortably, Elena leaned her head back on the seat and looked up at the dingy gray ceiling. If only that man behind us would stop snoring! She stole a glance at her brother. Carlos should not be here. He is going to be nothing but trouble. In a moment she leaned over him to look out the window. The bus was slowing down.

It halted with a jolt by a low wooden building that seemed to grow out of a sloping hill. The flashing red and yellow lights were above them, stretching all the way across the highway. Behind her, the snoring man awakened and growled, "What's going on here?"

The bus driver jumped into the aisle. "Stay in your seats," he said. "Immigration. It won't take long." He paused. "Did you all understand what I said?"

There were a few yeses and a few *sís*. Elena nodded, and the bus driver reached for his cap from above the dashboard and swung out the open bus door. Yes, she understood. Thanks to her friend Sylvia Lewis, in Playa Blanca, with whom she had practiced her English. Carlos, of course, spoke only Spanish.

He sat up again. "Now we are there, no?" Without waiting for an answer, he pushed across her into the aisle.

"Carlos, sit down!" She grabbed at his plaid shirt and drew him into his seat as a stocky uniformed man entered the bus.

It took only a few minutes for the officer to walk to the rear of the bus and back, but it seemed a long time to her, time for her to recall the stories told in Playa Blanca about the unrelenting meanness of these officials. Finally, she shook her head. How stupid she was being. Hadn't the officer in Tijuana looked at their papers and winked and called them "gringos?" Actually, that officer had been a bit too friendly. But she had answered his questions in a cool, businesslike way, avoiding his glances—and that had been that. She squared her shoulders as the uniformed man stopped in the aisle near her.

"You," he said, pointing at her. "Where were you born?"

"Los Angeles."

"And the boy?"

"He was born there, too. He's my brother. We're going to live with our father." If the man heard her, he showed no sign of it.

"Your papers," he said.

Elena held back her irritation at the man's rudeness and dug in her purse. The birth certificates were folded in her address book, along with her father's sealed envelope and the note Sylvia Lewis had written for her to a friend named Montalvo.

She watched the officer unfold the certificates. They would tell him only where her brother and she were born, and when. They would say nothing about that sad visit after her mother died when her father had come to Playa Blanca bringing the baby, Carlos. Before her father left Playa Blanca that time, he gave her Carlos' birth record and hers. "Guard these," he told her. He had also given her the sealed envelope. "Some old papers. Nothing of importance now, but take care of them for me." And from that day to this, she had.

The officer folded the certificates and returned them to her. "Where does your father live?" he asked more gently.

"In Los Angeles." Remembering the letters on her lap, she handed them to him and pointed to the return address.

He held up the top letter. "Is this the last one? It was mailed back in November." When she nodded, he said, "This is April. Haven't you had any word from him since?"

"No," she said, "but he will be there." Of course he will be there, she told herself.

"Well," the officer said, returning the letters, "good luck to you."

Elena smiled at Carlos and let out her breath. That was over!

Within minutes the bus was on its way again. It left the brightness of the border patrol's station and moved into darkness, its lights cutting shining strips in the hillside as it turned onto the road She was surrounded now by a cool velvet dark and the strong rhythm of the motor.

Almost immediately, Carlos was asleep again Elena stared at the envelopes in her hands. Then she leaned her head back, closed her eyes and sighed. Of course he will be there.

Chapter Two

Elena slept on and off during the last part of their journey When she was awakened by passengers pushing through the aisle, she was surprised to see that they were stopped and in a large dark garage with empty buses lined up around them.

"Come, Carlos," she said.

After they got their suitcase, they followed the other passengers into a brightly lit waiting room. Inside, she hurried to a booth marked Information.

"Emerald Avenue. Can you tell me how to get there, please?" she asked the woman behind the counter.

The woman stooped over and dragged out a thick book which she laid on the counter between them. She fumbled through the pages. "Emerald . . . yeah, here it is. It's out in Venice." She directed Elena to an intersection nearby where they should wait for a bus that would take them there.

Nearby. Elena shook her head as they walked ten long blocks through the gray dawn, Carlos open-mouthed as he stared at the height of the buildings that lined the streets. He pushed close to her as they walked by doorways where homeless men slept wrapped in newspapers and rags.

"Are they beggars?" he asked. "Will they hurt us?"

"No, no," Elena said with a reassurance she did not feel. "I think they are just poor people, people with no place to go."

They found the right intersection and stood by a lamppost to wait. It was almost daylight when the bus appeared in the distance. Carlos and Elena leaned over the curbing, waving eagerly until it came to a stop beside them. They shoved the suitcase in ahead of them and took the two seats behind the driver. Elena sat stiffly on the front half of the seat, wondering how soon they would get there. But the tall buildings and wide streets seemed to go on forever. Finally, the driver looked over his shoulder and said, "This is it."

They were stopped at a corner by a gasoline station. The driver pointed away from the open bus door. "Emerald's that way," he said. "About four blocks."

Carlos helped Elena with the suitcase and they waited at the corner for the signal to change. Across the street there was a row of small shops. The bright orange door of a restaurant called La Fonda caught Elena's eye and she felt a surge of gladness. Her father had written that he sometimes ate in a restaurant named La Fonda. That meant that they were almost there.

Ten minutes later she stopped on the sidewalk in front of a house with sagging porch steps. It might once have been blue, but it was more the color of old laundry now, grayish white. The numbers 1123 hung crookedly on a pillar. A wooden rocker with a tattered magazine was on the porch by a window. But where were all the plants her father said Señora Gómez kept on the porch. She looked up and down the block. This was the right address and it was the only two-story house. It had to be the right place. She walked to the door and knocked.

When no one answered, she knocked again. In a moment she heard voices and foot-steps and then the creaking of wooden stairs. The door opened, but only a few inches.

A woman's face framed by dry yellow hair looked out at her. "What the devil d'ya want? the woman grunted. "It's not even six o'clock."

"I'm sorry," Elena said. "I know it is early, but . . ."

"Well, go away and come back later."

"We can't. No, please don't close the door! We're looking for Miguel Vargas. He lives here.

The woman's eyes narrowed. She peered intently at Elena and then seemed to discover Carlos and the suitcase. "Think again," she said. My old man and me, we've lived here for more'n four months."

Elena caught her breath. Four months. And her father hadn't written for five. "He lived here with the Gómez family," she insisted. "Where did they go?"

"How would I know? You've come to the wrong place!" The woman stepped back and closed the door firmly.

"Lady, please . . . please," Elena called, but the only answer she got was the sound of the bolt as it slipped into place.

She turned away, then stopped and looked back. Somebody here should know some-thing! But what could the walls with their peeling paint, the windows with their ragged shades, or the bolted door tell her? Nothing. Nothing at all.

She sat on the top step and dropped her head onto her knees. In all the gray morning world, there was no sound but the whirr of cars on the distant boulevard and the drip, drip of mois-ture falling on the sidewalk from a nearby tree. A car drove down the street and muffled music from its radio reached her. The sound was like sighing, she thought, distant, sad. How alone it made her feel.

I should have stayed in Playa Blanca. Maybe I should have gone on working for Doctor Flores, even if he didn't always keep his hands to himself Of course, the pay wasn't enough to sup-port Carlos and me. Still I might have managed something. Or I could have married Alfonso. If I had, I would have a home of my own now. But I would also have five ready-made children.

Elena turned and once more looked wistfully at the closed door. When she was a little girl, her father often said, "Whenever you're scared, Elenita, look over your shoulder and I will be there." And she had known what he meant. That even though he was far away, she could count on him. But where was he today? All along she had been afraid that he might not be here, but she had forced that fear into a distant corner of her mind. She had told herself that there would be no problems. She had looked only on the good side. And now? Well, she thought, there's no one to blame. It was my idea to come here.

"Come on, Carlos," she called, gathering up her things. "Come on, and don't ask where we're going because I don't know!"

There was no answer.

She took a few more steps. "Hurry up, "she said, turning. But her brother wasn't there. "Carlos! Carlos, stop hiding!" She was tired and hungry, and she could stand nothing more. "Come here right now!"

Dropping the suitcase, she ran to the side of the house. Two or three dusty shrubs and some scrawny geraniums were growing there, but there was no sign of Carlos. Then she heard his voice.

"Papá," he was calling, "Papá, where are you?"

At once she felt relieved and then puzzled. Where was he? A creaking, rustling sound came from a jacaranda tree at the rear of the house and Carlos called in a stage whisper, "Here, Elena, up here."

Above her a window was raised with a slam and the yellow-haired woman pushed her head out and shouted, "Get outta that tree, you pint-size peepin' Tom!"

Elena yelled, "Carlos, get down! Right now!"

With a splitting sound, a limb of the jacaranda arched toward the ground. Carlos hung draped on his stomach over the branch, his feet thrashing wildly. For an instant she froze, then she raced to him and grabbed his legs. "I have you. Let go!"

"That does it!" the woman at the window yelled. "I'm comin' down after you!"

Elena steadied Carlos on the ground. "Are you all right?" When he nodded, she said. "See what you did? You broke the branch. Come on, run!"

She lifted the suitcase and, carrying it pressed against her, dashed down the street with her purse dangling on her arm and Carlos at her heels. They turned the corner and kept running. They crossed one street and then another. They kept on running until Elena knew she could not take another step and they stopped. She sat on the suitcase, trying to catch her breath.

Carlos dropped to the ground. "Where's Papá?" he panted. "You said you knew, but you don't. I don't think you know anything!"

"Stop that! You got us into this trouble. And now what are you doing? Making things worse!"

He looked at her for a moment, his black eyes seeming to darken. Tears filled them and spilled over. "I am very hungry, Elena," he said.

"So am I, but the food is gone, remember? Let me think for a minute." She looked around her at the unfamiliar houses on the unfamiliar street and fought back her own tears. She didn't know where she was; she didn't know where her father was; and she didn't know what she was going to do. Carlos was right. She didn't know anything.

No, that wasn't true. There was one thing she knew. She knew that this was the most disappointing morning of her life—and what was even worse, she knew, too, that it wasn't over yet.

As if to prove her right, a black and white car drew to a stop at the curb beside her. She groaned. The police! That ugly, yellow-haired woman must have called them! But how could they have gotten here so fast?

A tall man in uniform got out of the passenger side of the black and white car, slamming the door. He looked at his watch. "Say, young lady, what are you doing out here so early?"

She felt her face color. In Playa Blanca no respectable woman would be found sitting idly on the streets at such an hour. She swallowed and started to answer something when from inside the police car another man's voice said, "Looks to me, Sims, like they're lost."

"They?"

"Sure. There's a kid behind that tree."

"Carlos!" Elena called, and Carlos, his eyes on his feet, walked over to her.

"So what's up?" the officer called Sims said. "Are you lost?"

Elena shook her head. "No . . . not lost, not really."

"What's with the suitcase? What've you got in it?"

"My clothes and his," she said quickly, annoyed at the shakiness of her voice. She raised her chin. She would not be afraid. "My name is María Elena Vargas, señor, and this is my brother Carlos." She gave Carlos a little push and he stepped forward and extended his hand to Sims.

"Carlos Lorenzo Vargas," he said, "*su servidor.*"

Sims nodded somberly and shook Carlos' hand. "Well, Miss Vargas, tell me, where do you two live?"

Again, Elena brought out the letters and the birth certificates. She ended up telling him the whole story, even the part about the woman on Emerald Avenue. "But he did not break the branch, señor, not all the way. He only climbed the tree."

"Oh, I believe you," Sims said with a smile. Then, more seriously, "That's rough, your father's not being there. Could be he's following the crops. Up north, maybe."

"Picking the harvest?" she asked. "No, I don't think so. My father is a carpenter, a very good one. There must be another reason why he is not here."

"Well, until he shows up, do you have a place to stay?"

When she said no, he asked, "Any money?"

What did he mean, money? *Mordida?* Like the Playa Blanca police always expected? Were there bribes here, too? "Yes, I have money." She dug in her purse and held out her hand. "Eight dollars and fifty-two cents. Is that enough?"

"For a couple of hamburgers," Sims said, frowning. "But, anyway, it's something. Put it away." He swung around. "Bellini, come here. We have a problem."

Slowly, she put the money back. He had not taken it. Perhaps it was not enough. Well, she would wonder about that later. Right now she had to wonder what he meant by "problem."

The officer named Bellini, a stocky, curly haired man, got out of the car and Sims and he talked briefly. Bellini turned toward them and nodded, frowning.

What would they do? Elena wondered. Take them to jail? Of course, that's what would happen. She knew that her thoughts were getting the better of her, but even so she shuddered. And at the end of the shudder came a sigh. She would have to use the letter Sylvia had given her.

"If anything goes wrong and you need help," Sylvia had told her, "don't hesitate to call on my friends, the Montalvos." And she had answered blithely that nothing would go wrong. Now, she pulled the letter from her purse and handed it to Officer Sims.

He looked at the envelope, then gave it to his partner. "Gray Ridge Drive," Bellini said. "Not a bad address, not bad at all." He fumbled for a pair of glasses in his shirt pocket and with Sims looking over his shoulder, opened the envelope and read the letter. She knew exactly what it said:

"Dear Ana and Salvador: This note is to introduce María Elena Vargas. I have known Elena since she was nine. For the past ten years I have tutored her, and in that time we have become close friends. In a remote little village like Playa Blanca, a village that looks suspiciously on "gringas" who do nothing but paint and refuse to go to church, friends are not easy to come by, so Elena's companionship has been very precious to me. (Precious also is the memory of that long-ago summer when you, Ana, and David spent two weeks with me in Playa Blanca.)

"Elena is resourceful and self-reliant, so if this letter reaches you it will be because she is truly in need of help. Please do whatever you can for her and I will be grateful to you. Affectionately, Sylvia."

There was a rustling of paper as Bellini returned the letter to its envelope. Sims rubbed his chin. "Doctor Salvador Reyes Montalvo. Seems to me I know that name. A geologist, isn't he? Teaches at Eastmount? No? Well, anyway, I've read something about him somewhere."

Bellini said, "Maybe you have," and they walked a few steps away, where they talked again in lowered tones.

"Elena," Carlos whined, "Elena, I am hungry."

Carlos. For the moment she had forgotten him. When Sylvia had written that letter for her, they hadn't known that Carlos would follow her across Playa Blanca to the bus stop, begging to go with her. There was no mention of Carlos in Sylvia's letter. Would the Montalvos welcome him, too?

Writings

Novels: *Campfire Dreams*, Harlequin, 1987. *Pepita Talks Twice/Pepita habla dos veces*, Arte Público Press, 1995. *A Shell for Angela*, Arte Público Press, 1995. *The Girl from Playa Blanca*, Arte Público Press, 1995. *Leticia's Secret*, Arte Público Press, 1997. *Lupita and La Paloma/Lupita y La Paloma*, Arte Público Press, 1997. **Short Stories and Articles:** In *The Chicago Tribune*, *The Christian Science Monitor*, *The Boston Globe*, *The Washington Times*, *Newsday*, *The Detroit News*, *Michigan Magazine*, *Green's Magazine* and others.

Sandra María Esteves

Sandra María Esteves is the most important female writer to come out of the Nuyorican group of writers. A performance poet, Esteves's works have deep roots in community life and popular culture, and they also represent eloquent and passionate queries into the themes of feminism, machismo, racism, and biculturalism. She is a bilingual poet who cultivates an Afro-Caribbean identity in her life and verse, and so African and Taíno influences are evident in her art and work.

Esteves was born on May 10, 1948, in New York City, the daughter of a Dominican garment worker and a Puerto Rican sailor. She received her early education at a Catholic boarding school, where her Spanish language and Hispanic culture were targeted for obliteration by the strict, Irish American nuns. But that was on weekdays; her weekends were spent in the warmth and comfort of her Puerto Rican aunt's home. Thus, at an early age she discerned the language and culture conflicts that Hispanics experience in this country. Later in life these conflicts would form the basis for much of her poetry.

Esteves studied art at the Pratt Institute in New York City and when, after various interruptions, she graduated in 1978, her writing career was already firmly established. In the early 1970s, Esteves became part of the Civil Rights Movement and the movement to gain independence for Puerto Rico. In connection with the latter, she sang and recited her poetry with a socialist musical group, simply titled

El Grupo, whose recordings became anthems for the independence movement. The recordings also effectively launched Esteves's career as a poet. In the mid-1970s she became involved in the Nuyorican Poets Cafe and the performance poetry it sponsored under the leadership of writers Miguel Algarín, Tato Laviera, and Miguel Piñero. In a literary movement heavily directed by males, Esteves became a beacon of feminism. Her work as a painter followed a similar course as her writing and she became affiliated with the Taller Boricua (Puerto Rican Workshop), a socially-committed collective of graphic artists.

After a considerable portion of her works had been published in magazines and anthologies, Sandra María Esteves published her first book, *Yerba Buena* (The Good Herb), in 1980, to resounding reviews. *Library Journal* named the book the best small press publication in 1981. The title refers to mint, an herb that in Caribbean culture has medicinal qualities; her tropical and urban poems are meant to heal—mend the rifts of culture and gender conflict among Latinos and Latinas. Despite widespread interest among publishers in issuing her works, Esteves self-published her next collection of poems, *Tropical Rains* (1984), probably in order to control distribution herself. The book followed in the bilingual, urban vernacular of *Yerba Buena,* but did not have its impact.

Her latest work, *Bluestown Mockingbird Mambo* (1990), is a mature work that is a distillation of jazz and salsa, "sung" in a precisely stylized bilingualism and exuding a deep spirituality and humanism. Like her other works, the line structures and blank verse of the poetry demonstrate that they are meant to be recited and performed. Esteves's incantations come from both *santería* (an Afro-Catholic religion) and the cadences, threats, and caresses of speech heard in the Barrio. As Louis Reyes Rivera wrote, Esteves's words "conjure up both that Nuyorican way of refusing to accept English insistence on difference, and that Caribbean way of embracing the common ties—in this case, with that African beat, drum, tongue—that binds us."

Personal Stats

Nuyorican writer, graphic artist, art program director. **Born:** May 10, 1948, in New York City. **Education:** B.A. in Fine Art, Pratt Institute, 1978. **Career:** CETA artist, 1987–80; African Caribbean Poetry Theater Director, 1983–90; director, The Family Repertory Company, 1990; coordinator, literary programs, Bronx Council on the Arts, 1991 to present. **Memberships:** Associated Writing Programs, WritersCorp Project; Poets and Writers Inc. **Awards/Honors:** CAPS Poetry Fellowship, 1980; Best Small Press Publication, *Library Journal,* for *Yerba Buena,* 1981; New York State Council on the Arts Poetry Fellowship, 1985; Award for

Outstanding Achievement in the Latino Community from New York University, 1991; Edgar Allen Poe Literary Award from the Bronx Historical Society, 1992.
Address: 3750 Broadway, #31, New York, NY 10032-1527

Amor negro

from *The Americas Review,* Vol. XX, No. 3–4, Fall-Winter, 1992, p. 144

in our wagon oysters are treasured
their hard shells clacking against each other
words that crash into our ears

we cushion them
cut them gently in our hands
we kiss and suck the delicate juice
and sculpture flowers from the stone skin
we wash them in the river by moonlight
with offerings of songs
and after the meal we wear them in our hair
and in our eyes

Transference

from *The Americas Review,* Vol. XX, No. 3–4, Fall-Winter, 1992, p. 147–48

Don't come to me with expectations
Of who you think I should be
From some past when
You were going through changes
I'm not your mother who didn't hold you all day long
Or kiss away the rough cuts when you fell
I'm not your sister who wouldn't play with you
Mashing up your favorite toys on purpose
I'm not the lady upstairs who keeps you up all night
Playing Lawrence Welk Muzac
And I'm not your girlfriend who left you flat
The one who promised forever never to go
For whom you would never love another
Or the one who used you for sex
And forgot your first name
I'm not the one who beat you
For ten dollars and dinner
Or ate up your cookies and milk
Or gave you the wrong kind of presents
I'm not your neighbor who hates you
'Cause you have more roaches than them
Or the landlord who steals your rent
And leaves you out in the cold
I'm not the meter maid who gave you $300 in parking tickets

Or the kid who plugged your tires just for fun

Or the psycho who smashed your front windshield

Or the truck that hit your rear bumper and ran

I'm not the traffic court judge who insists you're the liar

Or the junkie who popped your trunk lock

And tried to steal your spare tire

I didn't take your virginity with empty promise

Or con you with a job for sex

And I'm definitely not the one who ripped off your mind

And did not allow you to speak your own tongue

Or tried to turn you slave or dog

No, I'm not the bitch who denies you your true history

Or tries to hide the beauty of yourself

I am not the colonizer or the oppressor

Or the sum total of your problems, I am not the enemy

I am not the one who never called you

To invite you to coffee and dinner

Nor the friend who never gave you friendship

Or the lover who did not know how to love

So when you come to me, don't assume

That you know me so well as that

Don't come with preconceptions

Or expect me to fit the mold you have created

Because we fit no molds

We have no limitations

And when you do come, bring me your hopes

Describe for me your visions, your dreams

Bring me your support and your inspiration

Your guidance and your faith

Your belief in our possibilities

Bring me the best that you can

Give me the chance to be

Myself and create symphonies like

The pastel dawn or the empty canvas

Before the first stroke of color is released

Come in a dialogue of we

You and me reacting, responding

Being, something new

Discovering.

Anonymous Apartheid

from *Bluestown Mockingbird Mambo,* Arte Público Press, 1990, pp.63–64

There is a stranger in our house
who looks half blind at us,
does not know our name,
assumes our earth is flat,
wraps a ball and chain around our tired legs,
barricades our windows with formless visions,
illusions of no consequence.
This stranger thinks we are alley cats, purring
in heat for violent attentions,
feeds us day-old fish and dead meat,
leaves our fruit basket empty,
does not speak our language, wear our colors,
nor understand the soul of these tender thoughts.
The stranger upsets our garden,
turning over seeds of potential into desert soil,
laying waste the promise of life's harvest,
denied, for no better reason than greed,
chopping down innocent buds to feed
their wealth of scavengers, and thieves,
growing fat from the treasures we are.
This stranger steals us from our mother,
separates us from our brothers and sisters,
does not listen to our million crying petitions,
cuts off our rebellious tongues,
laughs when our tears fall on stone,
orders us to kneel, though we refuse.
Each day the stranger drinks a nectar of blood at high noon, wears clothing spun from blood,
worships a heathen blood god made of gold,
destroys the covenant of humanity
for the sake of a synthetic blood mirror, cracked,
tarnished quicksilver, ungrounded and formless,
traveling a broken spiral of blood.
This stranger lives here uninvited,

an unwelcomed alien ravaging us in gluttonous consummation, throwing a soiled shroud over our
    altar,
expecting us to accept a life of disgrace.
Yet, we refuse.
There is a ruthless stranger in our house
who has no voice of its own,
mimics our words in crude scorn,
suggests we are low, worthless, incompetent,
grinning at itself
while we are held hostage in a doomed drama
where act one lasts more than five hundred years,
in plots of bigoted abuse,
dialogues of racial condescension, poverty,
transitions of rapes, muggings, lynchings,
scenes of jailhouse tortures and hangings,
life sentences to minimum security housing projects.
There is a stranger in our house
plundering our womb,
stealing our newborn with a dry knife,
drug-thirsty for their blood,
bargains in exchange for their lives,
tells us to throw away our weapons, love one another,
rejecting our religion,
forcing us to sell our worth,
poisoning the rich center of our spiritual essence,
speaking the lecherous tongue of split truth.
Yet we refuse, and will continue to refuse,
along with our planetary relatives who also refuse
this stranger in our house
who has no face.

Writings

Poetry Books: *Yerba Buena,* Greenfield Review Press, 1980. *Tropical Rains: A Bilingual Downpour,* African Caribbean Poetry Theater, 1984. *Bluestown Mockingbird Mambo,* Arte Público Press, 1990. **Poems:**   In *In Other Words: Literature by Latinas in the United States; Woman of Her Word: Hispanic; Write, Aloud: Voices from the Nuyorican Poets Cafe; Blackworld; Third Woman; Afro Realism; Heresies: Third World Women; Art against Apartheid;* and numerous other magazines, anthologies and textbooks. **Essays:**   In *Breaking Boundaries, Latinas Writing and Critical Readings; Conditions: Fourteen; Images and Identities: The Puerto Rican in Two World Contexts.*

Roberto Fernández

Roberto Fernández is in the vanguard of Cuban American literature, having made the transition from the literature of exile to a literature that is very much of the culture and social conditions of Cubans in the United States, and having made the transition from producing works in Spanish to writing in English.

Born in Sagua la Grande, Cuba, on September 24, 1951 (just eight years before the Cuban Revolution), Fernández went into exile with his family when he was only eleven years old. His family settled in southern Florida—not in Miami's Cuban community but in areas where Anglo-American culture was dominant. The environment seemed hostile to the young boy and consequently, periods of adjustment followed. This culture conflict would become evident in his writings. Nevertheless, the Fernández family also maintained close ties with the Miami community, and this too became subject matter for the writer. When he was an adolescent Fernández became interested in writing, and this interest led him to college and graduate school. There Fernández became a Spanish major specializing in linguistics; in his Ph.D. research, and later as a professor, he became an expert on the Spanish dialects spoken by Hispanics in the United States. This research and experience is evident in the dialogues and monologues Fernández creates in his novels and stories.

Fernández continued writing while he pursued his Ph.D. in Linguistics, which he completed in 1977. By that time, he had already published two collections of stories, *Cuentos sin rumbo/Directionless Tales*, (1975) and *El jardín de la luna/The Garden of the Moon,* (1976). After earning his Ph.D., Fernández began his career as an academic, writing Spanish-language materials for the science curriculum as a Research Associate of the U.S. Office of Education in 1976, and later as an Assistant Professor of Spanish at the University of South Alabama in 1978. He began teaching Spanish linguistics and Hispanic literature at Florida State University in Tallahassee in 1981, where he remains today as a tenured associate professor.

Although Fernández has built an impressive career as an academic, it is through his writing that he has realized most of his creative potential and he has been far more productive a writer of fiction than of scholarship. He is the author of four open-formed novels that have earned him a reputation for being a humorist and satirist of the Miami Cuban community. He is also a master of the nuances of Cuban dialect both in Spanish and English. *La vida es un special/Life Is on Special* (1982), *La montaña rusa/The Roller Coaster* (1985), *Raining Backwards* (1988), and *Holy Radishes!* (1995) are mosaics made up of monologues, dialogues, letters, phone conversations, and speeches. In composite, these forms of speech make up a continuing tale of the development of the Cuban exile community and the younger generations of increasingly acculturated Cuban Americans. In the pages of his books the author charts the goings-on at social clubs and coming-out parties, the movements of counter-revolutionary guerrillas in the Florida swamps, the emergence of a Cuban pope, the proceedings at poetry and art contests, and many other episodic bits that together create a broad and epic spectrum and portray a dynamic community caught between two cultures, two sets of values, two languages, and two political systems.

Raining Backwards, Fernández's first book published in English, became a small press hit, receiving outstanding reviews in major newspapers and magazines from coast to coast (*The New York Times, USA Today,* and *San Francisco Chronicle,* among them), and was optioned to become a feature film. The novel, which weaves a detective story into the principal story, is a collage of the gossip among Cuban exiles, boasts, newspaper clippings, excerpts from radio broadcasts, and evocations of a Cuban past that Fernández renders in a style of magical realism. *Publishers Weekly* called *Raining Backwards* "a spirited, appealing book, with . . . hyperbolic visions . . . like an *Under Milkwood* written by a Cuban William Burroughs."

Fernández's *Holy Radishes!* is a satirical Cuban American version of Gabriel García Marquez's *macondo.* In it, Fernández depicts a forgotten civilization living in exile in the Florida swamps. After their homeland was taken over by Communists, the previously privileged denizens of the fictional land of Xawa must face a new set of harsh realities in the Everglades. Sustained by memories of their bygone life in Xawa, they pursue their dreams to recreate that existence. Fernández peoples the novel with a host of memorable and quirky characters, including Nellie Pardo, a dreamer who envisions herself in a paradise called Mondovi.

> Raining Backwards
> is "a spirited,
> appealing book,
> with . . . hyperbolic
> visions . . . like an
> Under Milkwood
> written by a Cuban
> William Burroughs."
>
> **Publishers Weekly**

The recognition and acclaim that Fernández has won as a writer have not only resulted in the publication of more of his fiction, but in his serving as a guest writer at the University of Florida, the University of Texas at El Paso, Our Lady of the Lake University, the University of Houston, and the Chicago Public Library.

Personal Stats

Cuban American writer, professor of Spanish Linguistics. **Born:** Sagua La Grande, Cuba, September 24, 1951. ***Education:*** B.A. in Spanish, Florida Atlantic University, 1971; M.A. in Spanish Linguistics, Florida Atlantic University, 1973; Ph.D. in Spanish Linguistics, Florida State University, 1977. ***Career:*** Research Associate, U.S. Office of Education, 1976–78; Assistant Professor, Department of Foreign Languages, University of South Alabama, 1978–80; Assistant Professor, Department of Modern Languages, Florida State University, 1981–86; Associate Professor, Florida State University, 1986–present. ***Memberships:*** Associated Writing Programs, American Association of Teachers of Spanish and Portuguese, American Dialect Society and Modern Language Association. ***Honors/Awards:*** Cultural Award of the City of Miami for fiction, 1977; State of Florida, Division of Cultural Affairs, Artist Fellowship (Fiction), 1986; Cintas Fellowship (fiction), 1986. ***Memberships:*** c/o Arte Público Press, University of Houston, Houston, TX 77204-2090

Holy Radishes!

"Nellie," in *Holy Radishes!*, Arte Público Press, 1995, pp. 7–20

Nellie

Nellie was glad she hadn't burned herself this time. She unplugged the sizzling iron, put the starch underneath the kitchen sink, and began folding the freshly ironed clothes. She began placing the garments in two worn suitcases which rested open-mouthed at the foot of the bed. The luggage was spotted with faded stickers, echoes of long-ago sojourns—a faceless bullfighter battling half a bull, a Tower of Pisa which no longer leaned, and a Beefeater beheaded by time. First she packed the underwear, then her blouses; followed by skirts, shirts and slacks. On top, she carefully placed her favorite and only remaining evening gown, a royal-blue dress with brocades, pearls, and sequins. Though the dress had not felt the warmth of her flesh or heard the music and laughter of a ballroom for some time, Nellie brought it out to look at it for a moment when she ironed each day. She covered the clothes with moth balls, impregnating the house with the stench of time. Then, with a suddenness born out of her small hope, she slammed the suitcase shut and with a series of vigorous kicks made the luggage disappear underneath the bed.

She licked her index finger and flicked the iron, making sure it could be stored inside the closet without risking a fire. Delfina had warned her when she was a child to be careful of fire. At the time, Delfina had been trying to light a blaze under a kettle of water to boil Nellie's father's soiled shirts while Nellie, contentedly sucking on a mango, and always the observant child, watched her.

"See the fire, little girl?" Delfina asked. "In your path there is something charred by flames. Beware of anything that burns!"

Though the two years her family had spent in the bungalow seemed like twenty, Nellie could not bring herself to unpack their bags. Her daily routine of ironing and repacking helped to keep her faith from being snuffed out altogether. She hoped that this was not lasting, not permanent.

It was hot for January. Nellie took the cardboard fan she had found on her doorstep and escaped to the porch, where it was cooler. The front of the fan depicted a Scandinavian Christ resting by a riverbank shaded by tall beech trees, and holding a black sheep in his lap. On the back, a holy message was written in incipient Spanish: *PESCADOR ARRE PIENTA DIOS ENOHADO CON USTED VEN Y TIEMPLO PRIMERO VIVO LLAMAR REVEREND Y AMIGO AUGUSTUS B. FENDER. OLE! SE HABLA PEQUENO ESPANOL. (FISHERMAN, REPENT! GOD MAD WITH YOU. COME AND I SCREW FIRST LIVING. CALL REVEREND AND FRIEND AUGUSTUS B. FENDER. OLE! A SMALL SPANISH IS SPOKEN.)* Nellie wiped the rocking chair with a rag that hung from her left pocket and smelled of garlic, then sat down. She started to fan and rock herself in perfect synchrony. Her gaze was lost in the cane fields that surrounded the house and stretched beyond the horizon. Her eyes became cloudy remembering Rigoletto, attired in a light red sweater. His memory grew smaller and smaller until it became a tiny glowing speck on the edge of her mind.

Nellie remained on the porch with her eyes fixed on the fields until she heard the clanking and whirring of old bicycles approaching. School was out for the day and her children, happy to be free, were coming home. She hurried to supervise the cola-fueling operation and lament her fate to the children. After Nelson Jr. and María-Chiara had left, burping with satisfaction, she turned on the television, an old RCA whose picture faded in and out every five minutes, and began watching *Donna Reed,* her favorite show. The set did its best to produce a vision of family life, but the fuzzy picture soon became a downpour of tiny gray dots. It forced Nellie to rely on her ears to follow the plot. As best as she could tell, Donna and Dr. Stone were planning a trip to Europe. Donna wanted to go to Paris and her husband to London. In the last scenes the couple was in the midst of an argument. They suddenly hushed because Jeff and Mary had come home from school. Donna dried her tears with her apron and Dr. Alex Stone welcomed the kids with a big smile.

The theme music signaled that the show was over for today and that her husband, Nelson, would arrive in an hour. He worked as a stocker for Rosser and Dunlap Trucks and Rigs. It was the first real job he had found after arriving from Xawa; he held on to it, happily stagnant despite having once been the head of his father's vast business empire. For Nelson, his new environment was a labyrinth from which he didn't want to escape. He was frozen like a pre-Cambrian bug in a drop of amber.

Nellie, wearing her flaps, padded into the kitchen to prepare dinner. She walked in as if facing a firing squad. A note from Nelson was held in place on the refrigerator door by a magnet in the shape of an angry green worm holding an M-19 on its right shoulder and a tricolor flag with a lone star in its left. The note suggested: "After placing the pots, pans, and skillets on the burners, make sure to turn the burners on." Nellie usually forgot that final detail. She opened her cookbook and began reading the instructions:

SAUTEES-Sautee a la Criolla: cup olive oil, one diced pimento, one chopped bell pepper, one teaspoon sugar, one teaspoon oregano, one-half teaspoon cumin, one chicken-broth cube, 1½ cup thinly chopped onions, 5 garlic cloves, one can tomato sauce, 1½ teaspoon salt and one teaspoon vinegar. Nellie was overwhelmed by so much chopping, so many teaspoons, so much slicing. She closed her eyes and wished her fairy godmother would come to her rescue and turn the bell pepper into Delfina, the onion into Tomasu, and the garlic clove into Agripina. She closed her eyes again, but this time much tighter. Her godmother was obviously vacationing somewhere. Resigning herself to her fate, she opened the kitchen closet and took out a can of Kirby's Black Beans and opened it. She poured the contents of the can in the pot and turned the burner on low heat. She rinsed her hands, and her eyes examined the large scar which marred her pale forearm, reminding her of the battles she had fought with the house. Nellie rubbed the iron-burned flesh, thinking that the imitation tortoise shell bracelet which she had seen at W. T. Grant might camouflage the burn. She dried her hands with the garlicky rag and went to her room.

She pulled the suitcase with the bullfighter sticker from under the bed and dug around the clothes searching for her photo album. Nellie was reconstructing her old life with pictures Delfina sent in exchange for Gillette razor blades and flints which she could sell on the black market. Nellie enclosed them in each letter, padded with toilet paper to avoid the letter censor back home. The photos came from the old albums Delfina has found under a pile of trash by the curb a few days after Don Andrés' mansion was confiscated. Seated in front of her dresser, Nellie began combing her hair 100 times, a ritual she followed ever since she battled tinea when she was almost ten. With her free hand she flipped through her album.

On the first page was her favorite picture: "1940 Yacht Club Dance—The Odalisques' Conga." The note on the back of the photo read, "I also danced in the Ladies' Tennis club, the Air Club, and the Doctors' Club." Then 'Xawa-on-Deep River." And in much fresher ink: "To remember is to live again, but I feel like dying when I remember. Belle Glade, Florida, 1963. (Still in exile)." The Odalisques' Conga displayed eight delightful damsels, society's best. They all wore red transparent linen veils, velvet cassocks embroidered with silver thread and gold coins of different sizes to cover their convulsing navels. In the midst of the make-believe harem sat a sultan called Mario. He was a tall, dark gentleman with hairy arms which brought about nightmares, insomnia, and premature ovulations in the unsuspecting harem. Nellie never realized that her attraction to The Donna Reed Show had its basis in the similar secondary characteristics shared by the sultan and Carl Betz. But, why tell her? It would only cause her anxiety to know that she was unfaithful to Nelson every Monday through Friday from two to three in the afternoon.

The days of the Big Band era were rolling. It was the time of American actors, of smoking Lucky Strikes and dreaming yourself blonde, pale, and freckle-faced. From left to right, forming a bouquet enveloping Mario: Pituca, María Rosa, Loly, Cuquín, Helen, Ignacia, and Nellie, though, among themselves, they went by Joan, Ginger, Hedy, Betty, Debbie, Lana, and Irene.

The aroma of a nearby Kentucky Fried Chicken made Nellie recall Lana's premature death in '42. It was attributed to the chicken with which she slept. His name was Curly, and he was a gift from one of Irene's father's young farmhands who had fallen in love with Lana. The biped arrived in a shoe box with a note which said: "For Miss Ignacia. Now, you'll never be lonely. Truly, Juan Benson." This was the only way the poor farmhand could have gotten close to his beloved. In a few months Curly grew from a fuzzy yellow ball into a robust specimen with shiny feathers, fastly developing spurs, and firm comb. The bird accompanied Lana to every rehearsal of the conga ensemble and perched in the first seat of the second row patiently awaiting for the odalisques to finish their act. At night, Lana would dress the rooster in flannel pajamas and cover its comb with a diminutive cotton hat. But Curly was very demanding. Many were the parties Lana couldn't attend because of the unyielding biped. It loved to go to bed early—seven at the latest—and wouldn't sleep unless Lana was there. Irene (Nellie) secretly envied Lana and wished Curly could be hers. She became so sad that Don Andrés gave her a little pet of her own. Irene named it Rigoletto. One night after Curly was sound asleep, Lana left silently for a New Year's Eve party at the Yacht Club. When she returned the following year, Curly was nowhere to be found. The rooster had flown through an open bedroom window to the chicken coop where he joined all sorts of low-life hens. Lana found the bird three days later almost featherless and with a bleeding comb damaged by violent pecking. In its frenzy Curly had made amorous advances toward a peahen without realizing that her peacock was perched directly above.

It was that night that Curly was contaminated with lice carrying a deadly microbe. A week later, Lana woke up with a bleeding scalp from her nocturnal scratching. Irene had come to visit her to show her the new silk veils for the ball. Lana had greeted her with a big smile and a blonde wig that her father had bought for her on a trip to Key West. Three days after Irene's visit, Lana was found dead, a pool of dried blood under her wig, her brains exposed. A few days later when Juan Benson found out about his lady love, in despair he cut off the pinkie and ring fingers on his right hand with his machete.

Facing Lana in an exotic Middle Eastern pose and with the biggest coin in her navel was Hedy. Hedy and Irene played the piano every afternoon at Fabre's Academy of Music. Hedy wanted to be a concert pianist and play with the national symphony. She was jovial and always wore shorts, a legacy of her days at Mobile's Finishing School and a scandal for her hometown. It was while in Alabama that she met her boyfriend Rudy Jones. He was attending Springhill College. Rudy died during the Normandy landing, but not before he had given Hedy the only passionate night she was ever to experience. One afternoon, when Irene was accompanying Hedy in her personal rendition of "Claire de Lune," Elvirita, the instructor, tried to imprison her hands, using the lesson as pretext. Hedy and Irene escaped screaming from the ambush that Elvirita was launching from the island of Lesbos. Thus, Hedy abandoned a piano career that undoubtedly would have led her to Carnegie Hall. When Hedy was forty and still a spinster raising her younger siblings, she decided to stop mourning for Rudy. She married Senator Zubizarreta, the owner of La Campana Hardware Store. The husband forbade her to use shorts, forcing her to wear long, heavy black stockings to the beach. Finally exile gave her enough courage to have her marriage annulled.

Though she saw them often at Pepe's Grocery, Nellie didn't care for the remaining four odalisques. And the sultan? He was born, grew up, and died in the same old town. He never married because the responsibility of the annual odalisques conga line didn't leave him with much time for love. He had hardly finished one year's conga when he immediately started laboring on the variations for the next—more veils, more tambourines, less gold. His choreographies propelled him into national limelight. But he didn't allow fame to cloud his world vision, never accepting the many bribes that were offered by politicians and capitalists to have their daughters join his seraglio. Mario continued selecting his girls from Xawa's cream. He never suspected the many moments of secret joy he had given generations of dancing maidens, young girls whose fingers, in the midst of the night and the intimacy of their alcoves, went wild sinking uncontrollably beneath their panties as they dreamed of the hirsute sultan. When Mario died in a train accident, the Legion of Mary took a collection to build a monument to perpetuate his memory. The statue was sculpted from a single piece of Carrara marble by Gianni Galli. It bore the name, "The Surrendering of the Odalisques." The inscription read: "To you who filled our free time with the greatest of joys. We will not forget you, The Legion of Mary and the Ladies' Tennis Club."

She turned the page once more and time elapsed swiftly. Skipping the sleepless night when she felt the vacuum of her mother's absence, her coming-out party, her first cigarette, Nelson's first kiss through the living room window, she stopped at Nelson's graduation ceremony. It was 1944 and the allies were bombing Dresden. This time Nellie was in the center of the photo, elegantly dressed in a black silk gown, embroidered by her own hands. She had taken up embroidery to occupy her time while Nelson was away finishing his degree. They had been engaged for nine long years. Nellie sewed sixty-two blouses, knitted twenty-five sweaters for Rigoletto, embroidered thirty-two table cloths, and made all the Lent covers for all the saints of all the churches, monasteries, and convents in her diocese during those years. When she completed these tasks, she still had two more years before Nelson's return. To fill her time Nellie began the composition of five-hundred and four sonnets. All the poems were recorded in the Italian manner as prescribed by Marco F. Pietralunga (Pietrarca) in his *Viaggio All' Amore: The Muses Within Your Reach.*

The tenth sonnet of the one-hundred-four rhymed like this:
Your divine eyes, Nelson
are not what submitted me to love's yoke';
nor your swollen lips, the blind cupid's sweet nest,
where nectar springs,
nor your olive cheeks,
nor your hair darker than a chestnut;
nor your hands, which have conquered so many;
nor your voice, which seems more than human.

It was your soul, visible in your deeds,
which was able to subject mine,
so its captivity would last beyond death.
Thus, everything that has been mentioned can be
reduced simply to the power of your soul,
for by its commission each member performed its
ministry.

Pressed against the paper on both sides of the tenth sonnet were a pair of seductive, purplish marks.

As Nelson's commencement godmother, Nellie wore her hair loose in a cascade that started from her forehead and ran down her neck, finally coming to an end one half inch from her shoulders. Nellie, who still thought of herself as Irene Dunn's twin, had blossomed. Her physical attributes could have been listed in terms of apples—two in front and half of one in the rear. She had used heavy make-up around her eyes to accentuate their almond shape. Nelson, with golden spectacles and sporting a cap and gown, held a diploma in his right hand, trying to assume an air of sagacity. His business administration degree had cost him more than sweat, and given him a nervous stomach. Nelson's fear of having to head his father's businesses after graduation was the source of the stomach spasms which caused him to shower his peers with pineapple chunks, black beans, and salami before each exam. He became known as Black Vomit. That night, after the pre-scribed picture-taking beneath the loving arms of the Alma Mater, the radiant couple danced at the Montmartre. Rene Touzet's orchestra played "You Don't Need To Know," while Nelson held Nellie very tight against his chest. He murmured the lyrics in Nellie's ear while thinking of The Squirrel's roomy hips. Like any other Saturday, The Squirrel would surely be waiting for him until three o'clock in the morning, when the night was still young and her older clients were headed home to their suspecting wives. Nelson always left her a generous tip and a few pieces of bubble gum.

Nellie was about to flip the page when unexpectedly someone knocked at the door. She immediately thought it was the roving reverend bringing a new cardboard fan. But she was amazed to see a woman dressed in tight pants and a sleeveless blouse. Nellie strained her eyes to observe the woman better through the peephole, recognizing the lady who had diligently ordered around the Mayflower movers. She was obviously one of the people that had moved to the corner house, the one that had been vacant for years. Since no one answered, the tightly clad lady peeked through the window of the Florida room, shouting: "Hello, hello. Any one home?"

"My husband is not here," answered Nellie uneasily.

"My name is Mrs. James B. Olsen," she said, raising her voice.

"My husband is not here. He is working," Nellie answered.

"I ain't here to see your husband," a slightly irritated Mrs. James B. responded with a musical rhythm. "I'm your new neighbor. My name is Mrs. James B. Olsen II. May I come in?"

"Well, yes, of course. Excuse me, I am even losing my manners. Please, come in," Nellie said, opening the door.

"We've just moved to the white house. The one with the picket fence. We hail from Tallahassee. You know where that is? Where you from?"

"Oh, yes! The corner house. Do you have any children? We have a boy and a girl. The oldest is Nelson, Jr. and the youngest is the little María-Chiara. The boy goes to the junior high school." Nellie was feeling nervous and started scratching her head.

"Yeah! We've got ourselves a little couple, too. The boy's name is James B. Olsen III, and we call the little belle Missy, but she's really named after me. They're both in boarding school in Mississippi. James B. III goes to a military academy and Missy to pre-finishing school. You just can't send kids to public school no more, too many negroes." She had lowered her voice to utter the last three words.

"That is very bad because the children could have played together. Maybe in the summer. May I offer to you anything to drink?"

"Yes, coffee. But no cream, please. I like it black. Where are you from?" Mrs. James B. raised her voice for the last question and carefully enunciated each syllable.

"Please make yourself at home. I am from Xawa, but I was meant to be born in Mondovi."

"Oh, is that so! Oh! A picture album. I love albums! A picture is worth one-thousand words." Mrs. James B. started flipping through the album without first asking if she could.

"You can open it if you want," said Nellie after the fact.

"I could bring mine tomorrow. I have lovely family pictures. Actually, they aren't pictures but photographs. And there's a difference! Photographs of my great-great-grandma's plantation, Fairview. It had a beautiful wrought iron fence. The Yankees sacked it and burned it to the ground. My great-great grandma died trying to save the family heirlooms. But please, don't come to my house. If my husband knew I was here he would kill me. I've always been ahead of my time. Do you realize I was Leon High School's homecoming queen? There were lots of people that came to my crowning, even though it was the same weekend as the county fair. I had to compete with the Ubangi Woman, the Alligator Lady, the Bearded Lady, and the Quarter Man. I remember it as if it was today. I was crowned inside a giant redwood log. Boy, did I cry that day! I felt special and fearful of the great responsibility I was about to assume. My ladies in waiting—those are the girls that tended to my every wish—were throwing rose petals at my feet. I was crowned by the football team captain, Captain James B. Olsen II. His jersey was number 24, and it was retired. In the school year book he was chosen most likely to succeed, most athletic, best personality, and best all-around during his sophomore, junior and senior years—something really unique in American history. He was really dying to place that shining crown on my head. It was the week before we played the Marianna Bulldogs. We made this huge bonfire and burned a bulldog in effigy. An effigy is something like a big dummy, except you can be really nasty to it. Before we threw it in the fire, the big dummy was just mauled by the sharp teeth of our fighting Lions. Mr. James B. took the biggest bite and ripped off a flank. Do you want to know what we did next? We began pelting the smoking bulldog with marshmallows, and we shouted that he was no bulldog but a chihuahua, which is a small scrawny South American dog from Mexico. Then the Captain slowly climbed the steps to the podium and told my future subjects, 'It's surely nice for you to show up. Let me tell you that team made the trip here for nothing. Y'all gonna be eating hot dogs for breakfast tomorrow morning. We wanna have our best game and we're gonna try our hardest to do it.' The Lions went wild and the band started pumping them up even higher by playing 'You Ain't Nothing But A Hound Dog.' And right when I was gonna lead them into an uproar of GOOOOOOOOOOOOO BIGGGGGGGGGGGGG REEEEEEEEEEEEEEEEEED BEAAAAAAAAAAAAAAAAAT BULLDAWWWWWWWWWWWWWWWWGS, a tiny figure made her way through the pack. It was Mrs. Cornelia Williamson, James B.'s grandma, who grabbed the microphone. She was wearing a red sweatshirt with the words MY GRANDSON and the number 24. Then everybody heard her yell, 'Who's gonna win tonight?' The crowd didn't wait to answer her cracking voice. It roared L-E-O-N L-I-O-N-S. I never forgave her. It was the most important moment of my cheerleading career, and she ruined it for me. Her grandson carried her on his shoulders while the band played, 'When The Saints Go Marching In.' But let me tell you about James B. II. He fell for me all the way back in the seventh grade. Do you know what he wrote in my eighth-grade yearbook? He wrote: 'I wish I was a mosquito so I could bite you. But please don't squash me. Lots of love, JB II.' All those years he was longing for me and I only gave him tiny, little bits of hope. Like when he invited me to go to the pig races in Georgia and I made him wait for an answer the whole month! Actually, I really wanted to go 'cause they're a lot of fun, and Sugar, Uncle Blue's sow, was one of the contestants. James B. arrived early, driving his father's brand new pickup. He had just gotten his restricted license. I made him wait for forty-five minutes even though I had been ready for over two hours. James B. had used Brylcreem for the first time and had brushed his teeth at least fifteen times. He smelled of fluoride toothpaste and breath mint. He didn't dare to even hold my hand, and at the end of our date, he didn't know how to say goodbye. He leaned forward and said in a deep voice, 'I had a ball!' I'm lots of fun! Oh, something smells. Are you killing roaches or something? What is it?"

"Please, please make yourself comfortable. I will be right back with the coffee."

"And who are all these people?"

"Myself and a group of friends at a party," said Nellie from the kitchen.

"I just love your dresses. Ain't them adorable? Do you always dress like that in your country or just on Sundays? And who's the man wearing the turban? Are y'all his girlfriends?"

Nellie couldn't quite hear her since the water for the coffee was boiling, so she nodded from afar.

"I couldn't have shared my Mr. James B. Olsen with no one. Did I tell you he was chosen most athletic? He's always been my cup of tea. I was the captain of the cheerleading squad," she added while she wet her index finger to flip the page.

"The one with the toga is Nelson, my husband. That was the day he graduated from the university. And the man to his left is my father. He was the owner of many factories, including the one that made the best rum, and of the national railroad.

"I hate trains. They always wake me up in the morning with that awful whistle. I was thinking maybe you would like to come with me to W. T. Grant. They're having a clearance sale. On the way, we could stop at the Dairy Queen for some ice cream. Have you ever had ice cream?"

"Well, thank you very much. I wanted to buy a bracelet, and the ice cream is okay, too."

"What about tomorrow before Mr. James B. returns from baseball practice? If he catches you near our place, he'll hunt you down like a wild deer. He ain't very broad-minded."

"It will be a pleasure, Mrs. Olsen."

"Well, I'd better go back to prepare Mr. James B.'s supper. I'm going to perfume myself. I'm his horse doovers; it's French for snack. When he sees me, I drive him wild. He chases me all over the house, and when he finally catches me, he kisses me savagely while I scream, 'Go, go, go, go, big red.' Before I forget, did you ever meet Talihu Medina?"

"No."

"How about that. She being Filipino and all that. Anyway, I'm sure you'd have loved her, too. Many of my friends thought she was my maid. Can you imagine! When we went shopping, I managed to always go a few steps ahead of her. You know how short their legs are. As I told you, all of my friends thought she was my servant. I never told them so, but I didn't deny it either. I just smiled. She left when her husband, Sergeant Bahama Joe, was transferred to Eglin. Don't you forget, I'll come fetch you tomorrow morning. Well, like y'all say, 'sayonara.'"

Nellie was happy to have made a new friend. She went to the mailbox and found a letter from Delfina. They always came with the same stamp, a white dove surrounded by the word "peace" in many languages. She opened the envelope and saw her wedding picture. She took it out and put it on top of the night stand so she could show it to Mrs. James B. first thing in the morning. She walked to the kitchen whistling The Donna Reed Show theme song and opened her recipe book. She looked under "desserts" and started getting the ingredients to make her new friend a coconut custard. While measuring out the wrong amount of sugar, she realized she had forgotten to tell her that her name was Nellie.

Writings

Novels: *La vida es un special/Life Is on Special,* Ediciones Universal, 1981. *La montaña rusa/The Roller Coaster,* Arte Público Press, 1985. *Raining Backwards,* Houston: Arte Público Press, 1988. *Holy Radishes!* Arte Público Press, 1995. ***Short Stories:*** *Cuentos sin rumbo/Directionless Stories,* Ediciones Universal, 1975. *El Jardín de la luna/The Garden of the Moon,* Ediciones Universal, 1976. Also in *The Americas Review; Apalachee Quarterly; The Florida Review; Linden Lane Magazine; Cuban American Writers: Los Atrevidos, 20 cuentistas cubanos; Nuevos Horizontes; Cuentos hispanos de los Estados Unidos; Veinte años de literatura;* and numerous other magazines and anthologies. ***Scholarly Publications:*** *Biographical Index of Cuban Authors (Diaspora 1959–1979),* Ediciones Universal, 1983; articles on Hispanic dialectology of the United States in *Hispania, American Speech, Crítica hispánica, Actas del I Congreso Internacional sobre el Español de America.*

Cristina García

Cristina García is the first Cuban American woman to achieve main-stream success as a novelist. After nine years with Time magazine, García made a break from journalism in 1990 when she took a three-month leave of absence from the popular magazine in order to write—not about news and world events, but from her imagination and from her own experience. Having always been interested in politics and acutely aware of how her own circumstances had been profoundly shaped by the politics between the United States and Cuba, García was living in Miami when she found "all the issues of [her] childhood . . . bubbling up." The result of her exploration into these issues was the novel Dreaming in Cuban, *published in 1992 and nominated for a National Book Award the same year.*

García was born in Havana, Cuba, on July 4, 1958, and was brought to the United States when her parents went into exile after the Cuban Revolution. García was an excellent student and attended elite American universities, graduating from Barnard College with a degree in Political Science in 1979, and from Johns Hopkins University with a Masters degree in Latin American Studies in 1981. Two years later she landed a coveted job as a reporter and researcher with *Time* magazine, where she was able to hone her writing skills. She quickly ascended to bureau chief and correspondent at *Time,* before leaving the magazine in 1990 to pursue her career as a creative writer, first taking a leave of absence and later deciding not to return to journalism at all.

The highly acclaimed *Dreaming in Cuban* was the first novel to provide a broad sector of the American reading public with insights into the psychology of Cubans who were born or raised in the United States—a generation that grew up under the looming myth of Cuba's past splendor and its present evils under Fidel Castro, but that never had first-hand knowledge of their parents' homeland. The novel also closely examines women's perspective on the problems of living between two cultures.

As a journalist, García found herself growing tired of "telling the truth." One day she wrote a poem about three crazy women who kill themselves and the feeling of being liberated by her words prompted her to take a leave of absence from Time.

as reported in the Ann Arbor [Mich.] News, April 23, 1992.

Dreaming in Cuban chronicles three generations of women in the Pino family, and in so doing compares the lives of those who live in Cuba with those living in the United States. Celia, a revolutionary and a true believer in the Communist regime, has remained in Cuba with her daughter, Felicia, and her three grandchildren. Celia's equally committed, counter-revolutionary daughter, Lourdes, lives with her own daughter in Brooklyn, where she runs a bakery that also serves as a gathering place for militant exiles. The novel shows how the revolution and the resulting immigration and exile disrupted and fragmented Cuban family life.

First generation Americans, they live cutoff from a homeland their parents cannot forgive and their new country forbids them to visit. (*Time,* March 23, 1992)

The novel also highlights the competing value systems: Lourdes's correspondence with Celia is symbolized by photos of baked goods, which become ideological weapons.

Each glistening éclair is a grenade aimed at Celia's political beliefs, each strawberry shortcake proof—in butter, cream, and eggs—of Lourdes' success in America, and a reminder of the ongoing shortages in Cuba.

Lourdes's daughter, Pilar (who is, perhaps, the author's alter-ego), does not share her mother's ideology but wishes to go to Cuba to see the island for herself, visit her grandmother, and both symbolically and physically return to the matrix. Since she was a child, Pilar has had a psychic connection to her grandmother Celia, with whom she communicates in her dreams. Finally, both Lourdes and Pilar do visit Cuba, and Pilar experiences a critical transformation—although she comes to love Cuba, she realizes that she is very tied to New York. Her lot, which is representative of the lot of her generation of Cuban Americans, is to find a way to maintain her ties to Cuba—to "take back the island"—while not abandoning her new life.

Personal Stats

Cuban American journalist, novelist. Born: July 4, 1958, in Havana, Cuba. *Education:* B.A. in Political Science, Barnard College, 1979; M.A. in Latin

American Studies, The Johns Hopkins University, 1981. *Career:* Reporter and researcher (1983–85), bureau chief, (1987–88), correspondent (1988–90), *Time* magazine. *Awards/Honors:* National Book Award, 1992. *Address:* c/o Ellen Levine Agency, 15 E. 26th St., Ste 1801, New York, NY 10110-1505

Inés in the Kitchen

from *Little Havana Blues: A Cuban-American Literature Anthology,* Arte Público Press, 1997, pp. 126–31

Inés Maidique is twelve weeks pregnant and nauseous. Her back hurts, her breasts are swollen, and her feet no longer fit into her dressy shoes. Although she is barely showing, she walks around in sneakers to ease the soreness that has settled in every corner of her body. The eleven pounds she's gained feel like fifty.

Cristina García

When her husband returns home he'll expect her trussed up in a silk dress and pearls and wearing make-up and high heels. It's Friday and Richard likes for her to make a fuss over him at the end of the week. He'll be home in two hours so Inés busies herself preparing their dinner—a poached loin of lamb with mint chutney, cumin rice, ratatouille, and spiced bananas for dessert.

Richard will question her closely about what she's eaten that day. Inés will avoid telling him about the fudge cookies she devoured that morning in the supermarket parking lot. She hadn't wanted to eat the whole box, but bringing it home was unthinkable. Richard scoured the kitchen cabinets for what he called "illegal foods" and she was in no mood for his usual harangue.

With a long length of string Inés ties together the eye of loin and tenderloin at one inch intervals, leaving enough string at the ends to suspend the meat from the handles of the kettle. She slits the lamb in several places and inserts slivers of garlic. Then she sets about preparing the stock, skimming the froth as it simmers. Inés thinks about the initial excitement she'd felt when the blood test came back positive. She always knew, or thought she knew, she wanted a child, but now she is less certain.

The mint leaves give off a tart scent that clears her head with each pulse of the food processor. She adds fresh coriander, minced garlic, ginger root, honey, and a little lemon until the chutney congeals. Then she whisks it together with plain yogurt in a stainless steel bowl. Inés remembers the abortion she'd had the month before her college graduation. She was twenty-one and, like now, twelve weeks pregnant. The baby's father was Cuban, like her, a hematology resident at the hospital where Inés was finishing her practicum. Manolo Espada was not opposed to having the baby, only against getting married. This was unacceptable to Inés. After the abortion, she bled for five days and cramped so hard she passed out. Inés spent the summer working a double shift at an emergency room in Yonkers. Her child would have been eight years old by now. Inés thinks of this often.

Shortly before she was to marry Richard, Inés tracked down her old lover to San Francisco, where he'd been doing AIDS research with an eminent name in the field. Over the phone, Manolo told her he was leaving for Africa the following month on a two-year grant from the Department of Health. Inés abruptly forgot everything she had planned to say. Even if she'd wanted him again, it was too late. She'd already sent out her wedding invitations and Richard had put a down payment on the colonial house across from the riding stables. Manolo was going to Africa. It would have never worked out.

Ratatouille is one of Inés's favorite dishes. It's easy to prepare and she cooks big batches of it at a time then freezes it. The red peppers give the ratatouille a slightly sweetish taste. Inés heats the olive oil in a skillet then tosses in the garlic and chopped onion. She adds the cubed eggplants and stirs in the remaining ingredients one at a time. On another burner she prepares the rice with chicken broth, cuminseed, and fresh parsley. If she times it right, dinner will be ready just as Richard walks through the door.

Her husband doesn't know about Inés's abortion, and only superficially about Manolo Espada. It is better this way. Richard doesn't like it when Inés's attention is diverted from him in any significant way. How, she wonders, will he get used to having a baby around? Richard was the only boy in a family of older sisters, and accustomed to getting his way. His father died when Richard was eight and his three sisters had worked as secretaries to put him through medical school. Richard had been the great hope of the Roth family. When he told them he was marrying a Catholic, his mother and sisters were devastated. Janice, the oldest, told him point-blank that Inés would ruin his life. Perhaps, Inés thinks, his sister was right.

Inés strains the stock through a fine sieve into an enormous ceramic bowl, discarding the bones and scraps. She pours the liquid back into the kettle and turns on the burner to moderately high. Carefully, she lowers the lamb into the stock without letting it touch the sides or the bottom of the kettle, then she ties the string to the handles, and sets the timer for twelve minutes.

Other things concern Inés. She's heard about men running off when their wives become pregnant and she's afraid that Richard, who places such a premium on her looks, will be repelled by her bloating body. As it is, Inés feels that Richard scrutinizes her for nascent imperfections. He abhors cellulite and varicose veins, the corporal trademarks of his mother and sisters, and so Inés works hard to stay fit. She swims, plays tennis, takes aerobics classes, and works out twice a week on the Nautilus machines at her gym. Her major weakness is a fondness for sweets. Inés loves chocolate, but Richard glares at her in restaurants if she so much as asks to see the dessert menu. To him a lack of self-discipline on such small matters is indicative of more serious character flaws.

What of her husband's good qualities? Richard takes her to the Bahamas every winter, although he spends most of the time scuba-diving, a sport which Inés does not share. And he is intelligent and well-informed and she believes he is faithful. Also, he isn't a tightwad like so many of her friends' husbands, watching every penny, and he doesn't hang out with the boys or play poker or anything like that. Richard is an adequate lover, too, although he lacks imagination. He likes what he likes, which does not include many of the things that Inés likes. Once, in bed, she asked Richard to pretend he was Henry Kissinger. The request offended him deeply. If Richard rejected so harmless a game, what would he say to the darker, more elaborate rituals she'd engaged in with Manolo?

The loin of lamb is medium rare, just the way Richard likes it. Inés lets it cool off on the cutting board for a few minutes before slicing it diagonally into thick, juicy slabs. She sets the table with their wedding linen and china and wedges two white candles into squat crystal holders. Inés thinks back on the five years she worked as a nurse. She was good at what she did and was sought after for the most important cardiology cases. More than one surgeon had jokingly proposed to her after she'd made a life-saving suggestion in the operating room. But like most men, they assumed she was unavailable. Someone so pretty, so self-contained, they thought, must already be spoken for.

When Richard first started working at the hospital, Inés felt drawn to him. There was something about his manner, about his nervous energy that appealed to her. It certainly wasn't his looks. Richard was skinny and tall with fleecy colorless hair, not at all like the mesomorphic Manolo whose skin seemed more of a pelt. For three months she and Richard worked side by side on coronary bypasses, ventricular aneurysm resections, mitral valve replacements. Their manner was always cordial and efficient, with none of the macabre bantering one often hears in operating rooms. One day, Richard looked up at her from a triple bypass and said, "Marry me, Inés." And so she did.

When Inés was a child, her father had predicted wistfully that she would never marry, while her mother seemed to gear her for little else. Inés remembers the beauty pageants she was forced to enter from an early age, the banana curls that hung from her skull like so many sausages. She'd won the "Little Miss Latin New York" pageant in 1964, when she was seven years old. Her mother still considers this to be Inés's greatest achievement. Inés had sung and played the piano to "Putting on the Ritz," which she'd translated to Spanish herself. Gerardo complained to his wife about sharing Inés with an auditorium full of leering strangers, but Haydée would not budge. "This is better than a dowry, Gerardo." But Gerardo preferred to have his daughter, dolled up in her starched Sunday dress and ruffled anklets, all to himself.

Gerardo expected Inés to drop everything to play the piano for him, and for many years she complied. This became more and more difficult as she got older. Her parents separated and her father would call at all hours on the private phone line he'd installed in Inés's bedroom, pleading with her to come play the white baby grand he had rented just for her. Sometimes he would stroke her hair or tickle her spine as she played, tease her about her tiny new breasts or affectionately pat her behind. Inés remembers how the air seemed different during those times, charged and hard to swallow. Now her father is dead. And what, she asks herself, does she really know about him?

Inés turns off all the burners and pours herself a glass of whole milk. She is doing all the right things to keep the life inside her thriving. But she accomplishes this without anticipation, only a sense of obligation. Sometimes she has a terrible urge to pour herself a glass of rum, although she hates the taste, and she knows what it would do to the baby, or to burn holes in the creamy calfskin upholstery of her husband's sports car. Other times, mostly in the early afternoons, she feels like setting fire to the damask curtains that keep their living room in a perpetual dusk. She dreams about blowing up her herb garden with its fragrant basil leaves, then stealing a thoroughbred from the stable across the street and riding it as fast as she can.

Inés finishes the last of her milk. She rinses the glass and leans against the kitchen sink. There is a jingling of keys at the front door. Richard is home.

Writings

Novel: *Dreaming in Cuban,* Alfred A. Knopf, 1992. **Short Story:** In *Little Havana Blues: A Cuban-American Literature Anthology,* edited by Virgil Suárez and Delia Poey, Arte Público Press, 1997.

Lionel García

As a novelist steeped in the traditions of Texas tall-tale and Mexican American folk narrative, Lionel G. García has created some of the most memorable characters in Chicano literature. He has proven to be the most humorous and reader-friendly of the Hispanic writers.

Born in San Diego, Texas, on August 20, 1935, García grew up in the small town and neighboring ranches where Mexican Americans were the majority population. His father a paint-and-body man and his mother a teacher, García lived a middle-class home and did so well in school that he was one of very few Mexican Americans admitted to Texas A & M University at that time. While at Texas A & M, he studied biology but was also encouraged by one of his English professors to write. After graduating in 1956, he married his high school sweetheart, Naoemi Barrera (an educational diagnostician). The couple later adopted three children, Rose, Carlos, and Paul.

Early on García tried to become a full-time writer but was unsuccessful in getting his works published. From 1957–60, he served in the Army and, after being honorably discharged, returned to Texas A & M for his Doctor of Veterinary Medicine, which he received in 1965. He stayed on at A & M as a professor of anatomy from 1966–68, before beginning his career as a veterinarian in 1969. Throughout his life as a successful veterinarian in the affluent community near Clear Lake, where the Johnson Space Center is located, García continued writing, as well as spinning tales for his family and his clients, keeping alive the art of storytelling—much to the delight of all who know him.

In the early 1980s he once again attempted to publish, and found that there were many more opportunities to do so. In 1983 García won the PEN Southwest Discovery Award for his novel in progress, *Leaving Home,* which was published in 1985. This and his second novel, *A Shroud in the Family* (1987), draw heavily on his family experiences and small-town background; both are set in a quaint village very much like San Diego, Texas, where he grew up, and both follow the antics of children like those who surrounded him as a child. (All of these characters reappeared again in 1994 in his collection of autobiographical stories, *I Can Hear the Cowbell Ring.*) In part, *A Shroud in the Family* also shatters the myth of the "great" Texas heroes such as Sam Houston and Jim Bowie, who have become symbols of Anglo-Texans' victory over Mexicans. The work was García's contribution to the Texas Sesquicentennial celebrations. *Leaving Home,* on the other hand, focuses on a character who was inspired by one of his uncles, a lovable ne'er-do-well who almost had a career in professional baseball but ended up as a vagabond.

García's novel *Hardscrub* (1989) is a departure from his former works; it is a realistically drawn chronicle of the life of an Anglo child in an abusive family. *Booklist* noted that "The voices of children are memorable in this novel—they resonate with the willingness to observe with clear eyes the absurdity of the alcoholic, irresponsible adults in whose hands their upbringing has been placed." *Hardscrub* was awarded the two most prestigious prizes for fiction in the Southwest—the Texas Institute of Letters Award for the Best Novel and the Southwest Booksellers Association Prize for Fiction.

Lionel García's latest novel, *To a Widow with Children* (1994) is a heartwarming tale about a love triangle that becomes the talk of the town and the source of a lot of humor. Again, García set his story in pre-World War II, rural south Texas and populated it with a variety of quaint characters, including the all-knowing village priest, a resentful sheriff, the small-town gossip, old codgers, and, of course, the widow's five mischievous but astute children. *Publishers Weekly* commented that "A shimmering magic-realism informs lives that would otherwise seem discouragingly impoverished and devoid of hope in this whimsical, mid-20th century love story."

In the introduction to his collection of autobiographical stories, *I Can Hear the Cowbells Ring,* García finally acknowledges the real-life basis for so many of his interesting characters. *Library Journal* praised the collection of short stories (many of which had also appeared in newspapers, magazines, and anthologies), saying:

> The characters in the sketches are real, from the breast-beating grandmother to the brother who could not be cured of swearing. Hardship, cruelty, and tragedy are present but warmed by an unsentimental, rollicking sense of good humor and life.

His work well-received, it seems García has succeeded at what he considers the writer's job to be —"to present people as they are, usually to the surprise of the reader."

Personal Stats

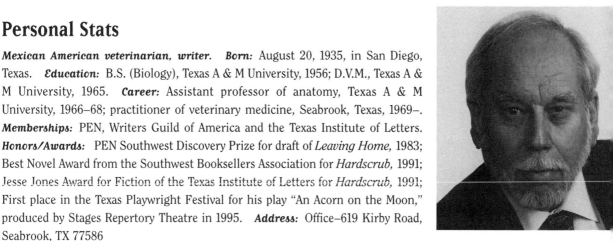

Mexican American veterinarian, writer. **Born:** August 20, 1935, in San Diego, Texas. **Education:** B.S. (Biology), Texas A & M University, 1956; D.V.M., Texas A & M University, 1965. **Career:** Assistant professor of anatomy, Texas A & M University, 1966–68; practitioner of veterinary medicine, Seabrook, Texas, 1969–. **Memberships:** PEN, Writers Guild of America and the Texas Institute of Letters. **Honors/Awards:** PEN Southwest Discovery Prize for draft of *Leaving Home,* 1983; Best Novel Award from the Southwest Booksellers Association for *Hardscrub,* 1991; Jesse Jones Award for Fiction of the Texas Institute of Letters for *Hardscrub,* 1991; First place in the Texas Playwright Festival for his play "An Acorn on the Moon," produced by Stages Repertory Theatre in 1995. **Address:** Office–619 Kirby Road, Seabrook, TX 77586

The Ringing of the Bell

"The Ringing of the Bell" from *I Can Hear the Cowbells Ring,* Arte Público Press, 1994, pp. 9–15

Author's Introduction

I was born and raised in San Diego, Texas, the county seat of Duval County. The long years of political turmoil have covered the little town like a black cloud. To those of you not familiar with its history, the town has a reputation for being bad. It was the county seat for political shenanigans dating back to the late 1800's. This is the courthouse where the infamous Box Thirteen from neighboring Jim Wells County was burned making Lyndon Johnson a Texas senator. This is where the Parr family ruled politically for decades. This is where State Officials sent four Rangers to live, giving up on the old adage of "one riot, one ranger." This is where State Officials who came down to investigate after one election could not help but be amazed when they discovered that the people had all voted in alphabetical order.

In my very early years we were an inseparable collection of eight children brought together to gain the protection of the pack. Of course we had a pecking order. I was the youngest and the least important. If any errand needed to be run, I ran it. If any disagreeable task needed to be performed, I was chosen. My brother Richard came after me, and then my sister Sylvia—they were above me, but not by much. Then came my grandmother's children, my uncles Juan and Matías, the two dominant males. Then came my aunts Cota (Eloise), Maggie, and Frances. Of the three aunts, Cota was the most dominant, and she fought often over leadership with her two brothers. The two branches of the family lived next to each other, separated by an empty lot.

We walked the hot, dusty, streets barefooted, our pockets full of marbles, spinning tops, mesquite sticks and balls, looking for a game to play. We were carefree then, getting up in the morning, leaving home after breakfast and not returning until dark, all dirty and sweaty, hoping some supper had been left for us.

As we crossed the yard by the light of the moon between my grandmother's house and ours, we could hear the voices of our elders, sitting on the porch at my grandmother's, my grandmother fanning herself, to shed the intense heat which had consumed her in the kitchen the whole day. By now she had annoited her arms and neck with camphorated alcohol, and the vapors of the camphor reached us from afar. Under the stars and amid the sounds of the locusts, our elders made beautiful talk about people alive or long dead.

Whenever there was disagreement as to a date, we would run to get Mercé, our insane uncle, who knew exactly when each member of the family present and gone was born. Mercé was an alcoholic and most of the time we could find him drunk, asleep in the semidarkness of his room, the lantern barely lit. Thrown on the bed, his clothes still on, snoring, the room reeking of tobacco and beer, he would have difficulty getting up, but he'd come. He loved company. If we didn't find him when we ran back home, our elders would say that Mercé was at a tavern, putting on his show of madness in exchange for a bottle of beer.

When Mercé was young he was sent to the insane asylum in San Antonio. There, in no time at all according to my grandmother, he memorized most of the streets in the city. If in the course of a conversation he had a fit, they would just let him go running through the streets as though nothing had happened. "Be careful," my grandmother would tell him. "Don't run into anything in the dark." Mercé would be gone, lost for the night. We would see him again the next morning, that is, if we didn't go sleep at his house.

It was easy to laugh and cry in the dark with the stories.

We never knew who would be there for the evening. Relatives of all shapes and forms—both physical and mental—would come. Some would stay until my grandmother couldn't keep her eyes open, others just long enough to take advantage of a free meal. Others would just happen by the street and join us. There was nothing quite so thrilling as to see a favorite storyteller approach. We knew we were in for a wonderful night of listening to tales of someone dying, dead, married, pregnant, jobless, toothless, penniless. The whole of human condition was played before our eyes and ears daily. I never realized until later how much of life I had witnessed or been revealed to me during those years.

I was raised amidst insanity with my uncle Mercé who loved me as a child and took me with him everywhere. I remember how his fits would start, sensing his changing mood, how with one hand he would yank at his ears because he heard voices that ordered him to curse and who to curse dragging me with the other around town. Some days, while he held me in his arms and took off with me, I felt there would be no end to his fits and that we were forever destined to pull at our ears and curse at the whole town. With Mercé, reality became an illusion for me. Then there was my aunt Pepa, also insane. Pepa took me by the hand, walking the streets in the daylight with a lantern like Diogenes, searching not for an honest man but for her dead husband and children. She would ask me if I could see them and I would lie and say that I could. We would then hurry to greet the apparition. The disappointment of not finding them was always followed by a smile, because she would try again in a few moments, and there would always be tomorrow. Pepa lived for tomorrow. "Tomorrow," she would say to me, "they will come." After a while I too could see her husband on horseback riding toward us. Some days I could see her children. With her, my illusions became reality.

We never had money, never owned anything except parts of toys—one roller skate; an old baseball given to us by our uncle Adolfo, the baseball player; an old iron hoop which Matías kept spinning, rolling on its side for miles with a little stick; a few marbles and tops. We could reenact any movie we had seen. We were the fastest guns in the west, shooting with our fingers. We had the fastest horses, that ran wild, as we made the noise of thundering hooves.

There is such beautiful innocence that comes with deprivation.

We were raised with traditions that become very meaningful as one grows older. In San Diego, the Spanish priests had brought over the European tradition of communicating with the townspeople through the church bell. The good news and the bad were passed on to us with the ringing of the bell as John Donne so eloquently said in his 1624 poem.

I remember that on Sunday mornings Father Zavala had us ring the large deep sounding bell an hour before Mass, and it broke out in repeated metallic peals that penetrated throughout the sleeping town. Every fifteen minutes he would nod and one of us—my uncles Juan or Matías, or my brother Richard and I—dressed in our starched red cassocks, wearing shoes for the first time that week, would all hold on to the large rope and tug at it with all our might, the weight of the swinging bell picking us up from the floor on the upswing.

Father Zavala himself would ring the large bell to announce the deaths in the little town and it would toll on and on, a woeful sound of death which bound the town together. He would ring the small bell for the death of a child, a higher, lighter, sadder tone announcing the unfairness of life. We would stop the game of marbles, tops, *la chusa*, or baseball to hear the sound fade away, reminded of our own mortality. My mother, Marillita, and my grandmother, María, would stop the old washing machine. The soulful peals would continue their mourning. No words needed to be spoken. We would run barefoot to the church to find Father Zavala resting against the wall, an old man exhausted from ringing the bell. He would straighten up, clear his throat, and announce the dead person's name.

Off we'd run back home, our feet burning on the asphalt under the scorching sun, reciting the name over and over to be sure we would not forget, would not announce the wrong name.

One time we did get it wrong, and my grandmother cried all afternoon for her favorite cousin until the self same cousin showed up, asking for a cup of flour. According to my grandmother, who loved to exaggerate, she clutched her heart and fell backwards into a chair. She thought she had seen a ghost she said. We had to stay away from her home for a while until she forgave us.

Regardless of who died, as far as my grandmother was concerned it was always a relative. It could be a cousin ten times removed on my grandfather's aunt's side. And she would cry, not wailing as when my grandfather died. But still she cried. And she would get my mother to start crying, both of them trying to dry the tears from their eyes with their soapy hands, feeding the wash into the rollers.

It was as my grandfather had said years before: my grandmother María should hire out for wakes and funerals to prime the mourners, to keep the wailing going.

We'd leave our marbles on the ground and run to the printer who was busy by now laying type for the *esquela,* the official death announcement. It stated the person's name, date of birth and death, relatives, and the dates and times for the rosary and for the funeral. The printer would dip the printing machine in the blackest ink he had, so that the letters would stand out against the gray background of the paper, rolling out from the press the color of death.

It was our job to distribute the *esquelas.* Holding on to the car door and standing on the running-board, we went about town, jumping off the car and running to slip a notice in the handle of every screen door. If the person was important, we got paid ten cents, a quarter.

That night Dr. Dunlap would go through town in his car with Clementina, his nurse, by his side and showing him where everyone lived who had called to complain of shortness of breath. Sometimes he had so many people to see that he wouldn't arrive at our house until well after our bedtime and he'd catch us asleep. But we would wake up just to see him. To us it was all a game, but to Dr. Dunlap it was work, and we ended up killing him from overwork when all the time we thought we were being kind to him.

When he took out his magical stethoscope, we were in awe. He didn't have to ask for silence. You could almost hear my grandmother's heartbeat as she sat straight in her large wicker chair like a queen. He would gently place the bell of the instrument on my grandmother's chest and move it around once in a while, asking questions of Clementina. Clementina translated the questions into Spanish. Had she eaten a lot of fried foods? No, sir. Never. We would laugh. Everything my grandmother ate had been cooked in lard. How long had she felt bad? Since this morning when she was kneading the dough for *tortillas* and she had heard the tolling of the bell. Finally, Dr. Dunlap would roll up the stethoscope around his hand, look my grandmother in the eye and tell her she had the heart of a young woman. What a joy it was. We could go out and play, knowing our grandmother would live to knead more dough.

I visit the cemetery in San Diego every time I go. It seems the proper thing to do, to go pay my respects to the people there I love so much: to my mother, Marillita; my father, Gonzalo;

my grandmother, María; and my grandfather, Gonzalo, who died suddenly coming out of the meat market, clutching his package of meat to his chest—witnesses said he was dead before he hit the ground. Next to them my uncle Juan, who became a musician, dead at thirty-three. My little sister, Belinda, died needlessly of dysentery. We baptized her with tap water because the priest could not come to the house to baptize her and give her the last rites. My uncle Mercé, insane but generous and kind, who knew everyone's birthday and cursed everyone in town. Next to him is Adolfo, his brother, the baseball player, buried in name only since shortly after he bought his tombstone, already a mindless old man, he was kidnapped from San Diego by someone who claimed to be his illegitimate son. He's buried in San Antonio. Then my great-grandfather, who lived to be almost one hundred years and spent a week in agony before dying while we played marbles outside his window. And my aunt Pepa, the crazy one, who lost all her children in one year.

The list goes on: García, Saenz, González, Garza, Arguijo, Flores, Everett.

The ringing of the bell never ends.

There is universality to mankind. There are no bad towns. A little town in south Texas is the little town in John Donne's England where someone also runs to the church to ask for whom the bell tolls.

Lastly, I discovered that regardless how great a poet John Donne was, he was not entirely right. Surely the bell tolls for everyone, but the other person's death does not diminish me. On the contrary, each one of us, by having lived, magnifies the soul of everyone else.

And now a word about these stories. All of them are testament to the love and joy of being raised as a Mexican American in deep south Texas. There is no other place like it in the world and I feel privileged to have been born and raised there. If fiction is the enhancement of reality through illusion, like for Pepa, then these stories are fiction. If you believe reality can be an illusion, like for Mercé, then these stories are true. Rest assured that none of them happened exactly as I have written. On the other hand, all that I have written is true.

Mercé

"Mercé" from *I Can Hear the Cowbells Ring,* Arte Público Press, 1994, pp. 50–55

Tío Mercé lived with us, setting him apart from the large group of uncles who would come by to get a handout meal or a cup of coffee—*tíos* like Adolfo, Nano, Juanito Everett, Gumercindo, Manuel Saenz, and Pacho. He would be the last to eat, my grandmother saving little bits and pieces from everyone's plate to complete a meal for him while he waited patiently out-side, sitting by the kitchen door. He slept at his mother's old abandoned house on the corner, an old unpainted house whose wood had turned gray and had grown a velvet-like covering as soft as a peach. He had one kerosene lantern to light his way around the house, but we never saw him use it. He must have realized that it was dangerous for him to light a fire. So Mercé slept in complete and shadowless darkness. When we went looking for him at night, we had to feel our way against the wall until we found, on the right, the closed door to his room. We could smell his presence in the darkness when we opened the door, the smell of Bugler, of Bull Durham, the cheap tobacco which he burned in cigarettes rolled in corn husks, of the stale yeast of beer he drank which permeated his body.

After a week or so of being close to him, my grandmother would ask him to take a bath. She would take out some clean clothes for him, and he would bathe in the shed behind the house where we had a shower that drained under the floor and into the back yard.

My grandmother, who in her innocence believed everything that happened had a cause or a cure, had an explanation for Mercé's affliction. She believed Mercé had drank a potion meant for someone else in a beer. Some scorned woman had meant to chemically castrate her man by lacing his beer, and Mercé, as a result, had lost his manhood. His naturalness, she called it, had never descended, whatever that meant. "You know what I mean, don't you?" she would ask, and we would all nod our little heads, wondering what she was talking about, no one wanting to ask and be the fool. Cota was the most astute of the bunch and even she could not explain to the rest of us what "undescended naturalness" meant. "It probably has something to do with his huevos," she would say and then dismiss the conversation and talk about something else. Juan and Matías would laugh, and then my brother and sister and I would go along with them to the creek to play and smoke, not thinking at all of the disease which afflicted Mercé. To us he was normal, except for those times, and we could forget them very easily.

"His naturalness is still in his head," my grandmother would explain, and we would go along with the theory. "If a man's naturalness does not descend, it stays in his head and he goes crazy."

"How do you know?" asked Matías.

"I just do," she would say, and that was the end of that.

So only María Saenz knew what she was talking about, and I'm sure it pleased her knowing no one would question her theory.

The truth was, undescended naturalness or not, Mercé was insane. He could be sitting down at the table or sitting outside whittling or rolling a cigarette and he would start to mumble. And then the mumbling would get worse, louder. He would shoot up, stare into space and begin to curse, softly at first, gathering momentum in time until he could be heard from blocks away. He would grab the lobes of his ears and yank them violently, as though some demon were inside his brain. He would do this over and over until it seemed he would never stop, until blood would come out of his ears, until we were afraid he would tear them off. If this happened in the small kitchen while we were all eating, there would be a small commotion with us trying to get out of his way as best we could and my grandmother shouting at him, trying to make him behave. Of course, she couldn't. Invariably, he would run into the streets, sometimes in the direction of the rectory and the convent where the priest and the nuns had been watching him from the window. The Mother Superior would hurry through the convent, closing the shutters to protect the sensitive ears of the younger nuns. Father Zavala, jaded from having to carry the burden of the sins from so many confessions, would merely walk away to the far side of the house so that he would not appear to have noticed. If we were around, my grandmother would yell at us to go catch him, try to turn him around toward the house, and bring him back. If we weren't there, he would travel as far as the seizure would take him, sometimes clear to the other end of town, and he would take several hours to return.

My sister Sylvia hated to bring her friends from school to the house because of Mercé. She lived in fear of embarrassment that he would go into a fit around one of her friends who did not know him. All the rest of us—Cota, Maggie, Frances, Juan, Matías, Richard and myself—didn't care. We liked to be around him. There was never a dull moment.

One day the inevitable happened. Two of Sylvia's classmates came by uninvited to see her after school. We were all showing off, behaving ourselves for once, sitting at the porch at my grandmother's house drinking tea when Mercé, freshly showered, his hair wet and plastered down, came out of the shed at a full trot, yanking at his ears and shouting obscenities. He ran past us without as much as giving us a look, took off into the street, and this time headed straight for the Luby house, a three-story mansion which belonged to the cattle and land baron, Jason Luby. Mercé ran into the fence and kept pushing against it. shouting obscenities at old Mrs. Luby. Mrs. Luby was peeking out through a window, watching a deranged man crashing against her fence and shouting things about her which surely weren't true. She never seemed to mind, however. She was used to seeing Mercé having insane fits, cursing her and other people in town. She died at a good age, but no telling how much longer she would have lasted without the barrage of insults.

Unfortunately, my sister Sylvia's friends had never seen Mercé have a fit, and when he passed by them at a trot, yelling his obscenities, they screamed and hid under the old wicker sofa my grandmother had moved from the living room to the porch and where she sat at night rubbing camphorated alcohol on her arms and neck. My sister Sylvia tried to calm her friends, but to no avail. The two girls crawled around under the sofa until they got stuck and we had to lift it to free them. They jumped up, dusted themselves, still screaming in horror at what they had just seen and heard, and ran off as fast as Mercé had done, but in the opposite direction, toward the convent and the protection of the nuns. Shortly afterwards, my sister Sylvia told my brother Richard and me that she could never get married as long as Mercé was alive. She was seven at the time and thinking ahead.

All of San Diego knew Mercé and knew of his affliction. He was accepted as part of the local cast of characters. Many times, Mercé would have a fit in the middle of town and run down the little main street, in and out of the C.O.D. Bar, through the pool hall and back out into the street, and no one even bothered to look at him. Most of the men were more interested in what *Tío Amando* had to say as he held court in front of the butcher shop.

Lionel García

When he was a young man, Mercé had worked as a wrangler for the Lubys. He would come by for me on his horse, place me in front of the saddle, and together we would ride into town. When he had a fit, the horse, used to it by then, would duck his head and move his ears around quickly like antennas, trying to find a position that would keep him from the full blast of Mercé's obscenities. The Lubys let him go. He was cursing the grand old lady too much.

Dr. Dunlap got us an appointment and we took him one Friday to the insane asylum in San Antonio to see what could be done for him. He had two fits in the car, brought on, I suppose, by the thought of being separated from us. My grandmother, riding up front with my mother and father, begged us to control him, but we couldn't. He kicked and scratched to try to get to his ears until the fits ended. The doctors insisted on keeping him, wanting to study his insanity. We were very depressed on the way back, hardly talking to each other. My grandmother was crying, saying she would have never brought him if she had known they were going to keep him.

After one month we missed him so much that we returned to the asylum to try to get him back.

When we drove in through the gate, we saw Mercé sitting on a bench rolling a cigarette. We yelled when we saw him. My father began to honk the horn. Mercé recognized us and came running. He jumped in the car and wouldn't get out. So my father drove around the circular drive and came back out on the street and we never looked back. We didn't talk to the doctors. It turned out to be the right decision. According to Mercé, the doctor's were not doing anything for him except watching him run around the grounds having fits. He came back fatter, but soon lost his weight running around town cursing everyone with seemingly renewed vigor.

In his older years he would sit around the yard whittling, talking to himself and smoking. When he got tired of that, he would take off for the taverns.

My father bought him a cow to take care of, to give him some responsibilities. Mercé enjoyed the cow. He would milk her in the mornings and then take her out through town looking for an empty lot with grass where he could put her out to pasture. Then he would go to the tavern where he would spend the day drinking what was offered to him. In the meantime, he would have a fit or two. Later, he would pick up the cow on his way home, staggering down the road, the animal anxiously leading him, her udder bursting with milk. We would then give him a hand with the milking, holding the lantern by the pail so that he could see better in his drunken state.

Some nights Mercé would return without the cow, having either forgotten about her or not remembering where he had left her. We would all go with my father and him to look for her, happy that we had something exciting to do at night and listening to the overlapping of the night sounds—the piercing wails of the dying locusts, the cowbell ringing in the hollowness of the dark, a solitary dog barking at a shadow somewhere. Then we would take up a favorite game, the counting of a hundred fireflies, while we sifted the still warm sand between our toes as we walked.

After the Lubys took the horse away from Mercé, he enjoyed taking me out for walks to town, holding my hand and, when he sensed me tiring, carrying me in his arms. When his fits got so bad that he could not keep control of me, my mother told him he could not take me any more. My mother was afraid he was going to drop me on my head during one of his fits and hurt me. And besides, I was hearing too many obscenities at too young an age.

When I got older, my father would lend us his old single shot .22 and we would go hunting together. We never killed anything. During his fits he would scare off all the animals around for miles and besides, it was not in his nature to kill. When we saw a rabbit, I would point it out to him. He would keep on walking and say, "We'll kill him on the way back." We would walk for as long as he felt I should go and not be tired.

"See, Mercé," I would say. "We never kill anything if we wait until we come back."

"We'll kill him tomorrow," he would say. Then when we returned, the rabbit was never there.

When I would come home late at night on college vacations, Mercé would be waiting for me early the next morning. I would go out and sit with him and we would talk about little things. When I asked him how he felt, how he was doing, he always answered "*bien*," that he was doing well. He never complained about the life he had brought him—his insanity. Acceptance ruled his life. His sane moments were so serene and calm that a stranger would have easily picked him out as the only sane person among a sea of relatives always in turmoil.

The cow had died by then and he had been left with no responsibilities. He was drinking more than ever. The last morning I spent with him, he got up as we spoke, started his fit, and ran away. Feeling it would be insulting to him for me to try to stop him, I let him go.

Inside my grandmother's house I saw the cot where he slept—she had moved him over to her house to keep a closer watch on him, to make sure he didn't die alone after he had discarded Dr. Dunlap's advice about not drinking. That was at Christmas, a sad time for all of us. But, I had thought then, what does a person like Mercé, the disfranchised among us, care about Christmas?

Shortly after I returned to school, my mother called to tell me Mercé had died. She did not want me taking time off from my studies to come to the funeral.

"He would have understood," she said. "It's too far to come and too much trouble."

This time Dr. Dunlap had insisted that he have no liquor. He was not allowed outside the house. In a few days he was dead. As courageous as he was, he could not stand to live a sober life.

Writings

Novels: *Leaving Home,* Arte Público Press, 1985. *A Shroud in the Family,* Arte Público Press, 1987. *Hardscrub,* Arte Público Press, 1990. *To a Widow with Children,* Arte Público Press, 1994.
Short Stories: *I Can Hear the Cowbells Ring* (collection), Arte Público Press, 1994; stories also published in *The Americas Review, New Growth, Cuentos Chicanos, Texas Monthly, Texas Magazine/The Houston Chronicle, Short Fiction by Hispanic Writers of the United States,* and elsewhere.

Victor Hernández Cruz

Victor Hernández Cruz is a Nuyorican poet who was discovered as a precocious street poet while still in high school in New York and in the mainstream has become the most recognized and acclaimed Hispanic poet. Despite his early acceptance into creative writing circles, culminating with Life magazine's canonizing him as one of the twenty-five best American poets in 1981, Hernández Cruz has resisted aestheticism and academic writing to remain an oral poet, a jazz poet, a poet of the people and popular traditions, a bilingual poet, and a poet of intuition and tremendous insight. Despite the steady stream of his verse published in magazines and in books, he is first and foremost a performance artist, creating poetry for oral delivery, and in so doing preserving and furthering the traditional, communal functions of poetry.

Born on February 6, 1949, in Aguas Buenas, Puerto Rico, Victor Hernández Cruz moved with his family to New York's Spanish Harlem when he was five. Later Cruz attended Benjamin Franklin High School, where he began writing poetry. In the years following graduation, his poetry appeared in *Evergreen Review, New York Review of Books, Ramparts, Down Here,* and many other magazines. In 1970 he began working with New York's poetry-in-the-schools programs, including the Teachers and Writers Collaborative. In 1973 Cruz left New York and took up residence in San Francisco, where he worked for the U.S. Postal Service and served as a visiting poet at area colleges. From 1973 to 1975, he became a traveling troubadour, covering the full expanse of the United States, from Alaska and Hawaii to Puerto Rico, reading and performing his works and continuing to write. Thereafter, he alternated living in San Francisco and Puerto Rico, dedicating himself to writing and accepting engagements to read his works at campuses, poetry festivals, and book fairs around the country. Aside from living off the royalties from his published works, Hernández Cruz also received support from the National Endowment for the Arts and the Guggenheim Foundation in 1980 and 1991, respectively.

Victor Hernández Cruz's poetry books include *Papa Got His Gun* (1966), *Snaps* (1969), *Mainland* (1973), *Tropicalization* (1976), *By Lingual Wholes* (1982), and *Rhythm, Content and Flavor* (1989). Classifying his poetry as Afro-Latin, Hernández Cruz is the consummate bilingual poet and experimenter who consistently explores the relationship between music and poetry in a multi-racial, multicultural context. Hernández Cruz has often been considered a jazz poet and an African American poet, but the April 1981 issue of *Life* magazine proclaimed him a national treasure by including him among a handful of outstanding American poets —without making reference to his race or ethnicity. He is one of the most innovative living American poets; he not only derives his work from the mountain songs of Puerto Rico, salsa, and other popular music, but also is inspired by modernists like e.e. cummings, Afro-American masters like Amiri Baraka, Taíno Indian culture, Hindu literature, and classical music. Hernández Cruz states that a strong concern in his work has been "the difference between a tropical village, such as Aguas Buenas, Puerto Rico, where I was born, and an immensity such as New York City, where I was raised. I compare smells and sounds, I explore the differences, I write from the center of a culture which is not on its native soil, a culture in flight, living half the time on memories, becoming something totally new and unique, while at the same time it helps to shape and inform the new environment. I write about the city with an agonizing memory of a lush tropical silence. This contrast between landscape and languages creates an intensity in my work."

His has been a borderless, polyglot odyssey through the world of oral poetic expression and performance that could never have been accomplished within the walls of academia. And his mixing and blending of Spanish and English— including the use of various dialects of both languages, which is so evident in his pioneering multilingual/multidialect work, *By Lingual Wholes,* has freed poetry of linguistic constraints while undermining the graphic representation of sounds in written language.

Richard Elman noted in *The New York Times* that in *By Lingual Wholes,* Victor Hernández Cruz's poems "often speak to us with a forked tongue, sometimes in a highly literate Spanglish. He gives things their proper names (bodega, *bacalao*).

Cruz's poems "often speak to us with a forked tongue, sometimes in a highly literate Spanglish. . . . He's a funny, hard-edged poet, declining always into mother wit and pathos."

Richard Elman in
The New York Times Book
Review, September 18, 1983

He's a funny, hard-edged poet, declining always into mother wit and pathos. . . . The amalgam poetry which emerges is finely drawn, without apology or inhibition." Hernández Cruz himself has said, "My work is on the border of a new language, because I create out of a consciousness steeped in two of the important world languages, Spanish and English. A piece totally written in English could have a Spanish spirit."

In a poetic essay included in *Red Beans,* Hernández Cruz proclaims that "National languages sail into each other" and that, because of the Latino presence in the United States, "the syntax of English is being changed." Clearly, Hernández Cruz is one of the catalysts of that change. But more than that, he proudly announces that the racial and cultural mixing that has taken place in the Caribbean is taking over American culture, transforming it and revitalizing it.

> *"My family life was full of music, guitars and conga drums, maracas and songs. My mother sang songs. Even when it was five below zero in New York she sang warm tropical ballads."*
>
> **Victor Hernández Cruz**

Personal Stats

Nuyorican writer. **Born:** February 6, 1949, in Aguas Buenas, Puerto Rico. *Education:* Benjamin Franklin High School, New York City. **Career:** Discovered as a poet while still in high school, worked as a postal worker thereafter, help various visiting-writer and visiting-professor positions at the Other Ways Project, Berkeley Unified School District, 1968–69; New York City public schools, 1970; the University of California-Berkeley, 1971–72; San Francisco State University, 1971; Creative Artists in Public Service (CAPS) in New York City, 1977; Mission Neighborhood Center, 1981 and others. *Memberships:* Before Columbus Foundation board of directors; San Francisco Poetry Center board of directors; *The Americas Review* editorial board; Puerto Rico PEN. *Awards/Honors:* New York City CAPS grant, 1977; National Endowment for the Arts Creative Writing Fellowship, 1980; New York Poetry Foundation Award, 1989; Guggenheim Fellowship, 1991. *Address:* c/o Arte Público Press, PO Box 2090, The University of Houston, Houston, TX 77204-2090

The Latest Latin Dance Craze

from *Rhythm, Content & Flavor,* Arte Público Press, 1989, p. 85

First
You throw your head back twice
Jump out onto the floor like a
Kangaroo

Circle the floor once
Doing fast scissor works with your
Legs
Next
Dash towards the door
Walking in a double cha cha cha
Open the door and glide down
The stairs like a swan
Hit the street
Run at least ten blocks
Come back in through the same
Door
Doing a mambo-minuet
Being careful that you don't fall

Victor Hernández Cruz

And break your head on that one
You have just completed your first
Step.

energy

from *Rhythm, Content & Flavor,* Arte Público Press, 1989, p. 18

is
red beans
ray barretto
banging away
steam out the
radio
the five-stair
steps
is mofongo
cuchifrito stand
outside down
the avenue
that long hill
of a block
before the train
is pacheco
playing with
bleeding
blue lips

Three Songs From The 50's

from *Rhythm, Content & Flavor,* Arte Público Press, 1989, p. 82–83

Song 1

Julito used to shine the soul
of his shoes before he left for
the Palladium to take the wax

off the floor while Tito Rodríguez
flew around the walls like a
parakeet choking Maracas
It was around this time that
Julito threw away his cape
because the Umbrella Man and the
Dragons put the heat on all the
Ricans who used to fly around
in Dracula capes swinging canes
or carrying umbrellas
Even if there was no rain
on the horizon
That same epoca my mother
got the urge to paint the
living room pink and buy a
new mirror with flamingoes
elegantly on the right hand
corner because the one we had
was broken from the time that
Carlos tried to put some respect
Into Julito and knocked the
party out of him.

Song 2

All the old Chevies that the
gringoes from up state New York
wore out
Were sailing around the neighborhood
with dices and San Martín de Porres
el negrito who turned catholic
Hanging in the front windows.

Song 3

There was still no central heating
in the tenements
We thought that the cold was
the oldest thing on the planet earth
We used to think about my Uncle Listo
Who never left his hometown
We'd picture him sitting around

cooling himself with a fan
In that imaginary place
called Puerto Rico.

Writings

Poetry Books: *Papa Got His Gun,* Calle Once Publications, 1966. *Snaps,* Random House, 1969. *Mainland,* Random House, 1973. *Tropicalization,* Reed & Cannon, 1976. *By Lingual Wholes,* Momos Press, 1982. *Rhythm, Content and Flavor,* Arte Público Press, 1989. *Red Beans,* Coffee House Press, 1991. **Anthologies:** *Stuff: A Collection of Poems, Visions, and Imaginative Happenings from Young Writers in Schools—Open and Closed,* co-edited with Herbert Kohl, New American Library, 1971. **Poetry:** In *The Americas Review, Evergreen Review, The New York Times Sunday Magazine, The Village Voice, The New York Review of Books, The San Francisco Chronicle, Ramparts, River Styx, El nuevo día, Claridad,* and numerous other periodicals, anthologies, and textbooks.

Oscar Hijuelos

Oscar Hijuelos is the first Hispanic writer to win the Pulitzer Prize for Fiction (1990). He is also the clearest example of the writers of a younger generation who benefited from studying creative writing in college, not only for the craft they learned but also for the contacts they made there that opened doors for them in the publishing industry. In Hijuelos's case, it was Donald Barthelme, from City College of New York, who helped launch the career of the then-promising but unproved writer.

Born on August 24, 1951, to Cuban American working-class parents in New York City, Hijuelos was educated in public schools and earned his B.A. in 1975 and an M.A. in 1976, both in English, from City College of the City University of New York. Hijuelos is one of the few Hispanic writers to have formally studied creative writing and to have broken into the Anglo-dominated creative writing circles, participating in prestigious workshops, such as the Breadloaf Writers Conference, and benefiting from highly competitive fellowships, such as the American Academy in Rome Fellowship from the American Academy and the Institute for Arts and Letters (1985), the National Endowment for the Arts Fellowship (1985), and the Guggenheim Fellowship (1990).

Hijuelos is the author of various short stories and four novels—*Our House in the Last World* (1983), *The Mambo Kings Play Songs of Love* (1989), *The Fourteen Sisters of Emilio Montez O'Brien* (1993), and *Mr. Ives' Christmas* (1995). His first novel follows in the tradition of ethnic autobiography and the novel of immigration, as it chronicles the life and maladjustment of a Cuban immigrant family in the United States during the 1940s. *The Mambo Kings Play Songs of Love,* the winner of the Pulitzer Prize, is more than just a story of immigration—it examines a period when Hispanic culture was highly visible in the United States and had a strong influence on American popular culture. This time was the 1950s, during the height of the mambo craze and the overwhelming success of Desi Arnaz's television show, *I Love Lucy.* Written in a poetic but almost documentary style, the novel follows two brothers who are musicians trying to ride the crest of the Latin music wave. While providing a picture of one segment of American life never seen before in English-language fiction, the novel also indicts, as does *Our House in the Last World,* womanizing and alcoholism as Cuban flaws.

In *The Fourteen Sisters of Emilio Montez O'Brien,* Hijuelos also examines gender roles in Cuban culture, and Hispanic culture in general. The novel received mixed reviews, being somewhat of a let-down after the heights of its Pulitzer-prize winning predecessor. In an interview in *The New York Times,* Hijuelos stated that he wanted "to portray a world in which women were very powerful. I took the idea of machismo and pushed it, getting inside the skin of the characters . . . I wanted to look behind the basic images of women." His latest novel, *Mr. Ives' Christmas,* released just in time for the Christmas season in 1995, was a complete departure for the author: the short highly-commercial novel comprised a psychological study that has nothing at all to do with Hispanic culture or themes.

At this point in his career, Hijuelos seems to have a singular path: he is not part of the immigrant generation of his parents nor is he one of the children of Cuban exile and he does not seem to have been stigmatized by the racism of growing up on the mean streets of New York. Clearly a product of the working class, Hijuelos is a whose style and focus are similar to those Italian American, Irish American, and Jewish American writers of the American Dream—writers fascinated with the mosaic of American culture and who use their backgrounds as intellectual material for creating literature. Hijuelos is part of this group of writers who are more thoughtful than passionate about their community's place in American society, more observer than participant, more individualistic artist than epic singer.

Personal Stats

Cuban American writer. **Born:** August 24, 1951, in New York City. **Education:** B.A. (1975) and M.A. (1976), in English from the City College of the City University of New York. **Career:** Advertising media traffic manager at Transportation Display Inc., 1977–84; full-time writer, 1984–present. **Membership:** PEN. **Awards/ Honors:** Stories in *Best of the Pushcart Awards III,* 1978; Cintas (Cuban American) fellowship for writing, 1980; Breadloaf Writing Conference scholarship, 1980; grant

> "The very best [critics] have seen beyond the social and cultural veneer of [The Mambo Kings]. Of course it's about Cubans and music, but I also wanted to do something about the way that memory works—like spinning a record, a TV rerun —that occurs again and again. . . . These two brothers . . . are ordinary human beings with complex inner lives —no stereotypes here."
>
> **Oscar Hijuelos**

from the Creative Artists Programs Service of New York City, 1982; grant from the Ingram Merrill Foundation, 1983; American Institute of Arts and Letters Rome Prize, 1985; National Endowment for the Arts Fellowship, 1985; Guggenheim Fellowship, 1990; Pulitzer Prize, 1990. **Address:** c/o Persea Books, 60 Madison Ave., New York, NY 10010

Cuba, Cuba, 1954

From *Our House in the Last World,* Persea Books, 1983

1

It was the summertime, and Alejo Santinio had sent Mercedes and Horacio and Hector down to Cuba by airplane. Mercedes had been homesick for Holguín and wanted to see her sisters, and for them and her mother to see the children. And there had been too much fighting in the house, a situation that was forgotten during their visit in Cuba, except that regrets about her life sometimes sent Mercedes to bed at two in the afternoon. Her sisters would comfort her, send the children out to play.

Horacio thought of Cuba as a place of small towns and hick farms. He did not see it with Mercedes's romantic eyes. Romanticism existed in the distant past and died with the conquistadors, gallant caballeros, and señoritas. Almost everyone from the past time was dead, save for the ghost he saw. Most of the people he would have admired were gone, down under the ground with the worms and stone. Teodoro Sorrea, the great artist, was someone he wanted to meet. And why? In his eyes, his grandfather was a first-class hustler. Not the saint Mercedes always made him out to be, but a dude who almost made a fortune off that tax-skimming scheme. But he had stalled for too long and dropped dead too soon. Maybe he would have sent Mercedes off to the university, and she would have become a great poet. Then Horacio would have been born in a beautiful house with much sunlight, and his head would not have been knocked around.

Horacio did not see Cuba as a place of romance. He could see under and through things. He saw Luisa's and Rina's nice houses on cobblestone streets. A farm of pigs, sheep, and flea-ridden dogs. Thick, festering bushes full of tiny, red, long-legged spiders, red ants, and thick-shelled beetles that sounded like hurled stones when they flew out and hit the walls. Termites with bodies like embers swarmed in the rotted tree stumps of the farm. And he saw aunts Rina and Luisa and their children: Paco, Rafael, and Delores, who belonged to Aunt Rina; Virginia and María, who were so pretty and attentive to their mother, Aunt Luisa, widowed some years before. He saw the ditches, pools of stagnant water, thick clouds of flies and mosquitoes. He saw the clogged-with-shit stone toilets that were made tolerable only by the strong fragrances of the fruit trees and blossoms. Cuba was in the nineteenth century—okay, a nice place, and not anything more. There

"In many ways a realistic novel, Our House in the Last World *also reflects certain Latin attributes that are usually termed 'surreal' or 'magical.' Although I am quite Americanized, my book focuses on many of my feelings about identity and my 'Cubanness.'"*

Oscar Hijuelos

was a lot of eating going on, some belching, food everywhere, unless you were poor and then worms grew long in your intestines.

He took trips into the country with Rina's husband, Uncle Manny. Trips to the steamy Neptuna, where the Frosty Cool Air Conditioning had broken down. He rode in the truck with Pucho, a mulatto who had been adopted by the family next door, went to Woolworths and came back and found a hacked-up iguana lying in the yard, black balls like fish larva spilling from its torn stomach.

The ghost was the only thing that really impressed Horacio. And Aunt Luisa's kisses. She was all right, good to everyone, especially to him. When they went places, whether to the beach or to the marketplace or to Rina's farm, she put her arm around him and liked to give him kisses. And with no demands! She was thin with a young face and long black hair. She and Aunt Rina had a dress shop, and in the afternoons, she paid Horacio a dollar to watch the store for an hour while she went home to take a nap. Then she would come back, and he could go off and wander around the town with its hot stone roads and square blue, pink, or white houses.

On the weekends they would go either to the beach or out to Rina's farm, about ten miles north of Holguín. This was a real farm with squealing pigs that rolled in the mud and fields of cane and fruit trees. The big event of the day was the cooking of the pig. There were three buildings on the farm: an old cool house from the days when they grew tobacco, a horse stable, and the main house. In front of the stable was a dirt road and a shallow declivity. At its bottom was a chopping block where the family cook would sit, casually hacking the heads off hens with a machete. The hens would run a few feet spurting blood like crazy and then drop, and the blood would settle in a thick pool of feathers and chicken heads that the dogs liked to eat. Then the cook would drop the chickens into a pot of boiling water so that the feathers could be easily pulled off. Flies everywhere. But that day Uncle Manny and the farmhand dragged out an immense pig weighing about ninety pounds, beheaded it, and then cleaved it in half. Horacio was sitting beside Aunt Luisa reading a funny book—*Superman in Spanish*— when Manny, square-shouldered and robust as a bull, called him over to help take the pig away. Horacio went over, and they tied a piece of rope around the pig's hooves and then pulled him toward a barbecue pit. It was hard work. Horacio was rewarded with a Coca-Cola.

The sides of pork were lying next to the pit when an iguana came along and burrowed his way into one of the haunches. Later, when Manny discovered the iguana nestled inside, he tried to pull it loose by its tail. But with its dinosaur teeth clamped into flesh, there was no way of jerking it free. So Manny and the cook dragged the side of pork across the yard and hauled it up onto one of the lower branches of a mango tree, then built a fire of leaves and twigs and newspapers underneath. The idea was to smoke the iguana out.

Everyone waited on the porch for the iguana to run away. There were columns of black smoke, burstings of fruit skins, withering leaves . . . and soon it let go and fell onto the ground. But suddenly it seemed as though hundreds of black flowers started raining down from the tree. They landed and spun around, creeping like fire in all directions. In fact, they were large, ugly tarantulas. There turned out to be a huge nest of them in the tree. Falling, they scurried in all directions and some went up the porch steps, under the chairs, under the skirts, and between shoes, and into the house. And soon everyone was after them with shovels and brooms and sticks. For an hour this hunt went on, and by then the sides of pork were cooking.

The meal was delicious, too greasy as always, too heavy because of the monstrous portions of black beans and starchy plantains. After dinner it was dull and relaxing to sit out on the porch listening to the "night bells," as the crickets were called, and to watch the stars rise over the field. It was boring but at least it was peaceful.

Before they had left to visit Rina and Luisa, the apartment walls had shaken from things and people smashing into them. Alejo's fist, a chair, a bottle, Alejo pounding the wall and knocking furniture aside, while Mercedes ran in circles inside the circular apartment and visitors tried to come between them but were pushed aside. Kindly visitors, like the three sisters from Oriente, had covered up Horacio's and Hector's eyes and ears with soft delicate hands, while Mercedes fled down the hall. But Horacio had called out, "Stop, you stop, stop, stop, you stop," so much that his voice had grown hoarse. Then for days the apartment had been quiet. No one had spoken, except Alejo, who had swallowed his manly pride trying to apologize for his outbursts. He had sent Horacio and Hector and Mercedes to Cuba because he loved the family and wanted to keep the family afloat.

Besides, Mercedes had promised her mother, Doña María, a chance to see the children. Now, during their visit, Doña María often sat on the porch in a wicker chair, holding Horacio's hand and smiling at him. She was suffering from heart disease. Her hair had turned white and her hands had begun to shake. Everything she had to say was like this: "You've made an old woman very happy with your visit, Horacio."

Kisses from the aunts, reassurances from Uncle Manny . . .

The evening ended around nine-thirty when yawning competed with the sounds of night. One by one, the family retired. Horacio and Hector and Luisa stayed in the same room on the second floor. The balcony of this room faced a field. The moon would rise at one side of the field just outside the window. Horacio liked to watch it, amazed that it looked the same as from New York.

They were sleeping the night Teodoro Sorrea's ghost came along. It was well after midnight. Luisa heard a noise and sat up in bed. She woke Horacio. By the balcony was Teodoro, now only a luminescence in the shape of a man, wavering like light rippling on water. "Dios mío," Luisa said, making the sign of the cross. Horacio could not believe his eyes. The ghost seemed to be spreading his arms open and sadness emanated from him. "Me estoy quemando," the ghost said. "I am burning." He stood on the balcony for a few minutes, turned away, and then disappeared. This was really the only thing about Cuba that made a lasting impression on Horacio.

■ ■ ■

2

And Hector? For him the journey was like a splintering film. He was so young, his memory had barely started. Impressions swooped upon him like the large-winged, white butterflies in the yard. There were quiet, floating dragonflies, star blossoms, hanging lianas, and orchids of sweet smells. The sunlight, *el señor del sol,* a friendly character who came out each day. Nightingales, dirty hens, sparrows, doves, chicks, crows in the dark trees. Orange-bottomed clouds shaped like orange blossoms, sun up in the sky, big hairy trees: acacia, tamarind, bread-fruit, banana, mango, cinnamon, mamey. Rainbows arching between trees, prisms inside puddles. . . . In town there were old carved church doors, Christ up to heaven, stagnant wells, a lazy turtle, the sleeping dog . . . bakery smells, white laundry sheets, a laundress. Taste of eating Hershey bar, taste of eating slice of pineapple, taste of eating chicken, taste of eating trees, taste of eating steak, taste of eating flowers, taste of eating sugar, taste of eating kisses, taste of eating fried sweet plantains. "Cuba, Cuba," repeated incessantly, "Cuba, Cuba . . . ."

Then something solid happened. He was sitting in the yard, examining a flower. The flower was purple with three oval wings and long red and yellow tendrils that ended in stars. There was a dog, Poochie, licking up his face. Then Poochie rolled over and his pathetic red dick slipped out from his heaving belly. Hector petted the dog's belly, and the dog rolled around on his back. Then Hector heard a noise coming from the bushes. A bird hopped from branch to branch. Poochie, wagging his tail, happily circled the tree and started leaping up and down, anxious to eat the bird. When Hector went to pet Poochie, the dog snarled and Hector began to cry. But in those days things did not bother him for very long. He went and sat on the kitchen steps. A breeze came in across the treetops from the east, and it felt good on his face. He was in his favorite sailor suit but without shoes, so his toes could play with the ants that teemed up under the floor tiles.

"Oh Hector! Hector!"

It was Aunt Luisa. She was in the kitchen, reading the dress-shop ledger book. The light of the afternoon printed a rectangle on the table and over her soft face. "Oh Hector, come and give your auntie a kiss and you'll get a delicious treat."

He kissed her and she laughed, patting his head.

"How affectionate you are," she said and pinched his cheeks. The he waited for the treat. He loved to eat, so much so that with each day he grew a little chubbier. His legs and belly were fat. His cheeks, so, so plump, were red. In the evenings he was always happy to sit on the floor with his female cousins, eating snacks given by Luisa. Chewing fried toast covered in sugar with his eyes closed, listening to Aunt Luisa's soft, pleasant voice as she answered in the half-light of the room. Chewing sounds and Luisa's voice mingled with the street noises outside: clop, clop, clop of horses, insects' songs, a dog barking, the murmur of spirits in the Cuban ghost land. Taste of sugar and bread. Luisa sighed as she put aside her sewing for the moment and leaned forward to touch Hector's face. "You're such a little blondie," she said.

Aunt Luisa fixed his drink, which he slowly drank down, savoring its taste. It was so good, with nutty, deep-forest flavors, sweet but not too sweet, with just enough bitterness to fill the mouth with a yawning sensation. He asked for more. She kissed him, poured another glass, and he drank that down. It went deep into his belly but shot up again, from time to time, into his sleep, night after night, for years to come. For some reason he would remember that drink, wondering what it could be, so Cuban, so delicious. Then one day, years in the future, Luisa would come to America, and he would find out its name.

He divided his time between the two aunts' houses, eating and drinking everything in sight: caramel sweets, hard candies, plates of fried pork in rice, bananas, sweet papaya ice cream, leaves, twigs, soda, crackers, honey-dripped flour balls, sour Cuban milk, Coca-Cola, and even water from a puddle. At Rina's house he would sit in a chair placed in front of Uncle Manny's work-shop and eat his lunch. Uncle Manny was an enormous man with white hair and wire-rimmed glasses. He had a horse face and liked to wear khaki clothing and read newspapers in an enclosure of prickly bushes. He was a bookkeeper but kept this little workshop in the backyard in order to do some silversmithing and watch repair on the side. Luisa and Rina sent him customers from the dress shop. The workshop: a pine shed, boxes of watch gears and tiny screws, coils of soft wire, and a burner used for heating a little pot of coffee. Smell of metal, rubber, silver, talcum, eucalyptus.

Now Hector was watching him melt silver in a tiny ladle over a flame. His demitasse of coffee steamed on the wooden counter. Swirling the silver around, Manny said, "You know what this is boy? Cuban blood." Hector looked at the steaming coffee, and Manny laughed. "Not the coffee boy, the silver. You have this in your veins." The silver swirling. "You know what you are, boy? You're Cuban. Un Cubano. Say it."

"*Cubano, Cubano,* Cuba, Cuba . . . . "

Hector sat watching Manny for a long time, wondering if the demitasse was full of the exotic, delicious Cuban drink. His eyes would dart between the ladle of Cuban blood and the coffee, and noticing this, Manny let him sip the dark espresso to which he had added sugar and dark rum. Hector spit it out, and Manny laughed again.

"Don't worry, you'll like it when you're older."

But he drank many other beverages: Coca-Cola and orange juice at Aunt Rina's. In town, at the bodega, some kind of crushed ice drink mixed with pieces of fruit and syrup. All so good, but not like what Luisa gave him. And he was always drinking Cuban water, especially on those trips he and Horacio took with Manny out to the countryside. Manny sometimes did the accounting for a pal of his who worked at a pharmaceutical warehouse. His pal used to give him free bottles of medicine and aspirin, which he would give to the poor *guajiros*—"hicks."

"How they can live like that," Manny used to say, shaking his head, "how they can live like that?"

And Manny would take the family up north to Gibara to go swimming. That was where, according to Mercedes, Hector got sick.

The whole family was together: Mercedes, Luisa, and Rina, the cousins, Manny, Horacio, and Hector. All the women sat under a big umbrella, reading fashion and Hollywood magazines with actors like William Holden and Cary Grant on the cover, while the men ran in and out of the warm ocean. The current whooshed Cuban sand between their toes. There were starfish by Manny's massive feet. His strong hands took Hector aloft onto his shoulders, real high up, the way Alejo used to do, back in New York. He was so high up, he could see all the palms and the Persian-looking cabanas and the weathered boardwalk, the sea all around him, a curly blue mirror.

Breaking the waves, Manny marched out into the ocean, his great chest of white hair foaming. The skies overhead, zooming by. Manny's voice: something about Christopher Columbus and a ship with huge white sails, Indians, skeletons under the water, and the edge of the world . . . And he was taking Hector out deep into the Cuban sea. Hector held on for his life, his arms around Manny's bull neck, until Manny pried his hands free and let him float off.

But down he went.

"Come on, niño, try, try, try, don't be afraid."

Hector swallowed more water, went up and down.

"Come on, niño."

But Hector went down and tasted salt and his throat burned, he swallowed and coughed, so that Manny finally brought him back to shore, where Luisa cured him with kisses.

When Hector started feeling sick, Luisa gave him more of the delicious Cuban drink, so good in his belly. But sometimes a weariness confused him and he stayed up at night, listening to the Cuban ghosts walking around in the yard. Or he could hear Mercedes speaking in whispers to Luisa. Sometimes his back ached or his penis felt shot with lead, and he could be in a room, drinking his treat, when he would hurt but remain quiet. If he did cry out, Luisa or Rina cured him with kisses. Mercedes always said, "You were so good, a quiet, quiet boy. If only we knew . . ."

A Cuban infection of some kind entered him. In any case, that was what Mercedes always said. What had he done? Swim in the ocean? Drink from a puddle? Kiss? Maybe he hadn't said his prayers properly, or he had pissed in his pants one too many times or cried too much. Maybe God had turned the Cuban water against him and allowed the *micróbios,* as Mercedes would call them, to go inside his body. Who knew? But getting sick in Cuba confused him greatly, because he had loved Cuba so much.

■ ■ ■

3

In her way Mercedes made sense of these things. This was what she said about that journey.

"We went there to see my poor mama, bless her soul. She was viejita, viejita, so old and happy to see us. There were other reasons we sent, for a vacation, you know. Alejo couldn't take that much time off, three months, so he sent us alone.

"When we got to Havana we took the train east to Holguín. That was a long trip, eight hours, but at least we got to see a little of everything: the big sugarcane plantations, the ranches, the mountains, the old colonial towns with their dusty train stations and the poor farmers going everywhere with their caged, dirty, white hens. Horacio was pressed against the window, looking at everything with big eyes, but Hector was too hot for the whole trip, inside a stuffy train. And, Dios mio, it was hot in those days. So believe me, we were happy when we finally came to Holguín.

"My sisters loved both of the boys very much, and they loved my sisters back. The boys were as happy as little mice and everything was pretty: the house, the town, and the flowers that were everywhere. I remember Manny . . . his children came to America last year on a boat from Mariel Harbor. He was a big man, so good, especially with the poor. He died in 1960, young, like anyone else who's any good in this world, but in those days he took us everywhere. To the movies and out to the farm and to the ocean, where maybe Hector got sick.

"I tried to be good, but it's impossible to watch the children all the time, with all the running around and playing. Horacio was good, quiet and minding his own business, but Hector . . . he made me go crazy down there. We would leave him in the yard in Luisa's house, saying, Stay put, but he wouldn't do that. Running around, he got into everything. I didn't mind that, but he went around drinking water out of puddles in the yard. There was dirty water down there, filled with little *micróbios,* which is why he got sick. We didn't know it then. He looked healthy, mi hijito, my little son. He was nice and chubby, and, little by little, he put on more weight. Horacio put on some weight, too, all those chorizos and plátanos omelets that he liked so much. So we didn't think anything about it. We went through the days in peace, Horacio having fun and Hector so curious and happy. Who knew that he would be so sick? I didn't.

"Alejo was writing me nice letters, saying nice things in them, saying for us to have a good time. The only thing he asked us to do was to visit his great grandmother, old Concepción. That's were Horacio and Hector got their light hair. From old Concepción. A long time ago, when Concepción was a young girl, maybe seventeen or sixteen years of age, walking in Santiago de Cuba, she met and Irish sailor by the name of O'Connor. He was very light and fair, with blond hair. He had sailed around the world about five or six times and was looking for a place to settle, was swept off his feet by Concepción, and eventually married her. So her name became Concepción O'Connor, and his blood passed down quietly through the generations until my sons were born.

"In any case, we went to see her one day. She was almost one hundred years old. But she was clean and still had all her senses. Her arms were thin, like young branches, and her hair was white, white. But she had young eyes, and was so happy to see us! She always sat in one place on the patio under an umbrella so that the berries dropping from the trees wouldn't hit her on her head. She was something of a celebrity, too, having been written up in the *Sol* and *Diario de la Marina* because she was so old and not yet dead. She was very happy to meet us, and when she saw Hector's little blond head, she got all happy . . . to think that more of the sailor was around!

"And I took the boys to see my old house. It was just like it used to be, so beautiful, except that now we couldn't go inside. A government man lived there and servants who wouldn't even let us peek around. There it was, a beautiful white house, so nice . . . the kind of house we could have all lived in if our luck was a little different, and if my poor papa did not die . . . .

"Still we have our fun. We went to the marketplace and saw a bullfight. And then I showed Horacio and Hector where a witch lived when I was a little girl, and we would pass the time watching the farmers going by on the road. Down the way there was a blind negro, un negrito muy bueno, who played the guitar and used to sing for pennies. For hours we would stand beside him or go riding around; every one of us had fun.

"But Hector became very sick and made trouble for me. I don't know what happened. Maybe it was the drinking water there or something in the food, but he got so sick, and Alejo blamed me for it. Maybe I should have known . . . .

One day we were at the beach at Gibara and Manny was taking everybody into the water. Hector was having fun on top of Manny's shoulders, going deeper and deeper into the water. You know how sometimes you can think of things, they come to you in a second? I was sitting under the umbrella, because the sun was bad for my skin, when I suddenly felt like a little girl, and as I watched everyone in the water, I had the idea that something was going to get me in trouble: I didn't want it to happen but couldn't tell what it would be. Just a feeling of wanting to stop something before it had started. Like knowing that there are bugs eating up your garden, but you can never find them. That was what it was like. When we left Cuba, Hector as sick but so happy and fat that we didn't know anything. He came back saying *Cuba, Cuba* and spent a lot of time with Alejo. He was a little Cuban, spouting Spanish."

Writings

Novels: *Our House in the Last World,* Persea Books, 1983. *The Mambo Kings Play Songs of Love,* Farrar, Straus and Giroux, 1989. *The Fourteen Sisters of Emilio Montez O'Brien,* Farrar, Straus and Giroux, 1993. *Mr. Ives' Christmas,* Farrar, Straus and Giroux, 1995. ***Short Stories:*** In numerous magazines and anthologies.

Rolando Hinojosa

Rolando Hinojosa is the most prolific and most proficiently bilingual Hispanic novelist in the United States. Not only has he created memorable Mexican American and Anglo characters, but he has completely populated a fictional county in the Lower Rio Grande Valley of Texas through his continuing narrative that he calls the "Klail City Death Trip Series."

Born on January 21, 1929, in Mercedes, Texas, to a Mexican American father and a bilingual Anglo-American mother, his paternal ancestors arrived in the Lower Rio Grande Valley in 1749 as part of the José Escandón expedition. Hinojosa was educated at first in Mexican schools in Mercedes and later in the segregated public schools where all of his classmates were Mexican Americans. He attended integrated classes in junior high. It was in high school that Hinojosa began to write, with his first pieces in English published in an annual literary magazine, *Creative Bits*. Hinojosa left the Valley in 1946 when he graduated from college, but the language, culture, and history of the area form the substance of all of his novels. The ensuing years saw a stint in the Army, studies at the University of Texas, re-activation into the Army to fight in the Korean War (an experience that informs his poetic narrative *Korean Love Songs* and his novel *The Useless Servants*), graduation from the University of Texas in 1954 with a degree in Spanish, and a return to the Valley (Brownsville) to teach before he went on to graduate school. In 1969 he obtained his Ph.D. in Spanish from the University of Illinois but he went back to teach at Texas colleges. Hinojosa has remained in academia in a variety of positions and universities; today he serves as Ellen Clayton Garwood Professor of English and Creative Writing at the University of Texas.

Although he has written throughout his life, Hinojosa did not publish a book until 1973: his *Estampas del Valle y otras obras* (which he recreated in English and published as *The Valley* in 1983) was the winner of the national award for Chicano literature, Premio Quinto Sol. From that time on he has become a prolific Chicano novelist, publishing one novel after another in his ongoing narrative that centers around the lives of two of his alter-egos, Rafa Buenrostro and Jehú Malacara. The individual installments in the series vary in style from poetry and dialogue to the picaresque novel and the detective novel. His titles in English alone include *Korean Love Songs* (1980), *Rites and Witnesses* (1982), *Dear Rafe* (1985), *Partners in Crime: A Rafe Buenrostro Mystery* (1985), *Claros varones de Belken/ Fair Gentlemen of Belken County* (1986, bilingual edition), *Klail City* (1987), *Becky and Her Friends* (1989), and *The Useless Servants* (1994). His original Spanish version of *Klail City,* (a selection from which follows), entitled *Klail City y sus alrededores* (1976), won the international award for fiction, Premio Casa de las Américas, from Cuba in 1976. It was issued in Cuba under this title and a year later it was published in the United States under the title of *Generaciones y semblanzas*. The book was also published in German two years later. Hinojosa's short stories and essays have been widely published, as have his installments of a satirical, running commentary on life and current events in the United States, known as "The Mexican American Devil's Dictionary." The commentary is supposedly created by another of Hinojosa's alter-egos, who is also one of the narrators of the "Klail City Death Trip Series"—P. Galindo (meaning "right on target," in Spanish).

Hinojosa's novels reject traditional linear plots and generic structures, concentrating rather on language and character revealed through language.

> My stories are not held together by the *peripeteia,* or the plot, as much as by what the people who populate the stories say and *how* they say it; how they look at the world out and the world in; and the works, then, become studies of perceptions and values and decisions reached by them because of those perceptions and values, which in turn were fashioned and forged by the place and its history.

Hinojosa has been hailed as a master satirist, an acute observer of the human comedy, and a Chicano William Faulkner for his creation of the continuing history of the people of Belken County, and for his work as a faithful recorder of the customs and dialects of the Lower Rio Grande Valley. Through his commitment to creating the fictitious world that has helped us understand Mexican American life so well, Hinojosa has become one of the best loved and most highly regarded Hispanic writers.

Hinojosa has an "unusual talent for capturing the language and spirit of his subject matter."

Lourdes Torres, Western American Literature, *fall, 1988*

The Hispanic Literary Companion

Personal Stats

Mexican American university professor, writer. **Born:** January 21, 1929, in Mercedes, Texas. **Education:** B.A. in Spanish from the University of Texas, 1953; M.A. in Spanish from New Mexico Highlands University, 1963; Ph.D. in Spanish from the University of Illinois, 1969. **Career:** Chairman of Modern Languages Department (1970–74), Dean, College of Arts & Science (1974–76), Vice President of Academic Affairs (1976–77), Texas A & I University; Professor, Chicano Studies and American Studies, University of Minnesota, 1977–1981; Professor of English and Creative Writing, University of Texas, 1981–present; Director, Texas Center for Writers, 1988–present. **Memberships:** PEN, Texas Institute of Letters, Academia Norteamericana de la Lengua, Modern Language Association. **Awards/Honors:** Premio Quinto Sol (national award for Chicano literature) Best Novel, 1972; Casa de las Américas Premio Mejor Novela, 1976; Southwest Council on Latin American Studies Award, 1981; University of Illinois Alumni Achievement Award, 1988. **Address:** c/o Arte Público Press, PO Box 2090, The University of Houston, Houston, TX 77204-2090

> *"I enjoy writing of course, but I enjoy the re-writing even more: four or five rewritings are not uncommon."*
>
> *Rolando Hinojosa*

Coming Home I

from *Short Fiction by Hispanic Writers of the United States,* edited by Nicolás Kanellos, Arte Público Press, 1993, pp. 73–76

It should come as no surprise that Belken County's largest, best known, and certainly most profitable whorehouse is to be found in Flora. Flora people have convinced themselves that they invented sliced bread; this goes for Texas Mexicans and Texas Anglos alike. For their part, the Flora Mexicans have also come to think of themselves as an integral part of the Flora economic establishment. No such thing, of course; at best, they've stopped resisting, have become acculturated, and, delusion of delusions, have assimilated. All this up to a point, of course, but still, they're an energetic folk and hell to deal and live with.

Flora is also the newest of the Valley towns; sprang up during that war the Anglos had between themselves in the 1860's; truth to tell, though, Texas Mexicans fought on both sides of that one. So, Flora was born yesterday and thus not as old as Relámpago or Jonesville or Klail; Klail City's real name is Llano Grande, the name of the grant. (General Rufus T. Klail came down here, took over the name, and then thought he'd swept away the traditions with the change. And so it goes . . .)

Anyway, the Texas Anglo and Texas Mexican citizenry of Flora are identical in many ways: noisy, trust God and give Him credit on Sundays, and believe in cash on the barrelhead from sunup to sundown. They also believe in other important things: leap years, for one. To their credit, Flora is unlike the other Valley towns in other respects and thus so are the Mexicanos who live and die there.

As for whorehouses, this is a lamentably recognized universality, but the Flora-ites claim it as a native invention. Just like that: judgment without explanation. To compensate, perhaps, the town of Flora also boasts of more churches per capita than any other Valley town. See? Admittedly, there is a cure for hiccups (water, air, a good scare); for polio (Drs. Salk and Sabin); but there's nothing you can do about stupidity. Takes more than a pill or a shot for that one. But the Flora-ites don't know this, and if they do, they choose to ignore it. Secure, then, in their ways.

Don Manuel Guzmán, Klail's lone Mexicano cop, was rolling himself a flake tobacco cigarette as he sat with some of the *viejitos*—the old men; men his age, then. He'd risen from the sidewalk bench, walked to the curb to stand under the corner lamplight. He spit-sealed his roll, lit it, and looked at his pocket watch: ten after twelve; a warm, foggy, December night, when out of the fog and walking straight at him, there came a woman, gun in hand.

Why, it was Julie, a young black whore from Flora. "Mist Manyul . . . c'n I talk to you?" And then: "Mist Manyul, I done shot Sonny . . . shot 'n killed him, Mist Manyul."

Don Manuel nodded, listened some more, and handed her his cigarette. She stared at it as if she'd never seen one before in her life. Don Manuel opened the front car door, and she slipped in and waited for him as he walked over to see the *viejitos* (Leal, Echevarría, and Genaro Castañeda), those old, well-known friends of the former revolutionary.

"What is it? You leaving now?"

"Got to." Pointing with his chin: "I'll see you here in about an hour or so; and if not here, I'll just drive on to Dirty Luke's."

"What'd she do?"

"She says she shot her husband . . . at Maria Lara's house . . . in Flora."

"She works there, does she?"

"Aha . . . but she lives here, in Klail. I got them a room at the Flats."

"Hmmm. What happened out in Flora this time?"

"You think the pimp held out on her?"

Don Manuel, slowly. "It's possible; I didn't ask her much, and it's probably best to leave her alone for a while."

"I think you're right there, don Manuel."

Old man Leal: "I know who she is. Her man works for Missouri Pacific; a switchman, right? Sonny . . . yeah, he plays semi-pro ball for the Flora White Sox . . . Yeah."

Echevarría: "Now don't tell me he didn't know about his wife workin' over to Flora?"

Don Manuel: "Oh, he knew all right. They've been married five-six years, I'd say."

Castañeda: "Married." Bland.

Leal: "Do black folks marry? Really?" Curious.

Echevarría: "Yeah, I think they do, once in a while." Not sure.

Castañeda: "Man was probably drinking." Abruptly.

Leal: "Why not?" A hunch of the shoulders.

Echevarría: "Yeah, why not?" Resignation.

Castañeda: "Did, ah, did Sonny pull a knife on her?"

Don Manuel: "Yes; that's what she says."

Leal: "How'd she get over *here* from Flora, anyway?" Admiration.

Don Manuel: "Took a bus, she says."

Echevarría: "A bus? There's a lot-a guts in them ovaries, yes sir."

Don Manuel: "I'm taking her to jail; I'll go ahead and drive her on over to Flora tomorrow sometime. She killed her man and they're probably looking for her about now. I think it's best she be alone for a while; cry herself to sleep, think about what she's done; sort things out, you know. But, she needs to be left alone for now; she'll have enough to do tomorrow with that Flora crowd, poor thing . . . Look, I'll see you all here or over to Dirty's."

With this, don Manuel got into his car—his, not the city's which didn't provide him with one, anyway—and then drove Julie Wilson to the Klail City workhouse.

"We goin' to jail, Mist Manyul?"

"Yes."

"I din mean to do it! Mist Manyol. I din mean to kill Son . . . you know that, Mist Manyul? But I kill him . . . . Oh, I shot that man . . . . I say, Son, don't you do it . . . I say, you back off now, you hear? But he din back off none. . . . He din 'n I shot him . . . got him in the chest I did 'n he plop down on the bed there. . . . I kill Son, Mist Manyul, an' you know that no one come to the room when I shot him? . . . Oh, I shot him and killed him, Mist Manyol . . . . He was drunk . . . all out drunk Sonny was and then I just up and shot him . . . . You taking me to Flora jail, Mist Manyul?"

"Takin' you to Klail City jail, Julie."

"Oh, thank you, Mist Manyul. I don't want to go to no Flora jail tonight, no I don'. . . . You takin' me there tomorrow? That it, Mist Manyul?"

"Yes . . . tomorrow . . . one of my sons will bring you hot coffee tomorrow morning and then I'll take you to Flora."

"Thank you, Mist Manyul . . . . I won't cry no more . . . I up 'n shot that man and he dead and he deserve it . . . he say he gonna cut me an' I say you back off, Sonny, back off . . . don' come over to here, Sonny, but he did and then I did . . . Mist Manyul, can I go to the bathroom now?"

"There's a bowl in the room."

"Oh, thank you, Mist Manyul."

Don Manuel Guzmán drove out to the corner of Hidalgo Street and, since his old friends weren't anywhere to be seen, he did a U-turn in the middle of the deserted main street and headed for Dirty Luke's. Beer time was over and now it was time for the coffee crowd to take over. The *viejitos*'d be there, waiting for him, and then he'd take them home, as always.

Tomorrow, early, *mañana may de mañana,* after bringing Julie a pot of coffee, he'd drive her to Flora; first though, he'd stop at María Lara's place and get some firsthand news.

He and María Lara had known each other for over forty years, and although there'd been an arrangement between them when both were in their twenties and healthy and vibrant and ready-to-go, their long friendship and a shared place of provenance (the Buenrostro family's Campacuás Ranch) was what kept them in close contact. He thought of the old ranch house and its Texas Ranger-burned-down-to-its-ashes church . . . The ashes were still there, fifty years later. The man shook his head slightly.

But now, headed for Dirty Luke's, he parked any old way and walked into the place; he sat and waited for Rafe Buenrostro to bring him his cup of coffee.

"Boy, turn the volume down; you're going to have the neighbors down on you."

"Yessing"

Coffee over, don Manuel says: "Going back to Hidalgo and First; when y'all get ready to go home, let me know."

The oldsters thank him, as always, and don Manuel leaves the car in front of Dirty's; he's going for a walk, and he'll eventually wind up on Hidalgo Street in Klail City; a town like any other in Belken County in Texas's Lower Rio Grande Valley.

Coming Home V

from *Short Fiction by Hispanic Writers of the United States,* edited by Nicolás Kanellos, Arte Público Press, 1993, pp. 77–79

Don Orfalindo Buitureyra is a quadrilateral lump of Valley loam and shit. Buitureyra is also a pharmacist, thanks to some pretty lax laws in the Lone Star State; there are other weaknesses in Orfalindo Buitureyra's arsenal: he's a sentimentalist and so much so that he goes on three-four day drunks (we call 'em *parrandas serias*), and then, later on, he wonders where those King Kong-sized hangovers come from; as said, forgetful, as most sentimentalists.

Anyway, the man will break out two or three times a year and here's the pattern: he'll drink alone for a while, and then he'll drink with some friends, and *then* comes the dancing (a solo effort) and then la pièce de résistance: He sings.

"I like to," he says. To tell the truth, he's so-so in that department.

On the other hand, there's no oratory, no public crying, declamations, patriotic speeches, etc. "That's for queers; get me?"

Sure, sure, don Orfalindo; no need to come to blows over a little thing like that, is there?

"Good! Just so's we understand each other. Know what I mean? Now, where was I?"

Singing.

"Right! Almost forgot . . . "

And he does. Actually, what he does is to sing along with the Wurlitzer. The following is tacit: if an Andalusian *pasodoble* breaks out, the floor belongs to don Orfalindo. The reader probably thinks people stop and stare; the reader is *wrong*. And no, it isn't that the drinkers are bored stiffer than the Pope; not at all. It's more like this: live and let live. Man wants to dance? Let him. Man wants to dance alone? Who's he bothering? Right!

To put it as plainly as possible: People simply leave him alone.

"They'd better; what if he poisons them, right?"

Jesus! I'd forgotten about that . . .

"Tscha! I'm just talking."

Don Orfalindo Buitureyra, it so happens, is a cuckold. A *cabrón,* a capricorn, antlered. You with me? This makes him the lump he is. And, he's a nice old guy, too. None of this is incompatible, and why should it be? A bit of a fool, like all of us, then, *but* he is a cuckold; in his case, a cuckold Made in Texas by Texas Mexicans.

"And the kids?"

"Oh, they're his, all right."

"Damn right they are: they got his nose, all-a them."

"And that lantern jaw, too; even that girl a-his has it."

"Hmmm; but he's a *cabrón,* and that stain won't go away.,

"We-ell now, that's something that don't rub off with gasoline. Goes deeper than that, you see."

This is all talk. Don Orfalindo is, *a la italiana, cornutto,* but not *contento.* If anything, he's resigned to it. A bit of Islamic resignation that.

"Look, his kids like him and love 'im. Isn't that enough?"

"Yeah, what the hell. Tell me this: just how long is that wife a-his gonna remain good looking? There's no guarantee of longevity, you know."

"Well, nothing lasts one hundred years, not even a man's faith, let alone his wife. Truth to tell, though, he'll wear those horns to his grave."

"How long she been running around now? Five? Six years? Give her two, three more; tops."

"Well, Echevarría, you ought to go into counseling and fortune-telling, ha!"

"Tscha! A matter of time is all. Look at him: dancing that *Silverio Pérez pasodoble* . . . Who's he bothering?"

"Well now, if it comes to bothering, you're right: he's not bothering anybody, but look out in the sidewalk there: there's some youngster watching him."

"So? Those aren't his kids; his are all grown up."

A newcomer said that; and he really doesn't belong in that table with the *viejitos*: "Out with it, then . . . who's his wife fooling around with?"

This is a breach; the inquisitor should know better.

The Wurlitzer blinked once or twice and then some *norteño* music came on: don Orfalindo went to the bar.

Not a peep at the table. Don Orfalindo's at the bar and orders another Miller Hi-Life. The men at the table look away, and the inquisitor excuses himself; to the john, he says.

Don Orfalindo takes a swig from the Miller's and then, without fail, he caps the bottle with his thumb. Conserves the carbonation, he says.

The *viejitos* at the table wave; he waves back. They're all friends; good men, really. The man who went to the john is still out there. It's hoped he doesn't ask many more questions. What would be the use?

First of all, being a cuckold isn't a profession; it's hard, cruel, but then it can happen to anybody: Napoleon, the President of the United States, one's best friend. No telling. There's don Orfalindo, for ex. Except for the oldsters at the table, few know and less remember *the reason* for don O.'s binges. As my neighbor says: "Who cares?"

"Don Manuel Guzmán ought to be dropping in pretty soon."

"Right as rain. Rafe! Rafe, boy, better heat up that coffee; don Manuel ought to be coming in any minute now."

"Yessing"

Don O. pulls away from the bar; on his way to the john. But here comes the Grand Inquisitor; they almost run into each other.

At the table, Esteban Echevarría, Luis Leal, don Matías Uribe, and Dirty Luke, the owner of the place, throw a glance at the pair. The four men, the *viejitos,* shake their heads; the inquisitor shouldn't even be at this table, he's forty years old and out of place with these men. He invited himself, then. Worse, it's don Manuel's chair.

Enter don Manuel. "Son, cut the volume, you're going to get the neighbors down on you."

Don Orfalindo is back at the bar, bottle in hand, thumb in cap. He spots don Manuel at the table.

"Begging your pardon, don Manuel, but I've been drinking."

"You want me to take you home, don Orfalindo?"

"Well, no; ah . . . not this minute. I just started this morning."

"Well, you take care now."

"Yessir; I'm going back to the bar now."

There'll be no dancing by don Orfalindo as long as don Manuel is in there. (A note of respect ace. to don O.) For his part, don Manuel sips at his coffee and, as he finishes, says to the others: "My car's out front; let me know when you're ready to go." He rises and walks out the front door.

The inquisitor is back, too, but the chair is no longer there.

As don Manuel walks out, don Orfalindo hits the floor: *Besos Brujos* (*letra* de R. Schiammarella; *con música* de Alfredo Malerba). Libertad or Amanda sings out: "Déjame, no quiero que me beses . . ."

Un tango, tangazo! Eyes closed, don Orfalindo Buitureyra glides away. Years, miles, and more years: it's that woman again: young, hardbodied, once married to a former military surgeon from Agualeguas, Nuevo León; the surgeon died as a result of a prescription handed him by the apprentice pharmacist Orfalindo Buitureyra years and years ago . . .

Besos Brujos; bewitched kisses, in English, doesn't cut it. Another long glide by the man and *then* a sudden severe cut to the right! *Bailando con corte!* Eyes closed, harder now. A smile? Is it? Yes!

The eyes remain closed. Yes; he smiles again, and one could almost say, almost say, that don Orfalindo Buitureyra is contented enough to be happy. And alive, and older, too.

But above all, happy; *y eso es lo que cuenta*. And that's what counts.

Writings

Novels: *Estampas del Valle y otras obras* (Sketches of the Valley and Other Works), Quinto Sol, 1972; revised edition published as *The Valley*, Bilingual Press, 1983. *Klail City y sus alrededores*, Casa de las Américas (Havana, Cuba), 1976, and Justa Publications (Berkeley, CA), 1977; re-written in English by Hinojosa as *Klail City*, Arte Público Press, 1987. *Korean Love Songs*, Justa Publications, 1978. *Claros Varones de Belken*, Justa Publications, 1981; translated as *Fair Gentlemen of Belken County*, Bilingual Press, 1987. *Mi querido Rafa*, Arte Público Press, 1981; re-created by Hinojosa in English as *Dear Rafe*, Arte Público Press, 1985. *Rites and Witnesses*, Arte Público Press, 1982. *Partners in Crime*, Arte Público Press, 1985. *Becky and Her Friends*, Arte Público Press, 1990. *Los amigos de Becky*, Arte Público Press, 1990. *The Useless Servants*, Arte Público Press, 1993. **Essays and Short Stories:** In *The Rolando Hinojosa Reader: Essays Historical and Critical*, edited by José Saldívar, Arte Público Press, 1984, and in numerous anthologies, textbooks, and magazines. **Translations:** Translated from the Spanish: *This Migrant Earth*, by Tomás Rivera, Arte Público Press, 1985.

Carolina Hospital

Carolina Hospital has been on the forefront of the development of a Cuban American aesthetic in literature. Not only does her poetry demonstrate the particular bilingual-bicultural nature of Cuban literary sensibility in the United States, but her editorial work has helped announce and define this aesthetic.

Born in Havana, just two years before the Cuban revolution, she accompanied her family into exile in 1961, and was raised and educated in Florida. Like so many other children of exiles, children who were transported into another culture and educated in a system where the language was different from that of their homeland, Hospital was part of a generation that knew only the United States as home, but that was constantly encouraged by parents and relatives to identify with an island they could only recreate in their imagination. The tension between their reality in the U.S. and a mythic Cuba created by the nostalgia of exiles, between the institutional English and Anglo-American culture of the outside world and the nurturing Spanish traditions inside the home, between growing up as an immigrant rather than an exile—all of these tensions dominate the works of Carolina Hospital and the generation of writers that she identified in her groundbreaking anthology *Cuban American Writers: Los Atrevidos.*

The lines in her poem "Dear Tía" reveal this tension between the present and the past, reality and nostalgia, the familiar and the foreign:

I do not write.
The years have frightened me away.
My life in a land so familiarly foreign . . .
I write because I cannot remember at all.

Before Hospital's works there was barely a consciousness of the corpus of Cuban American literature—the legacy of exile which is so dominant, especially in Miami. The prevailing political sentiment in Miami and other centers of Cuban exile had fought against the concept of a Cuban *Americanism,* since the exile community's identity depended on remaining distinctively Cuban and someday returning to their home. But Hospital braved the opposition, openly embracing English and bilingualism and recognizing the birth of a literature that was firmly planted on American soil and that is here to stay. In *Cuban American Writers: Los Atrevidos,* she declared that Cuban American writers were risk-takers, daring to belong to a future made up of a new reality.

> *Before Hospital's works there was barely a consciousness of the corpus of Cuban American literature—the legacy of exile which is so dominant, especially in Miami.*

Personal Stats

Cuban American educator, writer. Born: August 27, 1957, in Havana, Cuba. *Education:* Attended Miami Dade Community College and the University of Miami, 1976–78; B.A. and M.A. in English, University of Florida, 1979 and 1984, respectively. *Career:* Middle school teacher, Miami, 1985–86; Adjunct professor, Florida International University, 1987; Assistant Professor of English, Miami Dade Community College, 1987–present. *Awards/Honors:* Tinker Foundation grant, 1984. *Address:* English Department, Miami Dade Community College, South, 1101 SW 104th Street, Miami, FL 33176

Dear Tía

from *Decade II: A Twentieth Anniversary Anthology,* edited by Julián Olivares, Arte Público Press, 1993, p. 223

I do not write.
The years have frightened me away.
My life in a land so familiarly foreign,
a denial of your presence.
Your name is mine.
One black and white photograph of your youth,
all I hold on to.
One story of your past.
The pain comes not from nostalgia.

I do not miss your voice urging me in play,
your smiles,
or your pride when others called you my mother.
I cannot close my eyes and feel your soft skin;
listen to your laughter;
smell the sweetness of your bath.
I write because I cannot remember at all.

Papa

from *Decade II: A Twentieth Anniversary Anthology,* edited by Julián Olivares, Arte Público Press, 1993, p. 224

The two sat on the shoreline
under a piercing sun
ignoring the calls of their children
begging them to join them in play.
Both shared moments never lived
as wrinkled bodies crossed them
offering advice.
Without a glance they continued
almost whispering about a sacred man,
an outcast of their past,
an omen in their future.

Salvation Part II

from *The Americas Review,* Vol. XVII, No. 1, Spring, 1989, p. 52

A small boy plays on the street
with other children, unlike him.
He sheds no tears.
Nor bears a cross.
His heart does not bleed
the anguish of separation,
nor does his spirit despair.
No memories torment his passions . . .

A void
follows him in all his deeds.

Writings

Poems: In *The Americas Review, Cuban Heritage Magazine, Linden Lane Magazine, Bilingual Review,* and in anthologies, including *In Other Words: Literature by Latinas of the United States, Looking for Home,* and *Cuban American Writers: Los Atrevidos.* **Edited Works:** Special issue of *Cuban Heritage Magazine. Cuban American Writers: Los Atrevidos,* Linden Lane, 1989.

Angela de Hoyos

Angela de Hoyos is a pioneer of modern Chicano poetry; when there was little opportunity for her works to be published and recognized in the United States, she looked abroad for opportunities to publish her poetry. Finally in the early 1970s, as the Chicano literary movement was peaking, her work became part of that body of work and was partly responsible for its flowering. She was the first of the women poets to gather a following in the movement, and became an inspiration for other early writers who followed in her path.

De Hoyos was born into a middle-class family in Coahuila, Mexico, the daughter of a proprietor of a dry-cleaning shop and a housewife who had an artistic bent. After a tragic burning as a young child, de Hoyos was forced to convalesce in bed for many months, during which she entertained herself by composing rhymes. While she was still a child, her family moved to San Antonio and her interest in poetry continued. From her teenage years on, her education was informal, but supported by art courses she took in area institutions. In the late 1960s, de Hoyos began publishing poetry and entering her work in international competitions, for which she won awards. During the 1970s, her interest in literature and her awareness of the lack of opportunity for Chicano writers led her to found the small press M & A Editions in San Antonio, through which she issued not only her own work but that of such writers as Evangelina Vigil-Piñón as well. During the 1980s, de Hoyos also founded a cultural periodical, *Huehuetitlan*, which is still in existence. In addition to this intense literary life, de Hoyos developed a successful career as a painter. Her works, also inspired by Mexican American culture, are widely exhibited and collected in Texas.

De Hoyos has cultivated a free-verse, terse, conversational poetry—which at times takes dialog form—that provides a context for cultural and feminist issues within a larger philosophical and literary framework. De Hoyos, a student of writing in many languages and cultures, examines themes and issues from cross-cultural perspectives and her work is multi faceted. While her readers are always aware of these larger frameworks, the themes are perceived as being very specific and embodied in the actions and circumstances of real people. De Hoyos's poetry is socially engaged while at the same time humanistic in the best sense of the word. Her particular concerns are poverty, racism, and disenfranchisement, whether of a people, her people, of children, or women. Her particular mission is to give voice to those who cannot express themselves:

> "How to express your anguish
>
> when not even your burning words are yours."

De Hoyos is also a poet of humor and wit, creating piquant exchanges in verse between lovers and enemies, as is exemplified in her dialogues between Hernán Cortez and La Malinche.

Her most important book, *Woman, Woman*, deals with the roles that society has dictated for women and their struggle to overcome the limits of those roles. De Hoyos surveys history, from Aztec days to the present, and even casts an eye on the image of women in fairy tales, as in her poem "Fairy-Tale: Cuento de Hadas." Throughout *Woman, Woman*, de Hoyos sustains the dynamic tension that both unites and separates male and female. In her poetry, that tension is always erotically charged, always threatening to one or the other, always reverberating in the political. In *Woman, Woman*, de Hoyos has also perfected her bilingual style, innovatively mixing the linguistic codes of English and Spanish to reach beyond the merely conversational to the more philosophical—the choice of language and lexicon is not just a socio-linguistic one, it is also a deeply cultural one.

Throughout Woman, Woman, *de Hoyos sustains the dynamic tension that both unites and separates male and female. In her poetry, that tension is always erotically charged, always threatening to one or the other, always reverberating in the political.*

Personal Stats

Chicana writer, painter. Born: January 23, 1940, in Coahuila, Mexico. *Education:* Studied fine arts at San Antonio College, San Antonio Art Institute, the University of Texas at San Antonio and Ursuline Academy, San Antonio. *Career:* Oil painter and poet since the late 1960s. *Memberships:* Artists Alliance Center, San Antonio; Centro Cultural Aztlán, San Antonio; Centro Cultural, Literário e

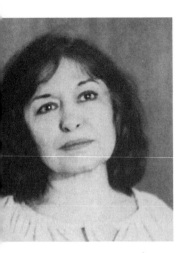

Artístico, Felqueiras, Portugal. **Awards/Honors:** Honorable Mention, Avalon World Arts Academy, 1966; Bronze Medal of Honor (poetry), Centro Studi e Scambi Internazionale (CSSI), Rome, Italy, 1966; Silver Medal of Honor (literature), CSSI, 1967; Diploma di Benemerenza (literature), CSSI, 1968; Diploma di Benemerenza (poetry), CSSI, 1969 and 1970; Distinguished Service Citation, World Poetry Society Intercontinental, India, 1970; Second Prize, International Poetry Competition, CSSI, 1974; Mención de Honor (obra literaria), La Rosa Blanca, Buenos Aires, Argentina, 1976; Diploma Honorífico, Centro Cultural, Literário e Artístico, Felgueiras, Portugal, 1976; Honorary Degree (Litt.D.), University of Danzig, Republik Danzig, 1977; Award for Artistic Accomplishment, Texas Institute for Educational Development, 1980; Fonapas Award, Secretaría de Relaciones Exteriores, Mexico City, 1982. **Address:** c/o M&A Editions, 4946 Luz Avenue, San Antonio, TX 78237

Woman, Woman

from *Woman, Woman,* Arte Público Press, 1985, p. 11

climb up
that ladder
bring down
the moon
or she
will tattle

tattle falsehood
to the skies
(and who
can tell
the truth
from lies?)

that it
is you
forever Eve
who rules
mere man
without
reprieve

Lesson in Semantics

from *Woman, Woman,* Arte Público Press, 1985, p. 21

Men, she said,
        sometimes
                in order to
                        say it
it is
        necessary
                to spit
                        the word.

How to Eat Crow on a Cold Sunday Morning

from *Woman, Woman,* Arte Público Press, 1985, pp. 46–47

you start on the wings
n i b b l i n g
                  apolegtic-like
because after all
        it was you
        who held the gun
        and fired pointblank
        the minute you saw the
        whites of their eyes
just like the army sergeant
always instructed you.

—Damn it, this thing's
gonna make me sick!

—No it won't. Go on. Eat the
blasted thing
                    (for practice)

because you'll be sicker
later on
                    when your friends
                    start giving you
an iceberg for a shoulder.

 . . . So the giblets are dry
and tough.
                    But you can
                    digest them.

It's the gall bladder
—that green bag of biliousness—
    wants to gag your throat
    in righteous retribution

refuses to budge
won't go up or down, just
                              sticks there
makes you wish that long ago
you'd learned how to eat
a pound of prudence
                    instead.

Writings

Poetry Books: *Arise Chicano! and Other Poems*, Backstage Books, 1975. *Chicano Poems: For the Barrio,* M&A Editions, 1976. *Selecciones,* (translations by Mireya Robles), Universidad Veracruzana, 1976. *Selected Poems/Selecciones,* (bilingual edition, with translations by Mireya Robles), Dezkalzo Press, 1979. *Woman, Woman*, Arte Público Press, 1985. **Poems:** In *The Americas Review/Revista Chicano-Riqueña, Puerto Norte y Sur, Tejidos, Real Poetry, American Poetry Society, Great American World Poets, Latin American Women Writers, Flor y Canto IV and V,* and numerous other magazines, textbooks, and anthologies.

Tato Laviera

Jesús Abraham "Tato" Laviera is the best-selling Hispanic poet of the United States and among the Hispanic poets he bears the distinction of still having all of his books in print. Since 1980, Laviera's career has included not only writing but touring nationally to perform his poetry, direct plays he has written, and produce cultural events.

Born September 5, 1950, in Santurce, Puerto Rico, at age ten he moved with his family to New York City, where they settled in a poor area of the Lower East Side. He found himself in an alien society and was able to speak very little English. But he eventually adjusted and went on to graduate high school as an honor student. Despite having no other degree except his high school diploma, Laviera's intelligence, persistence, and thorough knowledge of his community led to a career in the administration of social service agencies. After the publication of his first book, *La Carreta Made a U-Turn* (1979), Laviera gave up administrative work to dedicate his time to writing. In 1980 Laviera was received by President Jimmy Carter at the White House Gathering of American Poets. In 1981 his second book, *Enclave,* was the recipient of the Before Columbus Foundation's American Book Award.

All of Tato Laviera's books have been well received by critics, most of whom place him within the context of Afro-Caribbean poetry and U.S. Hispanic bilingualism. *La Carreta Made a U-Turn* is bilingual, jazz- or *salsa*-poetry that presents the reader with a slice of life drawn from the Puerto Rican community of the Lower East Side. As such, it examines both the oppression of the migrant community and its alienation through such popular culture forms as soap operas. It also examines crime and drug addiction, while nevertheless affirming the spiritual and social values of the community, and the place of art, poetry, and music in what many may consider the unlikeliest of environments. Laviera, here as in the rest of his books, acknowledges and supports the existence of a true Puerto Rican and Latino culture within the heart of the Metropolis and within the very belly of the United States. He further affirms that there is no need to return to an island or south-of-the-border homeland, for Latinos have made their home here and are transforming not only mainstream culture in the United States, but throughout the Americas.

In *Enclave* (1982), Laviera celebrates such heroes, real and imagined: Alicia Alonso, Suni Paz, John Lennon, and Miriam Makeba, share the page with the fictitious, half-Southern-Black-half-Puerto Rican Tito Madera Smith, the barrio gossip Juana Bochisme, and the neighborhood tough Esquina Dude. As in *La Carreta Made a U-Turn*, Laviera acknowledges in *Enclave* his debt to Afro-Caribbean music and poetry through his eulogies of *salsa*-composer Rafael Cortijo, of the famed poetry recitator Juan Boria, and of master poets Luis Palés Matos and Nicolás Guillén. *AmeRícan* (1986) published on the occasion of the centennial celebration of the Statue of Liberty, is a poetic re-consideration of immigrant life in New York City and the United States. *Mainstream Ethics* (1988) proposes transforming the United States from a Eurocentric culture to one that is ethnically and racially pluralistic in its official identity.

Laviera has also been a productive playwright, with works staged in New York's and Chicagos ethnic theater houses, such as the New Federal Theater at Henry Street Settlement, the Nuyorican Poets Cafe, and Teatro 4. His plays—all of which have remained unpublished, except for *Olú Clemente* (1979), co-written with Miguel Algarín—celebrate Afro-Puerto Rican heroes real and imagined. Besides *Piñones* (1979) and *Olú Clemente*, which are Afro-Puerto Rican poetic homages to baseball Hall of Famer Roberto Clemente, Laviera also created heroes in such works as *Here We Come* (1982), *La Chefa* (The Chef or Boss, 1984) and *Becoming García* (1984), where survival in the barrio is a central theme.

Important as Laviera's dramatic works may be, his greatest contribution is as a bilingual poet, combining both written and oral traditions. German critic Wolfgang Binder summed up the breadth and importance of Laviera's poetry:

> Tato Laviera is secure in a complex, contemporary manner: He writes convincingly and with a vast background of oral literature, in English, Spanish, Spanglish and in intralingual techniques mixing the languages. Not only is he aware of his Afro-Caribbean traditions, both on a folk level—in music, dance and mythology—and within a literary frame of reference, but he also celebrates all of these elements out of New

York, amalgamating them into a whole. Tato Laviera is a bilingual poet of the people, for the people, a poet of selfhood, sensuousness and life, of critical sanity, humaneness, warmth and triumphant joy. Above all, he is a poet of love and respect.

Personal Stats

Puerto Rican writer. *Born:* September 5, 1950, in Santurce, Puerto Rico. *Education:* Attended Cornell University and Brooklyn College. *Career:* Community worker and administrator of social services program until 1979, when he became a full-time writer. *Memberships:* PEN. *Awards/Honors:* American Book Award of the Before Columbus Foundation for *Enclave,* 1982; included in White House Gathering of American Poets, 1980. *Address:* c/o Arte Público Press, University of Houston, Houston, TX 77204-2090

AmeRícan

from *AmeRícan,* Arte Público Press, 1985, pp. 94–95

we gave birth to a new generation,
AmeRícan, broader than lost gold
never touched, hidden inside the
puerto rican mountains.
we gave birth to a new generation,
AmeRícan, it includes everything
imaginable you-name-it-we-got-it
society.
we gave birth to a new generation,
AmeRícan salutes all folklores,
european, indian, black, spanish,
and anything else compatible:
AmeRícan, singing to composer pedro flores' palm
       trees high up in the universal sky!
AmeRícan, sweet soft spanish danzas gypsies
       moving lyrics la española cascabelling
       presence always singing at our side!

AmeRícan, beating jíbaro modern troubadours
          crying guitars romantic continental
          bolero love songs!
AmeRícan, across forth and across back
          back across and forth back
          forth across and back and forth
          our trips are walking bridges!
          it all dissolved into itself, the attempt
          was truly made, the attempt was truly
          absorbed, digested, we spit out
          the poison, we spit out the malice,
          we stand, affirmative in action,
          to reproduce a broader answer to the
          marginality that gobbled us up abruptly!
AmeRícan, walking plena-rhythms in new york,
          strutting beautifully alert, alive,
          many turning eyes wondering,
          admiring!
AmeRícan, defining myself my own way any way many
          ways Am e Rícan, with the big R and the
          accent on the í!
AmeRícan, like the soul gliding talk of gospel
          boogie music!
AmeRícan, speaking new words in spanglish tenements,
          fast tongue moving street corner "que
          corta" talk being invented at the insistence
          of a smile!
AmeRícan, abounding inside so many ethnic english
          people, and out of humanity, we blend
          and mix all that is good!
AmeRícan, integrating in new york and defining our
          own destino, our own way of life,
AmeRícan, defining the new america, humane america,
          admired america, loved america, harmonious
          america, the world in peace, our energies
          collectively invested to find other civili-
          zations, to touch God, further and further,
          to dwell in the spirit of divinity!
AmeRícan, yes, for now, for i love this, my second
          land, and i dream to take the accent from

the altercation, and be proud to call
myself AmeRícan, in the u.s. sense of the
word, AmeRícan, America!

my graduation speech

from *La Carreta Made a U-Turn,* Arte Público Press, 1992, p. 17

i think in spanish
i write in english
i want to go back to puerto rico,
but i wonder if my kink could live
in ponce, mayagüez and carolina
tengo las venas aculturadas
escribo en spanglish
abraham in español
abraham in english
tato in spanish
"taro" in english
tonto in both languages
how are you?
¿cómo estás?
i don't know if i'm coming
or si me fui ya
si me dicen barranquitas, yo reply,
"¿con qué se come eso?"
si me dicen caviar, i digo,
"a new pair of converse sneakers."
ahí supe que estoy jodío
ahí supe que estamos jodios
english or spanish
spanish or english
spanenglish
now, dig this:
hablo lo inglés matao

hablo lo español matao

no sé leer ninguno bien

so it is, spanglish to matao

what i digo

¡ay, virgen, yo no sé hablar!

Writings

Poetry Books: *Enclave*, Arte Público Press, 1982. *AmeRícan,* Arte Público Press, 1985. *Mainstream Ethics*, Arte Público Press, 1988. *La Carreta Made a U-Turn*, Arte Público Press, 1992. **Published Plays:** *Olú Clemente* in *Nuevos Pasos: Chicano and Puerto Rican Drama*, edited by Nicolás Kanellos and Jorge Huerta, Arte Público Press, 1979. **Poems:** In *The Americas Review, Revista Chicano-Riqueña, Nuyorican Poetry, Herejes y mitificadores, Daedalus,* and numerous other magazines, textbooks, and anthologies.

Graciela Limón

For Graciela Limón becoming a novelist was the result of a long process of self-discovery and the fulfillment of a long-held dream. Born and raised in East Los Angeles the daughter of Mexican immigrants, the life of a writer seemed beyond reach to her. But ever since age twelve, when she read a novel based on Joan of Arc's life, she hoped to become a novelist:

> It wasn't that I wanted to be like Joan of Arc, but rather that I wanted to be like the person who had written the novel. After that, I read every historical novel that I could get my hands on, and by the time I was twenty years old, the idea of writing became part of me. I thought of it almost always.

Limón decided that it was more practical to teach rather than to write. She graduated from Marymount College in 1965 and went on to obtain an M.A. and a Ph.D. in 1969 and 1975, respectively. Her career as an educator was launched at the college level in 1969 at Marymount College, where she taught Hispanic literature and ascended to department administration. In 1990 Limón recovered her dream when, unable to find a publisher for her historical novel, *María Belén,* she paid for the edition herself. Later, this first novel (which was based on research of the Aztecs) was reworked into the well-crafted and highly received *Song of the Hummingbird* (1996).

Limón's novel *In Search of Bernabé* (1993) was the result of her travels to El Salvador as part of a delegation sent to investigate the deaths of Jesuit priests.

While she was there she witnessed first-hand the emotions, fears, and attendant sense of powerlessness that governed the lives of most Salvadorans during the long-lasting civil war. In the book, Limón gives a powerful and enlightening description of Luz Delcano's odyssey to find her son Bernabé amidst the chaos that followed the assassination of Archbishop Romero. By telling the story of Delcano and her son, Limón was successful in humanizing the political turmoil and international intrigue of the Salvadoran civil war, so much so that the novel was cited as a *New York Times* "critic's choice" and won an American Book Award.

The Memories of Ana Calderón traces the life of a Mexican immigrant, Ana Calderón, who struggles against the gender roles cast by both Mexican and American societies, and which are supported by Biblical teachings. The hand of fate deals Ana one blow after another, but her will is as unshakeable as the societal structures with which she wrestles. In the end there is a sunrise rapprochement, which a number of critics, especially feminist critics, found implausible and melo-dramatic, but that fits well within Ana Calderón's Catholic psychology. As *Publishers Weekly* said:

> What has begun as a sensitive exploration of one woman's attempt to come to terms with two cultures now becomes an increasingly chaotic portrait of a dysfunction-al family whose lives are fraught with melodrama . . . events are unbelievably resolved as the novel closes.

No such complexity of plot and thought are present in the beautiful evocation of life before and after the Spanish conquest of the Aztecs in *Song of the Hummingbird* (1996), the fictional memories of an Aztec noblewoman who is recounting her personal experiences of the fall of her people to a Catholic priest. Even the violence of battle and of sexual and religious rituals do not limit the poetry and grace of the main character's narrative flashbacks, nor do they limit her resolve not to accept Christian morality and not to tolerate the censure from the naive priest who thinks of himself as the older woman's father-confessor.

In all, Graciela Limón has created a gallery of unforgettably strong women who battle war, politics, and social mores with unbreakable resolve.

Personal Stats

Mexican American professor, writer. **Born:** August 2, 1938, in East Los Angeles, California. **Education:** B.A. in Spanish, Marymount College, Palos Verdes Estates, California, 1965; M.A. in Spanish, University of the Americas, Mexico City, in 1969; Ph.D. in Spanish, University of California—Los Angeles, 1975. **Career:** Assistant Professor, Modern Language Department, Marymount College, 1969–75; Associate Professor, 1975–80; Full Professor and Chair of Department, 1980–present.

Awards/Honors: Before Columbus Foundation American Book Award for *In Search of Bernabé*, 1994; Finalist, *Los Angeles Times* Book Award, 1994. **Address:** Modern Language Department, Loyola Marymount University, Los Angeles, CA 90045

The Memories of Ana Calderón

from *The Memories of Ana Calderón*, Arte Público Press, 1994, pp. 11–23

My name is Ana Calderón, and my story begins in a palapa close to Puerto Real in southern Mexico. Even though many years have passed, my recollections of the hut often come to me. Its roof was made of long interlaced fronds which were lashed to a supporting frame of poles hacked out of palm trees. Its floor was the black sand that had been washed ashore ages before our time. Our palapa was on the fringe of a cluster of dwellings, and even though we weren't really a part of the port city, still, its lights could be seen from where we lived. We could even see the ships that came down the coast from Veracruz.

My father's name was Rodolfo and like all the men of the village, he was a fisherman. My mother was named Rosalva. I don't remember her as well as I do my father, and that's because she died when I was twelve years old, but I know that I loved her very much. Although I have memories, even vivid ones of when I was a child, I've always thought that my life really began on the day that my little brother, César, was born. That happened on the day I turned ten.

I was listening to my Aunt Calista's voice calling out for me that afternoon, and even though it sounded heavy with frustration, I pretended not to hear her. I was sitting under the shade of a small palm tree, wiggling my toes in the sand, with my knees drawn tightly under my chin as I gazed at the emerald-colored water. I used to dream most of the time when I sat by the ocean.

When I heard Tía Calista calling me, instead of running to where she was, I closed my eyes trying to forget that my mother was having another baby. I didn't want to think of it. I knew that it meant that I would have to take care of another sister because, of all my mother's children, only the girls lived. Each of the boys had died. That began to happen after I was born.

Ever since I could remember, everyone always reminded me that I must have done something bad to my mother's womb when I was inside of it because after me two boys, one right after the other, died. It wasn't until Aleja came along three years later that we had a new baby. But even after her there was another boy, and he died too. So everyone convinced me that it had been me that had done it.

They said that no boy could live where I had lived. I knew my father resented me for what I had done to my mother's insides and that made me feel very lonely. So from as far back as

I could remember, I tried to let everyone believe that I didn't care what they said. But I did care. Sometimes I even shook all over just thinking of what I had done. So I decided when I was very little, that I would live inside of myself, down deep where no one could blame me for what had happened

Of the sisters, I was the oldest, and because of that I was expected to take care of the smaller ones. I didn't like it, but when I complained I was told that all girls were born to have babies, or to take care of them. My Tía Calista, my mother and my father really believed that, but even then I knew that there was another reason for what they told me. My mother had to wash clothes for the people of Puerto Real to help my father feed us, so somebody else had to watch my sisters. But I told myself that it wasn't that bad because when they reached two years or so, each one would go off on her own during the day. I don't remember exactly where they went. I think they spent their time playing with the neighbor children.

I had only turned ten, but already I knew how to deliver a baby and how to take care of it from the beginning until it began to walk. The only thing I couldn't do was feed it. For that I had to take the little girl to wherever my mother was washing clothes. I didn't have to say anything because she knew why I was there. She would stop what she was doing and sit under a tree. With her arms still dripping soap, she would uncover her breast and stick its rose-colored nipple into the baby's mouth. I remember that my mother's breasts were large. They were round and brown. They reminded me of the clay jugs in which we kept the water we drank.

Alejandra was born when I was three years old, and after her the ones that lived were five girls. My father I think, had lost hope of ever having a son until César came. He was the only one able to live to be a young man. Then when he was born, my mother stopped having babies.

There was also Octavio Arce. We called him Tavo. He was not my brother. I don't remember when he first came into our family. He was an orphan, and although no one in particular took him in, he spent most of his time with us. He even slept in our hut. He, Alejandra and I were like triplets. I mean we were hardly ever apart one from the other. That is, until we were grown-up people.

On the day of César's birth, Tía Calista was calling me, but I was dreaming of becoming a famous dancer, so I pretended not to hear her. Alejandra and Tavo were with me, but I had that special way of going inside of myself to be alone with my plans. I used to do that because I wanted to prepare for the day when I would show my father that I could be just as good as the son he longed for. I wanted to do that every day, but he hardly ever looked at me except to let me know with his eyes that he hated me because I was not a boy, and that he believed that I had poisoned the way for the brothers that followed me. But one day, I knew, I would make him see that he had been wrong.

On that day, I could hear my aunt's voice. I didn't want to answer because in my mind, along with my imaginings, I was also seeing my mother's legs spreading out. I could see the syrupy liquid that leaked out of her body, and even how it stained the rough sheet under her, making it stick to the sandy ground. I didn't want to go to the palapa, but I knew that if I didn't I would be sorry for it later on.

■ ■ ■

"Ana-a-a-a! Ana-a-a-a!"

The voice cracked under the strain of shouting.

"Where are you, *muchacha*? Ana-a-a-a! Your mother's time has come! *Por Dios, ¿dónde estás?* I need you! If you don't come right now, I'll beat the skin off your behind. Anaa-a-a! I know you're out there somewhere. The baby is coming, and I need you!"

Ana gazed at the shimmering water and the foamy waves as they slapped against the embankments of the harbor prison, far away. She could hear her aunt's exasperated call, but she didn't want to interrupt her thoughts. Ana could also hear Octavio's and Alejandra's giggling as their bare feet poked her rump, prodding her to run to the hut. Several minutes passed.

When Ana finally decided to respond, she pulled her legs out of the sand and, sprinting up as she always did, the girl danced from one palm tree to the other, from one low fern to the next. Nothing in her body or face indicated that she was in a hurry, or frightened, or worried. Instead, she jumped, springing as high up toward the tops of the trees as possible. At the height of each leap her body was suspended in mid-air, back arched, one leg poised straight out in front, the other gracefully held behind as she lifted her arms in a wide curve above her head. When Ana landed in the sand after each leap, her feet touched invisible springs that again pushed her straight up into the turquoise sky.

By the time she came within view of her family's hut, Ana slowed down, dragging her feet and tracing long tracks in the sand with the tips of her toes. When she crouched through the low entrance, her nostrils expanded with the pungent smell of her mother's body combined with the acrid smoke from the earthen fire crackling in the far corner. As soon as Calista saw the girl standing in the opening, she moved toward her and spoke in a muffled voice. She pinched the girl's underarm, making her flinch with pain.

"*¡Muchacha condenada!* Where have you been? You know that I need you! I suppose you've been dreaming again. Don't bother to answer. Just bring over those sheets, and put more water in the pot. *¡Muévete!*"

The girl moved with familiarity towards the corner her aunt had pointed out in the gloomy hut. When she found the sheets, she brought them to Calista. Ana crouched on her haunches to get a closer look at her mother, who was sweaty and dusty. She had both her hands clenched into fists, and she was biting one of them so that she would not scream.

"Scream, 'Amá, scream. They all do it. Why don't you?"

"*Cállate, malcriada!* Don't you see how much your mother is suffering? She went through the same thing just for you, and look at you! As if nothing were happening. Just wait until you have your own kids. Only then will you understand."

"I'm never going to have children, Tía."

"Ha! When we're young, we women all say the same thing. But in the end, no one asks us what we want, or don't want. Come, *Hermana,* push, push, just a little more, and it's over."

Her aunt's voice was husky with fatigue and what Ana thought to be resentment. Ana knew that the baby was close to coming. She was glad because she hated her aunt's words that assured her that she would be just like the other women in her family. These thoughts troubled Ana. She wanted to escape; she could hardly wait until she would be able to run out to the beach again.

Suddenly the smeared tiny body appeared from between her mother's legs. Calista took hold of the child while cutting the cord. A shrill cry tore at the gloom. Calista turned to look at Ana. It was an intense glare; her eyes were filled with a meaning that the girl was unable to understand. Calista saw the girl's bewilderment and, sighing heavily, looked down at the baby.

"*¡Santo Dios!* It's a boy! *Hermana ¡es un hombrecito!,* Maybe this time . . . . " Calista bit her lip and murmured to her niece, "Here, take him. You know what to do. But be careful with him, and give him right back to your mother."

Ana took her baby brother from Calista's hands and moved to the light where she could look at him. This was the first boy she had really looked at. As she wiped his body, her eyes lingered on his genitals, and she thought that his penis looked like a tiny handle. She felt a surge of affection for him, remembering that he had come into her life on her birthday. She told herself that he was a gift for her, and she hoped that he would not die. That would prove to everyone that she had not done anything wrong.

Ana slowly wrapped the boy in the threadbare blanket that had been used for each of the babies that had come before him. She was aware that her aunt was cleaning her mother, and she could hear the two women murmuring. But she could not make out what they were saying. When she was finished cleaning her brother, she took the child to her mother.

"Here, 'Amá. Can I leave now?"

Calista sucked at her lips in irritation. "*¡Muchacha, buena para nada!* You can hardly wait to go out and jump around like a *burra,* can you? You know how special it is to at last have a boy, and here you leave your mother . . . "

Ana didn't hear the rest of what her aunt said because she was out of the hut, sprinting toward the beach. She felt her heart beating, but she knew that it was not the running that was causing the pounding. It was because she did indeed see how special it was that their family now had a boy. Ana told herself that he had come to save her, and because of that he would be just like her. She and her brother had been born on the same day for a special reason. She was born to become a famous dancer, and he would grow to be someone important, too. Ana ran as fast as she could to find Alejandra and Octavio to tell them the news.

She knew where to find them. The three children had a favorite cove where they spent their time playing in the sand whenever they could escape from their hut and the dreary chores.

They would go there especially during the months when the priest who taught them how to read and write traveled to other villages to marry couples and baptize their children.

Ana arrived breathless. She found Octavio and Alejandra lying face up on the sand playing a game in which they pointed at clouds that looked like animals or plants.

"It's a boy!"

Ana's voice startled her sister and Octavio, causing them to jump to their feet. Neither wore shoes nor much clothing. Alejandra was the first to utter what sounded like a groan.

"Ahhg! Is it dead?"

"No! He's alive, and very pretty. Come on! Come and see him!"

Alejandra was annoyed. She stood erect, glaring at Ana, showing her dislike for her. She resented Ana's self-assurance and offishness, but most of all Alejandra was jealous of her sister's looks, which were so different from her own. Whereas Ana's skin was a coppery brown, hers was white; this was the legacy, said Calista, of a French grandfather. Ana's body was thin and sinewy, and her limbs tapered, as if she had been cast in a porcelain mold. Alejandra, on the other hand, was round and supple, and even though she was only seven years old, her small breasts were already beginning to protrude underneath her shear cotton dress. Ana was still flat-cheated. Her body retained the look of a boy rather than a girl.

Ana returned her sister's disapproving gaze for a few seconds. Then, suddenly disengaging her eyes from those of Alejandra, she turned to look at Octavio who was standing with his arms hanging limply by his sides. His mouth was open and he blinked his eyes, not knowing what to say. He blurted out the first thing that came to his mind.

"What do you think his name will be, Ana?"

Her answer was brisk. "I think I heard them call him 'César.'"

Octavio's skin was dark and his body was beginning to show that he would develop into a tall man. Although people guessed that he was only nine years old, there already was a transparent fuzz over his upper lip that glistened with perspiration from the excitement of hearing Ana speak. Whenever she spoke, his heart inexplicably beat faster.

Ana was staring at him. "Come on! Let's go see the new baby!"

It was Alejandra, however, who responded. "No! We can see him later. We're in the middle of playing a game. Come on, Tavo! I'm ahead of you."

Octavio looked at Ana as if expecting her to say something. Whenever he gazed at her, his face took on a faint smile, not so much with his lips as with his eyes. He felt drawn to the girl's energy and ability to recreate imaginary worlds that were beautiful to him. Secretly, he preferred the games devised by Ana to those of Alejandra.

"Well, why don't we change and instead play the game Ana was telling us about. The one with the Aztecs and the princess who is going to be sacrificed."

"Oh, no! I hate that one. She's always the beautiful girl who dies after she dances her head off. I think it's boring!"

Alejandra was showing irritation with both Octavio and Ana. She sensed that he liked her sister better and that whatever she did or thought of doing was wonderful for him. Alejandra, however, wanted him for herself, just like when Ana was away. Unable to think of how to get rid of her sister, Alejandra shouted out. "Ana, I think Tía Calista is calling you again."

"No, she's not. You're right, Tavo! Let's do the Ritual of the Humming Bird. You're the High Priest, and I'm Huitzítzilin . . ."

Ana, forgetting the baby and her mother, leaped through the air, her sheer cotton dress flowing in the warm breeze. Despite her young age, she had already invented a number of dances, each with a title, story line and characters. She often organized her sister and Octavio as part of her troupe, directing them to jump and kick and twirl.

Alejandra protested more than ever to the humming bird dance, knowing that it had two leading parts. The only role she could play was toward the end of the piece when she appeared briefly as an old sorceress. "Oh, no! Not that thing again! Huit . . . Huit . . . I can't even pronounce the dumb word! I'm fed up with you being the lady-of-the-something-or-another, and Tavo is always the warrior who's in love with you."

Ana and Octavio disregarded the girl's objections. Without an introduction or warm-up, they whirled about in the sand as the declining sun cast golden sparks in their hair. At first Alejandra sulked, plopping down on the sand with arms folded over her chest. Then she made faces at them as she mimicked their movements. Finally, losing patience, she jumped to her feet, stuck her tongue out at the dancing couple and ran off towards the hut where she knew she would find her mother, her new brother, and at least one of her other sisters or cousins with whom to play.

The two dancers didn't notice Alejandra's mocking gestures. Instead, they continued their ritualistic dance, just as Ana had imagined a high priest and a sacrificial virgin would do. They sprang and turned until their breath came in spurts and their chests heaved from the exertion. They ran from one end of the cove to the other, waving their arms in the air, gesturing and posturing until Ana, re-enacting the death scene, collapsed on the sand. Octavio, knowing his part, fell at her side, first on his knees, then finally on the imaginary onyx knife with which he would take his life after sacrificing the princess.

He was so out breath, however, that he lost his balance and fell on top of her. He had not meant to do that, but when he felt her body beneath him, an unexpected urge kept him there. Octavio felt bound to Ana, and he didn't want to be separated from her. He realized that he had never before felt such a sensation, but he liked what he felt, and he remained without moving.

She was also surprised and remained motionless for several seconds. Then, not knowing what to do, she wiggled to one side until Octavio slid off from on top of her. Still, their faces were very close and their breath intermingled. They were both quiet until their breathing stabilized. Then Octavio placed his hand on her chest, and without thinking he said "Ana, I wish we could be this way always."

As if his voice had been a musical note marking her next step, Ana jumped to her feet, laughing and swirling her dress. She ran away, shouting words that seemed aimed at the tops of the palm trees rather than at him. "We will always be this way."

■ ■ ■

My mother died in the middle of a scream. No one really knew exactly when it came, or the name of the sickness that afflicted her. I only remember that it began one morning when she whispered, "¡Aye! My head hurts so much! She wasn't speaking to anyone in particular. She said it as she handed César a cup of chocolate.

In the beginning, the pain in her head made her sigh almost constantly. Soon after, her sighing turned to moans; sometimes they sounded like short gasps. But the time finally came when her groans turned to screams that tore at the night like a sharp invisible knife.

Tía Calista came to be with my mother during those terrible days and nights, but no matter what brews she prepared, my mother's screaming only grew louder. All through those times, we children sat outside our hut along with our father as Calista and other women tried their concoctions, hoping to lessen my mother's pain. I asked my father several times what we would do if she died, but he kept quiet. He never answered my questions; he only stared at me with his resentful eyes. I remember that I didn't cry, despite the big hole growing in my stomach with each minute that passed.

On the last night, my mother let out a wail that I have never been able to forget. It was so loud and so desperate that its vibration caused the owls to flutter up from their roosts in the palm trees. I remember their dark silhouettes as they rose, angrily flapping their wings against the sky that was lit only by the brilliance of the stars. After that, my father was left alone to bring us up. César was two years old.

■ ■ ■

Ana's mother died in 1932. It had been a bad year for the fishing communities living near Puerto Real. The fighting and killing in central Mexico had overflowed Sierra Orizaba spilling onto the shores of the Gulf and spreading from northern Tamaulipas down to southern Campeche. People trapped in poverty talked of moving away to find a new way to live. No one seemed to know exactly what was happening. The weekly newspaper in Puerto Real described the executions of priests and collaborators who had been found to be in defiance of the constitution. Later on, drifters coming in from different parts of the country countered those reports with stories of their own. A stranger one day walked into the cluster of huts shouting *"Long Live the Cristeros!"* but few people really understood what his words meant.

Rodolfo Calderón was not involved in those events. His mind was taken with the grief of losing Rosalva and with the worry of caring for his eight children. Like everyone else, he saw that things were bad, that the situation around them was deteriorating day by day. Adding to his personal sadness, after his wife's death, bad luck afflicted Rodolfo even more when his boat struck a reef and was damaged beyond repair. The *panga* had been small, but it had provided him with a way to feed his family. Now, even that was gone. His two brothers offered to help him, but he saw that their lives were even more miserable than his. His sister-in-law Calista was helpful with the children, and he was grateful, but that wasn't enough.

He began to visit the busier streets of the port town in search of work. Instead, he found countless men without means of supporting their families as well as women who no longer could find a way to help their husbands. When he spoke to any of them, each seemed to have troubles greater than his own. At first, Rodolfo thought that it was their fault for not wanting to break away from the old ways. When he approached the cannery for a job, however, he discovered that wanting to work was not enough. He was rejected because he was unskilled with machinery and inexperienced in packing. He then turned to the cantina and restaurant, offering to be a waiter or even a cook, but he found out that there were several men ahead of him, waiting for just such a job to come up.

After several months, he gathered his children in the hut. Calista was there also. They sat in a circle on the sandy earth as if they were going to share a meal. No one spoke; they seemed to understand that something important was about to happen. The only sound was the crackling of a few twigs burning in the brasier.

As he peered into the face of each of his daughters, Rodolfo felt a tightness in his stomach. His eyes lingered so long on Ana's face that she began to bounce her crossed legs up and down nervously. It was a gesture she repeated often, and it annoyed him as did most of her traits. He turned away from her, trying not to think of the feelings that assaulted him whenever he looked at her, or even thought of her. Ana was his first child, and he knew that he should have loved her above the others, but he couldn't. He found it impossible to explain why he resented her, especially after his sons had died one after the other. He felt that the disappointment and bitterness that flooded him after each death had infected his heart, making him hate Ana as if it had been her doing.

Rodolfo stared at Rosalva, thinking of how brown her hair and skin were, and that she looked just like her mother when he first saw her. His eyes rolled over to Alejandra, and her determined look unsettled him; something in her eyes usually made him uncomfortable, yet she was his favorite. He turned to Zulma, and he told himself that she seemed filled with the energy of the ocean. He felt a little afraid. Rodolfo's eyes then met those of Jasmín and his heart leaped at the beauty he saw there. But he remembered how often she was ill. He stared at the two youngest, the twins Pilar and Cruz, as he began to speak in his usual quiet manner. "We're going north. I hear there's work in the fields of Sonora and plenty of jobs for everyone on the plantations."

Each of the children, from Ana to César, looked first at their father and then at each other not knowing what to respond. None of them had ever thought of life beyond the familiar shoreline between their hut and the town. Only Ana had dreamed of leaving Puerto Real, and even she was quiet. Tía Calista, astounded, was the first to speak.

"*Compadre,* no! It's a mistake, believe me. What are you going to do all the way across the world? You're from here, from this very sand on which we're sitting. The cord that connected you to your mother's womb is buried out there, right alongside this *palapa*. It's there, just like the cords of these children. I should know; I buried them with these hands. And what about the boys? Even though they didn't live, they're still your sons, and they're out there, too. *Compadre*, you can't leave them . . . or Rosalva."

Calista stopped speaking, but her breathing was hard; everyone could hear it. When Rodolfo didn't respond, she said more. "Besides, you're a man of the ocean. You'll die if you go where there's only dirt everywhere you look. I mean . . . what do you know of beans, or whatever it is that they plant up there?"

As if controlled by a single force, the eight small faces snapped from looking at Calista over to their father's face. Fastening their eyes on him, they waited for his response. Rodolfo's head, however, was hanging low over his chest, and it took him a while before he lifted it to speak. "I know nothing of seeds or of how to plant them in the earth, *Comadre*. But I must try. For their sake."

Rodolfo's face was covered with sweat and it glistened in the dimness of the hut. His children were looking intently at him. They saw his broad, bronzed face taut with worry. They sensed that he was thinking of their mother and the dead boys. The thatched roof cast a shadow accentuating his brow; it appeared to be cracked by a deep crevice that cut downward from his hairline elongating his nose. Rodolfo's dark mustache seemed to droop more than ever over his thick lips, and his slanted, black eyes had narrowed like slits in a brown mask.

"Listen to me, *Compadre.*" Calista felt compelled to speak again. "Hear my words as the older sister of your wife, God keep her in His company. Things will change, I'm sure. At least you know how to go about living here. And what about your brothers? Are you just going to leave them never to see them again? And, don't forget, *Compadre,* that even though I can't help provide the tortillas, you have me to help at least with the children. Except for Ana, they're all yet so little . . . *¡Por Dios!* . . . and all of them useless girls except for this one."

Calista put her arms around César, who was sitting next to her. The girls were familiar with being called useless, but they had never before seen their aunt's face so intense. Somehow it looked darker than ever. In the darkness of the hut, the deep wrinkles of her cheeks seemed like fissures in the brown coral they knew well, and her aquiline nose dipped sharply toward her chin.

Rodolfo again looked around at his brood, but he remained silent. The only movement in his face was when he nibbled at his upper lip, nervously tweaking his mustache.

"I have thought about it long enough. I've sold what was left of my gear, and with that money we'll have enough to take us to Veracruz. From there we'll make our way northward until we reach the Río Yaqui, where the planting is plentiful "

Calista had nothing more to say. She nodded vaguely, rose to her feet and left the hut. Rodolfo's children were silent, still not knowing what to say or do. Alejandra was the only one to speak. "What about Tavo?"

"What about him, Aleja?"

"Well, 'Apá, we can't just leave him. He's part of our family.

"I only have enough money for us. He'll have to stay behind."

Alejandra's head jerked to one side as if she had been slapped. Her face was filled with shock and disbelief because she could not even begin to imagine life without Octavia. "Then I'll stay, too." She was close to tears as she blurted out the words to her father.

"Alejandra, hush. It's impossible for you to stay. We're a family and we're staying together, and there's no more to be said."

After a few moments in which they all sat without saying anything, Rodolfo stood up and left the hut. As soon as she was sure that he was beyond hearing her, Ana sprang to her feet and let out a howl of joy. The other girls and César, not knowing how to react, also stood up and began to giggle. Only Alejandra remained squatting on the sand. She looked up at her older sister and said, "We can't leave Tavo behind."

Ana stopped in the middle of a whoop. "He'll come with us, silly. Nothing will hold him back."

Then, not knowing exactly why, the other girls and César began to yell and screech in wild joy. Inexplicably, they were elated at the prospect of leaving the place in which they had been born.

■ ■ ■

My dream was beginning to come true. I didn't know where we were going, but I felt that each step away from the palapa *would lead me to the fulfillment of what I knew was my destiny. And I would show everyone that I could do some good, after all.*

Unlike me, Alejandra was sad. She didn't share in my joy, especially when she saw that our father would not allow Tavo to come with us. On that last night, both of them begged my father to let him come with us. She cried and said she would not come unless he came along. Even Tavo wept as he asked over and again for the permission. But my father was firm; the answer was no.

When we were finished with the packing we laid down to sleep. Alejandra and I shared the same mat, so I was able to feel her turning over from one side to the other. I couldn't sleep either, not because of Tavo, but because I was so excited. After a few hours, I felt Alejandra leave the mate. I opened my eyes and saw that she had crawled over to where Tavo was lying, and I saw that she put her arms around him. He put his arms around her, too, and I knew that they would stay that way for the reast of the night.

Before the sun came out, we heard my father moving on his mat. When he blew his nose, we knew that it was time to rise and say goodbye to our aunts and uncles and cousins. I knew, also, that it was time to begin the road that would lead me to the world that I had imagined.

Writings

Novels: *María Belén; The Autobiography of an Indian Woman*, Vantage Press, 1990. *In Search of Bernabé*, Arte Público Press, 1993. *The Memories of Ana Calderón*, Arte Público Press, 1994. *Song of the Hummingbird,* Arte Público Press, 1996.   **Short Stories and Excerpts:** In *Hispanic American Literature*; *In Other Words: Writings by Latinas, Short Fiction by Hispanic Writers;* and others.

Max Martínez

Max Martínez's career as a writer spans the full course of the development of contemporary Chicano literature. In the late 1960s he became active in the Chicano literary movement in San Antonio, and by 1970 he was editing the Chicano Times *weekly newspaper, in which he also published commentary and short stories. In 1972, he founded and edited the short-lived* El magazín, *but left the periodical in 1973 when he moved to Denver to pursue a Ph.D. He later published stories in the highly influential pulp literary magazine,* Caracol, *and in* Revista Chicano-Riqueña.

Born on May 10, 1943, in Gonzales, Texas, a farm town some forty miles from San Antonio, Max (Maximiano) Martínez was raised in a rural, agricultural community similar to the one depicted in his two novels, *Schoolland* and *White Leg*. After graduating high school, he sought to escape the country life, where his lot as a Mexican American was limited, and he went to sea as a merchant marine. He was able to see a good portion of the world, including Spain, which left an indelible impression on his young mind. He returned to San Antonio and studied English and Philosophy at St. Mary's University, graduating with a B.AS. in 1972. By December 1973, he had finished a Master's degree in Comparative Literature at East Texas State University in Commerce, but rather than becoming a teacher, he once again experienced wanderlust and went off to New York to work as a stockbroker. This lasted almost no time at all. Having lived the life of a sailor, a stockbroker, and freelance writer, Martínez tried to settle down in 1975 into a more stable intellectual environment by studying for his Ph.D. in English at the University of Denver and, beginning in 1977, pursuing a career as a college professor at the University of Houston. But it turned out that neither was for him: he never finished his dissertation and he abandoned the tenure track at the university by the mid-1980s to dedicate himself to serious writing. This he has done to the present, taking various freelance writing jobs while penning some memorable works of fiction.

Aside from numerous stories published in a variety of literary magazines—as well as hundreds of "man-on-the-scene" commentary and thought pieces that he writes for a trade journal—the fruits of Martínez's labors have been four very different books. The first is a collection of his early short stories, The Adventures of the Chicano Kid and Other Stories (1983), in which he experiments with a variety of styles to depict the variety of Chicano life: a farm worker; a middle-class suburban businessman (today what would be called a yuppie); an educated, self-confident, modern Chicano in a face-off with traditional rural prejudice in the person of a Texas "redneck" (a frequent portrait of blue-color racism in most of Martínez's books); an old man snoozing on a park bench and bemoaning how things have changed; and others. The title story is a satire of nineteenth-century dime novels. "Faustino," also included in this anthology, is an outrageously inventive tale that portrays the levels of oppression in a stratified, rural setting, similar to Martínez's own hometown in central-Texas farm country. The humiliation Faustino suffers at the hands of an Anglo farm wife is later violently vented by Faustino on his own wife.

Schoolland (1988), Max Martínez's autobiographical novel, is a young boy's first-person account of the year of the great drought (1953), the same year that his beloved grandfather foretold his own death and began making preparations for it:

> Dying. I was thinking of dying. As old as I am, it's best to know I can die anytime now.

The novel is a coming-of-age tale but it is also a social protest that details the tragedy of bank takeovers of farmland—both boy and reader lose their innocence. Not only does the grandfather die, so does a Texas-Mexican way of life on the land.

Martínez's second collection of stories, *Red Bikini Dream,* also includes some autobiographical tales, but offers stories of non-Chicano experiences as well. The stories' characters include successful lawyers, drunken sailors, and even a middle-aged Jewish American couple on a dude ranch in Texas. The tension between "civilized" behavior and the desire to experience life unbridled and wild holds the varied stories together. Martínez again gives us glimpses of his own life as a struggling writer in New York, as a sailor, and as a child growing up in a fatherless home. The stories "offer a disturbing glimpse of the complex relationship between self and culture that underlies modern life," said *The Review of Contemporary*

Martínez "knows how to twist a wicked smile out of his characters, while making marvelous statements on who we are and where we are headed."

The Bloomsbury Review

Fiction. The Bloomsbury Review *stated that Martínez "knows how to twist a wicked smile out of his characters, while making marvelous statements on who we are and where we are headed." The title story, "A Red Bikini Dream," in which a woman's sexual fantasy comes to life and leads to her rape-murder has elicited a violent reaction, being viewed as misogynistic by Sharon Gibson, writing in the* Houston Chronicle *(September 9, 1990).*

White Leg is a well-crafted mystery novel narrated in the first-person by what can only be described as a somewhat charming "redneck," who commits murder and gets away with it. This is a powerful evocation of the dangerous politics and culture of small-town life in Texas. The ne'er-do-well protagonist slowly extracts himself from a plot crafted by some of the most powerful men in the county and his own treacherous, amoral wife. Peter Hammerle of *The San Francisco Chronicle* called the novel "a ride on a bullet train bound for hell."

Martínez's works have been praised for capturing the rhythm and nuance of rural Texas life, for their sensitive evocation of past times in central Texas, and for their array of interesting and diverse characters. They have been censured at times for their scenes of explicit sex and violence and for what has been seen as their victimization of women. Martínez wields a powerful pen that cuts so close to the bone of the reader that it is often hard to arrive at an objective judgment.

Personal Stats

Mexican American writer, professor. ***Born:*** May 10, 1943, in Gonzales, Texas. ***Education:*** B.A. in English and Philosophy, St. Mary's University, San Antonio, Texas, in 1972; M.A. in English, East Texas State University in Commerce, 1973; all but dissertation completed toward Ph.D. in English, University of Denver, 1975. ***Career:*** Assistant professor, English, University of Houston, 1977–83. ***Address:*** c/o Arte Público Press, University of Houston, Houston, TX 77204-2090

La Tacuachera

from *The Adventures of the Chicano Kid and Other Stories,* Arte Público Press, 1982, pp. 132–69

I

La Tacuachera stood atop the crest of a small hill five miles outside of Nixon on the road to Karnes City. Behind it and across the road in front of it were sloping terraced fields of rich black farm land. The tavern was situated in a gravel clearing surrounded by tall, ancient mesquite trees whose pale green leaves dulled the stinging heat of summer suns. In the back of the tavern, beyond the trees, the land lay fallow, overgrown with grass and weeds, rats and rattlesnakes. A narrow ribbon of cream-colored gravel extended beyond the half-moon of parking lot, circling around between the building and the trees. Approaching cars, turning off the black-top, produced a crunching rumbling announcement of their arrival.

As Nixon to the north was dry, *La Tacuachera,* located just outside the county line, sold the nearest legal beer. Bootleggers in town sold to teenagers and to those who could not find a ride to the tavern. Over the years, it had become a gathering place for people from Nixon and from a cluster of farm houses and a cotton gin known as Schoolland. The building was constructed out of stone up to waist level, and out of wood for the remainder. The sign above the entrance, supplied by a forgotten Coca-Cola salesman, read *Pleasant Hill Tavern.* Only the Anglos knew it by that name. The Chicanos of the area, mindful of some legendary or mythical occurrence, or perhaps remembering it as a clearing in which to rest after possum hunts, referred to it as *La Tacuachera.* More likely, the hunters never went beyond the tavern to their possum hunts.

No one really remembered when *La Tacuachera* began admitting Chicanos into the bar. It could be that it was always so, but the driveway around back, still used by Black people, served as a reminder. Of course, there were many who knew, but they seldom wanted to talk about it. When they did talk about it, it was with a laugh. When they, for some reason or other, remembered, when they chose to talk about it, it was said that Chicanos were allowed to open the back door, to poke in their heads, but they were not permitted to enter. The Chicano at the door would try to get the attention of the bartender. Failing to do so, he would have to ask an Anglo seated at a nearby table to please call the bartender. Once the bartender saw the waiting Chicano, the Chicano held up as many fingers as he wanted six-packs. There was no signal for brands and the bartender would bring him whatever kind of beer was handy or the kind he had overstocked. The transaction would be concluded at the back door, the bartender often keeping the Chicano's change as a tip because he would not want to go around the bar again to return it. But, that was a very long time ago for everyone. Black people, although permitted to drink inside, were not particularly welcomed and, after buying their beer and whiskey there, would drink it elsewhere.

It had been an uneasy period for those who remembered it, a period to which all of them resigned themselves. They accepted it without question. The patrons of *La Tacuachera,* white and brown, were embarrassed to think about it. They could neither defend nor condemn the arrangement. It was a time and an imperative which most-at least those who were old enough to have participated in it-deny having supported, refusing to accept either blame or guilt for an inherited system. They were quick to point out that the conditions of the past no longer prevailed and that it was time to concentrate on the present. Black people were allowed to enter and drink in *La Tacuachera,* an Anglo or a Chicano would emphatically point out, but they *chose* not to come in. What more could decent people do?

The man who owned and ran the place was pleasant enough. He was short, stocky, given to wearing bright-colored flannel shirts year around. What distinguished him from his customers was his face and hands which indicated a man who did not work in the fields. His wife helped him on busy evenings, Friday and Saturday nights. She was thin, almost frail-looking, but she had enough energy to evict a recalcitrant drunk and she was diplomatic enough to persuade two contenders to go outside for the fistfight necessary to settle their differences. The atmosphere at *La Tacuachera* was not belligerent, it did not have the reputation of the rough places that could be found in Gonzales or Karnes City. A man could confidently take his family there, although it was loud and often arguments dangled just below the cloud of cigarette smoke.

Fights, however, were not rare among the Anglos and among the Chicanos. They were seldom if ever mixed. There might have been a push-and-shove incident once in a while between a Chicano and an Anglo in the urinals, but it never developed into a fight. On those occasions when a fight was unavoidable, the participants knew they had to go behind the tavern, beyond the trees, into the darkness of the field. The path behind the trees was well-worn, leading to a rotting barn which was caved in at one corner. There were those who remembered the cock fights held there on Thursday nights. After the sheriff had stopped them, the barn served as a shelter for those wishing to settle an argument. After a thunderstorm destroyed part of it, the contestants had to battle in the open field, their falls cushioned by the soft earth and grass. No one was ever seriously hurt. A bloody nose was not common, although the would-be pugilists in their uncertain equilibrium, ended up quite sore from falling down so much.

The most serious incident anyone could remember was the time Juan Ríos suffered a bite from a startled rattlesnake. Juan Ríos went outside to watch a fight between his compadre Pablo Ramírez and his other compadre Samuel Gutiérrez. Before the first punch was thrown, as Juan Ríos moved back to give his compadres some room, the snake struck. The two fighters immediately lost interest in their argument. Juan's compadre Pablo, aggravated the snake bite when he tried to bleed the venom by cutting into Juan Ríos' calf. Juan Ríos ended up spending two weeks in the hospital, more as a result of his compadre's good will than the damage caused by the poisonous snake.

All in all, *La Tacuachera* was rowdy and boisterous, but good-natured. The people who came there were never involved in long-lasting feuds of any kind. In the fights, after a few wildly launched blows toward a blurry and elusive face in the dark, the cause of the fight was quickly forgotten and the antagonists would return inside, arm in arm, laughing, yelling for more beer. Invariably, when they returned to the subject of their recent fight, to the cause of it, the two friends would shed glistening, beer-soaked, male tears for the amusement of those present.

Inside *La Tacuachera,* next to the entrance on the left, was a long wooden bar. The varnish had been worn away long before. Elbows and sweat from the frosty beer bottles had coated it near the edges. It was lustreless and functional rather than colorful. There were still spots of varnish left and these islands would shine the reflection of the neon beer signs on the wall, bright colors framing lakes, rushing waterfalls, glittering trademarks, neatly dressed cowboys. Below the signs, upon a ledge, was a salty assortment of corn chips, potato chips, dried beef jerky, polish sausage, pickled pig's knuckles and feet, corn nuts, peanuts, cheese crackers and whatever else the salesman brought from San Antonio. The antique cash register would ring loudly, and this was followed by the dull thud of the erupting cash drawer. Under the bar were the beer coolers which contained the "coldest beer in Texas" as the sign outside proclaimed. Beside them, cases of warm bottles and cans were stacked, waiting their turn.

The belly-up bar was integrated. Chicanos and Anglos could lean freely against the bar without breaching an unspoken arrangement carried over from the past. In front of the bar, in an area as wide as the bar was long, were the Chicano tables. At the far end, all the way across, was the jukebox. To the left were two billiard tables, to the right was a clear passageway leading to the urinals outside of the building. Across the narrow walk-space adjacent to the Chicano area was the Anglo section. The tables and chairs were grouped together at one end leaving a glossy square of cement floor for dancing.

In the Chicano area, Spanish was the common language, English used more often than not to punctuate a joke. The jukebox mingled its twangy, mechanical country music dirges with the animated Chicano speech. The conversation of the Chicanos would often be interrupted by a piercing 'hoohuy' or an 'ajúa' from an exuberant celebrant. In later years, the owners of *La Tacuachera* added a few polkas and some corridos to the jukebox in recognition of the Chicanos.

The Anglo customers would bring their wives and children. None of the Chicanos did. For the Anglos, *La Tacuachera* and the weekend evenings they spent there was a family affair. The owners of the place, accustomed to it, began providing one of their bedrooms upstairs for unenduring, sleeping children, that they not be a burden on their drinking parents. The couples would dance to the music from the jukebox, except when a mischievous Chicano would play a firi-fidi-firi-fidi polka that would insinuate itself among the gringo selections. None of the Anglos would dance to the Chicano polkas, although they would dance to German polkas played by Myron Floren. While the Chicano polka played, an adventurous couple might dance to it, but most of the Anglos would return to their tables to wait. As things continued to change, the owners of *La Tacuachera* began booking third-rate country-western hands to play on weekends. They soon discovered that, inexpensive as the bands might he, it was not worth the cost and none of the customers noticed when the bands did not come anymore.

Friday and Saturday nights were the busiest at *La Tacuachera*. The Chicanos would rush home from their tractors, cotton-chopping, fence-mending and chicken-plucking at the packing houses. They would eat slowly but in anticipation of going out. After a bath, wearing freshly starched jeans and white shirts, they would speed toward the tavern. Just after sundown, before the pale blue of starlight begins to cool the night, there would be a crunch of tires on the gravel, sputtering mufflers, squeaky brakes, all signaling the arrival of the early Chicanos.

There was a gay, festive air in the gravel parking lot when several cars arrived simultaneously. The Chicanos would greet one another with handshakes as if it had been a long time since they had last seen each other. A small group might congregate beside the hood of a car. One would slip away to bring beers for everyone. After a sort of ritual introduction, someone would invite the rest inside the tavern. Once seated inside, the procession of arrivals would continue until the place overflowed with bodies and laughter, each new arrival greeted heartily by those already there.

The orders for beer kept the bartender busy; he seldom spoke to anyone on these evenings. There never seemed to be a shortage of money. No one who came to *La Tacuachera* and happened to be out of work or short on cash would be without a friend who made sure he had plenty of beer. These stretches of hard luck were brief and rare, the Chicanos knew. When he could, he would return the favor. Even if he didn't, it was always better to have a friend.

The talk was incessant, each member of a table vying for a turn to speak, no one ever satisfied with the little he got to say because someone always managed to interrupt. The conversation at the tables, and sometimes across tables, would include a recount of the activities of the past week, plans successfully concluded, plans gone wrong, jokes, legends, repetitions of past memorable events, gossip and chisme, raunchy sex-talk. It was never a matter of having to say something particularly funny. During the conversation, the crowd seemed attuned to the appropriate pause and then raucous, hearty laughter would erupt.

The Anglos would arrive much later than the Chicanos. They, too, would hurry home from the fields and the packing houses. However, they had to wait for their wives and children to get ready. For them it was a family gathering which had all but replaced the picnic, the reunion, the church social. For them, *The Pleasant Hill Tavern* was a place where they could meet and conduct the necessary social intercourse with friends and neighbors. It was the culmination of a week of hard work and isolation. The children would have other children to play with, the wives would exchange small talk, recipes, gossip, the men would discuss all but a few of the same things as the Chicanos. While the Chicano area was loud and noisy, the Anglo area was subdued but not at all somber.

When the Anglos began to arrive, as the door opened, the Chicanos would lift their eyes toward them. Upon seeing it was not an acquaintance, they would ignore the Anglos who would come into the tavern sternfaced, a condition made to seem all the more ominous and ill-humored by their squinty eyes and thin compressed lips. The Anglos, out of habit and tradition, avoided looking in the direction of the Chicano area. Occasionally, it could not be helped, and there would be a brief exchange which consisted of a nod, sometimes a forefinger salute. At the bar, which was neutral, Anglos and Chicanos could talk together, but never in a relaxed or free way, as they shared very little in common.

One could see two and sometimes three couples at each table in the Anglo area. The children would play in the dark corners, run up and down the staircase, and periodically they would make an appearance at their parents table to cadge small change for soda waters and chips. As the evening progressed, the couples would begin to dance out affection laden with alcohol. They considered it bad manners to ask someone's wife to dance, although it was permissible to swap dancing partners on the floor. Each time after the music, a husband would escort his wife back to the table.

Throughout the evening, noise and fellowship would continue to flow from the Chicano side. On the Anglo side, things were more restrained in keeping with the proper family atmosphere they strove to maintain. The men refrained from exchanging the off-color jokes they had heard in the fields. It was only when they went outside for some fresh air or to urinate that they would have more masculine conversation.

The people, white and brown, who came to *La Tacuachera* were friendly to outsiders, to those who were just passing through and needed to stop for a brief rest. They were friendly up to a point and beyond that, someone passing through would soon realize that he was nothing more than a stranger. They produced a simple, rustic, kind of excitement, peculiar to themselves, quaint perhaps to an outsider, but serious and nurturing to them. It was, finally, a closely guarded membership at *La Tacuachera*. To be a part of it, all one had to do was live in the area. A stranger could only observe but not share in the fullness of life that was *La Tacuachera*.

There were two exceptions. Ambrose Tench, who, it was said, would not live to see the age of thirty, lived in the area, in a shack on the outskirts of Nixon. He had such a reputation as a troublemaker that he was a permanent outsider at *La Tacuachera*. Ambrose Tench would be an outsider wherever he happened to be. The owner of the tavern had discouraged his business and was ill-at-ease when Tench came into the bar. The other exception, was Chango, whose real name was Joaquín, a native who no longer lived in the area. He returned as often as he could weekends and was thus included in *La Tacuachera* as though he had never moved away. It was assumed Chango lived in San Antonio because of the clothes he wore, but he never verified it, and the Chicanos were too polite to pry. He had friends there, had made new ones, and to many of them he still lived nearby.

■■■

II

Ambrose Tench was born four miles from where Chango was born. Both were born several months apart, in the same year in Schoolland, a once prosperous community surrounding a country store and a cotton gin. It was the cotton gin which served as the hub of the area, ginning for farms within a ten-mile radius. When the land started to give out, most of it going into the Soil Bank, the ginning equipment was dismantled and moved further south, near Refugio, where the soil was still producing plenty of cotton.

For many years after, only the dull grey-ribbed aluminum siding remained, slowly peeling away from the telephone-pole frames, exposing a dark, cavernous emptiness that made the children of Schoolland believe it was haunted by the ghost of a man who had been killed there. At one end of the gin, that facing the general store, the concrete loading platform still jutted out, strands of cotton still caught in the iron rims that made it look like a long bale. Not far from the loading platform, a misshapen, forgotten cotton bale lay on its side, the burlap having turned grey over the years, with large chunks of cotton pulled away from a corner. It resembled a mutilated loaf of bread.

The little cotton still grown in Schoolland was ginned either in Nixon or farther away in Gonzales. Only the shell of the building remained, a monument to the town that cotton was to have made. When someone set fire to the building, it was natural that Ambrose Tench was suspected. There was not enough evidence against Tench to charge him with anything and the owners of the gin shell were not overly concerned about it. The sheriff, however, while giving Tench a ride into town one day did ask him some questions about it.

Ambrose Tench had been the bully of Schoolland ever since he discovered he could make a fist and strike someone with it. He was thin, with sharp, angular features that made him seem taller than he actually was. His large, hooked nose had been broken several times, giving a peculiar distortion to his bony face. His eyes were set deep in their sockets, framed by a sharp, protruding forehead. His skin stretched so tautly over his face that one could swear it was not skin at all but waxen bone. Several anonymous people contributed to the further distortion of Ambrose Tench's face. A citizen of Houston had chipped in with a scar which started just below his right ear and extended down the side of his neck and curiously swept up around the hub of his Adam's apple. He had lost his lower teeth from a gum disease combined with the effects of several fistfights. His upper teeth were crooked, chipped, yellowed, with greenish-black half-moons just below the gums. They did not match the perfect evenness and whiteness of the lower plate which he purchased in Gonzales. When he smiled, which was not often, his face took on a perverse, ghoulish aspect.

His lower teeth had been already rotting and slipping away from their mooring in his gums when he had taken a trip to Corpus Christi. Tench had been sitting in Flippo's, drunker than usual, badgering the waitress. When the waitress could stand him no longer, she took a bowl of chicken noodle soup destined for an elderly tourist couple and poured it over Tench's head. As he stood up to attack her, the bartender came over carrying a piece of lead pipe wrapped in electrical tape. He told Tench to behave, pay his bill and leave quietly. The Chicana waitress suggested that he go to Robstown if he wanted to fight. There, the Mexicans loved to fight and they would be more than glad to knock the shit out of him. Upon hearing the suggestion, Ambrose Tench took a step toward the waitress, grabbing a bottle of ketchup from a nearby table. The bartender took a step forward which made Tench stop abruptly and momentarily lose his balance. He quickly stretched himself to his fullest height, which was just a little below the bartender's shoulders.

Tench said, "If there's anything I can't stand, it's uppity Meskins!"

Angrily pointing to the waitress, he fulminated, "I'm going to this Robstown place and every Meskin I see will pay for you, lady. I think I'll go out there and kick ass until I don't see your face anymore."

On his way out of the restaurant, the waitress made a reference to his grandmother. On his return to Schoolland, Ambrose Tench never mentioned anything beyond his encounter with the waitress and how the bartender had not dared to strike him. He was, however, without most of his lower teeth and he had to work steadily for four months to pay the dentist in Gonzales.

Ambrose Tench was a lazy, belligerent, unreliable worker. The landowners and share farmers of Schoolland knew it and would hire him only out of desperation during harvest season when there were not enough hands to go around. He would work for a day or two, draw his pay on some pretext or other, usually an argument or a fistfight, and go on a binge for as long as the money lasted. Hung-over, without having changed his clothing in days, Tench would return to ask his employer for an advance on his pay or for a loan. As no one trusted him, and as most were glad to be rid of him, he would have to look for another job.

Sooner or later, the farmers would regret having sent Ambrose Tench to work in the fields. Tractors would run out of gas in mid field with little or no plowing done. Cultivators would lose their feet. Tench could work, but someone had to watch him constantly. When other workers were in the fields, Ambrose Tench posed a different problem. Most of these workers would be Chicanos and Tench would intimidate them, demanding they do his share of the work or lie for him when he went into adjoining pastures to sleep. The Chicano workers generally ignored Tench. If, however, the worker was elderly or a youngster, Tench would punch and kick at them, causing more than a few to quit and seek work elsewhere. There had been a reluctance on the part of Chicanos to strike an Anglo, even one who needed it as much as Tench. The Anglos did not like the idea of a Mexican striking a white man, despite Ambrose Tench being embarrassing trash to them.

The landowners and farmers soon realized that Tench was not worth the trouble he caused. They could not depend on him to work alone and many Chicano workers would leave when they saw him appear in the fields. It was not long before they refused to hire him at all. When Tench found it impossible to obtain work in Schoolland, he became furious. He convinced himself that everyone, Anglos and Chicanos, were depriving him of work for no good reason. He decided to leave the area, but not before he had had his revenge. Tench set fire to a barn, killing two milk cows. It belonged to a retired Army officer who had only recently bought the farm and whom Tench did not know at all. The place happened to be close by. Next, he toppled a field gasoline tank and tried unsuccessfully to puncture it with an axe he found nearby. Afterward, on his way out of town, with his bindle dangling over his back, Tench was not entirely satisfied with his farewell to the area. On his way through Smiley at dusk, he saw don Miguel Ciarcía, an elderly widower whose custom it was to sit in front of the Red and White Grocery Store each evening. As Tench approached, don Miguel moved over to give him some room on the bench in front of the store. Tench grabbed don Miguel, taking him behind the store, broke what remained of the old man's teeth and cracked two of his ribs with a vicious kick. Satisfied that people would talk about him and not soon forget him, he left the area for more than three years.

The Tench family, until Ambrose became the last surviving member, was well liked and respected in Schoolland. The elder Tench drank a little more than the patrons of *La Tacuachera* thought prudent, but he gave insult to no one, was never a burden to friends, and his excess was a tolerable one. He had owned some watermelon land near Smiley. It was clean, sandy, fertile soil which could have provided a prosperous living for someone willing to work and astute enough for the business aspects of farming. Without anyone taking much notice and because of something no one was ever able to explain, old man Tench drank himself to death before Ambrose reached his twelfth birthday.

A neighboring couple took Ambrose Tench in after his father died. They were childless. The wife saw in him the child she had not been able to bear and the husband saw in Tench an unpaid field hand. The land left to the last Tench, at the petition of the neighbor, was to be held by him as Tench's guardian until Tench was old enough to care for it himself. It was an informal arrangement set up by a magistrate in Nixon.

By the time Ambrose Tench was fifteen years old, the land had been sold without him receiving a penny from the sale. Soon after, the good neighbor ordered him away from his foster home. Ambrose Tench, at fifteen, found himself alone and penniless as a result of two unrelated events. Tench was thin and sickly in appearance, given to preying upon the compassion of his foster mother. He would run to her for protection at the first sign of hard work. He was not producing the kind of work his foster father had envisioned when he agreed to take him in. He felt that he had something coming to him for his generosity and the only asset Tench had was his father's land. The farmer sold it, forging the deceased Tench's signature, and kept the money.

The neighbor was not in the least guilt-ridden over the theft of Tench's land and money. The way he figured it, it took plenty to feed and clothe the boy. Besides that, the boy was so scrawny he couldn't get a decent day's work out of him. It was not that the farmer was reminded of his crime each time he saw Tench and simply wanted to be rid of him who posed as a constant reminder. The neighbor ran Tench off his place for another private, more personal, reason.

The farmer caught Tench behind the outhouse on his hands and knees lifting the trap door. The farmer's wife had gone in there a few minutes before and Tench was looking up at her bare buttocks and other virtuous parts framed by the circular aperture of the toilet bench. The neighbor could not understand the combination of innocent curiosity and inchoate manhood that was rapidly transforming Tench. He was ready to shoot him on the spot and would likely have done so had not his wife come out of the coffin-like structure and intervened.

"Now, now, old man," said she, "he's just a boy."

"Boy, hell!" yelled the outraged old man. "He ain't no boy no more, woman. I saw that bulge on him. I tell you, he's dangerous!"

The old woman, who had submitted to sex with her husband only sparingly over the years and then only from a sense of unavoidable duty during their married life, did not completely understand the reason for her husband's anger. Nor did she completely understand what Tench was doing, exactly, although to her he was still a child and as such she was determined to he tolerant of him.

"Now, paw, don't be too harsh on the boy. He's just curious, that's all. I reckon all boys are like that at his age. It's only natural," she said, her toothless pink gums showing under her thin lips as she spoke.

"I'll just bet he's curious," the old man roared. "Get in the house, woman!"

"You watch yourself, old man. And watch that no harm comes to that boy," she said as she started up the path back to the house.

"Get in the god-damned house, I said!" He pointed to the house with an outstretched arm.

The old man turned to Ambrose Tench who cowered behind the outhouse, terrified of the beating he expected. The old man swung his arm toward the road in front of the house.

"Get off my place. Right now," he said. "And when you get down the road, way off where I can't see you, get on your knees and thank God I didn't shoot you like I should have."

Tench began to run along the ochre-colored gravel road as fast as he could, not bothering to stop to say the prayer his ex-benefactor had suggested. As abruptly as that, Ambrose Tench left his days of carefree, horny youth behind him and entered into a precarious manhood.

When he got to the paved farm-to-market road, he stopped to rest at the cattle pens belonging to the man who had bought his land. He perched himself on the loading end of the chute and started to think about his situation. He had no idea of how to find work. He would have to work, but the thought of it was not pleasing to him. He decided that work and how to support himself was something for another day, something that would probably just happen. Of more immediate concern was where to spend the night. It was already late afternoon. He could not tell how long he had been perched on the chute. As the afternoon turned to gold and the sting of the sun's heat left the air, Lou Horner stopped to ask him if he wanted a ride. Ambrose Tench was nearly in tears from desperation. He told Horner his sad story, wiping his dripping nose as he blurted out the words. Horner spared no affection for the old man because of a horse trade years earlier. He told Tench he could stay with him until he found what he wanted to do.

Lou Horner allowed Tench a few days to get settled. Mrs. Horner remembered Tench's mother as a kind woman and she took pity on his condition. Each night she would place a pallet on the floor of her son's room for Tench to sleep on. After about a week, sleeping late, saying nothing to the Horners about work or leaving, their son ran crying to them. He said Tench would take all of his clothes off at night, crawl into bed with him and demanded that he do dirty things. He also told them Tench had threatened to kill him if he did not or if he ever told anyone about it. Lou Horner was not a man to become upset or excited to a point where anybody noticed. He had come in for his mid-morning coffee when his son came to him. Tench was still asleep. He went into the bedroom to nudge him awake with his boot. Tench was annoyed to he awakened so early, but he went along with Horner and got into the truck. Horner drove him to the cattle pens where he'd found him and left him there. He told Tench not to come around his place anymore.

At the cattle pens, Tench considered what to do next. To his left, the road snaked along to Gonzales to which he had seldom been and which seemed like a foreign country to him. To the right, the road went to Smiley, about five miles distant. If he wanted work, he would have to go to the cafe or the gas station and make it known he was looking for work. Behind him, the gravel road went through Schoolland and ended in Nixon, some ten miles away. He was too frightened to risk walking toward Nixon which meant going past his ex-benefactor's place. After an hour of sitting with his feet dangling from the cattle chute, he jumped off and began walking toward Smiley. From there he would find a ride to Nixon. Nixon was larger and he felt he would more likely find something there.

He had to walk the five miles to Smiley because only one car passed by. It was full of Chicanos and as they passed they indicated they had no room for him. He cursed them, thinking one of them should have gotten out and waited where he stood while they drove him to town. Tench was raised in an atmosphere where Mexicans and Anglos did not mix very much, where the superiority of the Anglo is assumed if only because he owns the land and distributes the jobs. Tench's father had been particularly bitter about Chicanos and Tench inherited his attitude, focussing some of his own bitterness upon them. The lines between Chicanos and Anglos were clearly if subtlely drawn, but Tench was not content to leave well enough alone.

He reached Nixon that evening, realizing he had not eaten all day. He went into the drive-in, ordered two hamburgers with cheese, french fries and two cokes. After he finished, he told the waitress he did not have money to pay. She told the manager who came out to see him. He recognized him and told him to bring in the money some time. Tench thanked him, not quite understanding the reason. He found a shed behind the movie house and slept for the night. When he went back to the drive-in for breakfast, the owner came over to him and asked him for the money from the night before. Tench blurted out his story. The manager told him he could not afford to feed him. Out of respect for his father, he told Tench to forget what he owed from the night before. He advised that the best thing for him to do would be to go to the packing house and ask for a job. In a soft voice, Tench thanked the man for his kindness and began cursing him as soon as he was outside the drive-in. Before crossing the street, he picked up a rock and debated whether to toss it through the window.

At the packing house, they put him to work right away, moving barrels of chicken guts to a loading platform. It was wet, slippery, smelly work that permeated a man's clothes and was nearly impossible to scrub away. Tench lasted about two hours suppressing a constant urge to puke before leaving without bothering to ask for his pay. For several days after that, he did yardwork in exchange for food. He continued to sleep in the shed behind the movie house until the city marshal discovered him and suggested he find another place to sleep. He found an abandoned house whose owner never appeared. With his yardwork and the abandoned house which he considered a permanent place to live, Ambrose Tench was settled.

On Saturday, Tench waited at the IGA Grocery parking lot for his former foster parents to come into town. He wanted to speak to the old woman alone. She went into the store alone while her husband walked toward the Pool Parlor to play dominoes and talk. When she came out of the store, her arms full with a box of groceries, Tench ran up to her and fell in step, not offering to help with the box.

He said, "Ma'am, I got to talk to you."

She shook her head in a sad and confused way. She had expected he would approach her before this, and so did her husband. Her motherly feelings had been weighed against her wifely duty. Tench came out the loser.

"Ambrose," she said, "I'm sorry. I promised the mister. You can't come back. There's no more to discuss on the matter. It's already settled."

"That ain't exactly what I want, ma'am," said Tench.

"What is it you want, then? I thought . . ."

"It's my clothes, ma'am. These is all I got and I been wearing them for a long time. I can't take a bath without clean clothes."

The farmer's wife, a little relieved, said, "I see. Of course, you're right. But, you know the mister don't want you near the place. Besides, if he knew, he wouldn't want to give them to you. Out of meanness. He's still mighty upset. I'll see what I can do, though."

"Thanks, ma'am, I appreciate that."

"Yes, dear. Now, let's see. How to get them to you. I have it. My cousin Maude is coming to visit me tomorrow. I'll give them to her and you go to her house and get them."

"Yes, ma'am," said Tench and he took off running. The woman put the groceries on the truck bed and sat inside to wait while the old man finished playing dominoes.

Tench became known in Nixon and at first was offered plenty of work. He went through a succession of jobs, lasting at none for more than a few weeks. He began to develop a hatred of people, Mexicans in particular, reasoning that their intolerance of him was some fault of theirs and had nothing to do with him. After a year or more of living in the abandoned house he came to believe that there were too many people in Nixon. He found an old, abandoned shack with a good water well a mile or so off the road between Nixon and Smiley. There, he lived alone, found it to his liking, went in either direction to find work to supply his simple needs. He liked doing chores when he had to, working long enough to just get by, and he enjoyed not having anyone telling him what to do.

An old mongrel dog appeared on his porch one day. Someone had obviously driven him out of the city and left him. Tench tossed the remains of his supper at the dog. The next day, the dog was asleep on the porch, curled up as if he belonged there. Tench promptly named him "Bastard" and cut off one of his ears to show him who the master was. The dog remained faithful to Tench, silently suffering Tench's abuse, coming to know instinctively when Tench was in an evil mood and to stay away from him until it passed.

When Bastard stayed away longer than usual, Tench went looking for him. He walked to the nearest pasture where the dog went hunting for rabbits and armadilloes. He kept calling the dog's name. Tench feared the dog might have been bitten by a snake. He spent half the day walking the pasture, looking in every clump of cactus, finding no sign of him. He went to Nixon and walked every street in the city fiendishly planning to murder the person who would steal his dog.

When someone complained of Tench's quest, the marshal found him and asked what the hell he thought he was doing.

"I'm looking for my god-damned dog, is what I'm doing," Tench said defiantly.

"Well, you're making folks nervous. What's your dog look like, anyway?"

"Kind of sandy-colored. Missing one ear."

"Uh, that one," the marshal said, shaking his head.

"You do something to my dog?" Tench was beginning to let his fury loose.

"Had to, son. That damned animal was foaming at the mouth, shying away from water. Pretty sure it was rabies. Won't know till I get some tests back from San Antonio."

"Where's my god-damned dog?"

"Well, I shot him first off. Then, the Doc said he oughta be burned. Deputy Jeff and me did it last night. I'm real sorry, son. Probably caught it from a skunk somewhere."

Tench fell straight back on his buttocks, landing in an erect, sitting position on the paved street. He cried in an almost animal howl, beating on the pavement until his knuckles bled. The marshal placed his hands under Tench's arms and said, "Come on, son, I'll take you home." He was completely limp as the marshall picked him up, but he stayed on his feet when the marshall let go of him.

As the marshal led him to the waiting patrol car, Tench said, "Marshal?"

"What is it, son," said the marshal softly.

"Marshal, if you ever tell anyone I cried over that god-damned dog, I'll shoot your pecker off!"

The marshal never told anyone that Tench cried over his dead dog. Had he done so, no one would have believed it. In Nixon and Smiley, when people heard that the rabid dog belonged to Tench, some said he probably caught it after Tench bit him.

He saved enough money to buy a .22 caliber rifle at the Western Auto. He hunted rabbits when it rained too much and there was no work or, as time went on, when no one would hire him. Somehow, he managed to talk a used car dealer in Seguin into selling him a dilapidated pick-up truck on credit. He calculated he had to work twice as much to keep up the payments on it. He made two payments, driving all the way to Seguin to surrender the money in person, drove it for four months before two burly men found his shack, took the keys from him and repossessed it.

It was natural for Tench to start drinking, as if that too was part of his family inheritance. He began by going to *La Tacuachera,* standing in the rear driveway, near the urinals, waiting for the first person out to buy him a six-pack. More than a few were glad to oblige him on account of his father who had been a good friend at *La Tacuachera.* Tench was not like the other teenagers who had cars and drank beer on the way to dances and parties. Tench had no friends his own age.

When the six-pack was delivered to him, he would cross the barbed-wire fence into the pasture and drink all six hurriedly and alone. Afterward, he would weave and wobble along the road to Nixon until someone recognized him and took him home.

The news soon circulated that Tench was a mean drunk. In the few months he had his truck, he would drive slowly from the tavern to Nixon, sometimes stopping at the roadside rest area. By the time he reached the city limits, he would have finished all six beers. He would park his truck on the street in front of the movie theatre, not careful about denting someone's bumper. He stumbled up and down the sidewalks shouting obscenities at the after-movie strollers spending their last moments in town before going home. Tench often tried to goad a startled lover into a fight.

The fathers of the teenagers whom he threatened and intimidated were the ones who bought the beer for him. When they realized this, they stopped doing so. Tench tried to threaten the Chicanos into buying him beer, but the bartender made it clear that anyone buying Tench beer would no longer be welcomed at *La Tacuachera*.

It was customary for *La Tacuachera* to recognize the approaching manhood of certain sons of Anglo patrons by allowing them to buy their own beer before they were of legal age, provided they looked old enough and a parent was always present. Some could start drinking as early as eighteen, three years before their majority. No one would vouch for Tench and the courtesy was not extended to him, in spite of the fact that Tench looked a good ten years older than he was.

During the course of an odd conversation, someone mentioned that Tench had not been seen prowling around the back door of the tavern for some time. A quick survey among the drinkers present revealed that he had not been seen around Schoolland, Smiley nor Nixon. For the following three years, no one heard from or about Ambrose Tench. Some assumed he had gone to San Antonio or Houston and good riddance. Others, for personal reasons, hoped some generous soul had performed a service to the world by killing him. Still others thought the Army might have taken him. A veteran of the First World War dispelled that notion by averring that he would be drafted before the Army was desperate enough to take Tench.

On his twenty-first birthday, Ambrose Tench walked into *La Tacuachera*. He was dressed in a blue-gingham cowboy shirt with diamond-shaped mother-of-pearl buttons, a clean, starched, creased pair of new Levi's and brightly shined boots which squeaked when he walked. He wore a new, grey Stetson, the most expensive of the line, but which was cheapened because he tried to block it himself. He had also contributed a gaudy red silk hatband. He would have presented a neat appearance had he bathed at any time in the preceding few weeks. There was dirt under his raggedly cut fingernails and a black grease spot on his wrist.

Moses Jackson, eyeing him from head to toe, was the first to notice the jingling spurs with rowels two inches in diameter. Moses was about to ask Tench what the hell he was wearing spurs for when Tench noticed him staring and snarled.

"I'll knock your fucking head off!"

The still fresh bright red scar trailed down his ear to be swallowed by the dark blue bandana around his neck. It would be weeks before anyone saw the entire length of it and would see the curious hook it made over his Adam's apple. Remembering how he had been before his disappearance and the recent remark to Moses Jackson, no one was curious enough to ask about the scar.

Tench moved from the door, swaggering further into the tavern, turning left to the bar. He laid a twenty dollar bill on the bar, in a round puddle of water left by a beer bottle. He unsnapped the button of his breastpocket, took out his draft card and tossed it at Jake, the bartender. It flew past Jake and landed on the floor. Jake squatted to pick it up, did not bother to examine it, placed it on the bar for Tench to retrieve.

"What's your name, fella? You're new here," Tench said.

"Jake."

Tench raised a corner of his mouth in a twisted smile. He swivelled his head to look to both sides of the bar.

"This son-of-a-bitch you're looking at, Jake, is twenty-one. I can drink here now. I don't want any shit from you . . . ever."

"Law says I can serve you so long as you don't cause any trouble."

"That's right, Jake. I cause the trouble, get me? Give me a Lone Star and set up beers for everyone except the Meskins. I've come back home and I may stay. Don't know yet."

That was at six o'clock and by ten o'clock he had passed out once and had had his nose broken for the third time in his brief life. It was broken by a husky young husband, who spoke with a Polish accent, and who would not stand for Tench coming over to his table, grabbing his wife's buttocks and saying, "You're cute enough to fuck. How'd you like to have a real man?" The husband did not invite Tench outside as was customary. He simply half-stood from his chair and shot his fist across the table, landing it flat on Tench's beak nose. The blow knocked Tench out.

Tench lay on the polished cement floor for a long interval, preventing anyone from dancing. One of the wives became nauseous listening to the gurgling sounds issuing from Tench's nose and from looking at the bloodsoaked shirt. There was a pool of blood welling under his head, matting his hair. Except for the blood and the strange rattling of his nose, Tench looked peaceful, serene and restful.

Moses Jackson called the bartender and asked him to find one of Tench's friends to take care of him. There followed a debate as to whether Tench was seriously hurt and might need a doctor.

Jake scratched his head. "Ain't you folks his friends? I ain't never seen him before."

Receiving no reply, he asked again, bewildered. "None of you?" Again, silence. The men turned their backs or shifted positions in their chairs. Jake shook his head, placing his hands on his hips. "Well, it don't seem to me that none of the Mexicans is any friend to him. Not the way he spoke about them earlier."

Moses Jackson became impatient with the bartender. "Jake, just ask one of the Mexicans going home to take him to the doctor. My wife is gonna puke right here and now if you don't move him."

"I'll try," Jake said. "Can't promise nothing." He started for the Chicano area of the tavern. Before he got too far, Lou Horner, who had just come in to see Tench lying on the floor, called him back.

"Oh, Jake," Lou Horner said, "Can't you take him with you, drag him out somewhere, away from the ladies."

"He might die right in front of us. That would be awful!" Mrs. Horner said.

Mrs. Jackson sneered. "That might be the best thing for him."

The bartender dragged Tench, lifting him by the arms, away from the dance floor. He left him leaning against a stack of empties. Jake then hurried behind the bar for a wet mop to clean the blood from the floor. That done, with the mop still in hand, he walked to the Chicano area of the bar.

"Any of you boys going home want to take that man over there to the doctor?" he said.

No one responded.

"How 'bout you, Chencho? You oughta be ready to go home."

"Uh-uh! When that man wakes up, I think he's going to think the first man he sees killed him. He's going to want to kill me. I'm not that crazy, yet." Chencho laughed and the others at the table joined him.

Don Florencio Ramírez, who came *by La Tacuachera* each Friday and Saturday, drank just three beers and went home, stood up. He had been sitting at an adjacent table. As he stood he hitched up his trousers and adjusted his Stetson.

"I will take him home," he said, "if some of you will put him in my car."

Jake took a wet bar rag and wrapped it around Tench's head so as not to soil Don Florencio's car. Tench was breathing easier, though heavy with drunkenness. Jake beckoned a couple of Chicanos to help him carry Tench outside to the car. When nearing Nixon, Don Florencio tried to wake Tench to ask him where he was staying. Not being able to do so, he remembered where Tench had been living before his disappearance, took him there, deposited him on the porch and went home. Thus ended Tench's twenty-first birthday celebration.

From that time, Tench remained around the area, never leaving for very long. He bragged that he couldn't stand living out in the country by himself, saying that he had gotten used to city ways. He rented a two-room house sitting on a large lot separating the Black and Brown sections of Nixon. None of the Anglo property owners would rent to him in the white sections. He worked where he could, sometimes going away for a few weeks or months on a job. He was a more dependable worker, not as lazy as before, but eventually he would end up wanting to fight someone on the job.

He bought a used car just so he could go drinking every night. It was clear to him that he was not welcomed at *La Tacuachera* and he saved all of his bitterness and resentment until Friday or Saturday night. During the week, he would drive by, slowing on the curve, and continue on to Gillette, Yorktown, Kenedy or Karnes City. He drank as usual, becoming drunk very quickly, but he kept quiet there since he knew he was a stranger in these places and no one would take care of him. On the weekends, he would get drunk, leave a little earlier than usual in order to stop at *La Tacuachera* with the single purpose of fighting someone.

He was drunk enough, mean enough, when he arrived so all he had time to drink would be one beer. Tench soon realized that he was beaten more often than not. He gave up fighting Anglos when he received a dozen beatings in a row. He decided the Chicanos were smaller and thus he might improve his chances. The Chicanos who accepted his challenges also beat him. Tench was confused that the Anglos would allow the Mexicans to beat him. He felt that whatever else, Anglos ought to stick together.

When Milly Jones lost her husband in a tractor accident, Tench, who was not a friend of the family, having only known them by sight, attended the funeral. The service over, the casket lowered into the ground, the mourners began filing along the red clay path to where they parked their cars and trucks. Tench stood at some distance away, across the knee-high fence dividing the cemetery between the Anglos and Chicanos. He waited for the widow to leave.

As she was led along the path, leaning on her brother's shoulder with her mother's arm around her waist, Tench, with an obvious hangover and unshaven, walked up to Milly Jones and requested a few words with her. The two women and the man stopped, in their grief unable to anticipate what Tench could want.

"Miz Jones," he stammered, "I know you just lost your husband and everything. I don't expect an answer right away. I really don't. Anyway, what I'm trying to say, I would be glad to drop by your place, uh, if it's ok, tonight, to talk about it."

"Talk about what? Who are you?" Milly Jones asked.

"Ambrose Tench, ma'am. I thought you might know about me."

"No, Mr. Tench. I don't know about you."

Tench curled a corner of his mouth upward in a fiendish smile. "I'm a changed man, ma'am. Anybody will tell you that. And you just lost your man."

The brother tightened his grip on her and said, "I appreciate you trying to comfort my sister, Mr. Tench, but it won't be necessary to come by the house. We accept you sympathies, but it'll just be family at the house tonight."

Tench continued staring at Milly Jones, his head twisted at a nervous angle. "That ain't what I had in mind, ma'am. I mean, I didn't know the deceased except to say hello. I might be sorry for you, but he weren't nothing to me."

"I don't understand what you're trying to get at," she said, confused amidst her bereavement.

"Hell, it ain't that hard to figure out. Shit. Shoot, I'm talking about marrying, ma'am. I had my eye on you for a long time, but you always seemed to be doing all right by the deceased you all just dumped in that hole yonder. He ain't gonna do you no good lying in that hole, I can guarantee you that. Now, I know a sweet young thing like yourself cain't go without it for very long."

Milly Jones' mouth opened, anger colored her cheeks. Tench had prepared his speech, rehearsed it several times, now he was afraid to stop.

"I mean, I seen you walk and shake that behind of yours. Ass like that cain't do without no action for long, shit, I know that. I understand that. Now, I'm kinda known as a real stud. Not around here, of course, not much doing around here. In Houston, that's where, in Houston. They know me as a stud there. Ask anybody in Houston, they'll tell you."

"My lord!" said Milly's mother.

"You're sick!" hissed Milly Jones. She turned to her brother and said, "John, take me home, quickly, please."

The three walked down the path rapidly, almost running. John Jones, when they reached his car, stopped and looked into his sister's face. His anger caused his cheeks to twitch. He turned and started back to where Tench stood, taking long, slow strides.

"She change her mind?" Tench asked.

Through clenched teeth, John Jones said, "If you come near my sister again, I will kill you. You're crazy, an animal!"

He turned away without waiting for a response from Tench. Tench remained where he was, scratching his head. His anger began to rise. Tench ran toward the car just as it went out of the cemetery gate and onto the highway. He punched at a fencepost and said out loud to no one, "God damn it! It ain't like I asked her to shack up. I'da married her. What's the fucking problem?"

He ran to his car which he had not driven into the cemetery, preferring to park it on the shoulder of the highway. He wheeled it around, making his tires screech. He drove straight to Gillette, to a little tavern standing at the crossroads, yelling for a beer as soon as he walked in the door.

At that moment, Chango was driving out of San Antonio on Rigsby Avenue, past Loop 13, where it turns into Highway 87 heading toward Nixon.

■ ■ ■

III

Highway 87 southeast from San Antonio was a ribbon of blacktop, more grey than black, stretching unhurriedly along gentle risings of the terrain which seemed to have begun as hills but were somehow abandoned to become farms and ranches on either side of the road. What remained was a pleasant rising and falling ride flanked on either side by what appeared to be a continuous fence.

Chango left San Antonio early Friday afternoon. He had not been to Nixon for nearly two weeks and at the beginning of the week he faced an urgent assignment which might have to be taken care of that weekend. He waited patiently without receiving further word. When his deadline passed without a commitment on Friday morning, he packed a bag in the event he decided to stay for a few days, had his car serviced, and left after lunch.

Chango drove past the last houses on the edges of San Antonio, driving at a leisurely pace with the windows of his car opened, the wind swirling inside the car twisting his carefully groomed hair in all directions. He was tense and cautious driving the streets of the city. As soon as he saw open country, he leaned back, comfortable and secure, feeling a fresh resurgence of energy was the landscape turned into a quilt of dark brown, green, amber patches. He would smell the clean freshly-turned earth of the farmlands, he could almost taste the sweetness of the green unmowed hay. The air he drew into his lungs was different from that of the city which reeked of exhaust fumes and factory smoke, thick with quarrels and discontent, limp with uncertainties and futures that were only words. The air he now breathed, relaxed and unhurried, was an air of permanence, laden with history and regeneration. It was the air of his boyhood.

The boy hung upside down on the chinaberry tree, his thin legs bent over a branch close to the ground. His arms dangled, lifeless, in imitation of the Christian martyrs in a movie his parents had taken him to see.

The boy did not have brothers or sisters. The nearest neighbors with children his age were too far away to visit by himself. There were plenty of visits by his aunts and uncles who had children his age. By far, though, he preferred to be by himself. In his solitary existence he could invent worlds to entertain himself. He devised all sorts of games, dreaming up as many players as he needed. He planned elaborate excursions into the pasture behind his house, imagining himself at the head of vast armies or leading a safari into the wild and dangerous jungle where he had to shoot lions and tigers, elephants and snakes. When he did see a snake in the pasture, he would follow it for a distance to see it disappear into a gopher hole. He would not tell anyone about it and would return day after day to wait for it to come out again. They never did. He wondered if he had ever seen the same snake twice.

His mother called to him from the back porch as she dried her hands with her apron. It was time to walk the half-mile of dirt road to the paved highway where the yellow school bus stopped for him. He wiggled his legs. They began to slip from the tree, slowly, until they cleared the branch. He landed on his palms in a perfect handstand. With a slight push, his feet dropped to the ground. He jumped up as high as he could and landed straight and tall for his age. He combed his hair with the black pocket comb his cousin Andrés had given him. He inspected himself to see he had not soiled his clothes. His mother was easily upset if he dirtied his clothes before going to school. He never could get her to understand that desert pirates, waving funnylooking swords, had captured him on the hot wind-blown sands. He was lucky to get away in time for school.

The boy picked up a pebble and pitched it at the ancient chicken that somehow managed to escape the dinner table. He did not hit the chicken, nor did he mean to, but she squawked anyway, scurrying under the house.

Inside the house, his mother was not in the kitchen. He looked for her in the adjacent room. When he did not see her, he hurried to the table to drink the remainder of her coffee. His lunch was on a plate on the table, wrapped in a brown paper sack. He found his lunch pail with the color drawing of Roy Rogers and Trigger on top and on the sides. He dropped his tortilla and bean tacos inside it.

After he finished the coffee, he took the cup to the sink and rinsed it. As he did so, he looked at himself in the small mirror on the counter behind the sink. His coloring, which he took from his father, was dark brown, as dark as the soil they farmed. The boy noticed the recalcitrant cowlick sticking in the air behind his head. He wet his hands at the sink tap, plastered it down, but the impertinent tuft of hair refused to stay matted. His cousins made fun of him because of it. When his father took him to Tomás Aguilar for a haircut, he would tell him to cut it all off, to just leave a bald spot. All the men in the barbershop would laugh and he would perspire from embarrassment. He gave up on the cowlick and began to look for the leather book satchel his father had bought for him in Mexico. Upon finding it, he went into the next room which opened on to the front porch. His mother called to him from the bedroom.

"¿Hijo? ¿Dónde estás?" she said.

"Aquí, mamá. Ya me voy. Ahí viene el bos," he said.

"Espera. Tengo algo que decirte."

The boy remained by the screen door, his small fist on the doorknob, turning it to both sides. After waiting a few moments, he grew impatient, afraid he might miss the school bus. He opened the door, craning his head to look for a sign of the bus. Not seeing anything, he closed the door.

"Mamá, ahí viene el bos," he said in a sing-song voice.

"Sí, sí. Ahí voy. Espera."

The boy's mother came running into the room. She was as tall as his father, lighter-skinned than he, with long black hair which she braided every morning before doing anything else. When he was younger, she would let him brush her hair, which came down to her waist. As she came into the room, she wore a half-slip and brassiere. Her face was powdered and rouged, but she had not yet applied the red lipstick she used and which his father disapproved of. She smelled of strong eau de toilette. She had unrolled the braids of her hair and one of them slid across her breast like a long black snake.

It was rare for him to see his mother in underclothing. At twelve, he was old enough to be embarrassed. He averted his eyes, stared at his feet.

"Tu papá y yo tenemos que ir para San Antonio," she said. She told him his uncle Samuel was sick and that it would be after dark when they returned.

"Pon atención, niño," she said in a stern voice, "quiero que te vayas a quedar con tu tía Chona cuando salgas de la escuela. Le dices que dije yo que te cuide hasta que vengamos por ti."

The boy turned away from his mother, trying to hide the lump in his throat which made him want to cry. He hated his aunt Chona, hated to be in her house. He felt old enough to take care of himself.

"Yo no necesito a nadie que me cuide," he said sullenly.

"No le hace. Haz lo que te digo, ¿oíste?"

"Sí, mamá."

"Bueno. No se te vaya a olvidar, ¿oíste? Andale, antes de que se te pase el bos."

The boy ran out of the house with his head down, the pent-up tears flowing freely down his cheeks. He dreaded visiting his tía Chona. His father's brother had deserted her, going away to work in the oilfields on the Gulf. After less than a year, he had been killed in an accident and brought home to Wrightsboro for burial in the family plot. His father had felt responsible for his sister-in-law, the grass widow, even before his brother was killed. Afterward, as a true widow in the family, all of his relatives contributed to her welfare. She was old, bitchy, and she smelled. Her whole house smelled of cats and chicken shit as she seldom wiped her feet after feeding the chickens in back. He had stayed with her before and when she fed him, the food was never enough and was seldom fully cooked. She would serve him, almost throwing the plate at him, complaining about how much food cost and how little her relatives, meaning his father, gave her. He begged to stay with one of his school friends, like Frank or Adán, but his father told him it was something only for family.

He wiped his face and started skipping down the road to the highway, swinging his lunch pail in one hand and his book satchel in the other. He saw his father astride the tractor, working a few hours before leaving for San Antonio. The boy yelled at him. The father was furrowing parallel to the highway, going away from the boy. He waved to his father's back, hoping he might turn around and see him. He stopped by the mailbox on the gravel shoulder of the road. When the school bus arrived, he boarded it, but did not join in the yelling and laughing of the other kids. He felt sad.

The La Vernia crossroads were just in front of him, indicating he was halfway to Nixon. The white gravel of the easement hurt his eyes as the sun's reflection hit him. He squinted and slowed the car to negotiate the curve. As quickly as he approached it, he was out of the La Vernia city limit. Two miles away, he crossed the bridge which made him feel he was on home territory.

"Voy a jugar con Mateo, tía." said the boy.

No, señor. Se me queda aquí. Tu mamá dijo que te cuidara y aquí te quedas en esta casa."

The boy sat stiffly in a straight-back chair by the window, gazing at the world outside. Warm sunlight, filtered through encrusted dirt on the windowpanes, bathed his face. His aunt sat in a stuffed chair in the dimness of a far corner. He swung his right leg without hitting the chair. He did not want to give her an excuse to scold him. He was suffocating from the stuffiness of the room, the smell of the cats, all of which were in the room, curled about like fur cushions. He could smell his aunt across the room. He stood to go to the room in which he would sleep. His aunt stopped him.

"No sabe usted pedir permiso."

"¿Puedo ir al otro cuarto?"

"No. Vaya a darles de comer a los pollos."

"Ya voy," he said.

He went out the front door, around the side of the house, to the back yard. He was grateful for the fresh air. Even the stench of the chickens and the chickencoop was better than inside the house. He tried to vomit, but could not. He dreaded supper. Whatever it was, he would have to eat all of it. Luckily, she did not serve him much.

"Chango," a voice called from the unpaved street in a mournful singsong stretching his name to four syllables.

Chango ran to the front yard to meet Mateo. His aunt saw him through the screen door and came out to the porch. Her voice clucked at him.

"¿A dónde vas, huerco travieso?" she demanded.

"Aquí nomás voy a jugar con Mateo."

"¿Y quién es ese Mateo?"

"Mi amigo de la escuela."

"Yo no sé nada de familias que dejan a sus hijos andar sueltos de callejeros."

"Yo no soy callejero, oiga," said Mateo.

"Y malcriado también," she said. "Tú te me quedas en la yarda." With that, she returned inside the house.

"¿Qué pasó, Mateo?"

"Nada, Chango."

They sat on the grass, neither of them speaking. Chango hugged his knees, squinting at a sunflower facing him, bent over, springing from the ditch on the other side of the street.

"Vamos ir a campear tacuache a la noche. Yo y mi primo Julián. Vamos a ir con mi tío Lupe."

"Nomás vas ir a guachar. No te dejan tirar."

"Sí, de veras, me dijo apá que me podía llevar su carabina."

"No te creo, cabrón."

"Sí, a la brava. ¿Por qué no vas con nosotros?"

"Mi tía es muy pinche. No me deja ir. Comoquiera, vienen mis jefes más noche y tengo que estar aquí."

"Pos, mi tío te puede llevar pa' tu casa, tú sabes."

"No le hace. No me deja ir la vieja apestosa."

"Bueno. Entonces vale más irme. Mi tío viene después de la cena. Ahí te miro mañana."

"Andale. Ahí te miro."

Mateo went off, hopping and skipping along the gravel street. Chango finished feeding the chickens and came back to sit on the porch. He did not want to go inside the smelly house. His aunt came to the rusty screen door. She was angry.

"¿Acabaste lo que te mandé? ¿Qué te tardó tanto?"

"Pos, 'taba platicando con Mateo, tía."

"Mira, muchachito, vale más que te portes bien, porque si no, le digo todo a tu mamá que no me hiciste caso."

His aunt's house was on the edge of Smiley. In the distance, he could see the towering grain elevators beside the railroad track. He went inside a room piled with useless furniture, boxes and rags which were once clothes. There was a mattress on the floor with large holes in it from which sprang tufts of coarse cotton. He figured the rats must have chewed on it. There was a small window, partially blocked by some boxes. He started to sit on it, but it would not support him. Instead, he leaned against the wall, staring out into the horizon beyond the trees as the sun set in a bright orange-red ball casting a copper-gold glow over Smiley. Its final streaks were thick and heavy, disappearing in the darkness of the room, turning the blunt objects it contained into distorted, menacing shapes. And then it was night.

There was nothing to do, no one to talk to. The boy remained by the window. He could see a blue-greenish glow over Smiley now coming from the street lamps on the highway running through town. He was hungry but the thought of eating his aunt's cooking made him nauseous. He went into the front room to find her asleep in the stuffed chair. He knew from before that she would sleep there until morning. She had forgotten about supper. Luckily, his parents would take him home before morning. Hungry, and with a longing for something he could not explain, he went back to his room. He settled into the mattress without covers, nudged himself a comfortable valley, pretended he lay on a hammock outside a great house carved from the South American jungle, and fell asleep.

He startled awake, as if from a bad dream. It was chilly and musty in the room. His body inside his clothes was wet with perspiration. He was cold, trembling, his teeth chattered. He thought of getting up to get some of the rags he had seen earlier to use for covers. He thought there might he spiders tangled up in them and did not move from the mattress. As he became fully awake, he trembled more and became colder. The room felt hot in spite of his cold body.

He heard hushed voices somewhere in the house, not voices heard far away in the twilight of sleep, but hushed, purposely low voices. It was pitch dark where he lay and he was frightened. It was only he and his aunt asleep in the front room who inhabited the house. He started to call out to his mother, but he stifled the sound in his throat. Telling himself he was not a little boy anymore, he sat up on the mattress, cradling his head in his hands. He stood up and walked to the door. He opened it, the creaking of it alerting the voices in the other room. They stopped their hushed, whispered conversation to look at him.

The boy entered the light of his aunt's dim living room, his eyes having little difficulty adjusting quickly to the soft light. His aunt sat in the straight-back chair, on the edge of it, her face expressionless, blank, except for the redness of her eyes. She stared at the boy. Neither she nor the two men in the room said anything. All of them just looked at him. He had never seen the two men before. One of them stood a little behind her, with his hand on her shoulder, the other stood by the door, facing him at an angle. He remembered the disarray of his clothes from sleep. He smoothed his hair with both of his hands and then started to tuck in his shirt.

"Ven pa'cá, niño," his aunt said in a tender, soothing voice, unlike anything he had heard from her before.

"¿Qué pasa, tía?" he said, almost in a whimper. "¿Qué pasa?"

"Este es el señor Adames, y éste . . ." She could not finish the introduction. She lowered her head as the silent tears flowed from her eyes.

"Yo soy Pedro Zamora, aquí vivo cerquitas." He lowered his gaze to the floor when he finished speaking.

"Sí, señor."

"Mira, hijo, ven pa' cá," said Jaime Adames.

Pedro Zamora, seeing that the boy was reluctant to come forward, took a few steps from the door toward him. He touched his hand to the boy's cheek. He leaned over until his face was at the same level as the boy's, only inches away. The boy could smell the whiskey on his breath as he started to speak.

"Tu papá y tu mamá tuvieron un accidente."

The boy was too dazed to understand immediately.

"¿Dónde está mi mamá?" he cried. "Llévenme a verla."

"Ya traen a los dos, hijito," said Pedro Zamora.

"Entonces, no están muy malos, ¿verdad?"

From behind the two men, his aunt spoke in a firm, thought forced voice, pushing back the sobbing that was threatening to erupt.

"Niñito, tus padres duermen con Dios en el cielo."

"Bendito sea Dios," said Jaime Adames.

"Are they dead?" the boy asked in unaccustomed English.

The two men turned their faces away from him, tears welling up in their eyes. The boy was the only one not crying. His aunt resumed her crying, drawing in deep, labored breaths, giving full vent to the grief she had suppressed.

Sutherland Springs, with its one gas station and four houses, was to his right as he went over the horizon. He recalled being stranded there with his cousin, José, when a radiator hose broke. The sulphurous water they drank had reminded him of Smiley. He took the curve easily without having to slow down.

The boy remained with his aunt after the burial of his parents. He continued in school, steadily became accustomed to the smells of his aunt's house. He volunteered to do more and more of the cooking, which was fine with her. One of his uncles brought him his bed and his aunt did her best to fix up the room for him. Freed from the terror of having to stay with her for a day or two, facing the reality that she was now his guardian, she was not as fearsome, nor as bitchy. She became kinder to him, perhaps because he was an orphan or perhaps because she was not as lonely any longer. In any case, he came to respect her and to love her. They shared household duties, although more often than not, he had her share to do as well, but he did not mind. For his part, he was conscientious about what he had to do and for her part she accepted his willingness to be helpful and left him to himself as much as he wanted.

As he now lived in Smiley, he saw more of Mateo, grew very close to his family, especially Mateo's sister, Susana. He was fourteen when he discovered that he was very much in love with her. She was sixteen. At first, she had treated him and Mateo as children, telling them stories from the books she read in high school. Then, when he was not so eager to go off hunting or fishing with Mateo, preferring instead to remain in the coolness of the living room with her, listening to her talk, or just simply looking at her without saying anything, Susana realized he was in love with her. She would look at him and smile.

During the dog-days of August, when it was so hot everyone seemed to move through the harvest season with slow, lethargic steps, the boy went to visit Mateo to plan for the school opening the next week. He was always welcomed in their house and would just walk in without knocking.

The boy entered the house and called for Mateo. From the kitchen Mateo's mother responded.

"No está. Se fue con papá. Pero espérate, hijo, para que comas algo. Ya mero está la comida."

"Bueno, gracias, pero no tengo mucha hambre."

"Pero vas a comer comoquiera, ¿verdad?" It was Susana.

"I bet I can eat something," he said.

"It won't be ready for a while. Vamos pa' fuera, al columpio."

"Okay," he said.

Susana took him by the hand, led him into the kitchen and out the back door. Her mother smiled at them as they walked by. The back yard had a canopy made from large oak trees. They watered the lawn frequently. The grass was fresh, green and cool. An old tire hung from a thick oak branch, suspended by a long chain. Susana, bare-footed, wearing shorts and a T-shirt, picked up the tire, letting it drop down her shoulders and waist until she could sit on it. The boy dropped to the ground nearby, lying on his stomach, yanking out a leaf of grass to stick between his teeth. Susana swung to and fro, smiling at him each time she caught him looking at her. He would blush and turn his face to the grass.

"¿Por qué no me dices que me quieres, eh?" she said, matter-of-factly.

"Te quiero." He said so quickly, without thinking, surprising himself.

"Yo no sé si te quiero a ti, pero yo creo que sí te quiero."

"What are we going to do?" he asked.

"After what we've just said, tenemos que casarnos. ¿No crees?"

She slid out from the tire and knelt on the ground in front of him. His chest swelled. He could not bear to look at her, hearing again and again the words she had uttered. His forehead touched her knee.

"Mira," she said.

When he raised his head, she kissed him on the mouth.

"Ya," she said, laughing, "confórmate." She jumped up and went back into the house. At lunch, the both of them continued to look at one another, exchanging gestures, being giddy, communicating their secret to each other. Susana's mother noticed their strange behavior.

"Ustedes dos," she said, shaking her head, "parece que andan asoleados."

Mateo began to suspect that he was losing his friend to his sister. He and Mateo still spent as much time as ever together, but Susana was included in more of the things they did. The two of them held hands when Mateo was not looking. Susana would sneak quick kisses, pecking him on the cheek or the lips, but he could not return them for fear of being caught.

After Christmas, Susana began her last term in high school. They had not spoken of marriage any further. He knew he would marry her as soon as he could quit school. He was in the ninth grade, already having more schooling than most of his cousins. He had been working summers, weekends and after school ever since his parents died to take care of himself and his aunt. It was his aunt that would be the problem. The old woman talked of his mother and her wish that he be the first in her family to finish school and go on to college. As his legal guardian she would not allow him to quit.

He would be turning fifteen, he was in love, he wanted to marry Susana, but he knew he would have to wait. One morning he found an important patch of three whiskers on his chin. He felt himself become a man, but because of school and everything around him, he had to continue accepting treatment as a kid.

Susana did not seem to be as impatient as he. Her family, especially Mateo, was more or less understanding of his intentions, and while not approving of them in so many words, they did not object. That was enough for him.

Chango neared Stockdale. The highway veered to the right, by-passing the business district of the town, a block or two of stores. He remembered when the highway went through town. He also remembered that during watermelon season Stockdale would be the nearest place for lunch and cokes, and that the town bustled with trucks and workers-more people than he had ever seen.

"Susana, let's get married. Right away. We can elope."

"You haven't even finished high school," she said, irritated, cross with him.

"I can quit school."

"Don't be silly. You want to work in the packing house or the fields like everybody else?"

"What's wrong with that?"

"Everything. I want to travel, to see things. All I've seen is San Antonio and there is nothing there. Don't you ever dream of New York and Mexico City and Paris, France?"

"Sure, all the time. We might be able to go there some day."

"If I married you, we could never do anything or go any place. We would have to spend the rest of our lives in Smiley. Forever."

"It doesn't have to be like that, Susana. Look, I graduate in May. Tía wants me to go to college in San Antonio. We can have a big wedding, you can come with me and I'll get a job instead."

"I don't know how to tell you this, but I'm already married."

"I know we are, but I don't want to wait four more years."

"I'm going to marry someone else."

"We're already engaged."

"Not really. I thought I wanted to marry you, but I don't. I want to marry someone else."

"Why are you doing this to me?"

"I'm not doing anything to you. I want to get away, that's all."

"Then, why don't you go to hell," he said.

The following three months were pure torture for him. He could not bear to visit Mateo for fear of running into Susana with her intended, who now visited her regularly. He saw her mother at the Red and White. She started to say something to him, her face full of sympathy. Instead, she said hello to him and continued on without another word. So much of school was filled with Susana's presence, every hallway, every classroom. He could not go watch football practice in the late afternoons because she had often come from home to wait for him on the bleachers. They would sit, holding hands, not paying attention to the field. As he would not visit Mateo at his home, Mateo came by two or three times to see him. He and Susana had gradually excluded Mateo from their relationship and he realized how estranged he had become from him.

He never saw Susana again after the day she told him of her engagement. It was difficult but he managed to graduate from high school. He was listless, inattentive, almost in a constant daze. He thought of her virtually every minute of the day. After graduation, he left for San Antonio. He attended college for two months, found himself unable to concentrate on his courses and quit. He took a job which lasted six months until he found a better one. Then, the years lost their consecutive quality for him. They became mixed together, the events of his life seemed to have occurred in a random order without his being able to distinguish when a certain event happened and when another followed. Everything was outside the channel of time, coming back to him as the occasion suited, more imagined than real.

He was away for more than seven years. He returned only once in the second year for the burial of his aunt. When he arrived in Smiley, don Pedro Zamora had already arranged for the funeral. Afterward, he did not stay to dispose of her belongings and to sell the house. He quietly told don Pedro to keep what he wanted of her things and to give the rest away. Don Pedro seemed offended at the offer but kept it to himself. On the way back to San Antonio, he had stopped in Nixon, made arrangements with Jim Sturtevant, an attorney, to sell the house and lot, which his father had bought for her, and to forward the money to him.

It was odd, he thought, that he felt no grief at all upon his aunt's death. He had grown to care for her, had continued to send her money and made sure she lacked for nothing. Yet, he could not feel anything. The burial, with many of his uncles, aunts and cousins present, had been a dull, tedious experience. As soon as he arrived in Smiley he had been impatient to leave. After the funeral, his uncle Cipriano asked him to come to his house for the dinner which is almost a ritual commemoration for the deceased. He refused as politely as he could, not wishing to offend, not caring if he did. Before leaving, he drove by Susana's house. He was surprised to find it much smaller and less warm in appearance than he remembered, in disrepair, with a large gaping hole in the porch. It appeared to be abandoned. He could see Susana and himself in the back yard by the swing. The image of her face coming close to his for a kiss was bright and clear. He felt nothing. It was only a picture in his mind that meant nothing. Upon leaving Smiley, he had left a good part of himself, and on that brief return he realized he had lost what he had left behind.

The coldness he felt during his aunt's funeral continued to haunt him in ways he was not conscious of. He drank more, went on his assignments a bit more recklessly than before. He had a succession of girl friends who lived with him for a month to half a year, then they would go away, saying that his coldness and distance was more than they could stand. He stopped seeing women on a regular basis, living alone, enjoying the solitude of his life, realizing the selfishness of demanding companionship but refusing to give it in return.

He received a letter from Jim Sturtevant, the lawyer, informing him that after five years, he had a buyer for his property in Smiley. The offer was for less than it was worth and Sturtevant felt he ought to confer with him as soon as possible. The house had been rented for years, out of which the lawyer paid taxes, collected his fees, and sent him the remainder. Not wishing to return to Smiley after so many years, he scribbled "SELL" across the text of the letter and mailed it back to Sturtevant.

Two months after mailing the letter, he received an assignment in Victoria. The only way to get there, without chartering a small-engine aircraft, was to drive there on Highway 87. He did not like out-of-town assignments because he did not like being in unfamiliar territory. The one in Victoria was urgent, the fee was better than usual. He agreed to take it. He calculated he would need to spend the night, finish his work by mid morning or early afternoon the following day, and be back in San Antonio by nightfall.

The assignment went according to plan. On his return trip he stopped in Smiley. He had forgotten to eat lunch. Standing outside the Blue Goose Cafe where he parked were a few of his classmates who remembered him from high school. They seemed older to him, darker of skin, but they seemed happy and content with the way life was going for them. He invited them inside the cafe, offering to treat them to hamburgers or whatever the blue plate special might be. They accepted and he felt right at home with them. For a moment it felt as though they had been beside him all along. He was surprised to be wrong, to discover that he did share something with them. After they had eaten, someone suggested they go to Westhoff for a beer. He said he was on his way to San Antonio and told them *La Tacuachera* would be best.

His friends agreed quickly, saying anyplace but someplace. He offered to take some of them in his car and they were impressed by how expensive and new it was. He told them it was rented.

Upon entering the tavern, Jake, the bartender, recognized him. He had worked with Jake one summer at the grain elevators in Smiley. There were others, Chicano and Anglo, who remembered him or his father. Many of them came to shake his hand. He enjoyed a brief celebrity, a homecoming he had not expected. He drank more beers than he had had during the past year, enjoying himself, feeling no compulsion to restrict his drinking. He became maudlin, feeling a lump in his throat, as his friends recounted adventures they'd had together, or as the older men told him stories of his father, events he had put completely out of his mind upon hearing of his death. He found in the people and the land something he had willfully deprived himself of. The past only concerns people who have shared it with you, the land being more resistant to change, serving as a fixture which marks the past. By denying the people with whom he had shared so much, he had deprived himself of his own past, living in the recreations of solitary memory, which is not memory enough. The shared memories had more substance, were confirmations in fact that he had lived whereas alone his life had been a mere suspicion.

From that first time, Chango managed to return every few weeks to spend part of the day and most of the evening at *La Tacuachera*. Often, he rearranged his scheduled assignments so he could have Friday evening or Saturday free for his trips. As he recaptured his past he felt as though he had not been away at all. Some people would say it had been ages since they'd last seen him, but they would have said the same thing had he been gone for only a week or so.

Chango renewed many friendships and made new ones. His manner was even, well-spoken and polite. He was no longer the shy adolescent, as he was reminded, who could not look anyone in the eye. Now he was confident, smiling easily with self-assurance. His English was accentless as was his Spanish. He was not deferential when speaking to Anglos, as were many of the Chicanos. He spoke to them, without defiance, as equals. He did not join in the pretense, carried on by many rural Chicanos, that Anglos are inherently superior. His manner was controlled and no one minded, no one felt threatened by his presence.

There was a mystery about Chango which he would not resolve. He was well-dressed, though not flashy, he was never without money, standing for beer more than his rounds required but less than would be noticeable and embarrassing. When asked what he did in San Antonio, his answer was usually a funny remark, or a joke, or a question away from the subject. When pressed on it, he responded evasively by saying he "worked, had a job." He would not say what kind. Had it been someone else, the mystery concerning what he did for a living might have magnified into a crisis of friendship. There were speculations, ranging from his being a police officer to a master criminal. Don Isidro López settled it one Saturday night when Chango did not come by.

"Este hombre es decente con ustedes y con todo mundo. ¿Qué chingaos les importa más que eso?" he said. It settled the matter once and for all.

Chango liked to talk of the old times. It was not so much that he came to *La Tacuachera* to relive past experiences, or to retell the old jokes and anecdotes, things that are repeated over and over again as a kind of chronicle of life. What brought him back was the sense that here, among these people, his people, a man need never die. He could live so long as these friends remained alive to remember him and to pass on to their children memories of a man they'd never met, just as he knew stories and people long dead before he was born but who were as much a part of him as anyone he knew.

Toward closing time Chango would buy one or two cases of beer to take out. At the appointed hour he would pile the cases in the trunk of his car and drive in the direction of Nixon.

About a mile from the tavern, there was a roadside park, with a picnic bench, where he would pull over. Several cars would drive in behind him. He would open the trunk which gave out a dim light and remain drinking there with his friends until the pink of dawn defined clearly and grotesquely the spindly, black, distorted shapes of the mesquite trees on the other side of the fence. Chango never got drunk. He would drink as much or more than most but he remained sober always.

When the last of his friends could no longer take the beer and the late hour, Chango would get into his car and drive back to San Antonio. It did not occur to him to spend the morning sleeping at someone's house. He seldom saw any of his relatives, except when he drove to their homes for brief visits. His cousins his age had moved away and were scattered all over Texas. He could stay with his relatives, but as he did not visit for very long with them, he felt it would he an imposition. Among his friends, he was never invited and he never expected such an invitation. Chango knew the ways of the people, expected them, accepted them, respected them, and was gratified by them. It was something he found dependable, something of which he could be certain.

Coming up the first rise outside of Pandora, he could see the square grain elevator which was the major landmark identifying Nixon. It resembled a cigarette pack with four cigarettes evenly popped out, grey in color, unused for years but too expensive to take down. Chango was a little stiff from the hour's drive and hungry. Within minutes, he turned left at the only traffic light, a blinking red one, and drove to the Main Drugstore to stock up on cigarettes and have a hamburger. Afterward, slightly after three o'clock, he drove on to *La Tacuachera,* arriving there about three-thirty.

It would he nearly six hours before he would have his meeting with Tench.

■ ■ ■

IV

It was not quite dusk when Ambrose Tench left the tavern at the crossroads in Gillette. With the last of his money, he bought four bottles of beer. Once in his car, he tried to open one but found he did not have an opener. He went back inside the bar for one and discovered he did not have a nickel to pay for it. The bartender told him to take the opener and just leave. Tench pointed a finger at him, as if saying, I will be back, and left.

Tench was not as drunk as he should have been for having started so early. The angry rage over what happened with Milly Jones kept burning within him, preventing him from getting drunk. Midway between Gillette and *La Tacuachera,* he pulled to the side of the road to finish the last two beers. When he finished the last one, he cranked the car but it would not start. In the process, he flooded it. Tench got out, kicked one of the fenders. He stumbled onto the road shoulder to flag a car down for a push. Several cars drove by, their drivers seeing him weaving, and continued on without stopping. He cursed, shaking his fist at them. After waiting and realizing no one would stop for him, he started walking.

Chango had been at *La Tacuachera* since a little before four. He sat with a group of friends, talking, laughing, drinking beer. Tench walked two miles to *La Tacuachera.* When he arrived, he had sobered considerably, he was tired and sweating. He kicked open the door so violently that it shook on its hinges. The door swung to and fro. Tench remained standing, framed by the doorway, waiting for a comment from someone, anyone. Not receiving one, he took a step forward, raised his leg, coiled it around the door and shut it loudly with his foot. It slammed with such a noise that all conversation stopped. There was no longer the hum of human voices to be heard above the metallic, grating, music of the jukebox.

Ambrose Tench walked slowly to the corner of the bar. He surveyed all those in front of him. His eyelids drooping slightly, giving him a reptilian appearance, he swayed from the Chicano side to the Anglo side and back again. On the Anglo side, some stared at him, others grimaced and shook their heads. Most of the Chicanos bent their heads over their beers. Chicanos and Anglos alike had never seen Tench as he was. They knew the trouble he wanted was more than a fistfight would satisfy.

Chango had never seen Tench before. For all his trips to *La Tacuachera,* he had never been there to witness Tench's belligerent goading of people into fights. Apart from the bravado of kicking the door open, slamming it shut, and leaning with his back against the bar, Chango did not pay particular attention to Tench. Chango continued telling a series of new jokes he had heard in San Antonio. In the silence of the bar as the men watched to see what Tench would do next, Chango's voice sounded louder than usual. Tench fixed his gaze on Chango's table, watching as Chango told his new joke, moving his head in a circular motion to address each person at the table.

Ambrose Tench's jugular veins popped out like the terraces in the fields outside. His neck skin stretched tautly making his scar seem even more hideous. His jaws were clenched, his face turning into a sickly, discolored red, crisscrossed by white lines that made him look old and ghoulish. The narrow ribbon that was his mouth turned a pale, deathly white from the pressure. His eyes bulged forward deep from within their sockets as he stared at the Mexican he had not seen before. Chango's neat appearance and bright, even, teeth, which he could see in the gloom of the bar, became the focal point of all the reverses of his day.

Tossing his words over his shoulder, Tench yelled to the bartender in a loud voice to make sure everyone in the tavern heard him.

"Give me a god-damn beer, Jake. It better be a cold one, too, because I want to enjoy a real cold beer before I start kicking shit out of that Meskin' sitting over yonder."

Jake opened the beerbox and went deep for a cold one, wiping off the frost with his bar rag. He set the bottle on the bar within reach of Tench's arm. He knew there was no way to pacify Tench. Chango appeared to be in good condition as though he could take care of himself. Jake stepped back to watch. There was little else he could do. He did not even charge for the beer.

Ambrose Tench picked up the beer bottle by the neck, holding it between his thumb and forefinger, swinging it slightly, his eyes not turning for an instant away from Chango's table. With a strange, almost delicate motion, Tench raised the spout to his mouth, speaking before he took a drink. His voice had a hollow, echo-sound, as part of it reverberated inside the bottle. He was speaking in Chango's direction, although Chango appeared not to he paying attention to him.

"Take a good look at me, Meskin'. I'm the one that's gonna chug this beer and then I'm the one that's gonna take you outside and beat the hell out of you. Just 'cause I don't like your fucking face. What d'you think about that?"

Chango was still relaxed, not being able to take seriously the buffoon and the scene in front of him. He detected a mixture of fear and embarrassment throughout the building. All the Anglos were looking at him as if encouraging him to do something. A few of the Chicanos lifted their heads to look at him. These are blank, expressionless faces, speaking from roots Chango understood only too well. Thus far Tench had not said or done anything that a man had to respond to.

Chango thought Tench must be crazy. There could not be any seriousness in any of it. The people around him seemed concerned over something that was obviously a practical joke. At best, he thought, this man must be the community idiot, the person that no one pays any special attention to and the one who is tolerated so long as he does not lay a hand on anyone. Chango looked at Tench briefly and went back to telling his jokes, trying to draw his friends into more conversation when they did not laugh. From the expression on the faces around him, he slowly came to realize that something was about to happen.

"Parece que está loco. No le hagan caso," Chango said, annoyed.

"N'ombre, Chango, tú no lo conoces. Es muy desgraciado. Se ha puesto con varios aquí y les ha metido una chinguisa no más por ser cabrón. No sueltes el cabrón hasta que no lo dejes tirado. Cuídate."

Chango spoke up cheerfully.

"Saben que me he puesto con mejores que él. Tiene cara de puro cabrón. Ladra pero no muerde. No pica el baboso. Es uno de esos que les gusta hablar, es todo." Chango laughed confidently.

"Vale más que te salgas de volada, Chango, antes de que se acabe la vironga." The man who spoke was in earnest, fearing for his friend from San Antonio.

"N'ombre. No hay pedo. Si toca que se viene el puto, pos aquí traigo para él y para su abuela también." Chango intended the last to be funny, but no one laughed.

Tench finished the beer without moving it from his lips. He brought the bottle down to the bar with a loud dull thud. He burped obscenely, wiping his mouth with his sleeve. His eyes retained the same wild look as before when he first noticed Chango. Even as he had his head tilted back while drinking the beer, he had not taken his eyes off Chango. Ambrose Tench stretched his body to its full length.

"All right, Meskin', let's go. You and me, outside."

"Chango!" someone said, "¡córrele a la puerta!"

"No vale la pena, amigo," someone else said.

Chango brought his head up to look at Tench as if seeing him for the first time.

"Were you talking to me?"

"God-damn right I'm talking to you, Meskin'!"

"What do you want?" asked Chango, softly.

"What do I want? You, fella. You're the one I'm gonna kick around the parking lot. I feel mean. Kicking shit out of a Meskin' makes me feel so god-damn good! Come on, now, let's go. Outside."

Chango still had not been insulted beyond what he could easily dismiss. These were his friends, though. They might understand him running out the backdoor close by, but he would never be able to face them again. He had run away from Smiley once before. He had turned his back on these people a long time before and now he was back, making himself one of them again. He could not run. Yet, he could not afford to fight and draw attention to himself.

Tench and Chango kept staring at each other. Chango's face remained impassive. It was impossible to tell what went on in his mind. He knew that the least flicker of his eyes, twitch of his face, movement of his hands, and it would begin without his being able to do anything about it. The Anglos leaned forward in their chairs, watching the stagnating scene intently.

The fury that spit out his first words was subsiding from Tench.

"Don't think you can run out that back door, Meskin'. I'm already real mad. Now, if you make a try for it, I'm just gonna have to run right after you and I'm gonna catch you. You know I'm gonna catch you."

A small group of Chicanos started edging toward the door.

"Hold it right there, you! Sit the fuck back down. Nobody moves."

Jake kept polishing the bar, circling the same spot on the bar with his left hand. In his right hand, he held a piece of lead pipe covered with electrical tape. He hoped Chango would take Tench outside. The Chicanos sat down again.

"I just want to beat some shit out of you now, Meskin', but if you up and run on me, well, when I catch you, boy, when I catch up with you, it's gonna be a whole hell of a lot worse for you. I might just kill you, you know that? I don't think I ever killed anyone."

Chango still had difficulty believing what he was hearing. Suddenly, Chango's brown eyes fastened onto the wild, animal eyes that seemed suspended outside of Tench's face. Both men were unable to drop their glances. Chango's face became a mass of taut skin and nerve. Without breaking the trance which held his eyes fixed to Tench's, Chango began to rise slowly, evenly, from his chair.

He rose smoothly, gracefully, until he was firmly on his feet. Chango was taller than Tench. He stared down at an angle at him. He drew in a deep breath, expanded his chest, causing a slight strain on his tailored shirt. For what appeared to be a full minute, Chango, arms at his side, continued to face Tench. When he spoke, he was not angry or tense. He spoke evenly, in a measured voice.

"Don't push your luck."

"He talks," said Tench.

"I said, don't push your luck, redneck."

Upon hearing "redneck," Tench stepped forward and sidekicked a chair, sending it reeling, crashing, into a cluster of tables and chairs in the Anglo area, next to the dance floor.

"Go to 'im. Chango," someone said.

Tench turned in the direction the voice came from.

"You're next, motherfucker, you're next!" he shouted.

"Knock the shit out of him, Chango," said an Anglo.

"I'll be getting you, too, bastard!" said Tench.

"Cálmala, Chango," said an older Chicano. "Comoquiera pierdes."

Chango had not heard a word. It was only he and Tench in the bar. His mind and body waited for the right gesture to spring onto Tench, to tear him to pieces. Tench was a combination village idiot, maniac and bully. He had broken the peace and good feeling he came to *La Tacuachera* for. Tench spoiled the only tranquility he had enjoyed in many years. He had never wanted to rip another human being apart as much as he did now, as he realized this would be his last trip. If he ran, he could not face anybody here again. If he hurt Tench, they would forever be afraid of his violence. Tench was threatening to end what he enjoyed most in his life. As it was over in any case, the more he thought about it the more he wanted to hurt Tench, the more he wanted to yank Tench's arms from their sockets, to beat his brains out of his head with them.

"Dale en le madre al puto," yelled El Cucuy Sánchez.

"I heard that, Meskin'. You talk English around me, understand? I might decide to kill you, too!" said Tench.

Tench took another step forward.

"Come on outside, Meskin'," he said to Chango.

Chango did not move. He continued to stare at Tench.

"Redneck, you don't want to fool with me. You've run off at the mouth long enough."

The fury that was subsiding in Tench resumed full force. No one had ever stood up to him in his manner. He yelled at the top of his voice, in a pained, weird, animal squeal.

"I'll kill you right here, in front of your friends! You can't talk to me that way! Never!"

Seeing that Tench was no longer in his senses, Chango saw immediately that it was not to be a fight. The entire confrontation had suddenly changed. He saw that Tench was merely a bully trying to scare him. Chango could see now that he had been wrong about Tench's face. There had been no anger there, no hatred, no fury.

Chango now knew that it was fear in Tench's face. He had matched words with him and in doing so he had already beaten him. Tench was now terrified about what to do next. Chango knew Tench would fight and would get himself beaten senseless, perhaps killed. The one thing Tench could not stand was to be made a fool of. He had started a fight and it was over without any blows exchanged. Seeing Chango begin to relax his body, Tench became more terrified. He took another step toward Chango, with only the table separating them. Chango's friends had moved away.

"Redneck, I can wipe the floor with your face, except you'd probably dirty it. You're a loud-mouth, a bully. I guess these people around here always thought you were serious. You're yellow through and through. So, relax. If you promise to behave, I'll buy you a beer. There's no use trying your bullshit anymore, you're finished."

Chango returned to his seat, relaxing his gaze, turning it away from Tench. He picked up his beer and began drinking it slowly, smiling over the rim of the bottleneck, showing everyone his white teeth set in the dark brown face. He took a small sip, then tilted it up higher to take a larger draught. When he lowered the bottle to the table, a droplet of beer coarsed down his chin. He took a handkerchief from his hip pocket to wipe his mouth. When he finished wiping his chin, Chango started to laugh.

Tench was confused. His hands were still pressed together into impotent, useless, fists. He could not tell why Chango laughed. Chango looked up to become aware of the confused expression on Tench's face. He laughed all the more as if someone were tickling him, lifting one knee under the table.

Soon, a few of the Chicanos in the immediate area of Chango's table also started to laugh. The laughter began cautiously, more from the contagious nature of Chango's laugh. First, one Chicano snorted, unable to suppress the guffaw that swelled in his chest. Before long, two or three more Chicanos started to laugh, not knowing exactly why. At first, only Chango laughed openly and freely. The quiet, cautious laughter, begun more as a nervous release, gave way to uninhibited, uncontrollable belly laughter and the sound of it filled *La Tacuachera* on the Chicano side.

They laughed and pointed fingers at one another. Some covered their gaping mouths to conceal missing teeth, but they still pointed. When they realized how Chango had finally punctured Tench's puffed-up reputation, they pointed, first at Tench, then at Chango. With each pointing of a finger, there came a resurgence of laughter. The sound of the laughter was mixed with coughing.

Tench leaped in front of a small, elderly Chicano who held his sides in laughter. Tench yelled at him at the top of his lungs, trying to be heard above the laughing, making the meanest face he could muster.

"Old man, I'll kick the shit out of you."

Upon hearing this, the old man laughed even harder, placing one hand over his mouth to cover up his bad teeth. He pointed at Tench and as he did so, everyone started laughing again. Tench ran out the back door, his face contorted in what appeared to be anger, yelling something drowned out by the laughter.

Chango motioned to Jake to bring beers for everybody in *La Tacuachera.* When he approached to pay, Jake told him it was on the house. Again and again for the rest of the evening, someone would be unable to suppress a guffaw and *La Tacuachera* was sent into gales of laughter.

Writings

Short Stories (Collections): *The Adventures of the Chicano Kid and Other Stories,* Arte Público Press, 1982. *Red Bikini Dream,* Arte Público Press, 1990. **Novels:** *Schoolland,* Arte Público Press, 1988. *White Leg,* Arte Público Press, 1996. **Translation:** *Old Faces and New Wine,* by Alejandro Morales, Maize Press, 1981. **Short Stories and Essays:** In *Chicano Times, El Magazín, Caracol, Revista Chicano-Riqueña, De Colores, Rayas, Floricanto IV,* and *Floricanto V.*

Nicholasa Mohr

To date, Nicholasa Mohr is the only U.S. Hispanic woman to have developed a long career as a creative writer for the major publishing houses. Since 1973 her books for such publishers as Dell/Dial, Harper & Row, and Bantam, in both the adult and children's literature categories, have won numerous awards and outstanding reviews. Part and parcel of her work is the experience of growing up a female, Hispanic, and a minority in New York City.

Born on November 1, 1935, in New York City, to impoverished parents who had migrated there from Puerto Rico during the Depression, Mohr was raised in Spanish Harlem and educated in New York City schools. Her father died when she was just eight years old, and her mother became the sole provider for the family. Nicholasa's mother died before Nicholasa reached high school, but she had encouraged her daughter's budding artistic talent, a talent that took her to art school and led her into the creative life. Mohr graduated from the Pratt Center for Contemporary Printmaking in 1969. From that date until 1973 when her first book was published, she developed a successful career as a graphic artist. While studying art at the New School for Social Research, she met psychologist Irwin Mohr, whom she married; the couple later had two children, David and Jason.

Ultimately, it was through her artwork that Mohr came to the attention of Harper editor Ellen Rudin, who collected her prints. Rudin encouraged Mohr to convert the words and images in her prints into written language; Harper later published *Nilda*. The novel is the first woman's narrative in English of the Puerto Rican experience.

Nilda traces the life of a young Puerto Rican girl confronting prejudice and coming of age during World War II, and is so fresh and innovative in its depiction and language that it won the Jane Addams Children's Book Award and was selected by *School Library Journal* as Best Book of the Year. Although promoted by its publisher as a young adult novel, Mohr intended *Nilda* as a book for all ages, and it has truly served that purpose. Donald B. Gibson wrote in *Children's Literature*:

> There is no pity here, for the author is too much aware of the humanity of her characters and of the other implications of pity to be in any way condescending.

This statement could apply to all of Mohr's writings.

After *Nilda*'s success, Mohr was able to produce numerous stories, novellas, scripts including *El Bronx Remembered* (1975), *In Nueva York* (1977), *Felita* (1979), *Rituals of Survival: A Woman's Portfolio* (1985), *Going Home* (1986). For *Nilda*, *El Bronx Remembered*, and *Felita*, Mohr also provided original illustrations. After being promoted as a young adult author by the major publishing houses, it was difficult for Mohr to also have her feminist, very adult material considered for publication by those houses. Thus, in 1985 Mohr took her work to Arte Público Press to publish "The Artist," a highly autobiographical work, describing how a young woman launched her artistic career despite the negative sentiments of her family and her husband. The story was later re-written into a screenplay, but has not been produced. Another story in this anthology, "Zoraida," was also re-written as a play and received a reading at the Public Theater in New York.

Mohr's works have been praised for depicting the life of Puerto Ricans in New York with empathy, realism, and humor. In her stories for children, Mohr has successfully dealt with the most serious and tragic subjects—from the death of a loved one to incest—in a sensitive and humane way. "Mohr creates a remarkably brilliant tapestry of community life as well as of individual characters," wrote one critic in the *Bulletin of the Center for Children's Books*.

Mohr has contributed honest and memorable depictions of U.S. Puerto Ricans to the world of commercial publishing—where stereotypes have reigned supreme. In this and in her crusade to open the doors of publishing and the literary world to Hispanics, Nicholasa Mohr is a true pioneer.

Personal Stats

Nuyorican writer, visual artist. **Born:** November 1, 1935, in New York City. *Education:* Art Students' League, 1953–56, Brooklyn Museum Art School, 1959–66, Pratt Center for Contemporary Printmaking, 1966–69. *Career:* Artist-printmaker,

> "Few come up to Nilda *in describing the crushing humiliations of poverty and in peeling off the ethnic wrappings so that we can see the human child underneath."*
>
> **Marilyn Sachs,** New York Times Book Review, *November 4, 1973*

Nicholasa Mohr

1953–74; art instructor at schools in New York and New Jersey, 1967–74; writer, 1974–present; McDowell Colony, writer-in-residence, 1972, 1974, and 1976; New York City schools artist-in-residence, 1973–74; Distinguished Visiting Professor of Creative Writing, Queens College, 1988–90; Honorary Doctorate of Letters, State University of New York at Albany, 1989; writer-in-residence, Richmond College, The American International University, London, England, 1994–95. **Memberships:** PEN, Authors Guild, Authors League of America. **Awards/Honors:** *New York Times Outstanding Book of Juvenile Fiction,* 1973, 1974; *School Library Journal* Best Book, 1973, 1975, 1977; Jane Addams Children's Book Award, 1974; American Library Association Best Book, 1977; National Conference on Social Studies and Children's Book Council, Notable Book, 1977, 1980; American Book Award of the Before Columbus Foundation, 1981; Commendation from the State Legislature of New York, 1986. **Address:** c/o Arte Público Press, University of Houston, Houston, TX 77204-2090

A Time with a Future (Carmela)

from *Rituals of Survival: A Woman's Portfolio,* Arte Público Press, 1985, pp. 35–53

"A whole lifetime together, imagine! And now it's over." Edna spoke, holding back tears. "I don't know what I would do if I were Mama, honest."

"Poor Mama," murmured Mary, "she's had such a hard time of it. I'm glad that in these last few years they had each other. Papa was her whole life . . ." Mary stopped and began to sob quietly. Edna put her arms around Mary, who buried her head in her sister's bosom. "Oh Edna, it's so sad to see it all come to an end. The end of something so special."

"Come on, Mary." Edna very gently pushed Mary away from her. "Let's not get like this. Think of Ma. If she sees us crying, it'll be worse for her. We all have to figure this thing out calmly and rationally."

"I know." Mary wiped her eyes and swallowed. "It's . . . the finality of it that's so hard for me to bear, you know? But you're right, we're all Mom's got now, so it's up to us to decide what's best. At her age, it's like you say, she can't be left alone."

"That's more like it, and we can't stay here day after day indefinitely like this. I don't know how long Joe's mother is going to hold out with my kids. How about you? Exactly how long do you think Mark's gonna come home from work to take care of your three and do housework? That's why, when Roberto gets here, I'll discuss what Joe and I have agreed to. Then all three of us have to sit down and decide Mama's future."

Carmela had left her daughters seated in the kitchen, entered the small bedroom of her four-room flat and closed the door, shutting out their voices. She was sick of her daughters' tearstained faces, their wailing, crying and self-pity. Grown women, with families, acting like children. Carmela shook her head; it was all too much. Her whole body was tired; every bone, every muscle ached. She pulled back the bedspread, kicked off her shoes and lay down.

They had buried Benjamin two days ago, but her daughters had insisted on remaining with her both nights. And that meant Carmela had to make the daybed in the other room, share her own bed with one of her daughters, find more sheets, towels, dishes and all the extra work that was part of caring for others. She had not been able to rest; not as she should, by herself, alone with her private grief and deep sense of relief. There had been too many people at the funeral. Benjamin's friends from the union, neighbors and people she had not seen in years. Carmela felt her eyelids closing with a heaviness from lack of sleep. She had not really slept peacefully in over a week and, before that, for what had seemed like a timeless battle, she had hardly known sleep at all.

Her mind was still filled with him, with Benjamin. When they had laid Benjamin out in the casket, they had pinned a bright scarlet carnation on the lapel of his best suit. The rich red color of the flower contrasted sharply with the dry greyness of his skin and accentuated the dark purple lines of pain that the long illness had etched in his face. Carmela had asked the morticians to replace the red carnation with a white one; this change had made it easier to look at him.

She remembered her Freddie all too vividly. There are things one never forgets, always feels. Like my Freddie, Carmela nodded. His small casket had been laden with flowers. They had placed a bright red rose in his hands which were cupped together as if in prayer. For him, this had been the right color, matching his full red mouth which was fixed in a serene smile. He appeared to be sleeping and, for one long moment, Carmela had actually believed that Freddie would look up, his dark eyes smiling, and question her. "Where am I, Mami? What am I doing here?" And she would respond, "A bad dream, my baby. Freddie, you and me, we are both having a bad dream."

But it was no dream. Freddie's illness had been unexpected, swift and real. In a matter of days she had lost him. Not like Benjamin; more than a year of waiting patiently for him to die.

At first it had seemed no more than a bad cold. Freddie had a low fever and a sore throat. But he got sicker and his breathing became difficult, then unbearable. With each intake of air, he emitted a rasping, honking sound, and his small chest caved in, then extended until it seemed about to burst. Carmela was frightened and alone. Benjamin was on the night shift again. While the others slept soundly, Carmela dressed Freddie warmly. She went to a neighbor and asked her to look after the children until she returned from the clinic with Freddie. The bus was not there, and Carmela decided it would be quicker to walk the many long blocks to the emergency clinic. Even through the blankets she could feel Freddie struggling to breathe as she carried him as fast as her feet could take her. At the emergency clinic she explained with great effort in her halting English why she was there, and then waited for her name to be called.

The young doctor spoke gently to her. "You have a very sick baby. He must stay here, in the hospital. Understand . . . mother? Usted comprende? Si, very good." Carmela's head was spinning. She asked "But how? Why? He all right yesterday. He play with the brother and sisters. Por favor, doctor, give to me the medicine, and I take care of my baby in home. Mi casa is much better for him, yes?" The young doctor shook his head, "No! He's too sick to leave hospital." Lifting his hands, he covered his head and face, gesturing to her. "We have to put him in an oxygen-tent so he can breathe. He has pneumonia, understand? Muy enfermo niño . . . comprende, madre?" She felt the fear deep inside, shivering as if someone had replaced her blood with ice water. "Por favor, doctor, he never go away from me, he no talk good English too much . . . pero Freddie understands good everything. He no go in school . . . only cuatro, four years." The young doctor nodded reassuringly, "He'll be all right in hospital, Mrs. Puig, you go home to your casa. Take care of your other children. Then you can came back later and stay with Freddie. The nurse will give you all the information. Don't worry, no apures, we are going to take good care of your baby. Make him well. Go home, get some rest." As they took him away, Freddie had turned to her, wide-eyed and scared, fighting for breath.

As soon as Benjamin came home from work, Carmela returned, staying by Freddie's side for the better part of two days. Freddie was not improving, but he had not gotten worse. When he was awake, he smiled at her from under the oxygen tent and she smiled back, telling him all about the things she would get for him after he got well again.

When on the third day she had made her brief visit home to check on the others, Benjamin complained.

"Two days! Two days! I can't stay out another day. Woman, what am I gonna do for money to buy food, pay rent . . . when they dock me? I must get back to work. Freddie's all right now. He's in the best place, in the hospital with the doctors who know better than you what to do." This time Carmela fought back. "But if something should happen to him, I want to be there at his side. Freddie mustn't be alone." Benjamin was unshaken. "I can't be here with the kids, cooking, washing and doing your housework . . . just in case something happens! There's plenty men out there looking for jobs. I'll lose my job . . . woman! If you want to go when I'm not here, call in a neighbor or get a friend. How about Sara, you've done her plenty of favors, eh?" Carmela resisted. "What friends? When do I have time to make friends? Neighbors can't be staying here all day with our kids, and neither can Sara. Besides, she's alone with her own children and worse off than us. There's only you; nobody else can stay here except you. Ben . . . maybe you can ask for part-time work just a few more days until Freddie is over the crisis . . . maybe . . ." Benjamin shouted, "Stop it!" Full of his own fears, his mind raced with memories of his childhood in a time where death and starvation had dictated his existence. And for two days now, the words to a song he had not heard since he was a small boy would not leave his mind; they played on his lips over and over.

> First the tremors,
> then the typhoid
> follows hunger with every breath

we pray for joy, for better times
but the only relief is the promise of death!

The peasants of his tiny rural village would sing this song during the typhoid epidemic. Benjamin had lost his father, two older brothers and baby sister, leaving only his mother, older sister and younger brother. He was nine when he became head of the household. Sometimes he would get work at the fields or at the sugar refinery, working from sun-up to sundown, bringing home twenty-five, maybe thirty cents a day, depending on the work to be done. Other days he would work chopping wood, running errands and cleaning the hog pens, to be paid in food; usually leftovers, but enough so that they wouldn't starve at home. At thirteen, when his mother died, his sister found work as a domestic and he and his younger brother set out on their own.

"Absolutely not, woman! There's a goddam depression out there. Do you think I'm gonna let us all starve? I ain't selling apples or shoelaces in the street, not when I got a job to go to. And we don't take charity in this family. I go back to work tomorrow and you . . . you can do what the hell you want!" Carmela kept silent. Benjamin had a strong will and his fears justified his reasoning. She understood she could not persuade him.

Carmela had not wanted Freddie to die alone in the hospital, but that's how it had happened. For the next three days, she had only been able to be with him for a few hours, and always with the thought of the others that she left at home, unattended for the most part. That evening when Mr. Cooper, owner of the candy store, sent a message that the hospital had called on the public phone asking her to come right away, Carmela guessed what it was they would tell her.

"Too late. We did everything we possibly could." The young doctor was compassionate and visibly upset. "Double pneumonia . . . there was nothing we could give him. All of us did the best we could. We are all very, very sorry. Mrs. Puig, Freddie was a wonderful little boy."

That was in another lifetime, the time of the Great Depression, before the Second World War, before penicillin, antibiotics and miracle drugs. Today it would have been different; children don't have to die from that illness anymore. Medicine, in this lifetime, knows no limits. Look at an old man like Benjamin, eh? Kept alive, full of disease and tortured by pain beyond human endurance. And for what? No future, no hope, only the knowledge that each day he remained alive would be a torment for both of them.

Carmela opened her eyes and yawned, stretching her body. There was no sense in expecting sleep to come, take over and soothe away her weariness. Too much was still happening inside, repeating itself. The past was still the present and the present was not yet real.

When the doctor told her about Benjamin, she had insisted he be told as well. It was too much for her at this time; no longer did she have that kind of strength for others. Besides, Benjamin was a proud man, and it was only right. He had already suspected what the doctors confirmed; he was frightened, but not shocked. Calmly, Benjamin had told her he was resigned to the inevitable, but wanted to ask her for one last favor. And that request stirred and brought to the surface those deep and private feelings of hatred and revenge that can only be felt by one human being for another when they have been as close as Benjamin and Carmela. Then, as he spoke, Carmela felt herself spinning with rage.

"Carmela, no matter how sick I get, don't send me away. Let me die here in my own bed, Carmelita, here with you, by your side."

A tirade of words she had been nurturing, rehearsing and storing away for that day when she would leave him, walk out, walk out for good, choked Carmela. "Remember Freddie? Remember our son, Benjamin? How he died alone? In a strange place, in a strange bed. Without me by his side. I owed him at least as much as you ask of me. A baby, four years old with no one to comfort him from the fear of death, to guide him gently into the unknown. It all happened thirty-eight years ago, but I remember. And now, today, now . . . you want the right to die here, safe and secure in my arms. I didn't give birth to you! You selfish, hateful man, how well I know you!"

They had looked at each other silently. He, waiting for her to answer. She, unable to speak, afraid of that explosion of terrible words that would vent her rage. Now it was so easy to hurt him, to make him suffer as she had suffered the death and loss of her child. She couldn't speak, not one word left her lips. Carmela saw him old and tired, bracing himself against death, preparing himself and seeking her help. He spoke again, this time pleading.

"Promise, Carmela, that's all I ask of you. Just this favor and never will I ask you for another thing; I give you my word . . . just don't, don't send me away; no matter what, let me die at home."

Carmela had hidden her resentment and put aside her hatred. Instead, she responded as always, to the unspoken bond that existed between them, that dependency on each other.

And she had promised, "It'll be all right, Benjamin, you can remain at home. No matter how sick you get. Don't worry, I won't let them take you away. You can stay here with me . . . until it's over."

This pact, built on survival, was what held them together; it was what had cemented them to a lifetime of sharing without so much as a day's voluntary separation. That security, that dependency, was the foundation of their marriage; solid and tough, like a boulder of impenetrable granite.

For a full year she had nursed him, giving him medicine, caring for him as he got weaker, almost every minute of the day and night. In time, she had to bathe him, give him the bedpan and finally spoon-feed him. His body, at first, was still strong and straight. They had not slept together for many years and so Carmela had been amazed by his supple body, the muscular limbs and tightness of skin that was unusual for a man as old as Benjamin. But, as he got sicker and lost weight, his body became frail and bent; his skin hung loosely as if lightly tacked onto his bones.

The sleepless nights, when he called out to her for comfort not once, but constantly . . . the three flights she had to climb, loaded with bundles, began to rip Carmela apart. The burden of his illness gave her no time to rest. Completely exhausted, she decided to speak to him about her promise.

"Benjamin, maybe it's better for you in the hospital. Listen, think about it, please. They can care for you better there, give you stronger medicine, maybe, eh? Look, Benjamin, I'm so tired, because there's nothing more I can do for you. Please, I don't know how long I can hold out . . . please think about it. I promise, I'll be out to see you every day; every single day I'll be by your side at the hospital, I swear . . ."

"No, you promised me! And now you talk about sending me out! You said I could stay. Carmela, you've become hardhearted to say this to me. No!" His eyes had filled with tears. Like a child, he clung desperately to her, grabbing her hands, groping at her body. "Please, in the name of God . . . please don't send me away. Let me die here, with you . . . you promised!" Carmela had pushed him away, tearing at his fingers, shoving and struggling, unable to free herself from his fierce grip. "You promised! Now that I'm dying, I don't matter anymore . . . you can't send me away . . . you can't. "

"Selfish man, you deserve to die alone, just like my dead baby! It would be justice to send you away . . . away from me."

Again the words remained unspoken; instead, she said "All right, stop it! Stop! For God's sake, you can stay, I promise you. But I'm getting some help. I can't do it all alone. All right, I said you can stay! " Only then, after she had reassured him, had Benjamin released her.

Carmela had run away to the other side of the apartment and had put her hands over her ears to shut out his crying. But she still heard his loud sobbing and screaming.

"Carmela, Carmelita, you are a good woman!"

Carmela was able to get some help; a practical nurse came three times a week and later, every day. Benjamin journeyed each day on a long painful road that would lead to death. The kind of merciless journey that comes with cancer. The cancer had started in his lower intestines and finally ran rampant through his body, leaving him helpless, barely able to move. But still he clung to life, determined to put up a battle; fighting to survive was all he knew.

He would call out "Carmela . . . get me some water, Carmela, I don't want the nurse, tell her to leave. Do something for this pain! Carmela, give me something. Don't leave me, Carmela." And she would hope and pray that before he could utter her name once more, he would stop breathing.

Then, at last, he lapsed into a coma, feebly clinging to life. He would utter sounds and sentences which were, for the most part, unintelligible. Sometimes he screamed out the names of his own parents, brothers and sisters. Events of his childhood, memories of back home filled his mind and escaped from his lips. He spoke mostly in Spanish, laughing, crying and asking questions. No one knew what he wanted and, after two days, no one listened except Carmela. Maybe at this time, Carmela hoped, he would say something about their dead child; but in all his tangled words and gibberish, Freddie's name was never mentioned.

Her children had been at the apartment since their father's latest turn for the worse. That day, they all sat in the kitchen, drinking coffee and hot chocolate, waiting for him to die. They shared the vigil, taking turns at Benjamin's bedside. Late that evening, Roberto called his mother and when she returned, they found Benjamin staring blankly, not breathing. A look of peace spread over his face, as if the pain had finally disappeared. Gently, Carmela closed his eyes and mouth, kissed his dry lips and covered his face with the sheet.

Again, thoughts about the funeral, the people, the flowers and Freddie crowded Carmela's thoughts. It was as if her thinking pattern were following a cycle, winding up always with Benjamin's death.

Perhaps she was avoiding this latest part of the whole business? Carmela knew she had to deal with her children, grownups who still insisted on that relationship of mother and child. Now they felt themselves to be in charge, Carmela sighed, almost out of patience. She heard the front door and voices. That would be Roberto, and now her children would begin another discussion about her future.

She had been through their weddings, the birth of their children, marital disputes from time to time; always she had listened and given them her support. What they wanted now, and what they might ask of her, created an anxiety that drained Carmela's energy. In a few minutes she would get up and speak to them. Sooner or later they had to talk.

"Mama can come home with me, we'll find the room; Suzie and Gigi can double up . . ." Mary looked at her brother and sister nervously, then continued, "Mark won't mind, honest."

"No," Edna responded, "I think it's better if she comes with me; after all, we have the big house. Nobody will be put out for space."

"I wish I could say it's all right at my house, but the way things are with me and Gloria, well . . ." Roberto hesitated.

"We understand, don't worry," Edna said. "Besides, it's better for Mama to be with her own daughter."

"Financially, I can always help out, you know that," Roberto smiled.

"She's got Papa's pension and some savings; she's all right as far as that goes," Edna said, "but if we need anything more, I'll let you know."

"There's only one thing about her going with you," Mary said. "She's not gonna want to go way out to Long Island. Port Jefferson is too far away from everything for her."

"She'll get used to it. It'll take a little time, that's all. Anyway, you're far away yourself, Mary. Mount Vernon isn't around the corner! And your apartment isn't big enough for another person. Where are you gonna put her?"

"You know what I think? I don't think we are gonna get Mama out of this old apartment, period." Roberto nodded emphatically. "She's too attached to it. Remember the time they took a trip to Puerto Rico, back to Papa's town, to see about retiring there? Ma said she couldn't stand it. She missed the city, her friends, everything. How long have they been living here in this place? Twenty-six years or something like that, right?"

"It'll be better for her to leave here. Personally, I don't know how anybody can live here, in this city, if they can get out . . ." Edna shook her head, "The noise, the pollution, the crime! Oh, I know I wouldn't want my kids here. When we were kids, maybe it was different . . . it just seems worse today . . ."

"Mama said it's not too bad since they put up all the new middle-income buildings. She says it's better than ever with new shops and all kinds of interesting people around. Ma says she can go right to Broadway and buy anything she wants at any time of the day or . . ."

"Stop being so naive . . ." Edna interrupted. "Mary, how long can Mama stay by herself? She's sixty-six. In a few years, when she can't cope, then what? It'll be a lot worse to get her out of here. I'm not going to be commuting back and forth. And I know you, Mary . . . you too, Roberto, especially the way your marriage is going, who knows where you'll be, eh? No, we have to make a decision between us and stick to it. Now, listen to what Joe and I have planned . . ." Edna paused, making sure her brother and sister were listening. "Mama has a fairly good income from Papa's pension, so she won't be a financial burden to anyone. She's in good health, except for some arthritis now and then, but nobody ever hears her complain. And, she has some savings . . . all right, then. With a little more than half her savings we can convert the playroom area on the lower level of my house into living quarters for Mama. Like a kind of efficiency apartment, with her own kitchenette and half-bath. She won't need much more because she will have the rest of the house as well. This is necessary because we all know how independent Mama is. After that initial invest-ment, I won't charge her rent or anything. She can live there as long as she wants . . . I mean, for the rest of her days."

Roberto opened his mouth to speak, but thought better of it. Instead, he shrugged and smiled, looking at Mary. She smiled back. After a long silence, Mary said, "It sounds pretty good . . . what do you think, Roberto?" "Well, so far it's the best plan, and also the only plan. There's only one thing, like I said, Ma's gotta go for it." "She will," Edna said, "but it's up to us to convince her. The two of you better back me on this. Understand? We have to be united in this thing? Well?" Mary and Roberto nodded in agreement. "Good," Edna continued, "now, what to do with this place? Mama's got all kinds of pots and pans . . . look at all of this furniture and junk. I suppose she'll want to take some of this with her . . . let's see . . . "

Carmela sat up, put on her shoes and placed the bedspread neatly back on her bed. She heard the voices of her children. Well, she might as well get it over with. Carmela opened a bureau drawer, removed a small grey metal box and opened it. She searched among her valuable papers; the will she and Benjamin had made, the life insurance policy she had taken out on herself many years ago and still faithfully paid every month, some very old photographs, letters from her chil-dren as youngsters and from her grandchildren. Finally, she found the large manilla envelope with all the material she was looking for. She closed the box and put it back. Then she walked into the kitchen where her children were waiting.

"Ma, how you feeling?" Roberto kissed his mother lightly on the forehead.

"How about something to eat, Ma?" Edna asked. "Some tea? Or a little hot broth?"

"No," Carmela sat, holding the envelope in her hands. "I'm fine; I'm not hungry."

"Mama, you should eat more, you're getting too thin . . . it's not good for you. You should eat regularly, it could affect your . . ."

"Ma . . ." interrupted Edna, ignoring Mary, "we have to have a serious talk."

"I wasn't finished," snapped Mary.

"Mama's not hungry!" Edna looked directly at Mary. "All right?"

"Listen . . ." Roberto spoke. "Why don't I go out and get us all something to eat. Chinese or Cuban . . . so nobody has to cook."

"Sit down, Roberto." Edna then continued in a quiet, calm voice, "We have all the food we need here . . ."Turning to Carmela, she went on, "Mama, now that Papa isn't here anymore . . . we want you to know that you have us and you don't have to be alone. You are our responsibility now, just as if you had Papa. We all know this . . . don't we?" She turned to Mary and Roberto.

"Yes."

"Oh yes, Mama."

"We've all discussed this a great deal, just between ourselves. And, we've decided on a plan that we know you'll like. Of course, we want to talk it over with you first, so that we have your approval. But, I'm certain that when you hear what it is, you'll be pleased."

"Oh yes, Mama, wait until you hear what Edna . . . what we . . . oh, go ahead, Edna, tell her . . ." Mary smiled.

"Joe and I agreed and thought this out carefully. You . . . are coming to live with us, Mama. With me, Joe and the kids. We are the ones with a big house. Mary's in an apartment and Roberto doesn't exactly know where he's gonna settle; not the way things are right now. I know how proud you are and how independent, so you'll want to contribute something. Here's what we think . . . you know my house is a split level and there's room for expansion, right?"

Carmela felt an urge to open the envelope at that moment and tell them, so that Edna could stop talking nonsense. But instead, she listened, trying to hide her impatience.

". . . so that your savings, or part anyway, can pay for your private apartment. Of course, as I said, you don't need such a big area, because you can share the house with the rest of us. Outside, you can take a section of the lot, Mama, if you want to have a vegetable garden or flowers. The kids would love it, and of course Joe and I won't take a cent, you can live the rest of your days rent free. You know Joe's pleased, he wants you to feel welcomed in our home." Edna was almost out of breath. "Well, there, I've said my piece . . . now what do you think, Mama?"

All three waited for Carmela to respond. She held out the envelope.

"I've got something to show all of you." Carefully she removed its contents and spread several sheets of paper out on the kitchen table. "I suppose I should have said something before this, but with your father's illness and everything else . . ." Carmela gestured that they come closer. "Here we are . . . take a look. It's a co-op. The building's only been up about three years. Everything is brand new. My apartment is on the sixteenth floor, on the northwest corner, just like I wanted with lots of windows and it's got a terrace! Imagine, a terrace . . . I'm gonna feel rich . . . that's what. Look . . . kids, here are the floor plans, see? I got one bedroom, a living room-dining room, a brand-new kitchen. Oh, and here's an incinerator for garbage. They've got one on every floor and a community room with all kinds of activities. I heard from some of the people who live there, that there are some well-known experts, lecturers, coming in to speak about all kinds of subjects. The best part is that it's right here, around the corner, on Amsterdam Avenue. On the premises we have a drugstore, stationery and delicatessen. You know, I put my name down for this with a deposit right after Papa got sick. He hadn't wanted us to move, but once I knew how things would be, I went ahead. They called me just before Benjamin died, when he was almost in a coma, and asked if I could move in around the first of the month. I took a chance . . . I knew he couldn't last much longer, and said yes. That's in two weeks!" Carmela was busy tracing the floor plans with her fingers showing them the closets and cabinet space. "Here? See, I've paid the purchase, my savings covered the amount. You are all welcome to come and sit on the terrace . . . wait until you see how beautiful it is . . ."

"Mama . . ." Edna's voice was sharp, "what about what I just said? I finished explaining to you . . . a very important plan concerning your future. What about it?"

"I'm moving the first of the month, Edna," Carmela continued to look at floor plans. "But, I thank you and your husband for thinking of me."

"Is that it, Mama?"

"Yes, Edna."

"You already signed the lease, paid the money and everything?"

"Yes, all I have to do is move in, Edna."

"Well . . . I'm glad to see you figured it all out, Mama." Edna looked at Mary and Roberto; they avoided her eyes. "There's just one thing, eh? Who is gonna look after you when you can't . . . ?" You are sixty-six, ma! Sixty-six!"

"Not you, Edna." Carmela looked at her children. "Or you, Mary, or you, Roberto."

"Mama, I don't think you are being practical. Now, I'm too far away to be here if anything happens! If you get sick so is Mary. And as far as Roberto is concerned . . ."

"I'll manage."

"Manage? Please, Mama. Mary, Roberto, what do you have to say? Don't you think Mama should have asked us first about this? Mama, you should have spoken to us! After all, we are your children."

"I didn't ask any of you to come here when Papa was so sick, did I? I never called or bothered you. I took care of all of you once, and I took care of him . . . now, I want the privilege of taking care of myself!" There was a long silence and Carmela continued. "Thank you Edna, Mary, Roberto; you are all good children. But I can take care of myself; I've done it all my life."

"If that's the way you see it, Mama, I'm with you." Roberto said. "Right, Mary?"

"Okay . . . I guess . . ." Mary smiled weakly at Edna.

"All right, Mama." Edna stood up. "Go ahead . . . but remember, I tried my best to work something out for you. When something happens, you won't have anybody near you."

"I appreciate your good intentions, Edna, but it's all settled."

"When are you moving in, Mama?" asked Mary.

"I hope on the first, but since the landlord here knows me so well after twenty-six years, and we always paid our rent, I might be able to stay a few days extra, if things are not ready at the new place. I've already arranged everything with the movers and with the super of the new building and . . ."

They spoke for a while and Carmela talked excitedly about her new apartment.

"I feel better now that you all know . . . in fact," a feeling of drowsiness overcame her, "I think I might take a nap."

"Mama," Edna said, "we are all gonna have to leave soon, you know, get back to our families. But if you need us, please call."

"Good," Carmela smiled, "we should all get back to our own business of living, eh? The dead are at peace, after all. You were all a great help. Your husbands and children need you, and you too, Roberto . . . Gloria and the kids would like to see you, I'm sure."

"Go on, Mama, take your nap. Edna and I will cook something light, and then I think I'll call Mark to pick me up."

Carmela put everything back into her envelope and left. She closed her door and lay down, a sweet twilight state embraced her; it seemed to promise a deep sleep.

"Papa isn't even buried more than two days and she's acting like he's been dead forever." Edna was on the verge of tears. "She looks so happy . . . I don't understand it. You would think . . . Oh, I don't know anymore!"

"I'm sure she feels bad," Mary said, "it's just that she's also happy about her new apartment."

"She feels bad, all right. Mama doesn't want to show it, so that we don't feel worse than we already do," Roberto said.

"Well then, why is it that when Papa died she hardly cried. A few tears and moist eyes, but you can't call that crying! "

"Well, what do you want from her?" Roberto snapped.

"I don't know! She should be sorry . . . yes, that's what; I want her to be sorry!"

"What do you mean, sorry?!" Roberto whispered angrily.

"He was her husband of a lifetime, and my father, I . . ." Edna's voice became louder "want her to feel it!"

"Shh . . ." Mary snapped, "stop it!"

"How do you know what she feels inside? Leave her alone! It's always what you want? What about what she wants?"

"Go on, defend her. You've always been her favorite; mama's boy!"

"Quit that shit!" Roberto went towards Edna.

"For God's sake," Mary whimpered, "we're acting like kids . . . what's happening?"

"That's right, whimper like a baby, Mary." Edna began to cry, "that's all you know how to do. Everybody else has to make your decisions . . ."

"This is ridiculous," Roberto said, "I'm leaving."

"Go on . . . walk out, that's what you always do, you've done it to your own family now."

"Screw you . . . bitch!" Roberto called out, then slammed the front door.

"Come on, Edna, please stop it. What's the use of fighting? Mama's made up her mind. Let's make supper and forget about all of this. Roberto will come back after he cools off. You better call Joe; I think it's time we went home."

The two sisters began to open the refrigerator and pantry to prepare the evening meal. Mary turned to Edna, who was still sobbing quietly.

"What's the matter now?"

"I . . . wish she would be sorry . . ."

Carmela stood on the small terrace of her new apartment. She looked down at the city laid out before here. In between and over some of the buildings she could see the Hudson River and part of the George Washington Bridge. The river was dotted with sailboats and small craft that slipped in and out of sight. Overhead she had a view of a wide blue sky, changing clouds competing with the bright sun. Flocks of birds were returning home now that winter was over. Carmela took a deep breath. There was a warmth in the air; spring was almost here. In a couple of weeks she could bring out her new folding chair, lounger and snack table. Soon she would bring out her plants. New buds would begin to sprout, growing strong and healthy with the abundant sunlight and fresh air.

Carmela missed no one in particular. From time to time her children and grandchildren visited. She was pleased to see them for a short while and then was even happier when they left. In a few days it would be a whole year since Benjamin's death. It seemed like yesterday sometimes, and sometimes it was like it never happened.

She rarely thought about Benjamin. Memories of her days as a young girl became frequent, clear and at times quite vivid. Before Carmela had married at sixteen, she had dreamed of traveling to all the many places she had seen in her geography book. After school she would often go with her brothers to the docks of San Juan just to watch the freighters and big ships.

"When I grow up I'm going to work and travel on those ships."

"Carmelita, don't be silly, you can't. Girls can't join the navy or the merchant marine."

How she had wished she had been born a boy, to be able to travel anywhere, to be part of that world. Carmela loved the water; ocean, sea, river, all gave her a feeling of freedom.

She looked out from her terrace at the river, and a sense of peace filled her whole being. Carmela recognized it was the same exhilarating happiness she had experienced as a young girl, when each day would be a day for her to reckon with, all her own, a time with a future.

Writings

Novels: *Nilda,* Harper, 1973; Arte Público Press, 1986. *Felita,* Dial, 1979. *Going Home*, Dial, 1986. *Growing Up inside the Sanctuary of My Imagination* (autobiographical novel, adapted for television by ABC), 1994. *Old Letivia and the Mountain of Sorrows* (original fairytale), Viking, 1996. **Collections of Short Stories and Novellas:** *El Bronx Remembered: A Novella and Stories*, Harper, 1975; Arte Público Press, 1986. *In Nueva York*, Dial, 1977; Arte Público Press, 1988. *Rituals of Survival: A Woman's Portfolio*, Arte Público Press, 1985. *The Magic Shell,* illustrated by Rudy Gutierrez, Scholastic, 1995. *The Song of El Coquí and Other Tales of Puerto Rico,* co-authored and co-illustrated with Antonio Martorell, Viking, 1995. **Biography (Young Adult):** *All for the Better: A Story of El Barrio* (biography of social activist Evelina Lopez Antonetty), illustrated by Rudy Gutierrez, Raintree/Steck-Vaughn, 1996. **Short Stories and Excerpts:** In *The Americas Review, Children's Digest, Scholastic Magazine, Nuestro, Ethnic American Women,* and many other anthologies and textbooks.

Pat Mora

Of all of the Hispanic poets in the United States, Pat Mora has developed the broadest audiences for her poetry. Through its clean, crisp narrative style and healing messages, Mora's verse has reached out to both adults and young people. The result is that her poetry has been reprinted in more elementary, middle, and high school textbooks than any other U.S. Hispanic poet. While Mora is considered by some to be either a regional poet who celebrates life in the desert or a soft-spoken feminist, in reality she is a lyric, romantic poet who embraces many diverse segments of the reading public. This universality has led her to not only write poetry that explores the condition of women in the Southwest but also in Third World countries; it has led her to pen deeply humanistic essays; and it has even led her to create a richly diverse literature for children, encompassing Mexican folk traditions and even such modern, perplexing topics as adoption (Pablo's Tree).

Pat Mora was born and raised in El Paso, Texas, the daughter of an optician, Raúl Antonio, and a homemaker, Estella. She attended the El Paso public schools and received all of her higher education in this border city, including a B.A. and an M.A. in English from the University of Texas at El Paso. After graduating from college in 1963, she worked as an English teacher in the El Paso public schools and at El Paso Community College; eventually she made her way back to the University of Texas at El Paso as an instructor and, from 1981 to 1988, served as a university administrator and museum director there. In 1986, Mora received a prestigious Kellogg Fellowship to study cultural conservation issues nationally and internationally, which allowed her to spend almost one year in Pakistan. Subsequently, she became a consultant for the Kellogg Foundation, and in that capacity traveled to Brazil and other countries. In addition to the Kellogg honor, in 1994 Mora received a National Endowment for the Arts Fellowship to further the writing of her poetry, which resulted in the publication of her most recent book of verse, *Agua Santa: Holy Water* (1995). With her strong background in education and in exploring cultural development and conflict, as well as her ability to perform readings of her poetry, Mora has become one of the most popular speakers and guest presenters for educators around the country, which may help explain the popularity of her poetry among writers of curricula and the editors of primary and secondary English and language arts textbooks.

Pat Mora is the mother of three children (William, Elizabeth, and Cecilia), all from a first marriage (to William H. Burnside, Jr.). She re-married in 1984 to archeologist Vernon Lee Scarborough, with whom she traveled to Pakistan. When Professor Scarborough relocated from the University of Texas at El Paso to the University of Cincinnati, Mora made the transition from the west Texas desert to the icy North. Since moving to the Midwest, Mora has also become more interested in publishing children's literature and essays. *A Birthday Basket for Tía* (1992), *Listen to the Desert* (1993), *Pablo's Tree* (1994), *The Desert Is My Mother* (1994), and *The Gift of the Poinsettia* (1995) are all from that period, as are her autobiographical essays published in *Nepantla: Essays from the Land in the Middle* (1993).

In the late 1970s and early 1980s Mora began publishing her poetry in literary magazines such as *The Americas Review*. She was among the first Chicana writers to grab the reins of the Chicano literary movement and assume its leadership. It was her first books of poetry that firmly established her reputation as a lyric shaman and celebrant of biculturalism. For *Chants* (1984) and for *Borders* (1986), Mora received Southwest Book Awards, critical acclaim, and entry into the college and high school curricula. It is in the latter work that she employs the metaphor that unites much of her work—the border. Having lived on the U.S.-Mexican border most of her life, she is intrigued by borders and interprets them not only physically but philosophically, in broad terms. She came to see that being marginalized as a Mexican American was a type of border existence—imposing limits and separations. And Mora continued from there, using the metaphor to also describe the relationship between men and women.

While life on the border allows one a perspective from which to observe and understand two societies, it also makes one feel like the outsider. And so alienation becomes a condition of existence for the border-dweller:

> an American to Mexicans
> a Mexican to Americans
> a handy token
> sliding back and forth
> between the fringes of both worlds
>
> . . .
>
> of being prejudged
> bilaterally
> from "Legal Alien"

She also sees the border in terms of social classes and racism, where the skin color of Mexicans is a border to Anglos ("Mexican Maid") and where class differences even separate Mexicans from Mexican Americans ("Illegal Alien"). But in the dominant poems of *Chants,* Mora begins to see the border as a center of power, a place from which divisions can be bridged, wounds healed, and mutual understanding achieved. The border is no longer a margin and the people who live there are not marginal.

It is also in *Chants* that Mora employs another—often inhospitable—border: the desert. But she personifies the desert as a strong, enduring woman, like her grandmother and others who nurtured her as a child. Mora continually sees the strength of other Mexican women and their power to bridge gaps in society. Eventually she finds this strength in herself—in being a woman commanding respect in a university board room, speaking before an audience of educators, or in relationships with men. The poet's relationship with Mother Desert is magical in *Chants*: it transforms the poet into a shaman, who is able to tap the desert's mysterious power, its rhythms, its ability to heal (with herbs that grow there), its warmth, and its toughness:

> Desert women know
> about survival
> from "Desert Women"

"Mi Madre" (My Mother), the central poem in *Chants,* became the basis for one of Mora's award-wining children's books: *The Desert Is My Mother/El desierto es mi madre.* Behind this idea of the desert as a strong female/mother is the somewhat romantic idea that women are closer to nature than are men, that women feel the rhythms of nature and, just as the desert gives birth to flowers, women, too, give life.

"I write, in part, because Hispanic perspectives need to be part of our literary heritage . . . I also write because I am fascinated by the pleasure and power of words."

Pat Mora

Mora brings the power of the desert to her poetry readings as well, where she creates a mystical aura, often reading barefoot and in the calm, soothing voice of a shaman, or *curandera* (faith healer).

Another border that Mora negotiates in all three of her poetry books, including *Communion,* is the border between the past and the present. Again, she draws upon the strong women who preceded her in the United States and in Mexico: her Tía Loba, her grandmother, her mother, *curanderas,* and rebels. In her book of personal essays, *Nepantla,* Mora adds the Mexican colonial poet and intellectual, Sor Juana Inés de la Cruz, to her pantheon. Mora sees her role in passing on their wisdom to her own daughters and to society at large. "I write, in part, because Hispanic perspectives need to be part of our literary heritage; I want to be part of that validation process," said Mora in 1991. But hers is not a static vision; Mora insists on choosing the best from the past, casting a critical eye, and making necessary changes:

> To transform our traditions wisely, we need to know them, be inspired and sad-
> dened by them, choose for ourselves what to retain. But we can prize the past together,
> valuing the positive female and Mexican traditions. We can prize the elements of the
> past as we persist in demanding, and creating, change. (*Nepantla,* p. 56).

What Mora specifically chooses to reject from the Mexican past are the limited roles society has forced upon women, especially when it comes to controlling their sexuality. These rituals and practices are censured in her poems "Dream" and "Aztec Princess."

In *Communion,* her third collection of poems, Mora's metaphor of borders becomes most expansive, as she shows the similarities between Chicano/minority culture in the United States and the marginalized cultures of Third World. As the title indicates, Mora emphasizes the need for people to come together, heal the rifts, and create a global community— a communion:

> My community is not only my ethnic community but also all the like-minded souls
> seeking a more equitable world. *(Nepantla,* p.147)

In her travels, which she documents in this book, Mora not only sees that the race and class differences in countries around the world bear comparison with the minority condition in the United States, but she identifies the many faces of patriarchy that suppress women in many cultures ("Too Many Eyes," "Veiled," and "The Mystery").

In *Nepantla: Essays from the Land in the Middle* (1993), Mora expands upon the themes in her poetry as she turns her attention to the borders in her own life, one of which is the division (and conflict) between her professional-administrator life and her poet-writer life. The rift is even substantiated in the writing style, with the language oscillating between the discursive and the poetic.

Most of Pat Mora's poetry has attracted the attention of Chicano and feminist scholars and small press reviewers, who almost universally appreciate her shamanistic-healer stance and her idealistic desire to unite and heal. An unsigned review of *Chants* in *Dusty Dog Reviews* stated, "This is richly feminine poetry, in which a healthy, womanly sensuality is being continuously awakened like the living dawn that spreads its westward lights across the world, continuously unveiling a physical magic." Anya Achtenberg wrote in *Contact II,* "Healers, those who restore harmony by bringing together what seems to be separate, often suffer but possess great 'magic,' and Mora's is a healing voice." Jewelle Gómez wrote in *Hurricane Alice* that, "Mora has a powerful grasp of the music of everyday language, and she is not afraid of dark, complex feelings . . . . Mora's simplicity and economy create a haunting sense of timelessness." Gómez goes on to characterize the women in *Chants*: "None of these women have been bowed by the weighty roles chosen for them in this society. To be old, to speak only one language, are not stigmas; they are conditions in a natural transitory order . . . . This collection is rich, spirited, promising."

Mora's children's books, too, have met with almost universal acclaim. She is adept at creating sensitive portrayals of both Mexican American and Mexican cultures. Mary Sarber wrote (about *A Birthday Basket for Tía*) in *The El Paso Herald-Post*: "This is an outstanding addition to the growing body of literature that will help Hispanic children identify with their culture." What is also outstanding is that Mora's children's writing is bringing Hispanic culture to non-Hispanic children as well.

Personal Stats

Mexican American writer, teacher. **Born:** January 19, 1942, in El Paso, Texas. *Education:* B.A. in English, Texas Western College, 1963; M.A. in English, University of Texas at El Paso, 1967. *Career:* Teacher, El Paso, Texas, Independent School District, 1963–66; part-time instructor, El Paso Community College, 1971–78; part-time lecturer, University of Texas at El Paso, 1979–81; assistant to the vice president of academic affairs, University of Texas at El Paso, 1981–88; director, University Museum, 1988–89; full-time writer, 1989–present. *Honors:* Creative Writing Award from the National Association for Chicano Studies, 1983; *New America: Women Artists and Writers of the Southwest* poetry award, 1984; Harvey L. Johnson Book Award for *Chants* from the Southwest Council of Latin American Studies, 1984; Southwest Book Awards for *Chants,* 1985, and *Borders,* 1987; Kellogg National Fellowship, 1986 –89; *El Paso Herald Post* Writers Hall of Fame, 1988; Stepping Stones Award for Children's Environmental Literature for *The Desert Is My Mother,* 1995. *Address:* c/o Arte Público Press, University of Houston, Houston TX 77204-2090

Legal Alien

from *Chants*, Arte Público Press, 1984, p. 60

Bi-lingual, Bi-cultural,
able to slip from "How's life?"
to *"Me'stan volviendo loca,"*
able to sit in a paneled office
drafting memos in smooth English,
able to order in fluent Spanish
at a Mexican restaurant,
American but hyphenated,
viewed by Anglos as perhaps exotic,
perhaps inferior, definitely different,

viewed by Mexicans as alien,
(their eyes say, "You may speak
Spanish but you're not like me")
an American to Mexicans
a Mexican to Americans
a handy token
sliding back and forth
between the fringes of both worlds
by smiling
by masking the discomfort
of being pre-judged
Bi-laterally.

Immigrants

from *Borders*, Arte Público Press, 1986, p. 15

wrap their babies in the American flag,
feed them mashed hot dogs and apple pie,
name them Bill and Daisy,
buy them blonde dolls that blink blue
eyes or a football and tiny cleats
before the baby can even walk,
speak to them in thick English,
hallo, babee, hallo,
whisper in Spanish or Polish
when the babies sleep, whisper
in a dark parent bed, that dark
parent fear, "Will they like
our boy, our girl, our fine american
boy, our fine american girl?"

Fences

from *Communion*, Arte Público Press, 1991, p. 50

Mouths full of laughter,
the *turistas* come to the tall hotel

with suitcases full of dollars.
Every morning my brother makes
the cool beach sand new for them.
With a wooden board he smooths
away all footprints.
I peek through the cactus fence
and watch the women rub oil
sweeter than honey into their arms and legs
while their children jump waves
or sip drinks from long straws,
coconut white, mango yellow.
Once my little sister
ran barefoot across the hot sand
for a taste.
My mother roared like the ocean,
"No. No. It's their beach.
It's their beach."

Writings

Books of Poetry: Chants, Arte Público Press, 1984. *Borders,* Arte Público Press, 1986. *Communion, Arte Público Press, 1991. Agua Santa/Holy Water,* Beacon, 1995. **Book of Essays:** *Nepantla: Essays from the Land of the Middle,* University of New Mexico Press, 1993. **Children's Books:** *A Birthday Basket for Tía,* Macmillan, 1992. *Listen to the Desert/Oye al Desierto,* Clarion Books, 1993. *Pablo's Tree,* Simon & Schuster, 1994. *The Desert Is My Mother/ El Desierto Es Mi Madre,* Arte Público Press, 1994. *The Gift of the Poinsettia/El Regalo de la Flor de Noche Buena,* with Charles Ramírez-Berg, Arte Público Press, 1995 **Periodicals and Anthologies:** In *The Americas Review/Revista Chicano-Riqueña, Calyx, Bilingual Review, Kalliope, New America: Women Writers and Artists of the Southwest, The Heath Anthology of American Literature, The Norton Introduction to Literature, New Worlds of Literature,* and many others.

Judith Ortiz Cofer

Judith Ortiz Cofer is the first Puerto Rican writer to express—from a middle-class point of view—the disjuncture of migrating from island to mainland, and back again. Her poetry, novel, and autobiographical essays explore, even celebrate, the perspective she has gained from seeing life through the prism of two languages and two cultures. Through that prism, Ortiz Cofer has been able to analyze the varying and conflicting rituals in the education and rearing of children in Anglo-American and Hispanic cultures. She also comments on the gender roles in both cultures.

Judith Ortiz was born in Puerto Rico in 1952 into a family that was destined to move back and forth between Puerto Rico and New Jersey. Her father, Jesús Ortiz Lugo, was a Navy man, first assigned to the Brooklyn Navy Yard and then other points around the world. In Puerto Rico, young Judith attended San José Catholic School in San Germán and after the family moved to New Jersey in 1956, she went to public schools in Paterson, and later to Saint Joseph's Catholic School. In 1968, after her father retired from the Navy due to a nervous breakdown, the family moved to Augusta, Georgia, where Ortiz attended high school and later, Augusta College. She met Charles John Cofer at the college and they were married November 13, 1971. After graduation and the birth of her daughter Tanya, the family moved to West Palm Beach, Florida, where Ortiz Cofer earned an M.A. degree at Florida Atlantic University (1977). In 1977, the English-Speaking Union of America awarded her a scholarship to do graduate work at Oxford University. Among her many other awards are fellowships from the Florida Arts Council (1980), the Bread Loaf Writers Conference (1981), the Virginia Center for the Creative Arts (1985), the Witter Bynner Foundation (1988), and the National Endowment for the Arts (1989).

While pursuing her writing career and raising her daughter, Ortiz Cofer also held positions as a part-time instructor at universities and colleges in Florida and Georgia. She became one of the very few Hispanic writers ever chosen to teach at creative writing workshop-conferences when in 1991 she became a member of the teaching staff of the Bread Loaf Writers Conference Association. In 1992, her daughter raised and her writing career established, Ortiz Cofer secured a full-time position teaching creative writing and English at the University of Georgia. She has also lectured and given workshops at other universities, including Yale University, the University of Paris, and the University of Miami. Ortiz Cofer has read her works and given workshops at such prestigious venues as the Academy of American Poets, the 92nd Street YMCA in New York, the Modern Language Association Convention, and the Poetry Society of America.

While teaching English in south Florida area colleges, Ortiz Cofer began writing poetry, and her works soon appeared in such magazines as the *New Mexico Humanities Review, Kansas Quarterly, Prairie Schooner, Revista Chicano-Riqueña,* and *Southern Poetry Review.* Her collections of poetry include four chapbooks—*Latin Women Pray* (1980), *Among Ancestors* (1981), *The Native Dancer* (1981), *Peregrina* (1986); and two books—*Reaching for the Mainland* (1987), and *Terms of Survival* (1987). Her well-crafted poetry reflects her struggle as a writer to create a history for herself out of the cultural ambiguity of a childhood spent traveling between the United States and Puerto Rico. It is from a feminist perspective that she explores her relationship with her father, mother (Fanny Morot Ortiz), and grandmother, while also considering the different expectations that exist for males and females in both Anglo-American and Hispanic cultures. Her book of autobiographical essays and poems, *Silent Dancing: A Partial Remembrance of a Puerto Rican Childhood* (1990), in particular, addresses this question. Her only novel to date, *The Line of the Sun* (1989), is based on her family's immigration to the United States, and chronicles the years from the Depression to the 1960s. *The New York Times Book Review* praised the novel for the "vigorous elegance" of the language and called Ortiz Cofer "a prose writer of evocatively lyrical authority, a novelist of historical compass and sensitivity."

Personal Stats

Puerto Rican writer and teacher. Born: February 24, 1952, in Hormigueros, Puerto Rico. **Education:** B.A. in English, Augusta College, 1974; M.A. in English, Florida Atlantic University, 1977; English Speaking Union Fellow at Oxford University,

England, Summer Graduate School, 1977. *Career:* Bilingual teacher, Palm Beach County, Florida, public schools, 1974–75; adjunct instructor in English, 1978–80, and instructor in Spanish, 1979, Broward Community College, Fort Lauderdale, Florida; instructor, University of Miami English Department, 1980–84; instructor, University of Georgia English Department, 1984–87; instructor, Macon College Humanities Division, 1988–89; member, teaching staff, Bread Loaf Writers Conference, 1983, 1984, and 1991–present; assistant professor of English and Creative Writing, University of Georgia, 1992–present. *Memberships:* PEN, Bread Loaf Writers Association, Modern Language Association. *Honors/Awards:* Riverstone International Poetry Competition, 1985; New York Public Library System List of 25 Most Memorable Books of 1989 for *Line of the Sun;* Special Citation from the PEN Martha Albrand Award for *Silent Dancing;* Special Mention, *Best American Essays* anthology, 1990; Pushcart Prize in the essay category, 1990; New York Public Library System List of Best Books for the Teen Age for *Silent Dancing,* 1991; title essay in *Silent Dancing* chosen by

Joyce Carol Oates for *The Best American Essays,* 1991. **Address:** Department of English, University of Georgia, Athens, Georgia 30602

Casa

from *Silent Dancing: A Partial Rememberance of a Puerto Rican Childhood,* Arte Público Press, 1990, pp. 14–21

At three or four o'clock in the afternoon, the hour of *café con leche,* the women of my family gathered in Mamá's living room to speak of important things and to tell stories for the hundredth time, as if to each other, meant to be overheard by us young girls, their daughters. In Mamá's house (everyone called my grandmother Mamá) was a large parlor built by my grandfather to his wife's exact specifications so that it was always cool, facing away from the sun. The doorway was on the side of the house so no one could walk directly into her living room. First they had to take a little stroll through and around her beautiful garden where prize-winning orchids grew in the trunk of an ancient tree she had hollowed out for that purpose. This room was furnished with several mahogany rocking chairs, acquired at the births of her children, and one intricately carved rocker that had passed down to Mamá at the death of her own mother. It was on these rockers that my mother, her sisters and my grandmother sat on these afternoons of my childhood to tell their stories, teaching each other and my cousin and me what it was like to be a woman, more specifically, a Puerto Rican woman. They talked about life on the island, and life in *Los Nueva Yores,* their way of referring to the U.S., from New York City to California: the other place, not home, all the same. They told real-life stories, though as I later learned, always embellishing them with a little or a lot of dramatic detail, and they told *cuentos,* the morality and cautionary tales told by the women in our family for generations: stories that became a part of my subconscious as I grew up in two worlds, the tropical island and the cold city, and which would later surface in my dreams and in my poetry.

One of these tales was about the woman who was left at the altar. Mamá liked to tell that one with histrionic intensity. I remember the rise and fall of her voice, the sighs, and her constantly gesturing hands, like two birds swooping through her words. This particular story would usually come up in a conversation as a result of someone mentioning a forthcoming engagement or wedding. The first time I remember hearing it, I was sitting on the floor at Mamá's feet, pretending to read a comic book. I may have been eleven or twelve years old: at that difficult age when a girl is no longer a child who can be ordered to leave the room if the women wanted freedom to take their talk into forbidden zones, or really old enough to be considered a part of their conclave. I could only sit quietly, pretending to be in another world, while absorbing it all in a sort of unspoken agreement of my status as silent auditor. On this day, Mamá had taken my long, tangled mane of hair into her ever busy hands. Without looking down at me or interrupting her flow of words, she began braiding my hair, working at it with the quickness and determination which characterized all her actions. My mother was watching us impassively from her rocker across the room. On her lips played a little ironic smile. I would never sit still for *her* ministrations, but even then, I instinctively knew that she did not possess Mamá's matriarchal power to command and keep everyone's attention. This was particularly evident in the spell she cast when telling a story.

"It is not like it used to be when I was a girl." Mamá announced, "Then, a man could leave a girl standing at the church altar with a bouquet of fresh flowers in her hands and disappear off the face of the earth. No way to track him down if he was from another town. He could be a married man, with maybe even two or three families all over the island. There was no way to know. And there were men who did this. Hombres with the devil in their flesh who would come to a pueblo, like this one, take a job at one of the haciendas, never meaning to stay, only to have a good time and to seduce the women."

The whole time she was speaking, Mamá was weaving my hair into a flat plait which required pulling apart the two sections of hair with little jerks that made my eyes water; but knowing how grandmother detested whining and *boba* (sissy) tears, as she called them, I just sat up as straight and stiff as I did at La Escuela San José, where the nuns enforced good posture with a flexible plastic ruler they bounced off slumped shoulders and heads. As Mamá's story progressed, I noticed how my young aunt Laura had lowered her eyes, refusing to meet Mamá's meaningful gaze. Laura was seventeen, in her last year of high school, and already engaged to a boy from another town who had staked his claim with a tiny diamond ring, then left for Los Nueva Yores to make his fortune. They were planning to get married in a year; but Mamá had expressed serious doubts that the wedding would ever take place. In Mamá's eyes, a man set free without a legal contract was a man lost. She believed that marriage was not something men desired, but simply the price they had to pay for the privilege of children, and of course, for what no decent (synonymous with "smart") woman would give away for free.

"María la Loca was only seventeen when *it* happened to her." I listened closely at the mention of this name. María was a town "character," a fat middle-aged woman who lived with her old mother on the outskirts of town. She was to be seen around the pueblo delivering the meat pies the two women made for a living. The most peculiar thing about María, in my eyes, was that she walked and moved like a little girl, though she had the thick body and wrinkled face of an old woman. She would swing her hips in an exaggerated, clownish way, and sometimes even hop and skip up to someone's house. She spoke to no one. Even if you asked her a question, she would just look at you and smile, showing her yellow teeth. But I had heard that if you got close enough, you could hear her humming a tune without words. The kids yelled out nasty things at her, calling her *la Loca,* and the men who hung out at the bodega playing dominoes sometimes whistled mockingly as she passed by with her funny, outlandish walk. But María seemed impervious to it all, carrying her basket of *pasteles* like a grotesque Little Red Riding Hood through the forest.

María la Loca interested me, as did all the eccentrics and "crazies" of our pueblo. Their weirdness was a measuring stick I used in my serious quest for a definition of "normal." As a Navy brat, shuttling between New Jersey and the pueblo, I was constantly made to feel like an oddball by my peers, who made fun of my two-way accent: a Spanish accent when I spoke English; and, when I spoke Spanish, I was told that I sounded like a "Gringa." Being the outsiders had already turned my brother and me into cultural chameleons, developing early the ability to blend into a crowd, to sit and read quietly in a fifth story apartment building for days and days when it was too bitterly cold to play outside; or, set free, to run wild in Mamá's realm, where she took charge of our lives, releasing mother for a while from the intense fear for our safety that our father's absences instilled in her. In order to keep us from harm when father was away, mother kept us under strict surveillance. She even walked us to and from Public School No. 11, which we attended during the months we lived in Paterson, New Jersey, our home base in the States. Mamá freed the three of us like pigeons from a cage. I saw her as my liberator and my model. Her stories were parables from which to glean the *Truth*.

"María la Loca was once a beautiful girl. Everyone thought she would marry the Méndez boy." As everyone knew, Rogelio Méndez was no other than the richest man in town. "But," Mamá continued, knitting my hair with the same intensity she was putting into her story, "this *macho* made a fool out of her and ruined her life." She paused for the effect of her use of the word "macho," which at that time had not yet become a popular epithet for an unliberated man. This word had for us the crude and comical connotation of "male of the species," stud; a *macho* was what you put in a pen to increase your stock.

I peeked over my comic book at my mother. She too was under Mamá's spell, smiling conspiratorially at this little swipe at men. She was safe from Mamá's contempt in this area. Married at an early age, an unspotted lamb, she had been accepted by a good family of strict Spaniards whose name was old and respected, though their fortune had been lost long before my birth. In a rocker Papá had painted sky blue sat Mamá's oldest child, Aunt Nena. Mother of three children, stepmother of two more, she was a quiet woman who liked books but had married an ignorant and abusive widower whose main interest in life was accumulating wealth. He too was in the mainland working on his dream of returning home rich and triumphant to buy the *finca* of his dreams. She was waiting for him to send for her. She would leave her children with Mamá for several years while the two of them slaved away in factories. He would one day be a rich man, and she a sadder woman. Even now her life-light was dimming. She spoke little, an aberration in Mamá's house, and she read avidly, as if storing up spiritual food for the long winters that awaited her in Los Nueva Yores without her family. But even Aunt Nena came alive to Mamá's words, rocking gently, her hands over a thick book in her lap. Her daughter, my cousin Sara, played jacks by herself on the tile porch outside the room where we sat. She was a year older than I. We shared a bed and all our family's secrets. Collaborators in search of answers, Sara and I discussed everything we heard the women say, trying to fit it all together like a puzzle that once assembled would reveal life's mysteries to us. Though she and I still enjoyed taking part in boy's games—chase, volleyball and even *vaqueros,* the island version of cowboys and Indians involving cap-gun battles and violent shootouts under the mango tree in Mamá's backyard— we loved best the quiet hours in the afternoon when the men were still at work and the boys had gone to play serious baseball at the park. Then Mamá's house belonged only to us women. The aroma of coffee perking in the kitchen, the mesmerizing creaks and groans of the rockers, and the women telling their lives in *cuentos* are forever woven into the fabric of my imagination, braided like my hair that day I felt my grandmother's hands teaching me about strength, her voice convincing me of the power of story-telling.

That day Mamá told of how the beautiful María had fallen prey to a man whose name was never the same in subsequent versions of the story; it was Juan one time, José, Rafael, Diego, another. We understood that the name, and really any of the facts, were not important, only that a woman had allowed love to defeat her. Mamá put each of us in María's place by describing her wedding dress in loving detail: how she looked like a princess in her lace as she waited at the altar. Then, as Mamá approached the tragic denouement of her story, I was distracted by the sound of my Aunt Laura's violent rocking. She seemed on the verge of tears. She knew the fable was intended for her. That week she was going to have her wedding gown fitted, though no firm date had been set for the marriage. Mamá ignored Laura's obvious discomfort, digging out a ribbon from the sewing basket she kept by her rocker while describing María's long illness, "a fever that would not break for days." She spoke of a mother's despair: "that woman climbed the church steps on her knees every morning, wore only black as a *promesa* to the Holy Virgin in exchange for her daughter's health." By the time María returned from her honeymoon with death, she was ravished, no longer young or sane. "As you can see she is almost as old as her mother already," Mamá lamented while tying the ribbon to the ends of my hair, pulling it back with such force that I just knew that I would never be able to close my eyes completely again.

"That María is getting crazier every day." Mamá's voice would take a lighter tone now, expressing satisfaction, either for the perfection of my braid, or for a story well-told; it was hard to tell. "You know that tune she is always humming?" Carried away by her enthusiasm, I tried to nod, but Mamá would still have me pinned between her knees.

"Well, that's the wedding march." Surprising us all, Mamá sang out, *"Da, da, dará . . . da, da, dará."* Then lifting me off the floor by my skinny shoulders, she lead me around the room in an impromptu waltz—another session ending with the laughter of women, all of us caught up in the infectious joke of our lives.

The Woman Who Was Left at the Altar

from *Silent Dancing,: A Partial Rememberance of a Puerto Rican Childhood,* Arte Público Press, 1990, p. 22

She calls her shadow Juan,
looking back often as she walks.
She has grown fat, breasts huge
as reservoirs. She once opened her blouse

in church to show the silent town
what a plentiful mother she could be.
Since her old mother died, buried in black,
she lives alone.
Out of the lace she made curtains for her room,
doilies out of the veil. They are now
yellow as malaria.
She hangs live chickens from her waist to sell,
walks to the town swinging her skirts of flesh.
She doesn't speak to anyone. Dogs follow
the scent of blood to be shed. In their hungry,
yellow eyes she sees his face.
She takes him to the knife time after time.

Writings

Novel: *The Line of the Sun,* University of Georgia Press, 1989. ***Books of Poetry and Essays:*** *Latin Women Pray* (chapbook), Florida Arts Gazette Press, 1980. *The Native Dancer* (chapbook), Pterandon Press, 1981. *Among the Ancestors* (chapbook), Louisville News Press, 1981. *Peregrina* (poetry chapbook), Riverstone Press, 1986. *Reaching for the Mainland* (poems in the trilogy *Triple Crown* with two other authors), Bilingual Press, 1987. *Terms of Survival* (poems), Arte Público Press, 1987. *Silent Dancing: A Partial Remembrance of a Puerto Rican Childhood* (personal essays and poems), Arte Público Press, 1990. *The Latin Deli* (prose and poetry), University of Georgia Press, 1993. ***Poems:*** In *The Americas Review, Prairie Schooner, New Letters, Kansas Quarterly, Southern Poetry Review, Southern Humanities Review, Antioch Review, Kenyon Review, Georgia Review, Parnassus, Glamor,* and in many other magazines, journals and anthologies. ***Articles and Essays:*** In *Prairies Schooner, The Women's Review of Books, The Americas Review, Georgia Review, Missouri Review, Brújula/The Compass, The Pushcart Prize Anthology XV, Best American Essays, 1991,* and others.

Gustavo Pérez-Firmat

The creator of highly crafted, sensitive poems about exile, immigration, bilingualism, and biculturalism, Gustavo Pérez-Firmat is one of the most intellectual of those who are writing about the Cuban condition. His obsession with topics relating to biculturalism has also informed his literary scholarship, leading him to pen the most important book-length essay about being Cuban American. That essay is Life on the Hyphen: The Cuban American Way.

Pérez-Firmat was born in Havana, Cuba, on March 7, 1949, and relocated with his family to Miami after Castro came to power in Cuba. Pérez-Firmat received most of his formal education in Miami, obtaining a B.A. and an M.A. in Spanish from the University of Miami in 1972 and 1973, respectively. He went on to earn his Ph.D. in Comparative Literature (1979) at the University of Michigan, but Miami and the life of Cuban Americans remained central to his consciousness, even when he became a professor of Spanish and literature at Duke University in 1978.

Pérez-Firmat's basic condition—born in Cuba and transplanted to American soil in his youth—has made him a member of the new "Cuban-American" generation and has led to his theories about the dual perspective held by what he terms a "transitional" generation. For this poet/theorist, Cuban-Americans of his generation can be equally at home—or equally uncomfortable—

in both Cuba and the United States. They are cultural mediators, who are constantly translating not only language but the differences between the Anglo-American and Cuba/Cuban American world views. Since they have the unique ability to communicate with and understand both cultures, these Cuban Americans have taken on the role of translator not only for themselves but for society at large. Pérez-Firmat maintains, however, that this is only a transitional stage and that the next generation will follow a path similar to that of the children of European immigrants, who are simply considered ethnic Americans and are more American than they are anything else.

Pérez-Firmat has studied popular culture in the United states, particularly the phenomenal successes of other Cuban-Americans, such as Desi Arnaz and Gloria Estefan, and how they successfully manipulated both American and Cuban codes to speak to two audiences at the same time.

Themes of biculturalism are ever-present in Pérez-Firmat's poetry, but especially in his concept of language:

> The fact that I
>
> am writing to you
>
> in English
>
> already falsifies what I
>
> wanted to tell you

He is equally at home writing in English or Spanish, and also employs code-switching in his works. However, in many ways, he also feels alienated from both languages and the cultures they represent:

> I
>
> don't belong to English
>
> though I belong nowhere else

In his book-length memoir, *Next Year in Cuba* (1995), Pérez-Firmat documents the tension his generation feels between identifying with other Americans their age and identifying with their parents, who always looked forward to returning to Cuba. True to form, Pérez-Firmat re-created the memoir in Spanish (for publication in 1997).

While biculturalism forms the framework for Pérez-Firmat's poetry, it is not his sole theme. He is an expansive poet, a poet of love and eroticism, and of the daily, tedious rhythms of life. He chronicles both growing up and growing old; battles with family and battles with illness.

Pérez-Firmat's basic condition— born in Cuba and transplanted to American soil in his youth—has made him a member of the new "Cuban-American" generation and has led to his theories about the dual perspective held by what he terms a "transitional" generation.

Personal Stats

Cuban American professor, writer. **Born:** March 7, 1949, in Havana, Cuba. *Education:* B.A. and M.A. in Spanish, University of Miami, 1972 and 1973, respectively; Ph.D. in Comparative Literature, University of Michigan, 1979. *Memberships:* Modern Language Association, Association of Teachers of Spanish and Portuguese, American Studies Association, Phi Beta Kappa. *Career:* Professor, Spanish Department, Duke University, 1978–present. *Awards/ Honors:* American Council of Learned Societies Fellowship, 1981; National Endowment for the Humanities Senior Fellowship, 1985; Guggenheim Fellowship, 1986. *Address:* Spanish Department, Duke University, 205 Languages Building, Durham, NC 27706

Lost in Translation

from *Life on the Hyphen,* 1994, University of Texas Press, Mambo No. 1, pp. 21–22; Mambo No. 2, 46–47; Mambo No. 3, pp. 77–78; Mambo No. 4, p. 103; Mambo No. 5, 134–35; Mambo No. 6, 154–55

Mambo No. 1.

Take the phrase literally. Turn the commonplace into a place. Try to imagine where one ends up if one gets lost in translation. When I try to visualize such a place, I see myself, on a given Saturday afternoon, in the summer, somewhere in Miami. Since I'm thirsty, I go into a store called Love Juices, which specializes in nothing more salacious or salubrious than milk shakes made from papayas and other tropical fruits. Having quenched my thirst, I head for a boutique called Mr. Trapus, whose name-*trapo*-is actually the Spanish word for an old rag. Undaunted by the consumerist frenzy that has possessed me, I enter another store called Cachi Bachi-a name that, in spite of its chichi sound, is a slang word for a piece of junk, *cachi-vache.* And then for dinner I go to the Versailles of Eighth Street, a restaurant where I feast on something called Tropical Soup, the American name for the traditional Cuban stew, *ajiaco.* My dessert is also tropical, Tropical Snow, which is Miamian for *arroz con leche;* and to finish off the meal, of course, I sip some Cuban American espresso (don't go home without it). In this way I spend my entire afternoon lost in translation-and loving every minute. Translation takes you to a place where cultures divide to conga.

Spic'n Spanish

Mambo No. 2

Miami Spanish includes a term that, so far as I know, is unique to the city of sun and solecisms: *nilingüe.* Just as a bilingüe is someone who speaks two languages (say, Spanish and English), a *nilingüe* is someone who doesn't speak either: *"ni español, ni inglés."* Such a person is a no-lingual, a nulli-glot. My example of nilingualism is Ricky Ricardo. Ricky's occasional Spanish utterances are shot through with anglicisms: *falta* for *culpa, introducir* for *presentar, parientes* for *padres,* and so on. Sometimes the anglicisms seem deliberate (so that the monolingual viewers understand what he is saying), but at other times they're plain mistakes. A curious thing: as Ricky got older, his English didn't get any better, but his Spanish kept getting worse. Equally curious: the same thing happened to Desi Arnaz. In 1983 Arnaz was picked "king" of the Cuban carnival in Miami, Open House Eight. By then, his Spanish was as frail as his health. He now had an accent in *two* languages.

In Spanish to know a language well is to dominate it. But my mother tongue has it backward: people don't dominate languages, languages dominate people. By reversing the power relation, English comes closer to the truth. When someone speaks English better than Spanish, we say that he or she is "English-dominant," an expression in which the language, and not the speaker, has the upper hand. But in Ricky no language achieved dominance; English and Spanish battled each other to a tie (a tongue-tie). A *nilingüe* treats his mother tongue like a foreign language and treats the foreign language like his other tongue. T. W. Adorno once said: "Only he who is not truly at home inside a language can use it as an instrument." Ricky Ricardo is a multi-instrumentalist. He is homeless in two languages.

Desi Does It

Mambo No. 3

Going through her father's house after his death, Lucie Arnaz found a box of papers and memorabilia that she donated to the Love Library at San Diego State University, where Desi had lectured several times. The Desi Arnaz Collection contains a few home movies, an old film short entitled *Jitterhumba,* several drafts of *A Book,* and assorted notes that Arnaz took when he was working on his autobiography. Originally intending to write either a sequel to *A Book* (to be called *Another Book*) or a novel (probably to be called *A Novel*), Arnaz marked some of these jottings "Other Book" or "Novel." The notes contain not only many self-revealing moments and juicy gossip (like a list of Lucille Ball's alleged lovers), but also some of Desi's best quips.

Seeing Gary Morton, Lucy's second husband, on a TV talk show, he writes: "About Gary on TV with Lucy: Seems to be suffering from a massive inferiority complex to which he is fully entitled." To his children, Lucie and Desi, Jr., he once remarked: "The only reason you are here is because I woke up one night and couldn't think of anything else to do." About his famous quarrels with Lucy, he says: "Lucy and I had some great battles but at times when someone asked me why we fought, I had to answer, 'I don't know. She wouldn't tell me.'" Most pertinent, perhaps, are his thoughts on being a writer: "Writing a book is, I discovered, not an easy thing to do. It also proves that the brain is a wonderful thing. It starts up when you are born and stops when you sit down at the typewriter."

But my favorite is the simple aphorism "History is made at night." It seems appropriate that the box ended up at a place called the Love Library.

The Barber of Little Havana

Mambo No. 4

When I first became interested in the mambo some years ago, I was puzzled to find that a well-respected British reference work, *The Faber Companion to 20th Century Popular Music,* gave Pérez Prado's first name as Pantaleón rather than Dámaso. More puzzling still, after describing Pérez Prado's career in accurate detail, the entry concluded, "His elder brother Damos [sic] was also a band leader and composer who specialized in the mambo." Later I discovered that Pérez Prado actually had a brother named Pantaleón, who was also a musician. Still later, while going through some music magazines from the 1950s, I found Pantaleón had actually toured Europe claiming to be the Mambo King, an imposture that ended only when Dámaso threatened to take legal, rather than musical, steps.

For many years there has been a barbershop on Eighth Street in Miami called Barberia Pérez Prado. Its elderly owner bears a striking resemblance to Dámaso; some say he is Pérez Prado's brother, Pantaleón. But when questioned by visitors, the barber of Little Havana disclaims any connection. Will the real mambo king please stand up and grunt?

Mirror, Mirror

Mambo No. 5

One of the landmarks of Cuban Miami is a restaurant called Versailles, which has been located on Eighth Street and Thirty-fifth Avenue for many years. About the only thing this Versailles shares with its French namesake is that is has lots of mirrors on its walls. One goes to the Versailles not only to be seen, but to be multiplied. This quaint, kitschy, noisy restaurant that serves basic Cuban food is a paradise for the self-absorbed: the Nirvana of Little Havana. Because of the bright lights, even the windows reflect. The Versailles is a Cuban panopticon: you can lunch, but you can't hide. Who goes there wants to be the stuff of visions. Who goes there wants to make a spectacle of himself (or herself). All the *ajiaco* you can eat and all the jewelry you can wear multiplied by the number of reflecting planes-and to top it off, a waitress who calls you *mi vida.*

Across the street at La Carreta, another popular restaurant, the food is the same (both establishments are owned by the same man) but the feel is different. Instead of mirrors La Carreta has booths. There you can ensconce yourself in a booth and not be faced with multiple images of yourself. But at the Versailles there is no choice but to bask in self-reflective glory.

For years I have harbored the fantasy that those mirrors retain the blurred image of everyone who has paraded before them. I think the mirrors have a memory, as when one turns off the TV and the shadowy figures remain on the screen. Every Cuban who has lived or set foot in Miami over the last three decades has, at one time or another, seen himself or herself reflected on those shiny surfaces. It's no coincidence that the Versailles sits only two blocks away from the Woodlawn Cemetery, which contains the remains of many Cuban notables, including Desi Arnaz's father, whose remains occupy a niche right above Gerardo Machado's. Has anybody ever counted the number of Cubans who have died in Miami? Miami is a Cuban city not only because of the number of Cubans who live there but also because of the number who have died there.

The Versailles is a glistening mausoleum. The history of Little Havana-tragic, comic, tragicomic-is written on those spectacular specular walls. This may have been why, when the mirrors came down in 1991, there was such an uproar that some of them had to be put back. The hall of mirrors is also a house of spirits. When the time comes for me to pay for my last *ajiaco,* I intend to disappear into one of the mirrors (I would prefer the one on the right, just above the espresso machine). My idea of immortality is to become a mirror image at the Versailles.

English Is Broken Here

Mambo No. 6

Some years ago a Cuban radio station in Miami aired an advertisement promoting an airline's reduced fares: "Piedmont Airlines quiere limpiar el aire sobre sus bajas tarifas." Limpiar el aire? "clean the air?" This phrase is ungrammatical in two languages. First mistake: perhaps influenced by the Spanish *poner en limpio* (to clean up), the author of the ad must have thought that the English idiom was "clean the air" rather than "clear the air." Second mistake: he then decided that "clean the air" could be translated word for word into Spanish. Third mistake: he rendered "about" as "sobre," which in context sounds too much like "over" or "above." Hence: "Piedmont Airlines wants to clean the air above its low fares." But this sentence does have a certain flighty logic, especially considering that it went out over the airwaves. Piedmont's cleanser act is an interlingual utterance that remains up in the air, that cannot make up its mind whether to land in the domain of Spanish or English.

Another comedy of grammatical errors will bring us back to earth: there is a Cuban-owned pizza chain in Miami called Casino's Pizza. When Casino's was launched (or lunched) a few years ago, its publicity campaign included a bilingual brochure. I quote the first sentence of the Spanish text: "Su primera mirada, su primer olor, su primer gusto le dirá que usted descubrió La Pizza Ultima." Since "La Pizza Ultima" (the last pizza) doesn't make much sense in Spanish (it should have been "la última pizza" anyway), upon first reading this anglicized sentence, I had the impression that the final phrase was an incompletely digested translation of "the ultimate pizza." In order to check out my hunch, I went to the English text: "Your first sight, your first smell, your first taste will tell you that you've discovered La Pizza Ultima."

So what happened to my hypothetical Ultimate Pizza? It seems to have been eaten in translation. The same phrase that sounds like an anglicism in Spanish is offered as a hispanicism in English! Food for thought: the English phrase presupposes a Spanish phrase that presupposes an English phrase that doesn't exist. This is a paradox-lover's pizza, one that consumes itself in the cracks between languages. Like the Piedmont ad, "La Pizza Ultima" refuses to be English but cannot be Spanish. If Beny Moré is the "bárbaro del ritmo," the authors of these ads must be *bárbaros* of barbarism. Sometimes the American dream is written in Spanglish.

Writings

Poetry Books: *Carolina Cuban*, Bilingual Review Press, 1986. *Equivocaciones*, Editorial Betania, 1989. *Bilingual Blues* (Poems, 1981–1994), Bilingual Review Press, 1995. **Essay:** *Life on the Hyphen: The Cuban-American Way*, University of Texas, 1993. **Memoir:** *Next Year in Cuba*, Anchor Books, 1995. *El año que viene en Cuba* (translated), Arte Público Press, 1997. **Scholarly Books:** *Idle Fictions: The Hispanic Vanguard Novel, 1926–1934*, Duke University Press, 1982. *Literature and Liminality: Festive Readings in the Hispanic Tradition*, Duke University Press, 1986. *The Cuban Condition: Translation and Identity in Modern Cuban Literature*, Cambridge University Press, 1989.

Miguel Piñero

Miguel Piñero was a real-life outlaw who developed what he called an "outlaw" aesthetic in his poetry and plays. While imprisoned at Sing Sing, he wrote the first drafts of his award-winning play, Short Eyes, which would greatly influence realism on the American stage and television. Piñero was also one of the creators and promoters of a "Nuyorican" (New York Puerto Rican) literature that he and other writers popularized through readings and performances at the Nuyorican Poets Cafe on New York's Lower East Side.

Born on December 19, 1946, in Gurabo, Puerto Rico, Piñero migrated with his parents (Miguel Angel Gómez Ramos and Adelina Piñero) to New York City and was raised on the Lower East Side, where he attended public schools and became involved in street life at a very early age. Piñero grew up to be the leader of one of the most powerful gangs in New York, and became an astute and dangerous criminal. At age thirteen, he was sentenced to three years in prison for theft; by age fifteen he had become a heroine addict; at age twenty-four, he was sent to New York State Prison at Ossining (Sing Sing) for armed robbery.

At Sing Sing, Piñero was influenced by African American jailhouse poets and he began writing and reciting poetry. During his last term in prison, he enrolled in Clay Stevenson's theater workshop. It was then that Piñero began writing his revolutionary play, *Short Eyes*. Upon his release, he joined a theater company made up of ex-convicts, The Family, where he further developed the play. *Short*

Eyes was produced v the company's director, Marvin Felix Camillo, at the Riverside Church, where it was discovered by New York Shakespeare Festival Producer Joseph Papp, who gave the play an off-Broadway premiere. Critics hailed Piñero as a bright new face on the theater scene and saw the play as brutally realistic. It went on to win the prestigious New York Drama Critics' Award, for Best American Play of the 1973–74 Season.

The success of *Short Eyes* effectively launched Piñero's career not only as a serious playwright, but also as a script doctor specializing in street dialect for such television police dramas as *Kojak, Baretta,* and *Miami Vice.* It was, more than anything else, Piñero's ear for the vernacular that rang true in his plays and screenplays and that became the model for hundreds of writers who followed in his footsteps. He also turned his attention to full-length drama, writing television movies and episodic shows for TV programs including *Miami Vice.* Piñero also became a stock actor in crime dramas on television, contributing an extra dose of realism and his real-life experience to the shows. In Hollywood, his producers and directors exploited his considerable talents, using his language and insight as models for creating the stereotypes of street people and Hispanics that are often projected into America's living rooms.

It was during this period of success that Piñero married (1977) and divorced (1979) Juanita Lovette Rameize, but not before the couple adopted a son, Ismael Castro.

Piñero's plays develop an aesthetic of the streets and of life seen from below—from the vantage point of the "outlaw," the individual who lives outside established society and its laws. He created dramas about the criminal underworld, about prostitutes and pimps, about homosexuals and other marginalized denizens of the big city. *Short Eyes,* in fact was a play about the hierarchy in prison, where a child molester is supposedly considered the lowest of the low.

Although they are often humorous and sometimes ironic, Piñero's plays take aim at the comfortable aesthetics of the middle-class theater-goers. The raw language and sexual situations and the proud display of a code of honor among pimps, prostitutes, and criminals, are not Runyonesque in the least, but represent a genius striking back: Piñero was raised in dire poverty and violence, and he blamed the larger, established society for the exploitation of Third World peoples. In the play *Paper Toilet,* included in this anthology, the man who is locked in the toilet stall is the middle-class spectator/voyeur in the audience—the last laugh is on him (and the theater-goers) because they have paid Piñero to insult, scandalize, and make fun of them.

It was in his highly acerbic poetry that Piñero was able to use his native Spanish tongue to attack American racism, exploitation of the poor, colonialism (in

"I really got hooked on theatre. . . . It was like a shot of dope."

Miguel Piñero to The New York Times' Mel Gussow.

Puerto Rico), greed, and materialism—and do so without concern for the audience, the response of the critics, or the backing of theater producers. It was through his poems that he translated his wrath, literally spitting on the American flag and celebrating his addiction to drugs. He glorified his alternative lifestyle, but also foresaw his early death from it. Even at its most impudent, his poetry is a hurtful reaction to being victimized.

As a successful American artist, Piñero had the potential to ascend to the upper class, but he rejected mainstream values and its measures of achievement. He continued his life as a street urchin and outlaw, as an alcoholic and drug addict, and as a bisexual adventurer, until those roles resulted in his early demise. Piñero died at age forty-one of cirrhosis of the liver.

Personal Stats

Puerto Rican playwright, screenwriter, poet, actor. **Born:** December 19, 1946, Gurabo, Puerto Rico. **Died:** June 16 (some sources say June 17), 1988, New York City. **Education:** High school equivalency diploma, theater workshops in prison. **Career:** Playwright, 1970–88; Hollywood film and television screenwriter and actor from 1974–88. **Awards/Honors:** New York Drama Critics' Circle Award for Best American Play of the 1973–74 Season, Obie Award of 1974, and Drama Desk Award of 1974 (all for *Short Eyes*). Guggenheim Fellowship, 1984.

Paper Toilet

from *Outrageous: One Act Plays by Miguel Piñero*, 1986, Arte Público Press, pp. 9–34

Paper Toilet is a one-act play that takes place in a subway toilet. The rumble of trains is heard.

The People in the Play:

MAN 1: Middle aged.

MAN 2: Early twenties.

MAN 3: Middle aged vice cop.

MAN 4: Late twenties.

BOY 1: 15 years old.

BOY 2: 14 years old.

MAN 3: You know, I am the same way, I can't piss if someone is watching me or if I believe someone is watching me or talking to me. I guess it has to do with something from early childhood.

MAN 4: You should go see a therapist.

MAN 3: They have peeing therapists?

MAN 4: They have all kinds of therapists, it's big business nowadays to specialize in some kind of therapy.

MAN 2: Really?

MAN 4: Yes, no kidding around. I once heard of a therapist who specialized in nose picking.

MAN 2: Jesus H. Fucking Christ, will you shut up and let me pee?!!

MAN 4: I didn't know I was holding you back.

Silence. Pause. MAN 4 takes a look at MAN 3's penis. MAN 3 catches him. MAN 4 smiles and looks at the ceiling. MAN 4 takes another long look at MAN 3's penis again. This time he turns his head away before being detected. Once more he takes another look at MAN 3's penis. MAN 2 catches him.

MAN 2: Hey, whacha gonna do, suck out his dick with your eyes?

MAN 4: Who me?

MAN 2: Yeah, you, who else is here standing gawking at his dick? I'm talking to you mister . . . don't act funny with me. I know your type. You come into these places waiting for school boys to come in, and stare at them . . . you ain't gonna deny it are you? Well, where are you going? Go on, run. Go on, run, fairy . . . all alike . . . sick . . . freaking faggots . . . they come into these places to play hide and seek with other people's cocks . . . gotta watch them.

MAN 3: The cocks?

MAN 2: No, them freaks. You know what I mean.

MAN 3: No, I don't know.

MAN 2: Take it from me, I know. I been coming to these places long enough to know what I'm talking about.

MAN 3: I guess so.

MAN 2: Well, I know so.

MAN 3: I guess you do.

MAN 2: What you reading, the sports? Who won last night's game between . . .

MAN 3: I am not reading anything at all . . . I'm trying to take a piss in peace . . . if you want to read the paper while you pee, here, read it.

MAN 2: Shove it.

MAN 1: I would like to read it.

MAN 3 begins to exit. MAN 2 simulates masturbation. MAN 3 enters again.

MAN 3: Well . . . well . . . my . . . my . . . you have a big one for a white man. Can I clean it for you . . . here I have some kleenex tissues. They're supposed to be good for anything . . . even life juice. Here let me help you . . . ah, don't be shy . . . don't be embarrassed. Everybody should jerkoff now and then . . . it's good for the spirit and not to mention the wrist . . . you know what I mean?

MAN 2: No, thanks, I got a handkerchief, thank you.

MAN 3: No need to reward me, put your wallet back in your pocket. Just let me hold it for a while, that'll be reward enough for me.

MAN 2: Shut up.

MAN 3: No need to shout . . . oh, the man in the stall . . . well, don't worry about him, he's probably looking to do the same thing, just like little ole me . . . now ain't that something?

MAN 2: Shut up and look at this. Does this look like money to you?

MAN 3: No, it looks like a badge.

MAN 2: That's just what it is . . . you are under arrest . . . soliciting for the purpose of an unnatural sex act.

MAN 3: This has to be an act.

MAN 2: No, it's very real my friend.

MAN 3: If it's for real, I ain't no friend of yours. *(Goes into fit of cursing.)*

MAN 2: Oh, shut the fuck up, already will you? Ain't you ever been locked up before? Every nigger in New York has been in jail and that's the way God meant it to be. Wow, it stinks in here. Hey, you in there, you in that combat zone, why don't you flush that stink out to the river before it hits the streets and I have to come back and summons you for polluting the air.

MAN 3: Ha, ha . . . very funny, you're a real comedian ala Bob Hope . . .

¹AN 2: The air is gonna get so bad I'm gonna have to call Ralph Nader on you . . . ha . . . ha . . .

MAN 3: Jesus Christ . . .

MAN 1: Did you call my name out in vain?

MAN 3: Everybody's a comedian on the day I get arrested, shit!

MAN 1: That's what I'm doing.

MAN 2: Do it in good health.

MAN 1: Well, some come to sit and think . . . I came here to shit and stink.

MAN 2: You sure accomplished what you set out to do, mister. Okay, come on, let's go, come on, on the double.

MAN 3: What, I'm back in the army now.

MAN 1: Holy shit! No fucking toilet paper! You pay to get in here and they don't have the decency to protect you from the toilet paper thieves . . . shit . . . shit . . . shit . . . the newspaper . . . saved by the daily.

A young boy enters fast talking with another who is excited.

BOY 1: Boy, I bet there's a thousand dollars in that purse.

BOY 2: The way she fought for it and screamed and carried on, there must be a whole lot more than that. Man I bet there's a million . . .

BOY 1: I'd settle for twenty dollars.

BOY 2: Me too.

BOY 1: Let's check the motherfucker out, man. Open up the damn thing.

BOY 2: Okay, don't rush . . . man, don't rush man, be cool . . . be cool.

BOY 1: Be cool, are you kidding me? Shit, that bitch just gave us the fight of the century for this shit here and you tell me to be cool. Man, you better be cool and open up that damn thing, brother.

BOY 2: I dragged that old bitch down them stairs kicking.

BOY 1: She screamed like a fucking police siren. What a mouth.

BOY 2: Man, I almost had to stomp that bitch's back string loose before she cut loose of that damn bag.

BOY 1: Let's see what we got, brotherman.

BOY 2: Kicked her head in . . .

BOY 1: The regular junk . . .

BOY 2: Wrestled all over the platform, almost fell into the tracks.

BOY 1: Welfare card.

BOY 2: Should have let her fall . . . let the train deal with her.

BOY 1: Nothing in the little wallet . . .

BOY 2: Boy, lucky for us that the fucking strap broke or we'd be still struggling with that old big black mother jumbo.

BOY 1: My father always says, son, with people's wives . . . brothers . . . sisters . . . fuck over their whole generation . . . but don't fuck with their money.

BOY 2: My mom says, don't fuck with a wino's bottle or a junkie's cooker.

BOY 1: My father always says, son, take this advice, it's the only one that I can give freely, with confidence and experience, then he shows me a pack of scars all over his body . . . cuz if you take this advice, boy, about not fucking with other peoples money, especially when they need it badder than you, you best be cool, and you'll live to see my age. Then he takes a toke and passes out and that bottle be as empty as his advice.

BOY 2: Later for your pop, man. I can't seem to find any bread in this purse, man.

BOY 1: The hag has to have something in the bag. Like nobody fights like that for nothing, man.

BOY 2: Nothing, man, not a fucking thing, shitfuckbitchfaggot-motherfuck!

BOY 1: Man, the way that bitch fought for the fucking purse, I thought we had hit Rockerfella's grandmother, man.

BOY 2: It's your fault . . .

BOY 1: My fault?

BOY 2: 59 cents . . . 59 cents. Ain't this a kick in the motherfucking ass?

BOY 1: My fault, what you talking, nigger? You crazy shit, how the fuck can this be my fault, motherfucker?

BOY 2: You said that she was a bet, man. You said she a bet.

BOY 1: Man, the way she were holding on to that damn thing, man, what else am I to think, shit, man, be cool . . . man, she had to have something in there.

BOY 2: Maybe in the lining of the purse.

BOY 1: Yeah, rip it open brother . . .

BOY 2: Motherrrrffffuuuckkkerrrrr!

BOY 1: Damn, no way, man, she had to have something there . . . the bitch held on to it too tight, man, to, be nothing . . . maybe a welfare check.

BOY 2: There ain't nothing in there . . . what if we had gotten busted for that . . . man, that's getting busted for nothing.

BOY 1: Man, I didn't force you to go with me . . . I ain't got no gun.

BOY 2: Man, this is the last time I ever listen to you on anything again . . . the motherfucking last time, brother.

BOY 1: Man, fuck you.

BOY 2: Fuck you too, shit . . . you ain't nothing man.

BOY 1: Man, fuck you, and if you don't like it, jump, faggot.

BOY 2: Motherfucker, put your hands down before I put your jaw down.

BOY 1: Man, throw what you got, punk, and throw your best shit, 'cause you ain't saying a pound, punk . . .

BOY 2: Man, what you gonna do, you gonna fight me with your hands or with your mouth?

BOY 1: If you move your hands, I'm gonna move your teeth . . .

BOY 2: You got more shit with you than this fucking toilet.

MAN 1: Boys . . .

BOY 1: Who the fuck you calling "boy"?

BOY 2: Man, you better dig yourself, faggot.

MAN 1: I don't mean it in any manner that's derogatory, gentlemen.

BOY 1: What the hell you talking about, nigger?

BOY 2: Speak up when a man talks to you, sucker.

MAN 1: Excuse me, please, I meant no harm. I apologize, I really mean it. Believe me, I meant no harm whatsoever . . . I was only trying to capture your attention.

BOY 1: What you say?

BOY 2: Say he wanna rap.

MAN 1: I couldn't help overhearing about your little, let's say, financial adventure and about the frustrating results. I'd like to engage you in a little business.

BOY 1: Man, what the fuck you talking about, sucker?

BOY 2: He say he peeped into our comb, man.

BOY 1: Man, you better learn to mind your own business, you could get all hurt up doing shit like that.

MAN 1: I didn't mean to pry, just that your failure . . .

BOY 2: Man, my father is a failure, but not me, motherfucker. I ain't no failure.

BOY 1: Not yet, anyway.

MAN 1: I have a proposition to make . . .

BOY 1: He got a what to make?

BOY 2: I think the dude wanna play the skin flute, man.

BOY 1: Say man, are you a faggot or something?

MAN 1: I might be a motherfucker, but I'm not a faggot, young man?

BOY 1: What the deal, man?

BOY 2: We ain't icing nobody for nobody.

MAN 1: What was that?

BOY 1: What the deal?

MAN 1: Oh, the deal, yes, the deal, the deal is nothing that will get any of you in any kind of trouble. What I would like is . . . I would like to obtain that newspaper that I left on the floor over there. I . . . I . . . was reading an important article.

BOY 1: Cut the shit, you want the paper, huh? Why don't you come out and get it yourself?

MAN 1: Obviously because . . .

BOY 1: Man, you ain't got no shit paper and you wanna cop the news to do the job, right?

BOY 2: But we ain't upping the motherfucker unless you is upping something for it.

MAN 1: I was planning to offer a reward.

BOY 1: Like what, motherfucker?

BOY 2: Better be good . . .

MAN 1: Well, it is my newspaper. I left it behind.

BOY 2: Now you wanna use it for the behind.

MAN 1: I said that I would buy it from you at a very reasonable price.

BOY 1: Like what?

MAN 1: One dollar.

BOY 1: One dollar, are you serious, man?

BOY 2: Naw, man he just joking, ain't you mister?

MAN 1: Apiece . . . one dollar apiece.

BOY 1: That hold my interest a little bit.

BOY 2: . . . Cuz you know the old saying, "finders keepers, losers weepers."

BOY 1: That old saying and, besides, we were planning to read the paper, anyway.

BOY 2: That's right, so like we couldn't cut it loose for nothing.

MAN 1: I understand and I apologize for making such a meager offer for such a valuable piece of merchandise. It was unthinkable.

BOY 1: So, why you say it then?

MAN 1: So, in that light, I will offer each of you two dollars . . . consider it a reward.

BOY 1: *(Whispers.)* I think that dude has 'some bucks.

BOY 2: *(Whispers.)* I do too. dollars for a newspaper, that unreal.

MAN 1: Well, do we have a deal?

BOY 1: Hey, man, you got any more money on you?

BOY 2: Well, man, answer up, mister.

MAN 1: I don't have any real money on me.

BOY 1: What you got, counterfeit, motherfucker?

They grab the man's pants and begin a tug of war with them. They are cursing and threatening to end up with his pants.

BOY 1: And, motherfucker, you better stay in that fucking toilet.

BOY 2: Goddamn, we hit the number, fifty motherfucking dollars, bro.

MAN 1: Please, let me have my pants back.

BOY 1: Boy, you beg a lot, don't you, motherfucker?

BOY 2: He sure do, you a begging fool . . .

MAN 1: Please, keep the money . . . just give me back my pants.

BOY 1: You want the newspaper too?

MAN 1: Yes.

BOY 2: Then, be cool.

A big, rugged looking woman enters.

WOMAN: I thought I'd find you creeps in one of these places counting my money.

BOY 1: Counting your what, bitch?

BOY 2: Money? What motherfucking money you talking about, 59 cents? Is that what you call money?

WOMAN: Where's my money?

BOY 1: Here . . . here, lady, here's your freaking bag. Now get the fuck out of here before we rip you off again.

BOY 2: Rip her off again, for what? The bitch ain't got shit.

WOMAN: Rape . . . me . . . rape me, really? . . .

MAN 1: Lady, would you ask them to give me my pants.

BOY 1: Shut up in there, faggot.

BOY 2: You heard the man, don't make us repeat ourselves, motherfucker.

BOY 1: Get that clear, now mister. We ain't playing no games.

WOMAN: And neither am I. Now I want my money.

BOY 1: Lady, there ain't no money to give you, cuz you had no money to take in the first place.

WOMAN: First you take my money. Now you tell me that there wasn't none. Then you say you gonna rape me off again.

BOY 1: Rape, who said anything about rape? Shit, you must be crazy, bitch. To think anyone would wanna fuck you. Shit, bitch, you look so bad, I wouldn't fuck you with his dick. Shit, lady, you so old, I'd end up with lock jaw on my wood.

BOY 2: Purple balls . . . imagine her on the bed naked. You's a sorry sight, lady. Shit, you spoil a wet dream.

BOY 1: And you stink bad, too.

WOMAN: If you don't give me my money I'll scream and tell the cops that you armed robbery me and tried to rape me, too.

MAN 1: I'll be your witness, lady.

WOMAN: Man, shut the fuck up and flush that damn thing out of here.

BOY 1: Man, if you don't shut up, you'll be reading about yourself in the motherfucking newspaper you wanted so bad.

BOY 2: "Man drowns in subway toilet bowl."

WOMAN: Now give me my money, fellas, cuz once I start hollering, even God gonna come down and check it out too.

BOY 1: Tell him Satan is waiting for him.

BOY 2: And he ready to deal.

WOMAN: Fuck God, deal with me, you little bunch of faggots.

BOY 1: And, lady, you can scream rape all the fuck you want, cuz no one in their right mind, cop or judge, would ever believe we try to rape something as ugly as you, not even if you swear to that on a stack of bibles ten feet high.

She sails into them screaming, fist flying, cursing. They slap her upside the head with the newspaper and hit her with the pants. She throws one on the floor.

COP 1: Okay, hold it . . . what the hell is going on in here?

WOMAN: They armed robbery me and they tried to rape me, officer.

COP 1: They tried to do what?

BOY 1: You don't believe that?!

BOY 2: She try to kill us.

COP 1: That I believe . . .

COP 2: What the hell are you doing in the men's toilet, lady? Is this part of the women's liberation movement or something?

WOMAN: It's nothing. They robbery me and try to rape me. Help me arrest them. I demand that you arrest them now.

COP 1: Be quiet, lady, will you please?

A row of accusations begins between the boys and the woman.

MAN 1: Would anyone care to give me my pants or the newspaper, please?

COP 1: Hey you in there, shut up or we'll run you in for obstructing justice . . . you hear me, Mack? . . . and flush that damn thing.

MAN 1: But officer, I need that newspaper.

ALL: SHUT UP!

More accusations and arguments.

COP 2: Hold it, lady, hold it, lady!

COP 1: You two guys, shut the fuck up right now.

BOY 1: But officer . . .

COP 1: Not another fucking word, you hear me?

BOY 1: Yes, sir.

BOY 2: Be cool, bro, be cool.

WOMAN: They trying to be cool, so they can escape into the tracks.

BOY 1: She crazy.

COP 1: What did you say?

BOY 1: I didn't say anything, officer.

BOY 2: Be cool, man, be cool.

COP 1: Listen to your friend, be cool.

WOMAN: They beat me and robbed me.

COP 1: Lady, please be quiet. We'll get to the bottom of this as soon as we get some cooperation.

COP 2: Okay, now, what the hell you doing in the men's toilet?

WOMAN: I was robbery by them there two boys. They beat me, they try to rape me . . .

COP 2: Lady . . . lady, hold it. We're here to get the facts, not fantasies. Please stick to what really happened.

WOMAN: That's what really happened. They try to rape me . . .

BOY 2: The only thing we raped was your pocket book.

BOY 1: Now, who not being cool!

COP 1: So, you snatched her purse, huh?

BOY 2: Man, I didn't say that, you did.

COP 2: How would you like a size 9 up your ass, kid?

COP 1: Lady, if they try to rape you, they don't belong in a prison, but in a mental health institution.

WOMAN: They robbed me and beat me up.

BOY 1: That's a lot of shit. You were doing all the beating up.

BOY 2: Man, she almost killed us.

COP 1: Maybe we arrived too early, huh?

COP 2: Maybe we did.

COP 1: You think if we step outside for a while, they'll finish each other up?

COP 2: I don't know, but I feel that this is going to be one of them nights.

COP 1: Any of you got a knife?

BOY 1: We don't carry weapons of any kind.

COP 1: Yeah, I bet both of you sing in the choir on Sundays.

BOY 2: As a matter of fact, we do.

COP 1: Jesus.

BOY 1: He saves.

COP 1: Oh, shut up, will ya?

COP 2: Kid, we're trying to be nice guys. Why not just take our word for it that if you keep opening your trap, we're not going to be nice guys and you're gonna start screaming police brutality. So keep your fucking mouth shut.

BOY 1: Yes, sir.

COP 1: Do you understand?

BOY 1: Yes, sir.

BOY 2: Yes, sir.

COP 1: Good, now back to you, miss. Why are you in the men's toilet?

WOMAN: Because this is where they ran to escape from me.

MAN 1: Can I say something?

COP 1: Later . . . right now, keep pushing and keep your mouth shut.

MAN 1: I'm going to write my congressman about this.

COP 1: Write to the fucking mayor, mister.

COP 2: You wanna pen? Here, use the fucking toilet paper.

MAN 1: There isn't any toilet paper. That's what I'm trying to tell you.

COP 1: Well, I guess that's your tough luck, isn't it?

COP 2: Now, keep out of this investigation.

WOMAN: Now, what I was saying is that these two birds here . . .

COP 2: Watch your language, lady, please.

WOMAN: You're New York City cops and you're telling me to watch my language?!

COP 1: Lady, don't give us a hard time, please.

> *Enter vice cop.*

VICE COP: What's this, what's all this about?

COP 1: Who are you?

VICE COP: Police Vice Squad.

COP 1: Got some identification, sir?

VICE COP: Here, what's that, a play thing?

COP 1: Sorry, sir.

VICE COP: Now, what's all this about?

COP 1: That's what we're trying to figure out.

WOMAN: And they ain't doing it, telling everybody to shut up all the time, not giving anyone a chance to say anything at all. These two are not what I call cops.

COP 1: No, lady? What do you call a cop?

WOMAN: A flatfoot.

COP 1: Jesus, lady, get with the times. They now call us pigs.

COP 2: Pride, integrity, guts.

BOY 1: That's a lot of bullshit.

VICE COP: Who are they?

COP 1: We're trying to find out who's making a complaint. They for assault. Her, for armed robbery and attempted rape.

VICE COP: Rape. Ahahahahah. You're kidding.

COP 1: I wish we were. She insists that they tried it.

COP 2: Do you believe it?

VICE COP: They must be crazy or awful horny.

COP 1: Okay, once again, what did they hit you with?

WOMAN: With the newspaper.

COP 1: Assault with a dangerous instrument.

COP 2: Got it.

WOMAN: They also try to strangle me with them pants over there.

COP 1: Attempted murder. Take the pants too.

COP 2: Got it.

COP 1: Okay, lady, come on to the precinct and sign a complaint. On second thought, why not just meet us there.

BOY 1: Look, man, we snatched the book, but we didn't try no rape, man.

COP 1: Don't worry about it.

VICE COP: Wait a second, not so fast, there's got to be a law about this somewhere. There's just got to be.

COP 1: Well, sir, it is against the law to steal.

COP 2: And assault . . .

VICE COP: Not that, her.

COP 1: There's no law about looking that ugly, sir.

COP 2: Come on, let's go.

VICE COP: No, she ain't going no where.

COP 1: What are you talking about?

VICE COP: There's got to be a law about this down at central.

COP 1: What is he talking about?

COP 2: Why ask?

VICE COP: I'm talking about her.

COP 1: What about her? . . . she's the complainant.

VICE COP: I'm talking about, what I'm talking about . . .

BOY 1: What you rappin' about?

VICE COP: None of your business.

BOY 2: You heard the man, none of your B.I. business, man. Now, keep tight before you get both of our asses kicked, man!

COP 1: Shut up.

VICE COP: Don't tell me to shut up.

COP 2: He didn't mean you, he meant them.

BOY 2: Man, you gonna get us in big trouble with your big mouth, man.

VICE COP: He can speak for himself.

COP 1: Yeah! I meant them, Jesus!

VICE COP: Now, what I'm talking about is as simple as this.

COP 1: This hasn't been simple, believe me.

WOMAN: Talk straight, will you?

BOY 1: He speak with fork tongue.

WOMAN: They all speak with fork tongue.

BOY 2: Man, if they beat up on me, I'm gonna brain you, bro.

BOY 1: Boy, you ain't doing nothing to me.

BOY 2: We'll see about that.

COP 1: You two can fight at the precinct. We got some gloves.

BOY 1: That cool with me.

BOY 2: Not with me. I ain't no prize fighter, man.

BOY 1: No, man, you's a punk who talk much shit.

COP 1: Shut up, all of yous, please. Now, sir, what is it with this woman?

VICE COP: What I'm talking about is simple.

COP 2: You already said that. I'm still confused.

VICE COP: Yes, well, what I mean is . . . what I'm trying to say is that, can't you understand that there is something wrong here. I mean, well, that is, that er . . . er . . . er . . . that . . . I think that I mean I feel that there is something wrong here. Don't you see it. I mean it's perfectly clear to me. Can you see it?

COP 1: To tell the truth . . . no . . .

VICE COP: That's why you're a transit cop working the graveyard shift.

COP 1: I resent that.

VICE COP: Big deal, you resent the truth.

COP 1: I'm taking them in.

VICE COP: No, wait, you can't. There's something wrong here and it has to be straightened out immediately . . . I mean how can you let her get away with this crime.

COP 1: What crime are you talking about?

WOMAN: Crime? I didn't commit no crime. What are you talking about, mister? You better make yourself clear before I sue you for false accusation. I didn't commit no crime. The crime was committed on me, mister. Now, get that right in your head.

COP 2: She's right.

BOY 1: What about us?

BOY 2: What about us?

COP 1: If you guys don't shut the fuck up, I'm going to smack the living shit out of you.

COP 2: Hold it . . . . hold it, not here.

WOMAN: Just let me at them . . . .

COP 2: Calm down, everybody, calm down. Please, let's get down to the bottom of this. Please explain yourself, officer, and please make it as brief and as clear as you possibly can. Thank you.

COP 1: Yes, please.

BOY 1: Hey, man, keep that monster cool.

BOY 2: Be cool, bro, be cool. Please, I just got a cap on my teeth, bro, and if they knock it out, my old man is gonna kill me.

BOY 1: Yeah, okay, bro?

VICE COP: Man, if we let her out of here without arresting her, we're all gonners for sure . . . don't you see that?

COP 1: No.

WOMAN: He's crazy.

COP 2: Lady, please . . .

WOMAN: He's crazy, he's insane, out of his motherfucking mind!

VICE COP: If we let her get away with this, who knows what will happen next.

COP 2: What will happen to what . . . to who . . . what are you talking about?

COP 1: Oh, let's not start on that again, please. Let's keep it clear.

COP 2: You mean it's clear to you?

COP 1: No . . .

COP 2: What will happen to what? Let's start there.

VICE COP: To our society, man, to our society. What do you think I was trying to tell you all the time? What will happen to our society if we allow this woman to walk out of this men's toilet free without charging her with something . . . something that we can stick on her. Let's think . . . let's put our heads together.

COP 1: I wonder if your head is together.

COP 2: How long you been on the vice squad?

VICE COP: Peeping tomasina . . . that's it, peeping tomasina. There must be a law like that somewhere in the books downtown . . .

COP 1: About a woman in the man's toilet?

COP 2: You got to be kidding.

COP 1: I don't think he is.

COP 2: You're serious?

VICE COP: Of course, I'm serious.

COP 1: He's serious.

VICE COP: You better believe that I'm serious. What will become of society if we allow things like this to go unpunished? What? Tell me what? Men in women's toilets . . . women in men's toilets . . . next thing we know, women will be in men's toilets standing up taking a piss. Can you imagine that, can you? No, but I can.

COP 1: I bet you can.

VICE COP: You bet I can. I been working this beat long enough to know all the perverted thoughts and actions that take place in people's minds. I know them all . . . but I'm, strong, I stick to my guns . . . women standing up taking a piss, men sitting down . . . it can turn your stomach just thinking of it . . .

COP 2: I'll try not to.

VICE COP: You take this as a joke, but you are not realizing the seriousness of it. What will become of our children, our beautiful boys and girls? They'll be in a constant identity crisis. What will become of your daughter, if she walks into a toilet and finds a man putting on a sanitary napkin, what? . . . or your son, if he walks into the john and there's this stupid looking broad with one leg up in the air taking a piss? Think about things like that and you'll see the seriousness of it . . . think about it for one minute.

COP 1: I did . . . we've leaving.

VICE COP: That's only the better part of the signs, for the worst is yet to come.

COP 1: Repeat that.

VICE COP: I said that ain't all. There's more to be imagined . . . if we let this . . . this pervert go . . . what about the signs?

COP 1: Signs, what signs?

VICE COP: The signs on the doors.

COP 2: There are also other signs that one should take heed to, if you know what I mean.

VICE COP: Yes, I do.

COP 2: You do?

VICE COP: Of course, I do. I understand everything there is to understand, but do you understand about the signs on the doors? The signs on the doors that indicate whether it's a men's room or a ladies' room . . . kings and queens . . . caballeros and caballeras . . . those signs on the toilet doors that are the most important thing that has come out of a civilized society, that's what. No . . . no, sir, not me. I am not taking part in this communist conspiracy to rid our society of the men and women signs on the toilet doors . . . not me, I am a true spirit of the revolution . . . long live Betsy Ross.

> Man 4 enters.

VICE COP: Hold it, hold it, right there . . .

MAN 4: (In high feminine voice.) Who me? . . . (In husky voice.) I mean, who me?

VICE COP: Yeah, you come 'ere.

MAN 4: Yeah, what can I do for you? Good evening, officers . . . come on, I ain't got all day.

VICE COP: Hold it, I'm a police officer, too.

MAN 4: Is he?

VICE COP: Why you ask them . . . don't you believe me . . . don't I look like a cop to you?

MAN 4: No.

VICE COP: No?

COP 1: That's why you're a detective.

COP 2: Detectives are not supposed to look like cops.

VICE COP: Yeah, but everybody I know knows when a detective is around.

BOY 1: Everybody I know knows too.

MAN 4: Look, I wanna take a leak. Is there something wrong about that?

VICE COP: Don't be a wise guy . . . wasn't you in here before? Didn't I chase you out of here before?

MAN 4: Me . . . hell, no. Why would I be chased out of a men's toilet for? That makes no sense to me.

COP 2: Welcome to the club.

MAN 4: Now, what can I do for you . . . officer?

VICE COP: Nothing, nothing at all . . . it's just that you . . . you look so familiar.

MAN 4: Ain't never seen you before in my life.

VICE COP: Yeah, well, you better come back later or go to another toilet.

MAN 4: Listen, I paid a quarter to get in here to take a leak.

VICE COP: There is police business going on in here . . . so you better turn around right now and leave.

MAN 4: Police business in a subway toilet?

VICE COP: What makes you think that the law ends at subway toilet doors . . . in a toilet, even in a toilet the long arm of the law does not rest for one minute . . . and in here in this very toilet, mister, there is urgent police matters being taken care of, matters that may affect the future of our great democratic nation . . .

MAN 4: Is he serious?

COP 1: I think so.

WOMAN: He's crazy . . . call a cop, will ye, this man is crazy.

VICE COP: Shut up, you pervert, expounding communist . . .

MAN 4: Yes, well, good night, officers . . . *(In a high feminine voice.)* good night, honey . . . byeee.

VICE COP: It's him, that lousy faggot. I knew it was him. I just knew it. I bet he's part of her group. They all are . . . I am putting this woman under arrest . . . come on, lady, let's go. Put out your hands, you degenerate . . . pinko bulldyke.

MAN 1: Hello, God bless America, can I have my pants, please?

VICE COP: Are you making fun of me, mister? You better watch your step . . . if you wanna stay out of trouble, keep it clean.

WOMAN: Get your hands off me, you crazy honky . . . get them off me. Ain't you gonna help?!!

VICE COP: She is under arrest.

BOY 1: Right on, put her in the same cell with us.

COP 1: Shut up, punk.

COP 2: What we going to do?

VICE COP: She is under arrest. Now, either of you can take the collar. It's a credit. I'll share it with you . . . you can have an assist.

COP 1: No, you can have it by yourself.

COP 2: Yeah, you can have it. After all, you pointed the violation out to us, didn't you?

VICE COP: Yes, but I am willing to give you credit.

COP 1: No thanks.

COP 2: Yeah, thanks, but no thanks . . . let's go . . .

COP 1: Come on, boys, on the move . . .

COP 1: Take her, she's yours.

WOMAN: This nut is arresting me?

COP 2: Don't worry about it, lady, you have to go to the station, anyway, don't you? Well, this way you go in his car.

COP 1: And under his care . . .

VICE COP: *(Singing.)* "God bless America, land of the free . . . etc . . ."

The woman begins to fight and curse him out.

COP 1: All right, let's take them downtown.

COP 2: Downtown? The station is uptown.

COP 1: Yeah, I know, but it sounds more dramatic to say downtown. "Okay, the game's over let's go downtown, we're booking you."

COP 2: After him, I can see what you mean . . .

They exit with all the people under arrest and protesting their innocence.

Silence.

MAN 1: Hey, is these anybody out these? Hello, this is a man in trouble . . . is there anybody there? . . . shit . . . shit . . . shit . . .

Silence.

MAN 1: Help . . . .help . . . helppppppppppppp . . .

Curtain.

Writings

Published Plays: *Short Eyes: The Killing of a Sex Offender by the Inmates of the House of Detention Awaiting Trial,* Hill and Wang, 1975. *The Sun Always Shines for the Cool, Midnight Moon at the Greasy Spoon, Eulogy for a Small Time Thief,* Arte Público Press, 1984. *Outrageous One Act Plays,* Arte Público Press, 1986. **Produced Plays (and year first produced):** *All Junkies* (1973). *Sideshow* (1975). *The Gun Tower* (1976). *The Sun Always Shines for the Cool* (1976). *Eulogy for a Small-Time Thief* (1977). *Straight from the Ghetto* (with Neil Harris, 1977). *Paper Toilet* (c. 1979). *Cold Beer* (1979). *Nuyorican Nights at the Stanton Street Social Club* (1980). *Playland Blues* (1980). *A Midnight Moon at the Greasy Sppon* (1981). **Poetry:** *La Bodega Sold Dreams,* Arte Público Press, 1980. Also in *Revista Chicano-Riqueña, Nuyorican Poetry,* and other periodicals and anthologies. **Other:** *Nuyorican Poets: An Anthology of Puerto Rican Words and Feelings,* edited with Miguel Algarín, Morrow, 1975.

Dolores Prida

Dolores Prida has created plays that speak to Hispanics of every heritage. More than any other playwright, she has been able to identify the themes that cut across Hispanic life in the United States and she addresses these with humor and pathos. Because of her characteristic insight and ability, at least two of her plays have been repeatedly performed: Coser y cantar *and* Botánica.

Dolores Prida was born to Manuel Prida and Dolores Prieto on September 5, 1943, in Caibarién, Cuba. After Castro came to power, her family was among the first to resettle in the United States; the Pridas moved to New York in 1961. In her late teens already, she quickly set out to earn a living from writing in Spanish, and over the years she has worked as an editor, freelance writer, translator, and promotional copy-writer for newspapers, magazines, and publishing houses. From 1965–69, she studied Spanish-American literature at Hunter College. She also became part of a group of young Hispanic immigrant writers in New York who called themselves "La nueva sangre" (the new blood). The group ran workshops for literary creativity and exchange, published a short-lived magazine, and assisted in the publication of various books of poetry by its members—including two of Prida's books, *Woman of the Hour* (1971) and *The IRT Prayerbook* (1974), which was a collaboration with Puerto Rican photographer Roger Cabán.

It was not until 1976 that Prida received institutional support for her writing, with the award of a Cintas Fellowship for Literature. It was then that she began experimenting with theater, and in 1977, one of her most successful plays, *Beautiful Señoritas,* a musical satirizing the stereotypes of Latinas in popular culture, was produced by the DUO Theatre in New York. Lynn Feinerman said the work's "most powerful weapon is laughter. At times, hilarious, exciting and voluptuous, it leaves the tart aftertaste of satire." In 1980 *Beautiful Señoritas* was presented in a special performance at the National Organization for Women (NOW) convention in San Antonio, Texas.

Prida continued to write a remarkable series of plays, experimenting with the conventional musical comedy form. Like *Beautiful Señoritas,* the plays were staged at the DUO Theater as well as other venues in the United States and Puerto Rico. She first adapted Bertholt Brecht's *Three Penny Opera* to New York's Barrio life; it received rave reviews at the DUO Theater production at INTAR in 1979. Her 1980 bilingual musical comedy, *La era latina* (The Era of the Latins), toured to more than thirty Hispanic neighborhoods for open-air staging by the Puerto Rican Traveling Theater, and received a special award at the Third World Theater Competition in Caracas, Venezuela, in 1981.

Prida's foray into bilingual theater next led her to write her most important and far-reaching work, *Coser y cantar* (Sewing and Singing), which is a highly experimental, psychological play about bilingualism-biculturalism and the conflicting roles that Hispanics, especially women, must mediate in U.S. society. Prida illustrates the tensions and contradictions between two sides of an uprooted Latina by portraying each side in its own character: "She," the English speaker and the Americanized part of the woman's psyche, and "Ella," the Spanish-speaking, "old country" counterpart, argue throughout the one-act play, exposing the problems of living in two worlds.

Two other Prida plays were successfully produced at the DUO/INTAR theater in 1981: *Crisp!* is a musical adaptation of the Spanish classic *Los intereses creados* (Vested Interests) by Jacinto Benavente, and *Juan Bobo* is a bilingual, musical play for children. After this prolific showing, Prida became an INTAR Playwright-in-Residence in 1982–83. In 1985, she once again experimented with the musical comedy format, a la Broadway, with *Savings,* which deals with the subject of urban "gentrification." In her 1986 play *Pantallas* (Earrings), Prida trades in the musical comedy form for a more serious treatment. The play is a black comedy, running the gamut between TV's Spanish-language soap operas (*novelas*) and nuclear disasters.

Her latest play, *Botánica* (1990), is a comedy that nevertheless seriously considers culture conflict and generation gap in Hispanic society. Some heavy-hitting themes (tradition versus modernity, spirituality and traditional knowledge versus science and technology, assimilation versus genocide) underpin a lively dialog in New York-Puerto Rican Spanish. Like *Coser y cantar,* the play has tapped into

> "Prida's drama affirms the quest for personal and cultural definition by asserting the strength derived by individuals from the community."
>
> **Wilma Feliciano in the Latin American Theater Review,** *Fall 1994*

Hispanics' deep-rooted worries and fears, and so much so that it won a perennial place on the playbill of the Spanish Repertory Theater in New York.

Prida cannot be understood from the context of Cuban exile; her theater is not "political" in that sense. Nor is she simply superimposing Hispanic themes and content on conventional American theatrical forms, and thus making a "Cuban American" or "Hispanic American" theater. Hers is truly a search of how to best develop a Hispanic theater in the United States, ensuring the survival of the language and culture on stage.

Personal Stats

Cuban American playwright, freelance writer. **Born:** September 5, 1943, in Caibarién, Cuba. **Education:** Attended Hunter College, majoring in Spanish literature, 1965–69. **Career:** Editor of magazine for Schraftfts Restaurants, 1961–69; international correspondent, Collier-Macmillan International, 1969–70; assistant editor, Simon & Schuster, 1973–74; director of information services, National Puerto Rican Forum, 1971–73; managing editor, *El Tiempo magazine,* 1973–74; arts and science editor, *Vision* magazine, 1975–76; executive senior editor, *Nuestro* magazine, 1977–80; freelance writer/editor/translator, 1980–83; director of publications, Association of Hispanic Arts, 1983–90; full-time writer/playwright, 1990–present. **Memberships:** The Dramatists Guild, National Association of Hispanic Journalists. **Awards/honors:** Cintas Foundation Fellowship, 1976; New York Council on the Arts CAPS (Creative Artistic Public Service) grant, 1979–80; Special Award, Third World Theater Competition, Caracas, Venezuela, 1981, for *La era latina*; INTAR Playwright-in-Residence, 1982–83; Doctor of Humane Letters, Mount Holyoke College, 1989; Manhattan Borough President Excellence in the Arts Award, 1989. **Address:** c/o Association of Hispanic Arts, 173 E. 116th Street, New York, NY 10029

Coser y cantar

A One-Act Bilingual Fantasy for Two Women 1981

from *Beautiful Señoritas & Other Plays,* edited by Judith Weiss, Arte Público Press, 1991, pp. 48–67

Characters

ELLA, una mujer

SHE, the same woman

The action takes place in an apartment in New York City in the present/past.

Set

A couch, a chair, and a dressing table with an imaginary mirror facing the audience is on each side of the stage. A low table with a telephone on it is upstage center. In the back, a low shelf or cabinet holds a recordplayer, records and books. There are back exits on stage right and stage left.

Stage right is ELLA's area. Stage left is SHE's. Piles of books, magazines and newspapers surround SHE's area. A pair of ice skates and a tennis racket are visible somewhere. Her dressing table has a glass with pens and pencils and various bottles of vitamin pills. SHE wears jogging shorts and sneakers.

ELLA's area is somewhat untidy. Copies of Cosmopolitan, Vanidades and TV Guías are seen around her bed. ELLA's table is crowded with cosmetics, a figurine of the Virgen de la Caridad and a candle. A large conch and a pair of maracas are visible. ELLA is dressed in a short red kimono.

Important Note from the Author

This piece is really one long monologue. The two women are one and are playing a verbal, emotional game of ping pong. Throughout the action, except in the final confrontation, ELLA and SHE never look at each other, acting independently, pretending the other one does not really exist, although each continuously trespasses on each other's thoughts, feelings and behavior.

This play must NEVER be performed in just one language.

Coser y Cantar was first performed at Duo Theater in New York City on June 25, 1981 with the following cast:

ELLA   Elizabeth Peña

SHE   María Normán

It was directed by María Normán. The play has had many subsequent productions throughout the U.S. and in Puerto Rico. It was first published in Tramoya, the theater magazine of Universidad Veracruzana and Rutgers University, Issue No. 22, Jan.–Mar. 1990.

ACT I

In the dark we hear "Qué sabes tú", a recording by Olga Guillot. As lights go up slowly on ELLA's couch we see a naked leg up in the air, then a hand slides up the leg and begins to apply cream to it. ELLA puts cream on both legs, sensually, while singing along with the record. ELLA sits up in bed, takes a hairbrush, brushes her hair, then using the brush as a microphone continues to sing along. Carried away by the song, ELLA gets out of bed and "performs" in front of the imaginary mirror by her dressing table. At some point during the previous scene, lights will go up slowly on the other couch. SHE is reading Psychology Today magazine. We don't see her face at the beginning. As ELLA is doing her act by the mirror, SHE's eyes are seen above the magazine. She stares ahead for a while. Then shows impatience. SHE gets up and turns off the recordplayer, cutting off ELLA's singing in mid-sentence. SHE begins to pick up newspapers and magazines from the floor and to stack them up neatly.

ELLA: (With contained exasperation.) ¿Por qué haces eso? ¡Sabes que no me gusta que hagas eso! Detesto que me interrumpas así. ¡Yo no te interrumpo cuando tú te imaginas que eres Barbra Streisand!

SHE: (To herself, looking for her watch.) What time is it? (Finds watch.) My God, twelve thirty! The day half-gone and I haven't done a thing .... And so much to be done. So much to be done. *(Looks at one of the newspapers she has picked up.)* . . .Three people have been shot already. For no reason at all. No one is safe out there. No one. Not even those who speak good English. Not even those who know who they are . . .

ELLA: *(Licking her lips.)* Revoltillo de huevos, tostadas, queso blanco, café con leche. Hmmm, eso es lo que me pide el estómago. Anoche soñé con ese desayuno.

ELLA *goes backstage singing "Es mi vivir una linda guajirita". We hear the sound of pots and pans over her singing. At the same time,* SHE *puts on the Jane Fonda exercise record and begins to do exercises in the middle of the room. Still singing,* ELLA *returns with a tray loaded with breakfast food and turns off the record player.* ELLA *sits on the floor, Japanese-style, and begins to eat.* SHE *sits also and takes a glass of orange juice.*

SHE: Do you have to eat so much? You eat all day, then lie there like a dead octopus.

ELLA: Y tú me lo recuerdas todo el día, pero si no fuera por todo lo que yo como, ya tú te hubieras muerto de hambre. (ELLA *eats.* SHE *sips her orange juice.)*

SHE: *(Distracted.)* What shall I do today? There's so much to do.

ELLA: *(With her mouth full.)* Sí, mucho. El problema siempre es, por dónde empezar.

SHE: I should go out and jog a couple of miles.

ELLA: *(Taking a bite of food.)* Sí. Debía salir a correr. Es bueno para la figura. *(Takes another bite.)* Y el corazón. *(Takes another bite.)* Y la circulación. *(Another bite.)* A correr se ha dicho. (ELLA *continues eating.* SHE *gets up and opens an imaginary window facing the audience.* SHE *looks out, breathes deeply, stretches.)*

SHE: Aaah, what a beautiful day! It makes you so . . . so happy to be alive!

ELLA: *(From the table, without much enthusiasm.)* No es pare tanto.

SHE: *(SHE goes to her dressing table, sits down takes pen and paper.)* I'll make a list of all the things I must do. Let's see. I should start from the inside . . . . Number one, clean the house . . .

ELLA: *(Still eating)* Uno, limpiar la casa.

SHE: Two, take the garbage out.

ELLA: Dos, sacar la basura.

SHE: Then, do outside things. After running, I have to do something about El Salvador.

ELLA: Salvar a El Salvador.

SHE: Go to the march at the U.N.

ELLA: *(Has finished eating, picks up tray, gets enthusiastic about the planning.)* Escribir una carta el editor del *New York Times.*

SHE: Aha, that too. *(Adds it to the list.)* How about peace in the Middle East?

ELLA: La cuestión del aborto.

SHE: Should that come after or before the budget cuts?

ELLA: *(With relish)* Comprar chorizos mexicanos para unos burritos.

SHE: *(Writing.)* See that new Fassbinder film. (ELLA *makes a "boring" face.)* Find the map . . . (SHE *writes.)*

ELLA: *(Serious.)* Ver a mi madrina. Tengo algo que preguntarle a los caracoles. *(Splashes Florida Water around her head.)*

SHE: *(Exasperated.)* Not again! . . . *(Thinks.)* Buy a fish tank. *(Writes it down.)*

ELLA: ¿Una pecera?

SHE: I want to buy a fish tank, and some fish. I read in *Psychology Today* that it is supposed to calm your nerves to watch fish swimming in a tank.

ELLA: *(Background music begins.)* Peceras. *(Sits at her dressing table. Stares into the mirror. Gets lost in memories.)* Las peceras me recuerdan el aeropuerto cuando me fui . . . los que se iban, dentro de la pecera. Esperando. Esperando dentro de aquel cuarto transparente. Al otro lado del cristal, los otros, los que se quedaban: los padres, los hermanos, los tíos . . . . Allí estábamos, en la pecera, nadando en el mar que nos salía por los ojos . . . Y los que estaban dentro y los que estaban afuera solo podían mirarse. Mirarse las caras distorcionadas por las lágrimas y el cristal sucio—lleno de huellas de manos que se querían tocar, empañado por el aliento de bocas que trataban de besarse a través del cristal . . . . Una pecera llena de peces asustados, que no sabían nadar, que no sabían de las aguas heladas . . . donde los tiburones andan con pistolas . . .

SHE: *(Scratches item off the list forcefully.)* Dwelling in the past takes energies away.

ELLA: *(ELLA looks for the map among objects on her table. Lifts the Virgen de la Caridad statue.)* ¿Dónde habré puesto el mapa? Juraría que estaba debajo de la Santa . . . *(ELLA looks under the bed. Finds one old and dirty tennis shoe. It seems to bring back memories.)* Lo primerito que yo pensaba hacer al llegar aquí era comprarme unos tenis bien cómodos y caminar todo Nueva York. Cuadra por cuadra. Para saber dónde estaba todo.

SHE: I got the tennis shoes—actually, they were basketball shoes . . . But I didn't get to walk every block as I had planned. I wasn't aware of how big the city was. I wasn't aware of muggers either . . . I did get to walk a lot, though . . . in marches and demonstrations. But by then, I had given up wearing tennis shoes. I was into boots . . . .

ELLA: . . . Pero nunca me perdí en el subway . . .

SHE: Somehow I always knew where I was going. Sometimes the place I got to was the wrong place, to be sure. But that's different. All I had to do was choose another place . . . and go to it. I have gotten to a lot of right places too.

ELLA: *(With satisfaction.)* Da gusto llegar al luger que se va sin perder el camino.

Loud gunshots are heard outside, then police sirens, loud noises, screams, screeches. Both women get very nervous and upset. They run to the window and back, not knowing what to do.

SHE: There they go again! Now they are shooting the birds on the trees!

ELLA: ¡Están matando las viejitas en el parque . . .

SHE: Oh, my God! Let's get out of here!

ELLA: . . . Y los perros que orinan en los hidrantes!

SHE: No, no. Let's stay here! Look! They've shot a woman riding a bicycle . . . and now somebody is stealing it!

ELLA: ¡La gente corre, pero nadie hace nada!

SHE: Are we safe? Yes, we are safe. We're safe here . . . No, we're not! They can shoot through the window!

ELLA: ¡La gente grita pero nadie trace nada!

SHE: Get away from the window!

ELLA: (*Pausa.*) Pero, ¿y todo lo que hay que hacer?

> *They look around undecided, then begin to do several things around the room, but then drop them immediately.* SHE *picks up a book.* ELLA *goes to the kitchen. We hear the rattling of pots and pans.* ELLA *returns eating leftovers straight from a large pot.* ELLA *sits in front of the mirror, catches sight of herself. Puts pot down, touches her face, tries different smiles, none of which is a happy smile.* SHE *is lying on the couch staring at the ceiling.*

ELLA: Si pudiera sonreír como la Mona Lisa me tomarían por misteriosa en vez de antipática porque no enseño los dientes . . .

SHE: (*From the couch, still staring at the ceiling.*) That's because your face is an open book. You wear your emotions all over, like a suntan . . . You are emotionally naive . . . or rather, emotionally primitive . . . perhaps even emotionally retarded. What you need is a . . . a certain emotional sophistication . . .

ELLA: . . . sí, claro, eso . . . sofisticación emocional . . . (*Thinks about it*) . . . sofisticación emocional . . . ¿Y qué carajo es sofisticación emocional? ¿Ser como tú? ¡Tú, que ya ni te acuerdas como huele tu propio sudor, que no reconoces el sonido de tu propia voz! ¡No me jodas!

SHE: See what I mean! (SHE *gets up, goes to her dressing table, looks for the map.*)

ELLA: (*Exasperated.*) ¡Ay, Díos mio, ¿qué habré hecho yo para merecérmela? Es como tener un . . . un pingüino colgado del cuello!

SHE: An albatross . . . you mean like an albatross around your neck. Okay, Okay . . . I'll make myself light, light as a feather . . . light as an albatross feather. I promise. (SHE *continues to look for the map.*) Where did I put that map? I thought it was with the passport, the postcards . . . the traveling mementos . . . (*continues looking among papers kept in a small box. Finds her worry beads. That brings memories. She plays with the beads for a while.*) . . . I never really learned how to use them . . . (ELLA *continues searching elsewhere.*) Do you know what regret means?

ELLA: (*Absentmindedly.*) Es una canción de Edith Piaff.

SHE: Regret means that time in Athens, many years ago . . . at a cafe where they played bouzuki music. The men got up and danced and broke glasses and small dishes against the tiled floor. The women did not get up to dance. They just watched and tapped their feet under the table . . . now and then shaking their shoulders to the music. One Greek man danced more than the others. He broke more glasses and dishes than the others. His name was Nikos. It was his birthday. He cut his hand with one of the broken glasses. But he didn't stop, he didn't pay any attention to his wound. He kept on dancing. He danced by my table. I took a gardenia from the vase on the table and gave it to him. He took it, rubbed it on the blood dripping from his hand and gave it back to me with a smile. He danced away to other tables . . . . I wanted to get up and break some dishes and dance with him. Dance away, out the door, into the street, all the way to some cheap hotel by the harbor, where next morning I would hang the bed sheet stained with my blood out the window. But I didn't get up. Like the Greek women, I stayed on my seat, tapping my feet under the table, now and then shaking my shoulders to the music . . . a bloodied gardenia wilting in my glass of retsina . . .

ELLA: No haber roto ni un plato. That's regret for sure.

The clock strikes the hour. Alarmed, they get up quickly and look for their shoes.

SHE: (Putting boots on. Rushed, alarmed.) I have to practice the speech!

ELLA: (Puts on high heels.) Sí, tienes que aprender a hablar más alto. Sin micrófono no se te oye. Y nunca se sabe si habrá micrófono. Es mejor depender de los pulmones que de los aparatos. Los aparatos a veces fallan en el momento más inoportuno.

They stand back to back, each facing stage left and stage right respectively. They speak at the same time.

SHE: (In English.) A E I O U,

ELLA: (In Spanish.) A E I O U.

ELLA: Pirámides.

SHE: Pyramids.

ELLA: Orquídeas.

SHE: Orchids.

ELLA: Sudor.

SHE: Sweat.

ELLA: Luz.

SHE: Light.

ELLA: Blood.

SHE: Sangre.

ELLA: Dolphins.

SHE: Delfines.

ELLA: Mountains.

SHE: Montañas.

ELLA: Sed.

SHE: Thirst.

Freeze. Two beats. They snap out of their concentration.

ELLA: Tengo sed.

SHE: I think I'll have a Diet Pepsi.

ELLA: Yo me tomaría un guarapo de caña. (SHE *goes to the kitchen.*)

ELLA: (*Looking for the map. Stops before the mirror and looks at her body, passes hand by hips, sings a few lines of "Macorina" and continues to look for the map behind furniture, along the walls, etc. Suddenly, it seems as if* ELLA *hears something from the apartment next door.* ELLA *puts her ear to the wall and listens more carefully. Her face shows confusion.* ELLA *asks herself, deeply, seriously intrigued.*) ¿Por qué sería que Songo le dió a Borondongo? ¿Sería

porque Borondongo le dió a Bernabé? ¿O porque Bernabé le pegó a Muchilanga? ¿O en realidad sería porque Muchilanga le echó burundanga? *(Pause.)* . . . ¿Y Monina? ¿Quién es
Monina? ¡Ay, nunca lo he entendido . . . el gran misterio de nuestra cultura! (SHE *returns
drinking a Diet Pepsi. Sits on the bed and drinks slowly, watching the telephone with intense
concentration. ELLA's attention is also drawn to the telephone. Both watch it hypnotically.)* El
teléfono no ha sonado hoy.

SHE: I must call mother. She's always complaining.

ELLA: Llamadas. Llamadas. ¿Por qué no llamará? Voy a concentrarme para que llame.
(Concentrates.) El teléfono sonará en cualquier momento. Ya. Ya viene. Suena. Sí. Suena. Va a
sonar.

SHE: *(Sitting in the lotus position, meditating.)* Ayer is not the same as yesterday.

ELLA: Estás loca.

SHE: I think I'm going crazy. Talking to myself all day.

ELLA: It must be. It's too soon for menopause.

SHE: Maybe what I need is a good fuck after all.

ELLA: Eres una enferma.

SHE: At least let's talk about something important—exercise our intellects.

ELLA: ¿Como qué?

SHE: We could talk about . . . about . . . the meaning of life.

ELLA: Mi mamá me dijo una vez que la vida, sobre todo la vida de una mujer, era coser y cantar. Y yo me lo creí. Pero ahora me doy cuenta que la vida, la de todo el mundo: hombre,
mujer, perro, gato, jicotea, es, en realidad, comer y cager . . . ¡en otras palabras, la misma
mierda!

SHE: Puke! So much for philosophy.

Both look among the books and magazines. ELLA picks up Vanidades *magazine, flips
through the pages. SHE starts reading* Self *magazine.*

ELLA: No sé que le ha pasado a Corin Tellado. Ya sus novelas no son tan románticas como antes.
Me gustaban más cuando ella, la del sedoso cabello castaño y los brazos torneados y los ojos
color violeta, no se entregaba así, tan fácilmente, a él, el hombre, que aunque más viejo, y a
veces cojo, pero siempre millonario, la deseaba con locura, pero la respetaba hasta el día de
la boda . . .

SHE: I can't believe you're reading that crap.

ELLA: *(Flipping through the pages some more.)* Mira, esto es interesante: ¡un test! "Usted y sus
Fantasías". A ver, lo voy hacer. *(Gets a pencil from the table.)* Pregunta número uno: ¿Tienes
fantasías a menudo? *(Piensa.)*

SHE: Yes. (ELLA writes down answer.)

ELLA: ¿Cuán a menudo? *(Thinks.)*

SHE: Every night . . . and day.

ELLA: *(Writes down answer.)* ¿Cuál es el tema recurrente de tus fantasías?

SHE: *(Sensually mischievous.)* I am lying naked. Totally, fully, wonderfully naked. Feeling good and relaxed. Suddenly, I feel something warm and moist between my toes. It is a tongue! A huge, wide, live tongue! The most extraordinary thing about this tongue is that it changes. It takes different shapes . . . It wraps itself around my big toe . . . then goes in between and around each toe . . . then it moves up my leg, up my thigh . . . and into my . . .

ELLA: ¡Vulgar! No se trata de esas fantasías. Se trata de . . . de . . . de ¡Juana de Arco!

SHE: I didn't know that Joan of Arc was into . . .

ELLA: Ay, chica, no hablaba de fantasías eróticas, sino de fantasías heróicas . . . a lo Juana de Arco. A mí Juana de Arco me parece tan dramática, tan patriótica, tan sacrificada . . .

SHE: I don't care for Joan of Arc—too hot to handle! . . . ha, ha, ha. (Both laugh at the bad joke.)

ELLA: (Picking up the chair and lifting it above her head.) Mi fantasía es ser una superwoman: ¡Maravilla, la mujer maravilla! (Puts chair down and lies across it, arms and legs kicking in the air, as if swimming.) . . . Y salver a una niña que se ahoga en el Canal de la Mancha, y nadar, como Esther Williams, hasta los blancos farallones de Dover . . . (Gets up, then rides astride the chair.) ¡Ser una heroíne que cabalgando siempre adelante, hacia el sol, inspirada por una fe ciega, una pasión visionaria, arrastre a las multitudes para juntos salvar al mundo de sus errores!

SHE: Or else, a rock singer! They move crowds, all right. And make more money. How about, La Pasionaria and her Passionate Punk Rockers!

ELLA: (Disappointed.) Tú nunca me tomes en serio.

SHE: My fantasy is to make people happy. Make them laugh. I'd rather be a clown. When times are as bad as these, it is better to keep the gathering gloom at bay by laughing and dancing. The Greeks do it, you know. They dance when they are sad. Yes, what I really would like to be is a dancer. And dance depression . . . inflation . . . and the NUCLEAR THREAT . . . AWAY!

ELLA: (To herself, disheartened.) Pero tienes las piernas muy flacas y el culo muy grande.

SHE: (Ignoring ELLA's remarks.) Dancing is what life is all about. The tap- tapping of a hundred feet on Forty-Second Street is more exciting than an army marching off to kill the enemy . . . . Yes! My fantasy is to be a great dancer . . . like Fred Astaire and Ginger Rogers!

ELLA: ¿Cuál de ellos, Fred Astaire o Ginger Rogers?

SHE: Why can't I be both?

ELLA: ¿Será que eres bisexual?

SHE: (Puts her head between her legs, as if exercising.) No. I checked out. Just one.

ELLA: ¿Nunca has querido ser hombre?

SHE: Not really. Men are such jerks.

ELLA: Pero se divierten más. ¿De veras que nunca te has sentido como ese poema?: " . . . Hoy, quiero ser hombre. Subir por las tapias, burlar los conventos, ser todo un Don Juan; raptar a Sor Carmen y a Sor Josefina, rendirlas, y a Julia de Burgos violar . . ."

SHE: You are too romantic, that's your problem.

ELLA: ¡Y tú eres muy promiscua! Te acuestas con demasiada gente que ni siquiera te cae bien, que no tiene nada que ver contigo.

SHE: (Flexing her muscles.) It keeps me in shape. (Bitchy.) And besides, it isn't as corny as masturbating, listening to boleros.

ELLA: (Covering her ears.) ¡Cállate! ¡Cállate! ¡Cállate! (Goes to the window and looks out.) (Pause.) Está nevando. No se ve nada allá afuera. Y aquí, estas cuatro paredes me están volviendo . . . ¡bananas! (ELLA goes to the table, takes a banana and begins to eat it. SHE plays with an old tennis racket.) Si por lo menos tuviera el televisor, podría ver una película o algo . . . pero, no . . .

SHE: Forget about the TV set.

ELLA: ¡Tuviste que tirarlo por la ventana! Y lo peor no es que me quedé sin televisor. No. Lo peor es el caso por daños y perjuicios que tengo pendiente.

SHE: I don't regret a thing.

ELLA: La mala suerte que el maldito televisor le cayera encima al carro de los Moonies que viven al lado. ¿Te das cuenta? ¡Yo, acusada de terrorista por el Reverendo Sun Myung Moon! ¡A nadie le pasa esto! ¡A nadie más que a mí! ¡Te digo que estoy cagada de aura tiñosa!

SHE: You are exaggerating. Calm down.

ELLA: Cada vez que me acuerdo me hierve la sangre. Yo, yo, ¡acusada de terrorista! ¡Yo! ¡Cuando la víctima he sido yo!

¡No se puede negar que yo soy una víctima del terrorismo!

SHE: Dont' start with your paranoia again.

ELLA: ¡Paranoia! ¿Tú llamas paranoia a todo lo que ha pasado? ¿A lo que pasó con los gatos? ¡Mis tres gatos, secuestrados, descuartizados, y luego dejados en la puerta, envueltos en papel de regalo, con una tarjeta de Navidad!

SHE: You know very well it didn't happen like that.

ELLA: ¿Y la cobra entre las cartas? How about that snake in the mail box? Who put it there? Who? Who? Why?

SHE: Forget all that. Mira como te pones por gusto . . . Shit! We should have never come here.

ELLA: (Calming down.) Bueno, es mejor que New Jersey. Además ¿cuál es la diferencia? El mismo tiroteo, el mismo cucaracheo, la misma mierda . . . coser y cantar, you know.

SHE: At least in Miami there was sunshine . . .

ELLA: Había sol, sí, pero demasiadas nubes negras. Era el humo que salía de tantos cerebros tratando de pensar Además, aquí hay más cosas que hacer.

SHE: Yes. Más cosas que hacer. And I must do them. I have to stop contemplating my navel and wallowing in all this . . . this . . . Yes, one day soon I have to get my caca together and get out THERE and DO something. Definitely. Seriously. (Silent pause. Both are lost in thought.)

ELLA: I remember when I first met you . . . there was a shimmer in your eyes . . .

SHE: Y tú tenías una sonrisa . . .

ELLA: And with that shimmering look in your eyes and that smile . . .

SHE: . . . pensamos que íbamos a conquistar el mundo . . .

ELLA: . . . But . . .

SHE: . . . I don't know . . . (SHE goes to her table and picks up a bottle of vitamins.) Did I take my pills today?

ELLA: Sí.

SHE: Vitamin C?

ELLA: Sí.

SHE: Iron?

ELLA: Sí.

SHE: Painkiller?

ELLA: Of course . . . because camarón que se duerme se lo lleva la corriente.

SHE: A shrimp that falls asleep is carried away by the current?

ELLA: No . . . that doesn't make any sense.

SHE: Between the devil and the deep blue sea?

ELLA: . . . No es lo mismo que entre la espada y la pared, porque del dicho al hecho hay un gran trecho.

SHE: Betwixt the cup and the lip you should not look a gift horse in the mouth.

ELLA: A caballo regalado no se le mire el colmillo, pero tanto va el cántaro a la fuente, haste que se rompe.

SHE: An eye for an eye and a tooth for a tooth.

ELLA: Y no hay peor ciego que el que no quiere ver *(Both are lethargic, about to fall asleep.)*

SHE: *(Yawning.)* I have to be more competitive.

ELLA: *(Yawning.)* Despues de la siesta.

They fall asleep. Lights dim out. In the background, music box music comes on and remains through ELLA's *entire monologue.*

ELLA: *(Upset voice of a young child.)* Pero, ¿por qué tengo que esperar tres horas para bañarme? ¡No me va a pasar nada! . . . ¡Los peces comen y hacen la digestión en el agua y no les pasa nada! . . . Sí, tengo muchas leyes. ¡Debía ser abogada! ¡Debía ser piloto! ¡Debía ser capitán! ¡Debía ser una tonina y nadar al otro lado de la red, sin temer a los tiburones! *(Pause. Now as a rebellious teenager.)* ¡Y no voy a caminar bajo el sol con ese paraguas! ¡No me importa que la piel blanca sea mas elegante! . . . ¡No se puede taper el sol con una sombrilla! ¡No se puede esperar que la marea baje cuando tiene que subir! *(As an adult.)* . . . No se puede ser un delfín en las pirámides. No se le puede cortar la cabeza al delfín y guardarla en la gaveta, entre las prendas más íntimas y olvidar el delfín. Y olvidar que se quiso ser el delfín. Olvidar que se quiso ser la niña desnuda, cabalgando sobre el delfín . . .

SHE: *(Lights up on* SHE. *Needling.)* So, you don't have dreams. So, you can't remember your dreams. So, you never talk about your dreams. I think you *don't want* to remember your dreams. You always want to be going somewhere, but now you are stuck here with me, because outside it's raining blood and you have been to all the places you can possibly ever go to! No, you have nowhere to go! Nowhere! Nowhere! *(ELLA slaps* SHE *with force. The clock strikes twice. They awaken. Lights come up fully.* SHE *slaps herself softly on both cheeks.)* A nightmare in the middle of the day!

ELLA: Tengo que encontrar ese mapa. *(They look for the map.)*

SHE: *(Picks up a book, fans the pages. Finds a marker in one page. Reads silently, then reads aloud.)* "Picasso's gaze was so absorbing one was surprised to find anything left on the paper after he looked at it . . . " *(Thinks about this image. Then softly.)* Think about that . . .

ELLA: Sí. Claro. Así siento mis ojos en la primavera. Despés de ver tanto árbol desnudo durante el invierno, cuando salen las primeras hojas, esas hojitas de un verde tan tierno, me da miedo mirarlas mucho porque temo que mis ojos le vayan a chupar todo el color.

SHE: I miss all that green. Sometimes I wish I could do like Dorothy in "The Wizard of Oz" close my eyes, click my heels and repeat three times, "there's no place like home" . . . and, puff! be there.

ELLA: El peligro de eso es que una pueda terminar en una finca en Kansas.

SHE: . . . I remember that trip back home . . . I'd never seen such a blue sea. It was an alive, happy blue. You know what I mean?

ELLA: A mí no se me había olvidado. Es el mar más azul, el más verde . . . el más chévere del mundo. No hay comparación con estos mares de por aquí.

SHE: . . . It sort of slapped you in the eyes, got into them and massaged your eyeballs . . .

ELLA: Es un mar tan sexy, tan tibio. Como que te abraza. Dan ganas de quitarse el traje de baño y nadar desnuda . . . lo cual, por supuesto, hiciste a la primera oportunidad . . .

SHE: . . . I wanted to see everything, do everything in a week . . .

ELLA: *(Laughing.)* . . . No sé si lo viste todo, pero en cuanto a hacer . . . ¡el trópico te alborotó, chiquitica! ¡Hasta en el Malecón! ¡Qué escándalo!

SHE: *(Laughing.)* I sure let my hair down! It must have been all that rum. Everywhere we went, there was rum and "La Guantanamera" . . . And that feeling of belonging, of being home despite . . .

ELLA: *(Nostalgic.)* ¡Aaay!

SHE: ¿Qué pasa?

ELLA: ¡Ay, siento que me viene un ataque de nostalgia!

SHE: Let's wallow!

ELLA: ¡Ay, sí, un disquito!

SHE *puts a record on. It is "Nostalgia habanera" sung by Olga Guillot. Both sing and dance along with the record for a while. The music stays on throughout the scene.*

BOTH: *(Singing.)*

"Siento la nostalgia de volver a ti

más el destino manda y no puede ser

Mi Habana, mi tierra querida

cuándo yo te volveré a ver

Habana, como extraño el sol indiano de tus calles

Habana etc . . . . "

ELLA: ¡Aaay, esta nostalgia me ha dado un hambre!

SHE: That's the problem with nostalgia—it is usually loaded with calories! How about some steamed broccoli . . .

ELLA: Arroz . . .

SHE: Yogurt . . .

ELLA: Frijoles negros . . .

SHE: Bean sprouts . . .

ELLA: Plátanos fritos . . .

SHE: Wheat germ . . .

ELLA: Ensalada de aguacate . . .

SHE: Raw carrots . . .

ELLA: ¡Flan!

SHE: Granola!

ELLA: ¿Qué tal un arroz con pollo, o un ajiaco?

SHE: Let's go!

> *They exit out to the kitchen. Lights out. Record plays to the end. We hear rattling of pots and pans. When lights go up again, they lie on their respective beds.*

ELLA: ¡Qué bien! ¡Qué rico! Esa comida me ha puesto erótica. I feel sexy. Romántica.

SHE: (With bloated feeling.) How can you feel sexy after rice and beans? . . . I feel violent, wild. I feel like . . . chains, leather, whips. Whish! Whish!

ELLA: No, no, no! Yo me siento como rosas y besos bajo la luna, recostada a una palmera mecida por el viento . . .

SHE: Such tropical, romantic tackiness, ay, ay, ay.

ELLA: Sí, . . . y un olor a jasmines que se cuela por la ventana . . .

SHE: I thought you were leaning on a swaying coconut tree.

ELLA: . . . Olor a jasmines, mezclado con brisas de salitre. A lo lejos se escucha un bolero: (Sings.) Te acuerdas de la noche de la playa

Te acuerdas que te di mi amor primero . . . "

SHE: . . . I feel the smell of two bodies together, the heat of the flesh so close to mine, the sweat and the saliva trickling down my spine . . . (Both get progressively excited.)

ELLA: . . . y unas manos expertas me abren la blusa, me sueltan el ajustador, y con mucho cuidado, como si fueran dos mangos maduros, me sacan los senos al aire . . .

SHE: . . . And ten fingernails dig into my flesh and I hear drums beating faster and faster and faster!

> *They stop, exhaling a deep sigh of contentment. They get up from bed at different speeds and go to their dressing tables.* ELLA *lights up a cigarette sensually.* SHE *puts cold cream on her face, slowly and sensually. They sing in a sexy, relaxed manner.*

ELLA: "Fumar es un placer . . .

SHE: . . . Genial, sensual . . .

ELLA: . . . Fumando espero . . .

SHE: . . . Al hombre que yo quiero . . .

ELLA: . . . Tras los cristales . . .

SHE: . . . De alegres ventanales . . .

ELLA: . . . Y mientras fumo . . . "

SHE: *(Half laughs.)* . . . I remember the first time . . .

ELLA: Ja ja . . . a mí me preguntaron si yo había tenido un orgasmo alguna vez. Yo dije que no. No porque no lo había tenido, sino porque no sabía lo que era . . . Pensé que orgasmo era una tela.

SHE: I looked it up in the dictionary: orgasm. Read the definition, and still didn't know what it meant.

ELLA: A pesar del diccionario, haste que no tuve el primero, en realidad no supe lo que quería decir . . .

SHE: It felt wonderful. But all the new feelings scared me . . .

ELLA: *(Kneeling on the chair.)* . . . Fuí a la iglesia al otro día . . . me arrodillé, me persigné, alcé los ojos al cielo—es decir al techo—muy devotamente, pero cuando empecé a pensar la oración . . . me di cuenta de que, en vez de pedir perdón, estaba pidiendo . . . aprobación! . . . permiso para hacerlo otra vez!

SHE: . . . Oh God, please, give me a sign! Tell me it is all right! Send an angel, una paloma, a flash of green light to give me the go ahead! Stamp upon me the Good Housekeeping Seal of Approval, to let me know that fucking is okay!

ELLA: ¡Ay, Virgen del Cobre! Yo tenía un miedo que se enterara la familia. ¡Me parecía que me lo leían en la cara!

> They fall back laughing. The telephone rings three times. They stop laughing abruptly, look at the telephone with fear and expectation. After each ring each one in turn extends the hand to pick it up, but stops midway. Finally, after the third ring, SHE picks it up.

SHE: Hello? . . . Oh, hiii, how are you? . . . I am glad you called . . . I wanted to . . . Yes. Okay. Well, go ahead . . . *(Listens.)* Yes, I know . . . but I didn't think it was serious. *(Listens.)* . . . You said our relationship was special, untouchable . . . *(Whimpering.)* then how can you end it just like this . . . I can't believe that all the things we shared don't mean anything to you anymore . . . *(Listens.)* What do you mean, it was meaningful while it lasted?! . . . Yes, I remember you warned me you didn't want to get involved . . . but, all I said was that I love you . . . Okay. I shouldn't have said that . . . Oh, please, let's try again! . . . Look . . . I'll . . . I'll come over Saturday night . . . Sunday morning we'll make love . . . have brunch: eggs, croissants, Bloody Marys . . . we'll read the *Times* in bed and . . . please, don't . . . how can you? . . .

ELLA: *(Having been quietly reacting to the conversation, and getting angrier and angrier* ELLA *grabs the phone away from* SHE.) ¿Pero quién carajo tú te crees que eres para venir a tirarme así, como si yo fuera una chancleta vieja? ¡Qué huevos fritos ni ocho cuartos, viejo! ¡Después de tanta hambre que te maté, los buenos vinos que te compré! ¡A ver si esa putica que te has conseguido cocina tan bien como yo! ¡A ver si esa peluá te va a dar todo lo que yo te daba! ¡A ver si esa guaricandilla . . . *(Suddenly desperate.)* Ay, ¿cómo puedes hacerme esto a mí? ¡A mí que te adoro ciegamente, a mí, que te quiero tanto, que me muero por ti! . . . Mi amor . . . ay, mi amor, no me dejes. Haré lo que tú quieras. ¡Miénteme, pégame, traició-name, patéame, arrástrame por el fango, pero no me dejes! *(Sobs. Listens. Calms down. Now stoically melodramatic and resigned.)* Está bien. Me clavas un puñal. Me dejas con un puñal clavado en el centro del corazón. Ya nunca podré volver a amar. Mi corazón se desangra, siento que me desvanezco . . . Me iré a una playa solitaria y triste, y a media noche, como Alfonsina, echaré a andar hacia las olas y . . . *(Listens for three beats. Gets angry.)* ¿Así es como respondes cuando vuelco mi corazón, mis sentimientos en tu oído? ¿Cuando mis lágrimas casi crean un corto circuito en el teléfono?! ¡Ay, infeliz! ¡Tú no sabes nada de la vida! Adiós, y que te vaya bien. De veras . . . honestamente, no te guardo rencor . . . te deseo lo mejor . . . ¿Yo? . . . yo seguiré mi viaje. Seré bien recibida en otros puertos. Ja, ja, ja . . . De veras, te deseo de todo corazón que esa tipa, por lo menos, ¡sea tan BUENA EN LA CAMA COMO YO! *(Bangs the phone down. Both sit on the floor back to back. Long pause.* ELLA *fumes.* SHE *is contrite.)*

SHE: You shouldn't have said all those things.

ELLA: ¿Por qué no? Todo no se puede intelectualizar. You can't dance everything away, you know.

SHE: You can't eat yourself to numbness either.

ELLA: Yeah.

SHE: You know what's wrong with me? I can't relate anymore. I have been moving away from people. I stay here and look at the ceiling. And talk to you. I don't know how to talk to people anymore. I don't know if I want to talk to people anymore!

ELLA: Tu problema es que ves demasiadas películas de Woody Allen, y ya te crees una neoyorquina neurótica. Yo no. Yo sé como tener una fiesta cinmigo misma. Yo me divierto sola. Y me acompaño y me entretengo. Yo tengo mis recuerdos. Y mis plantas en la ventana. Yo tengo una solidez. Tengo unas raíces, algo de que agarrarme. Pero tú . . . ¿tú de qué te agarras?

SHE: I hold on to you. I couldn't exist without you.

ELLA: But I wonder if I need you. Me pregunto si te necesito . . . robándome la mitad de mis pensamientos, de mi tiempo, de mi sentir, de mis palabras . . . como una sanguijuela!

SHE: I was unavoidable. You spawned me while you swam in that fish tank. It would take a long time to make me go away!

ELLA: Tú no eres tan importante. Ni tan fuerte. Unos meses, tal vez unos años, bajo el sol, y, ¡presto! . . . desaparecerías. No quedaría ni rastro de ti. Yo soy la que existo. Yo soy la que soy. Tú . . . no sé lo que eres.

SHE: But, if it weren't for me you would not be the one you are now. No serías la que eres. I gave yourself back to you. If I had not opened some doors and some windows for you, you would still be sitting in the dark, with your recuerdos, the idealized beaches of your childhood, and your rice and beans and the rest of your goddam obsolete memories! *(For the first time they face each other, furiously.)*

ELLA: Pero soy la más fuerte!

SHE: I am as strong as you are! *(With each line, they throw something at each other pillows, books, papers, etc.)*

ELLA: ¡Soy la más fuerte!

SHE: I am the strongest!

ELLA: ¡Te robaste parte de mí!

SHE: You wanted to be me once!

ELLA: ¡Estoy harta de ti!

SHE: Now you are!

ELLA: ¡Ojalá no estuvieras!

SHE: You can't get rid of me!

ELLA: ¡Alguien tiene que ganar!

SHE: No one shall win!

Loud sounds of sirens, shots, screams are heard outside. They run towards the window, then walk backwards in fear, speaking simultaneously.

SHE: They are shooting again!

ELLA: ¡Y están cortando los árboles!

SHE: They're poisoning the children in the schoolyard!

ELLA: ¡Y echando la basura y los muertos al río!

SHE: We're next! We're next!

ELLA: ¡Yo no salgo de aquí!

SHE: Let's get out of here! (*Another shot is heard. They look at each other.*)

ELLA: El mapa . . .

SHE: Where's the map?

Black out.

Writings

Published Plays: *Beautiful Señoritas and Other Plays,* Arte Público Press, 1991. **Produced Plays (and year first produced):** *Beautiful Señoritas* (1977). *The Beggars Soap Opera* (1979). *La era latina* (with Víctor Fragoso), 1980. *Coser y cantar* (1981). *Crisp!* (1981). *Juan Bobo* (1981). *Savings* (1985). *Pantallas* (1986). *Botánica* (1990). **Poetry Books:** *The IRT Prayerbook,.* (with Roger Cabán), Nuevasangre, 1974. *Treinta y un poemas,.* Fancy Press Editors, 1967. *Women of the Hour,* Nuevasangre, 1971. **Poems:** In *La nueva sangre* and other periodicals. **Other:** Screenwriter for television and documentary films.

Tomás Rivera

Mexican American writer Tomás Rivera was one of the principal founders of Chicano literature and the author of the universally acknowledged classic of that literature, . . . y no se lo tragó la tierra/And the Earth Did Not Devour Him (1971). His short stories, poems, and essays, in both English and Spanish, provided direction for the development of Chicano literature. Rivera was not only dedicated to literary work, he was also devoted to opening the doors of academia to Hispanics and other minorities and he was an exemplar of the academic humanist and administrator. His life ended too soon when he suffered a fatal heart attack in 1984, shortly after becoming the first Hispanic president of a university in the California system. Unfortunately, his works were found to be in disarray and a novel the he had proclaimed to have written, La casa grande, has never been found among his papers and archives.

Born in December, 1935, into a family of migrant workers in Crystal City, Texas, Rivera had to fit his early and college education in between the seasons of field work. Nevertheless, he did very well academically, earning a B.A. and an M.Ed. from Southwest Texas State College in 1958 and 1964 (respectively), an M.A. in French Literature and a Ph.D. in Romance Languages (with a concentration in

Spanish) from the University of Oklahoma, both in 1969. He went on to build an impressive career as a college professor and administrator, and quickly rose to the highest level of administration when in 1979 he became the Chancellor of the University of California—Riverside.

Rivera's outwardly simple, but inwardly complex work, . . . *y no se lo tragó la tierra,* is experimental Latin American fiction, which demands that the reader take part in unraveling the story, determining the meaning, and in coming to his/her own conclusions about the characters' identities and relationships. Rivera constructed a narrative using the straightforward, but poetic, language of migrant workers. The central character, who remains nameless, searches for his identity by reconstructing conversations and stories he overheard in his family. Daniel P. Testa in *Modern Chicano Writers* (Prentice-Hall, 1979), calls it a "fascinating composite of stories and anecdotes of personal and collective . . . situations." The stories unfold over the course of one year, but it is a metaphorical year representing the central character's whole life. In many ways, . . . *y no se lo tragó la tierra* is the most influential book in the Chicano search for identity. Critic Juan Bruce-Novoa summed up the particular genius of the work:

> Though narrative, [his work] is no expository, but, rather, strangely impressionistic. It is a measure of Rivera's talent that the reader thinks that s/he has read a detailed depiction of reality, so much so that many have used the book as an accurate sociological statement of the migrant condition. What Rivera achieves is the evocation of an environment with a minimum of words, and within that environment, the migratory farm workers move with dignity, strength, and resilience.

Rivera was a pioneer of Chicano literature: Through his personal and scholarly activities, and through his essays, such as "Chicano Literature: Fiesta of the Living" (1979) and "Into the Labyrinth: The Chicano in Literature" (1971), he helped create its overall concept, promoted its authors, and established it as a legitimate part of the college curriculum. Rivera believed in literature's ability to both reflect and build community. He envisioned Chicanos defining themselves through literature, which became a central metaphor in his poems and stories. The short story "Zoo Island" (included in this anthology) chronicles the struggles of a people to define themselves, put themselves on the map, as it were—which they achieve through force of will. Rivera saw the migrant workers as embodying this search for identity:

> I wanted to document the spiritual strength, the concept of justice so important for the American continents. Within the migrants I saw that strength. They may be economically deprived, politically deprived, socially deprived, but they kept moving, never staying in one place to suffer or be subdued, but always searching for work; that's why they were "migrant" workers. I see that same sense of movement in the Europeans who

"Rivera has a clear eye for the cruel ironies of life. In the world his characters inhabit, people are often victimized by the very hopes they nurture, hopes that spring from the positions in life which they endure."

Ralph F. Grajeda in Modern Chicano Writers

came here and that concept of spiritual justice. It was there. And the migrant workers still have that role: to be searchers. That's an important metaphor in the Americas.

The life of the migrant worker also provides the setting for one of Rivera's most mystical and profoundly poetic stories, "The Salamanders," which he originally wrote in Spanish as "Las Salamandras" before rewriting it in English. It is a deceptively simple tale of a migrant worker child who confronts original sin and guilt.

In 1989 Rivera's stories were collected and published under the title, *The Harvest/La cosecha,* which was also the title of one of his stories, and in 1990 his poems were collected and published as *The Searchers.* By any account, Rivera remains the most outstanding and influential figure in the literature of Mexican peoples in the United States, and his works are fast achieving a place in the canon of Spanish-language literature in the world. In 1996, an award-winning feature film based on ... *y no se lo tragó la tierra* was released in theaters and broadcast nationally on the Corporation for Public Broadcasting.

Personal Stats

Mexican American educator, writer. **Born:** December 22, 1935, in Crystal City, Texas. **Died:** May 16, 1984, in Fontana, California. **Education:** A.A., Southwest Texas Junior College, 1956; B.A., Southwest Texas State College (now the University of Texas at San Marcos), 1958; M.Ed., Southwest Texas State College, 1964; M.A. in Romance Languages and Literatures, University of Oklahoma, 1969; Ph.D. in Romance Languages and Literatures, University of Oklahoma, 1969. **Career:** English and Spanish teacher in public schools of San Antonio (1957–58), Crystal City, Texas (1958–60), and League City, Texas (1960–65); teacher, Southwest Texas Junior College, Uvalde, Texas, 1965–66; instructor of Spanish, University of Oklahoma—Norman, 1968–69; associate professor, Sam Houston State University, 1969–71; professor of Spanish, University of Texas at San Antonio, 1971–77; associate dean, College of Multidisciplinary Studies, University of Texas at San Antonio, 1973 –76; vice chancellor for administration, University of Texas at San Antonio, 1976–77; vice president of Academic Affairs, University of Texas at El Paso, 1977–79; chancellor, University of California—Riverside, 1979–84. Visiting professor at Trinity University, San Antonio, Texas, 1973. **Memberships:** American Association of Teachers of Spanish & Portuguese; National Association for Bilingual Education; Modern Language Association; Phi Theta Kappa; Sigma Delta Pi; board of directors of the Times-Mirror Corporation and the Ford Foundation. **Awards/Honors:** Premio Quinto Sol (National Award for Chicano Literature) for ... *y no se lo tragó la tierra,* 1970.

Zoo Island

from *The Harvest: Short Stories,* bilingual edition, edited and translated by Julián Olivares,
Arte Público Press, 1989, pp. 113–20

Jose had just turned fifteen when he woke up one day with a great desire of taking a census count, of making a town and making everybody in it do what he said. All this happened because during the night he had dreamed that it was raining and, since they would not be working in the fields the next day, he dreamed about doing various things. But when he awoke, it hadn't rained at all. Anyway, he still had the desire.

The first thing he did when he got up was to count his family and himself—five. "We're five" he thought. Then he went on to the other family that lived with his, his uncle's— "Five more, and that's ten." Next he counted the people living in the chicken coop across the way. "Manuel and his wife and four more—that's six." And, with the ten he already had—"that's sixteen." Then he took into account the coop where Manuel's uncle lived, where there were three families. The first one, Don Jose's family, had seven, so now there were twenty-three. He was about to count the second family, when they told him to get ready to go to the fields.

It was still dark at five-thirty in the morning, and that day they would have to travel some fifty miles to reach the field overgrown with thistle that they had been working on. And as soon as they finished it, they would have to continue searching for more work. It would be way after dark by the time they got back. In the summertime, they could work up to eight o'clock. Then add an hour on the road back, plus the stop at the little store to buy something to eat . . . "We won't get back to the farm till late," he thought. But now he had something to do during the day while they were pulling up thistle. During the day, he could figure out exactly how many there were on that farm in Iowa.

■ ■ ■

"Here come those sonsabitches."

"Don't say bad words in front of the kids, Pa. They'll go around saying 'em all the time. That'd really be something, then, wouldn't it?"

"I'll bust them in the mouth if I hear them swearing. But here come those Whities. They don't leave a person in peace, do they? Soon as Sunday comes, and they come riding over to see us, to see how we live. They even stop and try to peek inside our chicken coops. You saw last Sunday how that row of cars passed by here. Them all laughing and laughing, and pointing at us. And you think they care about the dust they raise? Hell no. With their windows closed, why, they go on by just as fine as you please. And here we are, just like a bunch of monkeys in that park in San Antonio—Parkenrich."*

"Aw, let 'em be, Pa. They're not doing nothing to us, they're not doing any harm—not even if they was gypsies. Why you get all heated up for?"

"Well, it sets my blood a boiling, that's all. Why don't they mind their own business? I'm going to tell the owner to put a lock on the gate, so when they come they can't drive inside."

"Aw, let it go, it's nothing to make a fuss over."

"It sure is."

"We're almost to the field. Pa, you think we'll find work after we finish here?"

"Sure, son, there's always a lot of work. They don't take us for a bunch of lazy-bones. You saw how the boss' eyes popped out when I started pulling out all that thistle without any gloves on. Huh, they have to use gloves for everything. So, they're bound to recommend us to the other landowners. You'll see how they'll come and ask us if we want another field to work."

"The first thing I'll do is jot down the names on a list. Then, I'll use a page for each family, and that way I won't lose anybody. And for each bachelor, too, I'll use a page for each one, yeah. I'll also write down everybody's age. I wonder how many men and women there are on this farm, anyway? We're forty-nine field hands, counting the eight and nine-year-olds. Then, there's a bunch of kids, and then there's the two grandmothers that can't work anymore. The best thing to do is to get Jitter and Hank to help me with the counting. They could go to each coop and get the information, then we could gather up all the numbers. Too, it would be a good idea to put a number on each coop. Then, I could paint the number above each door. We could even pick up the mail from the box and distribute it, and that way the folks could even put the number of their coop on the letters they write. Sure, I bet that would make them feel better. Then we could even put up a sign at the farm gate that'll tell the number of people that live here, but . . . what would we call the farm? It doesn't have a name. I gotta think about that."

It rained the next day, and the following day as well. Therefore, Jose had the time and the opportunity to think over his plan. He made his helpers, Jitter and Hank, stick a pencil behind their ear, strap on a wrist watch—which they acquired easily enough—and shine their shoes. They also spent a half day reviewing the questions they would put to each household head and to each bachelor. The folks became aware of what the youngsters were up to and were soon talking about how they were going to be counted.

"These kids are always coming up with something . . . just ideas that pop into their heads or that they learn in school. Now, what for? What're they going to get out of counting us? Why, it's just a game, plain tomfoolery."

"Don't think that, comadre, no, no. These kids nowadays are on the ball, always inquiring about something or other. And you know, I like what they're doing. I like having my name put on a piece of paper, like they say they're gonna do. Tell me, when's anybody ever asked you your name and how many you got in the family and then write it all down on paper. You better believe it! Let them boys be, let 'em be, leastways while the rain keeps us from working."

"Yeah, but, what's it good for? I mean, how come so many questions? And then there's some things a person just doesn't say."

"Well, if you don't want to, don't tell 'em nothin.' But, look, all they want to know is how many of us there are in this grove. But, too, I think they want to feel like we're a whole lot of people. See here, in that little town were we buy our food there're only eighty-three souls, and you know what? They have a church, a dance hall, a filling station, a grocery store and even a little school. Here, we're more than eighty-three, I'll bet, and we don't have any of that. Why, we only have a water pump and four out-houses, right?"

"Now, you two are going to gather the names and the information. Ya'll go together so there won't be any problems. After each coop, you'll bring me the information right back. Ya'll jot it down on a sheet of paper and bring it to me, then I'll make a note of it in this notebook I got here. Let's start out with my family. You, Hank, ask me questions and jot down everything. Then you give me what you wrote down so that I can make a note of it. Do ya'll understand what we're going to do? Don't be afraid. Just knock on the door and ask. Don't be afraid."

It took them all afternoon to gather and jot down the details, then they compiled all the figures by the light of an oil lamp. Yes, it turned out that there were more fieldhands on the farm than there were people in the town where they bought their food. Actually, there were eighty-six on the farm, but the boys came up with a figure of eighty-seven because two women were expecting and they counted them for three. They gave the exact number to the rest of the folks, explaining the part about the pregnant women. Everyone was pleased to know that the farm settlement was really a town and bigger than the one where they bought their groceries every Saturday.

The third time they boys went over the figures they realized that they had forgotten to go over to Don Simon's shack. They had simply overlooked it because it was on the other side of the grove. When old Don Simon had gotten upset and fought with Stumpy, he asked the owner to take the tractor and drag his coop to the other side of the grove, where no one would bother him. The owner did this right away. There was something in Don Simon's eyes that made people jump. It wasn't just his gaze but also the fact that he hardly ever spoke. So, when he did talk everybody listened up so as not to lose a single word.

It was already late and the boys decided not to go see him until the next day, but the fact of the matter was they were a little afraid just thinking that they would have to go and ask him something. They remembered the to-do in the field when Don Simon got fed up with Stumpy's needling him and chased Stumpy all over the field with his onion knife. Then Stumpy, even though he was much younger, tripped and fell, tangling himself in the tow-sacks. Right then, Don Simon threw himself on Stumpy, slicing at him with his knife. What saved Stumpy were the tow-sacks. Luckily, Stumpy came out of it with only a slight wound in his leg; nonetheless, it did bleed quite a bit. When the owner was told what had happened, he ran Stumpy off. But Don Simon explained that it wasn't much to make a fuss over, so he let Stumpy stay but the owner did move Don Simon's coop to the other side of the grove, just like Don Simon wanted. So, that's why the boys were a little afraid of him. But, like they told themselves, just not riling him, he was good folk.

Stumpy had been riling Don Simon for some time about his wife leaving him for somebody else.

"Excuse us, Don Simon, but we're taking up the farm census, and we'd like to ask you a few questions. You don't have to answer them if you don't want to."

"Alright."

"How old are you?"

"Old enough."

"When were you born?"

"When my mother born me."

"Where were you born?"

"In the world."

"Do you have a family?"

"No."

"How come you don't talk much?"

"This is for the census, right?"

"No."

"What for, then? I reckon ya'll think you talk a lot. Well, not only ya'll but all the folks here. What ya'll do most of the time is open your mouth and make noise. Ya'll just like to talk to yourselves, that's all. I do the same, but I do it silently, the rest of you do it out loud."

"Well, Don Simon, I believe that's all. Thanks for your cooperation. You know, we're eighty-eight souls here on this farm. We're plenty, right?"

"Well, you know, I kinda like what ya'll are doing. By counting yourself, you begin everything. That way you know you're not only here but that you're alive. Ya'll know what you oughta call this place?"

"No."

"Zoo Island."**

The following Sunday just about all the people on the farm had their picture taken next to the sign the boys had made on Saturday afternoon and which they had put up at the farm gate. It said: **Zoo Island, Pop. 88½**. One of the women had given birth.

And every morning Jose would no sooner get up than he would go see the sign. He was part of that number, he was in Zoo Island, in Iowa, and like Don Simon said, in the world. He didn't know why, but there was a warm feeling that started in his feet and rose through his body until he felt it in his throat and in all his senses. Then this same feeling made him talk, made him open his mouth. At times it even made him shout. The shouting was something the owner never managed to understand. By the time he arrived sleepy-eyed in the morning, the boy would be shouting. Sometimes he thought about asking him why he shouted, but then he'd get busy with other things and forget all about it.

*Brackenridge Park Zoo.

**Reference to "Monkey Island," Brackenridge Zoo.

The Salamanders

from *The Harvest: Short Stories,* bilingual edition, edited and translated by Julián Olivares, Arte Público Press, 1989, pp. 87–90

What I remember most about that night is the darkness, the mud and the slime of the salamanders. But I should start from the beginning so you can understand all of this, and how, upon feeling this, I understood something that I still have with me. But I don't have this with me only as something I remember, but as something that I still feel.

It all began because it had been raining for three weeks and we had no work. We began to gather our things and made ready to leave. We had been with that farmer in Minnesota waiting for the rain to stop but it never did. Then he came and told us that the best thing for us to do was to leave his shacks because, after all, the beets had begun to rot away already. We understood, my father and I, that he was in fact afraid of us. He was afraid that we would begin to steal from him or perhaps that one of us would get sick, and then he would have to take the responsibility because we had no money. We told him we had no money, neither did we have anything to eat and no way of making it all the way back to Texas. We had enough money, perhaps, to buy gasoline to get as far south as Oklahoma. He just told us that he was very sorry, but he wanted us to leave. So we began to pick up our things. We were leaving when he softened up somewhat and gave us two tents, full of spider webs, that he had in the loft in one of his barns. He also gave us a lamp and some kerosene. He told my dad that, if we went by way of Crystal Lake in northern Iowa, perhaps we would find work among the farmers and perhaps it had not been raining there so much and the beets had not rotted away. And we left.

In my father's eyes and in my mother's eyes, I saw something original and pure that I had never seen before. It was a sad type of love, it seemed. We barely talked as we went riding over the gravel roads. The rain seemed to talk for us. A few miles before reaching Crystal Lake, we began to get remorseful. The rain that continued to fall kept on telling us monotonously that we would surely not find work there. And so it was. At every farm that we came to, the farmers would only shake their heads from inside the house. They would not even open the door to tell us there was no work. It was when they shook their heads in this way that I began to feel that I was not part of my father and my mother. The only thing in my mind that existed was the following farm.

The first day we were in the little town of Crystal Lake everything went bad. Going through a puddle, the car's wiring got wet and my father drained the battery trying to get the car started. Finally, a garage did us the favor of recharging the battery. We asked for work in various parts of that little town, but then they got police after us. My father explained that we were only looking for work, but the policeman told us that he did not want any gypsies in town and told us to leave. The money was almost gone, but we had to leave. We left at twilight and we stopped the car some three miles from town and there we saw the night fall.

The rain would come and go. Seated in the car near the ditch, we spoke little. We were tired. We were hungry. We were alone. We sensed that we were totally alone. In my father's eyes and in my mother's eyes, I saw something original. That day we had hardly eaten anything in order to have money left for the following day. My father looked sadder, weakened. He believed we would find no work, and we stayed seated in the car waiting for the following day. Almost no cars passed by on that gravel road during the night. At dawn I awoke and everybody was asleep, and I could see their bodies and their faces. I could see the bodies of my mother and my father and my brothers and sisters, and they were silent. They were faces and bodies made of wax. They reminded me of my grandfather's face the day we buried him. But I didn't get as afraid as that day when I found him inside the truck, dead. I guess it was because I knew they were not dead and that they were alive. Finally, the day came completely.

That day we looked for work all day, and we didn't find any work. We slept at the edge of the ditch and again I awoke in the early morning hours. Again I saw my people asleep. And that morning I felt somewhat afraid, not because they looked as if they were dead, but because I began to feel again that I no longer belonged to them.

The following day we looked for work all day again, and nothing. We slept at the edge of the ditch. Again I awoke in the morning, and again I saw my people asleep. But that morning, the third one, I felt like leaving them because I truly felt that I was no longer a part of them.

On that day, by noon, the rain stopped and the sun came out and we were filled with hope. Two hours later we found a farmer that had some beets which, according to him, probably had not been spoiled by the rain. But he had no houses or anything to live in. He showed us the acres of beets which were still under water, and he told us that, if we cared to wait until the water went down to see if the beets had not rotted, and if they had not, he would pay us a large bonus per acre that we helped him cultivate. But he didn't have any houses, he told us. We told him we had some tents with us and, if he would let us, we would set them up in his yard. But he didn't want that. We noticed that he was afraid of us. The only thing that we wanted was to be near the drinking water, which was necessary, and also we were so tired of sleeping seated in the car, and, of course, we wanted to be under the light that he had in his yard. But he did not want us, and he told us, if we wanted to work there, we had to put our tents at the foot of the field and wait there for the water to go down. And so we placed our tents at the foot of the field and we began to wait. At nightfall we lit up the lamp in one of the tents, and then we decided for all of us to sleep in one tent only. I remember that we all felt so comfortable being able to stretch our legs, our arms, and falling asleep was easy. The thing that I remember so clearly that night was what awakened me. I felt what I thought was the hand of one of my little brothers, and then I heard my own screaming. I pulled his hand away, and, when I awoke, I found myself holding a salamander. Then I screamed and I saw that we were all covered with salamanders that had come out from the flooded fields. And all of us continued screaming and throwing salamanders off our bodies. With the light of the lamp, we began to kill them. At first we felt nauseated because, when we stepped on them, they would ooze milk. It seemed they were invading us, that they were invading the tent as if they wanted to reclaim the foot of the field. I don't know why we killed so many salamanders that night. The easiest thing to do would have been to climb quickly into our car. Now that I remember, I think that we also felt the desire to recover and to reclaim the foot of the field. I do remember that we began to look for more salamanders to kill. We wanted to find more to kill more. I remember that I liked to take the lamp, to seek them out, to kill them very slowly. It may be that I was angry at them for having frightened me. Then I began to feel that I was becoming part of my father and my mother and my brothers and sisters again.

What I remember most about that night was the darkness, the mud and the slime of the salamanders, and how hard they would get when I tried to squeeze the life out of them. What I have with me still is what I saw and felt when I killed the last one, and I guess that is why I remember the night of the salamanders. I caught one and examined it very carefully under the lamp. Then I looked at its eyes for a long time before I killed it. What I saw and what I felt is something I still have with me, something that is very pure—original death.

Writings

Novels: . . . *y no se lo tragó la tierra/And the Earth Did Not Devour Him* (bilingual edition), Quinto Sol, 1971; Arte Público Press, 1987; *This Migrant Earth,* English language translation by Rolando Hinojosa, Arte Público Press, 1985; . . . *y no se lo tragó la tierra* (Spanish-language only), Arte Público Press, 1996. **Collections of Short Stories and Poetry:** *Always and Other Poems,* Sisterdale Press, 1973. *The Harvest/La cosecha,* Arte Público Press, 1989. *The Searchers: Collected Poetry,* Arte Público Press, 1990. *Tomás Rivera: The Complete Works,* edited by Julián Olivares, 2nd edition, Arte Público Press, 1995. **Stories and Essays:** In *El grito, Revista Chicano-Riqueña, Melus, El espejo/The Mirror, Aztlán: An Anthology of Mexican American Literature, A Decade of Chicano Literature,* and numerous other anthologies, magazines, and textbooks.

Floyd Salas

Floyd Salas is one of the pioneers of the contemporary Hispanic literary movement in the United States. He was one of the first novelists to break into print with major commercial publishers and has continued to produce powerful prose that graphically depicts such diverse aspects of urban Latino life as boxing, the underworld of petty criminals, the drug and hippy cultures, and the campus protest movement during the Vietnam War. Salas also wrote the most passionate and memorable autobiography of U.S. Hispanic literature to date, Buffalo Nickel (1992).

Salas was born on January 24, 1931, in Walsenburg, Colorado, into a family that traces both its maternal and paternal lines back to the original Spanish settlers of Florida and New Mexico. When he was still very young, the family relocated to California, and in pursuit of work opportunities, moved around so much that Salas attended six different high schools in four years. One of the most tragic events of his early life was the death of his mother, Anita Sanchez Salas, from a protracted illness during his high school years. Following her death, Salas became a juvenile delinquent and wound up spending 120 days on the Santa Rita Prison Farm; it was a grueling experience that led him to foreswear his delinquent ways to avoid problems with the law. The experience also served as material for his first novel, which graphically depicts prison life. In 1956, Salas won the first boxing scholarship ever given to the University of California, Berkeley, where he discovered literature. A number of writing scholarships and fellowships followed, including a Rockefeller grant to study at the Centro Mexicano de Escritores in Mexico City in 1958.

Upon returning to California from Mexico, Salas worked on Bay Area campuses as a creative writing instructor and became active in the campus protest movement and immersed himself in the drug and hippy subcultures. These experiences later became grist for his novels *What Now My Love* (1970) and *State of Emergency* (1996). His first published book, *Tatoo the Wicked Cross* (1967), however, was made possible by his winning the prestigious Joseph Henry Jackson Award and a Eugene F. Saxton Fellowship, which were awarded him based on his early drafts of that novel. *Tatoo the Wiked Cross* is an exposé of the brutality of juvenile jail, as seen by a street youth (*pachuco*) who is raped and abused; the brutalized protagonist ends up commiting murder. The raw power and passion of Salas's narrative left reviewers believing that Salas had experienced this brutality first-hand, but he actually based the story on tales he had heard about "the rape of a little kid in Preston Reform School . . . the boy then put lye in the food of his attackers and caused them much misery." The overwhelming acclaim the novel received from reviewers led Salas into a career as a writer. *The Satudrday Review of Literature* gave the most important canonizing response to *Tatoo*: "One of the best and certainly one of the most important first novels published in the last ten years."

Tatoo the Wicked Cross was followed by a novel of modest proportions, *What Now My Love?* (1970), which told the story of the escape of three hippies involved in a drug bust where policemen are shot. The novel follows their flight to Tijuana and their penetration of the border town's drug underworld. Salas's adventure story and insightful depiction of the drug subculture garnered praise from *The Los Angeles Times*: "A brilliant second novel by an indomitable writer." *The New York Times* concurred: "Remarkably spare and stirring . . . a hellbent sprint from the law and the author follows it with excellent timing. A little stunner."

With Salas, life and literature are always closely entwined. His next years were occupied in chasing the drug culture: "I made the world's pot scenes, following the hippy trail from San Francisco to Marakesh, writing a novel about my radical experiences in the Bay Area called *Lay My Body on the Line*." The novel was eventually published by a small press in 1978 to an almost negligible critical response. His personal battle with drugs, his dysfunctional family, and the break-up of his own marriage led Salas to a long hiatus from publishing.

In the early 1990s, through writing his memoir *Buffalo Nickel*, Salas came to terms with his family's dramatic history of widespread drug addiction and suicides (a total of six). The work depicts his own agonizing love-hate relationship with his older brother, a small-time prize-fighter, drug addict, and petty criminal. The memoir leads the reader into the underworld of pimp bars, drugs, and crime, and

"I wrote What Now My Love? *because I had a story to tell about smoking pot. I had been an early martyr for pot, and it cost me my wife and son."*

Floyd Salas

depicts Salas's struggles to escape the chaos of his family life by becoming a writer. The work was so well received that Salas was awarded a California Arts Council Fellowship for achieving excellence. Ishmael Reed wrote, "The high quality of the prose in this novel-like memoir ranks with that of the other memorable family dramas, *Native Son, Fences* and *Long Days Journey into Night*." Andrew Vachss called the memoir, "a biography with the narrative force of a fine novel . . . lyrical, compelling and insightful . . . a tortured soul's search for manhood."

After three decades in the vanguard of Hispanic literature of the United States, Floyd Salas still packs a wallop, or as Vachss said, "Salas has lived his entire life in the ring and he still packs the Equalizer."

Personal Stats

Writer, teacher, boxing coach. **Born:** January 24, 1931, in Walsenberg, Colorado. *Education:* California College of Arts and Crafts, 1950–54; Oakland Junior College, 1955–56; University of California, 1956-57; B.A. and M.A. in English, San Francisco State University, 1963 and 1965, respectively. **Career:** Professor, Creative Writing, San Francisco State University, 1966–67; State Coordinator of Poetry-in-the-Schools, San Francisco State University, 1973–76; Lecturer in English, University of California, Berkeley, 1977–78; Professor, Creative Writing, Foothills College, 1979 to present. *Memberships:* PEN Oakland, PEN Center West, USA Amateur Boxing Federation, Northern California Veteran Boxers Association. *Awards/Honors:* Rockefeller Foundation Fiction Scholarship to study at the Centro Mexicano de Escritores, 1958; Joseph Henry Jackson Fiction Award, San Francisco Foundation, 1964; Harper & Row Eugene F. Saxton Literature Fellowship, 1965; National Endowment for the Arts Fellowship, 1977; University of California, Berkeley James P. Lynch Memorial Fellowship for outstanding teachers, 1977; University of California, Berkeley Bay Area Writers Project Fellowship, 1984; California Arts Council Fellowship, 1993. *Address:* c/o Arte Público Press, University of Houston, Houston, TX 77204-2090

Kid Victory

from *The Americas Review*, Vol. XXI, No. 3–4, Fall—Winter, 1993, pp. 19–34

Fear drains me when I step through the ring ropes and look over at the guy I'm going to fight. I haven't been in a gym in twelve years and don't know if I've still got it.

Muscles ripple on his long, white body. Built rangy like me, but bigger by fifteen pounds at one-forty and twenty-five years younger, I know I'm going to have my hands full.

I turn away so I won't have to look at him and see this guy staring at me from the spectator stands next to the ring, under the wall of dirty windows.

Typical looking street kid, growing up downtown, he's got on a cream-colored felt hat, sitting right on top of his head like a gangster, a shiny polyester sport shirt and gabardine slacks, polished shoes and vest, with no coat, and a thin mustache touched up with eyebrow pencil to make it show on his white lip.

The boxing club's in a downtown section of Oakland, full of seedy bars, vice cops and whores, black pimps and dope fiends, up on the second floor of an old brick building, right across the landing from a taxi dance, a dollar a tune, and you can rub up all you want. It's an old, high hall just like the taxi dance, with a whole wall of dirty windows facing the one-way traffic on Twelfth Street below.

Two rings and the spectator stands are on the left half of the room by the windows and bare floor, mirrors and punching bags on the right. The locker room and two showers are behind the bags, with posters of past fights all over the walls and a few cracker-box sayings on signs like, "The fighter with a big head will get it knocked off."

The bell rings and I forget The Kid, move out with tingling legs to meet the long-waisted Okie, hands up by his freckled face, coming to get me.

I skip away and around the ring, and when he comes after me, skip back in, pop him with a quick jab, then skip back out before he can counter, and I think I can handle him. No more fear, I'm not as rusty as I thought.

I keep dancing around, popping him with jabs every time he gets in range, sometimes hitting him with a quick one-two and an occasional left hook, don't try to hit him hard, he's an amateur and I'm an ex-college champ, so I relax and take it easy on him. He's too slow for me, fifteen pounds worth. Even at age forty-five, I'm too quick.

I keep moving, throwing light shots that mainly hit their mark, beating him with the jab and a counter right hook to the ribs under his jab, out-punching him. But then he catches me in a corner and charges like a football lineman, and when I cover up with my arms, hits me in the nuts!

"Hey, man! Take it easy! I'm not punching on you!" I say and shove him back, see Art over in the corner laugh, but The Kid frown. It hurt but not that bad even though I'm not wearing a cup and I dance out into the ring again and, when he tries to charge me again, skip away and say, "Take it easy."

But he charges me again, gets me with a one-two and when I cover, hits me in the nuts again.

"Goddamnit!" I say, wincing at the sharp pain, and shove him back with both hands, but can't move because it hurts too bad. Then when he charges me again, without moving away, I dance back into the ropes and spring off them like a slingshot, stick out a straight right lead, catch him right on the button with a "smack!" and wobble him back, almost knock him down.

To keep from dumping him, I purposely don't hit him with all my strength. I'm just trying to teach him not to cheat, even if he's losing. When I connect, I hear a cry of admiration and glance out at The Kid on the stands, grinning.

But Okie charges in again and catches me with a stiff one-two to the forehead and I dance away and say, "Alright, man, if that's what you want," when the bell rings.

■ ■ ■

Though I'm panting hard and trying to get my breath, I walk over to Okie in the corner with Art and say, "Hey! Lighten up, man!"

But he keeps his freckled face turned to Art and doesn't even look at me. Art glances out of the corner of his eye like he doesn't want me in the corner with him and his boy so I walk away, still trying to catch my breath.

I walk around the ring, feeling weak as a kitten, trying to get my wind back, breathing deeply, holding the air in my lungs as long as possible so the oxygen will get into by bloodstream and revivify me, when I see The Kid staring at me with big eyes.

Turning at the neutral corner, I then see this little fighter with a powerful body and blue-toned cheeks, gotta be a bantamweight like me when I'm in shape, glowering at me from the next ring, where he's shadow boxing, from under a heavy head of stiff hair. One eye's squinted as if he's not sure he really believes I'm that good, which makes me feel good.

I haven't boxed in twelve years and I'm only an ex-college champ, but I've kept myself in pretty good shape by running three times a week, more or less, don't smoke and barely drink so I've got it under control and I could have knocked Okie down, maybe out, stopped him on a TKO with that straight-right shot, if I'd put all my power in it. I'm still taking it easy on him, even if he did hit me in the nuts, though I'm panting hard, trying to get my wind back.

But he charges out and hits me in the nuts the first time we meet in the middle of the ring and I skip away, aching and angry, and when he charges in again, stay right there and when he throws a jab hit him with a right hook to the ribs with all my strength and make him grunt and back off, stay away until the pain goes away and he can breath again.

I look him right in his pale eyes so he'll know what I mean, but after a few seconds, he charges again and this time, keeps his left low to protect his ribs. I feint with a jab at his stomach to keep his left down, then loop an overhand right over his low left and pop him right on the button, stop him right in his tracks, and freeze him straight up.

I could knock him cold with a follow-up left hook, but hold off and wait until his eyes lose their glaze and can focus on me again, then I skip away, tap him on the headgear with light jabs a few times and keep out of his range until the bell rings. Then I walk up to him and grin and throw my arm around him. He's had enough and I don't think of going a third round. I'm too tired anyway.

He jerks his head around, staring at me with those watery green eyes, surprised I'm not mad at him. But it's just a sparring match to me, just fun. I'm not out for his blood, just don't want him to get mine. I feel pretty good for an old man, haven't done badly at all.

I turn away and see The Kid with his head tilted back so he can see better, staring at me with bright eyes, and I'm amazed when Blue Beard parts the ropes for me to climb out of the ring.

"Thanks," I say, but he doesn't smile. He just spreads them with his knee and his hand. Still there's respect in it. Yet, when I walk down the ring steps and Art takes off my gloves and I feel so weak I could melt down and spread out on the floor like a pool of butter, he keeps glowering at me from up in the ring as he shadow boxes, like he's trying to scare me.

■ ■ ■

Then The Kid comes down off the stands and watches me punch the bags.

I wish he wouldn't. I'm so tired and out of shape, I can hardly hit the little speed bag. Can't keep my arms up, they're so weak, haven't been used like this in years. I was never good at it anyway. So, after two sloppy rounds of barely getting in twenty punches without missing and having to keep starting over again, I finally get through and go over to the heavy bags, pick an empty one and start working on that with the next bell.

But The Kid follows me over, stands a few feet away, sighting on me from his hat brim, making me feel self-conscious and I have to fake it. I lean against the bag with my body like I'm fighting in close, then, with my hands down, loop sloppy hooks from my sides, like I'm bobbing and weaving with my body, feeling so weak, I'd quit if The Kid weren't standing there, neat and shiny in his dress-up clothes. But I stick it out two whole three-minute rounds, getting slower and slower with each punch, heaving a sign of relief when the bell finally rings.

I turn away so I won't have to look The Kid in the face and notice Blue Beard standing on the other side of The Kid with a smirk on his face.

He shakes his head like I'm over the hill, and when I try to jump rope and can barely get through ten spins without catching one of my feet, he snorts, then bursts out laughing when I trip, trying to start again.

I have to grin myself, I'm so embarrassed, but The Kid looks down at the floor like he's embarrassed too, and I put the rope away and sit down to rest, too tired to even try anymore when Blue Beard stands right in front of me, looks at himself in the mirror, and starts jumping rope.

Bare-chested, his flat, wide muscles rippling over his whole body, he shows off for me. The rope whirs so fast, it looks like his feet barely touch the floor. Yet, he's hardly breathing, let alone breathing hard, when I was panting like a choo-choo train for one lousy round. His body's so much better than mine at twenty years younger, I guess he can probably beat me and tremble at the thought of fighting him.

The next day, I barely get dressed in my sweats and out into the gym, where I stand next to Art and start wrapping my hands, when Blue Beard comes out of the locker room, walks over by us and starts shadow-boxing in front of the mirror and flexing his muscles.

When I don't look up from my wraps at him, he stops, steps over next to me, puts his fist against my jaw and says, "Hey, Old Man, I won fifteen out of eighteen fights as an amateur before I turned pro."

I gently but firmly push his fist off my jaw and say, "Sounds good to me," then notice The Kid sitting in the stands, watching.

Blue Beard doesn't bother me by calling me an old man. In the gym, anybody over thirty who fights is an old man. And most people think I'm in my thirties because I take care of myself, have a good grain and raw vegetable and lean meat diet, and I'm smooth-skinned and unwrinkled —young faces run in my family. Thinning hair and the slightest puffiness on my hips are my only signs of age. I don't mind looking thirty and take pride in surprising people when I say how old I am.

"As a pro, I won my first eleven fights with eight kayos," Blue Beard says.

I look at the little guy. He's my size and weight, in better shape but not built better, just differently, both of us with muscles, but him with wider shoulders, me with a thicker chest.

"That's damn good," I say, guessing he's trying to set me up, get me to brag, too, then choose me, but I'm not ready to fight him yet and I try to keep it polite.

"Damn good, if it's true," Art says and laughs. "But it could all be bullshit. Right, paisano?"

"No, paisano," Blue Beard says and turns away, starts shadow boxing in front of the mirror, next to Art's equipment booth, where his boxing supplies are, gloves hanging from nails by their laces, old headgear, jump ropes, dirty handwraps and smelly old T-shirts.

Blue Beard's not graceful like I am. I'm a better boxer, if twenty years older. His jabs are straight and strong, but awkward, not smooth. He's got me a little scared, though, and I watch him as he jumps. "Whir-snap, whir-snap, whir-snap, whir-snap," the rope goes as somebody else pounds on the speed bag with a "ratatattat" and another guy thumps the heavy bag with a "thud, thud, thud."

"He won his first eleven fights when he first came over from Italy, but he's lost four straight decisions since," Art says. "He's on a losing streak and mean, tries to whip everybody in the gym. Nobody'll spar with him. Stay away from him."

I look at Art. Swarthy and fine-featured, he looked like the Italian movie star Vitorio Gassman when he was a young contender and now, in his mid-thirties, looks like Omar Shariff, the Egyptian actor. His curly hair has turned gray from drinking and smoking and he weighs 205 instead of 147, almost sixty pounds over his fighting weight, when he was called Slim. I appreciate him trying to help me, but I look at Blue Beard and don't say anything.

I know Blue Beard's after me, one of the few guys in the gym his weight who can probably give him a work-out. He's trying to soften me up with his nickel-psychology, scare me, and halfway succeeding.

■ ■ ■

Every day, Blue Beard watches me punch the bags, then shakes his head and laughs, and I can see The Kid lower his eyes and turn away. So I train hard.

I never see The Kid work out himself, though, and one day, when I'm punching the big bag, Art walks by and I stop him and ask, "See that kid over there. Does he fight?"

"He's got no balls. Been hanging around here for six months now and never so much as punched a bag," Art says and tilts his head to one side, watches me pop the bag with left jabs, then sneers and says, "That's no way to jab. It's all arm, you don't have your weight in it. Step in when you punch so you get power."

I step in and hit the bag with a stiff left and he says, "Throw three," and when I do it quick but without much power, he says, "Naw, naw," and shakes his head and walks away. I see Blue Beard smirk and The Kid look down.

But I keep at it and stay off the liquids and watch what I eat and come every day and start getting in shape. Soon, I can go a whole round on the speed bag without missing, popping it like a machine gun, and can do it three rounds in a row. When I finish, I look around and see The Kid staring at me, grinning.

I get it down on the double-end bag, too, after a month. I dance around it and hit it with lots of jabs and quick, long-armed combinations, jab-cross hook. And there's The Kid looking at me from under the brim of his hat, not saying anything, never working out himself, just watching me.

■ ■ ■

Blue Beard and Okie are in the ring waiting for the bell when I walk out into the gym from the locker room, where Art's taking a piss and jiving with some guys back there. I think of going back to tell him, but he knows Okie's up there—It's his fighter—and I change my mind with the bell. I want to see this. There's bound to be fireworks, with two bad actors in there.

Sure enough, they meet right in the middle of the ring and start slugging. Blue Beard throws a jab and Okie, taller by three inches, catches Blue Beard with a one-two and Blue Beard then cuts loose with both hands and hits Okie with four looping hooks, backs him into the ropes, and swarms all over him, hits him with some solid shots to the head, jolts him, and I look around for Art but only see The Kid looking at me.

Blue Beard keeps punching and wobbles him, though Okie manages to slide down the ropes and get away. I hope Blue Beard will lighten up on him like I did, and I look around for Art again, but only see The Kid

Blue Beard stays on him, drives him back, catches him in a corner and hits him with another solid shot, wobbles him again, and I know he's going to knock him out, unless Art shows up. I don't want to butt-in if I can help it. Managers don't like that.

I look around again but only see the kid and Blue Beard's manager Dago. But he just stands down below his corner, looking up from his round face, gray hair combed straight back, long red nose hanging down and his belly sticking out, not even moving when Blue Beard hits Okie really hard with an overhand right and staggers him. I get the urge to jump up there myself. It's true, then, what Art said, that he's mean. But this is only a work-out, not a professional fight, and when he catches Okie with two more hard shots and Okie's hands drop, leaving him defenseless, and he takes another shot to the face, I jump up the steps and shout, "Back off, man! Back off!" and when he keeps punching, leap through the ropes and run across the ring and grab his arms.

"Lighten up, man! You'll hurt him!" I say.

But when he looks over his shoulder and sees that it's me, he spins around and hits me with a hard left hook to the jaw.

I jump back right away and hold up my arms.

"Leave him be, man! You got him!" I say and skip back out of range as he charges in again and barely get away when Art jumps into the ring and grabs him.

"No, paisano," he says and holds onto him.

Blue Beard stops struggling but says, "You better get out of here, Old Man, or you're next."

I'm tempted to take him up on it. But I jumped in there when neither of them were my fighters and he feels justified, so I turn around and step back through the ropes, then go down the stairs and look up at him from outside the ring.

He watches Art lead Okie through the ropes in his corner and down the steps, then turns to me and says, "You want some, too, Old Man!"

I stare up at him. We must be the same size, five-five, and the same weight. I'm down to 119 all the time now, and even 117 after a work-out. So, I'm in fair boxing shape, and when he sticks out his blue-hued chin and glares at me with his little brown eyes, and says, "Do you?" I feel the blood rush to my head and I say, "Yeah! I want some!"

"He just stopped Okie in the first round, man. What's the matter with you?" Art says as he unties Okie's gloves.

"He hit me, then added insult in injury by choosing me, acting like he can take me, like I'm afraid."

He loosens the laces on a glove, then jerks it off.

"He'll try to kill yuh, man. He doesn't like you buttin' in like that."

"I don't care," I say.

"You're crazy?" he asks and jerks the other glove off.

"I don't like what he did to your boy," I say and avoid looking at Okie.

Art squints. There's always a little dark spot, like a speck of dirt on the inside corner of one eye, like some permanent scar tissue from boxing.

"Don't get hurt over it," he says and I'm surprised. I always thought he'd like to see me get it, since I never acted afraid of him, twenty wins as a pro or not. I could always see a grudging kind of respect for me, but now he's actually trying to protect me.

"I'm stronger now, Art," I say. "I learned how to shift my weight forward, too, even when I punch fast. I hit a little bit, myself. I want to give it a try."

"You sure or crazy?"

"Sure," I say just as Blue Beard calls out: "You chickenshit or you gonna fight?" and I answer, "Fight!" and nod at Art.

He steps over to Dago and says something, and Dago says, "Your boy comes in to get in shape. My boy comes to earn a living. Your boy can fight or night. My boy fights."

Art turns back to me and says, "Alright. Go get your gloves and headgear. Make sure you wear a cup. And when he comes at you, run!"

■ ■ ■

I go back to the gray locker room with the old peeling wallpaper, take off my sweatshirt, so I'm down to a loose-fitting green tank top which will give me plenty of room in the arms and cut down on sweating and fatigue, get my gloves and headgear, but sit down for a moment between the battered green lockers.

What am I doing it for? For Okie? He hit me in the nuts because I was better than him. To punish the little beast, Blue Beard, for being a killer? Maybe, but I'm no cop, and it wasn't any of my business.

Mainly, I'm doing it for myself, I figure. Because he chose me threatened me, same as said he could kick my ass, and I'm going to see if he can or not. It's pride, I have to admit it. I set myself up as a Good Guy by jumping in the middle of his fight when it was none of my business, technically, and now I'm so scared I'm weak, feel like laying down on the massage table and not going out there. I don't even know if I can last the round better than Okie, who, if anything, is in better shape, and Blue Beard's out to get me for butting-in now, not just on general principles any-more. So he'll be twice as mean as he was to Okie, which means trouble.

The bell rings ending a round. I should go in and get my gloves on. But I'm not ready. I try to steel myself, first. I'm stronger now and faster than both of them, have more grace and tal-ent, if not power and drive. If I'm older, I'm smarter. If I can only keep from getting tired.

I know another thing. I'm not the only one afraid. Art was so good as an amateur champion, other managers wouldn't let their fighters fight him. And he looked like a contender when he turned pro, with 20 straight wins and 17 knockouts, until a real contender knocked him out in his twenty-first fight. Then a week later, when he was discouraged to find he could get it, too, a ten-round middleweight main-eventer dropped him in the gym, and he slapped his gloves against the canvas and cried and never fought again. I'm not the only one scared.

When the bell rings again, I stand up and go out to the ring, as ready as I'll ever be, and Art's frowning.

"Look, if he traps you and presses on you, take a half-step back with your right foot, twist your body sidewards so you're holding his body off with your left shoulder and arm, and your right arm's free, drop it down to your hip and turn back and drive an uppercut to his gut. That'll take some steam out of him."

"Thanks, Art," I say and know I'll need it. I can see The Kid watching me from the stands, his felt hat down low, his eyes looking up past the brim, probably thinking I'm crazy to get in there with Blue Beard after he stopped Okie.

■ ■ ■

I need everything I've got. Art has to wash down my mouthpiece and doesn't stick it in my mouth until after the bell rings, and when I turn around, the little beast is already charging down on me, his face a scowl in his black headgear, and scares me to death, then smacks me right in the left eye with a right hook and sends a flash of painful light through it, then cuts loose with a barrage of punches to my face, trying to knock me out before I can even get out of the corner.

They sting but they don't stun me. I'm not dizzy. I still have my senses and try to stick out a jab to keep him off.

But he backs me down the ropes like he did Okie and catches me in a neutral corner and cuts loose again, going for the kill.

But this time my head's down and my hands up and I catch the shots on top my head and on my shoulders and, inside his wide hooks, cut loose with a short left hook, all my shoulder in it, that catches him right on the chin and stuns him.

His eyes widen and he stops punching, stares at me, gives me a second to slip out of the corner. I don't realize it's a mistake until I skip out into the ring, where I can see him still just standing there. Meaning, I could have gotten him then if I went all-out and had the confidence I wouldn't punch myself out and could last the whole three rounds. But, I couldn't take the chance. I didn't want to be a sitting-duck, if I didn't get him.

It's too late now, and when he comes charging out of the corner, screaming, "Yaaaaaaa!" I skip away like a water mosquito.

Art waves at me to slow down, I'm wasting energy, but I've just escaped with my life and I'm not about to sit there and let him hit me. I'm going to stay away from the little beast. Even

Blue Beard waves at me to come on and punch on him, too, trying to make me fight.

But when he traps me in the corner again and hits me with a good right hook to the head, I counter with a left hook over it and catch him right on the chin and all my fear vanishes. I'm in a fight now and I don't care.

Then when he screams and charges the next time, I step in with all my weight like Art showed me and spear him right on the chin with a left jab and snap his head back. When I see I can keep him off with the jab, I stand right in the middle of the ring and fight him every time he charges. I make no attempt to skip around, just stand there toe to toe with him so I won't get tired, and try to beat him to the punch with a stiff jab every time he rushes in, keep pumping it in his face and hold him off until the bell rings.

■ ■ ■

"Did he hurt you with that first punch?" Art asks in the corner.

"The punches hurt but he didn't stun me," I answer between deep breaths.

"Well, you stunned him and should've finished him then. Now, he's strong and even meaner. Keep sticking him with that jab and move away."

"I'm too tired to run, Art," I say and take a deep breath to ease the ache in my chest. "I better stand in the middle of the ring and fight him."

He squints that eye with the dark speck in it again and then says, "Alright, but remember to keep that left going. Don't forget to shift your weight so you can get momentum in those combinations."

When Blue Beard charges me in the corner at the bell for the second time, I slug it out with him and drive him off, then, my hands down at my sides, I'm so tired, I hit him with three, quick right hand leads. I see his eyes widen when I hit him and know the shots hurt. I do belt for my weight, partly because of the quickness and accuracy and also because I've got big hands for my size and long-armed build, with big knuckles on them like a sledge-hammer.

But I've discovered his main weakness and I use it with my jab the rest of the round and mostly keep him off. But he keeps driving in even after I hit him and gets me with a couple of smashes to the face and blood trickles out my nose. I'm too tired to fight back and I'm afraid he's going to knock me out.

Thank God the bell rings and I turn back to my corner, feeling like I can't last another second. His superior body is getting to me now. Age is telling. I need the rest bad.

■ ■ ■

"You alright," Art asks.

I take a deep breath, blow it out, and say, "just tired," and take another deep breath. But I notice after the third one that I'm catching my wind. The tiredness is going away. I feel better now than I did after the first round.

Art wipes the blood from my nose, washes out my mouthpiece and barely gets it in my mouth when the bell rings and the little beast comes charging at me again.

He scares me all over again. But this time, I pop him with a one-two, left-right, right in the face and snap his head back. But he screams, "Yaaaaaa!" and charges me anyway, and though I stick my left in his face, he keeps coming and drives me back to the ropes, pins me on them with his arms and elbows, presses against me with his whole body. I'm sure he's going to get me now. I can't even move, but I make myself turn and take a half-step back along the ropes, like Art said, keep him off with my left shoulder and arm, then drive a right hook to his gut, make him grunt and get time to get off the ropes.

He charges me right away again though and pins me on the other side of the ring, the same way, keeps me pinned so I can't turn and step back. He's wearing me down. He's going to get me. I shift my weight to the left like I'm going to try and get off that way and when he presses against me, shift my weight back to the right, shove his right shoulder with my right glove at the same time, and slide out along the ropes to my right and get away from him.

I'm exhausted but I pop him with two jabs from the middle of the ring when he comes at me and keep him off, but drop my arms, I'm so tired, and he screams and throws a looping right hook at my open chest. I'm too weak to get my arms up in time to block it, so I just twist my body and catch the punch on my shoulder muscle without even trying to life my arms, then shoot a quick, loose straight right lead out with just my arm and catch him in the face, surprise both him and me when he blinks and stops punching like he's stunned.

I see he's hurt. It's my only chance, do or die and right now otherwise he'll get me for sure. I throw it once, twice, three more times knock him back against the ropes and chase him down them, catch him in the corner and won't let him out. This is the last round and I fight with every bit of strength I've got.

He cuts loose with both hands when I come in and bangs me good, stuns me, makes my legs buckle, but I trade straight shots with him, right and left crosses, with both hands, and mine are cleaner and in a tighter pattern inside his, getting him right on the chin, while his are only hitting my headgear.

He wobbles, his knees buckle now, and he ducks down and covers his face, so I drop my hands to my hips and fire with ripping hooks to the body, take his head shots, but beat him to the punch and get more powerful punches in, pound on his body, going to take this strong man out when he suddenly catches me right on the button with a looping right and everything blurs into slow motion, like I'm under water. I can hear the ocean roar.

I think I'm going down. My legs turn to mush, but I keep punching instead of grabbing or covering up or trying to get away. I keep catching him to the body, feel the punches thump into his ribs and dig into his guts, and the whooziness passes, and he suddenly grabs his stomach with the gut shots and falls to his face on the canvas and rocks back and forth in pain.

I can't believe it. I've stopped the little monster when I couldn't go another second. As Dago rushes into the ring to pick up his fighter, I step out of the ring and float down the steps and bounce around on the floor like I'm on a pogo stick, way up on Cloud Nine, spacey as in a dream when The Kid suddenly appears next to me and raises my glove and says, "My man! My man!"

■ ■ ■

I can't believe it either when The Kid comes out of the locker room a few minutes later dressed in a tight-fitting black bathing suit that shows his pale white legs, low-topped white tennis shoes, and a short-sleeved woolen dress gaucho.

"Where you going?" I ask.

"To fight," he says.

"With who?" I ask but he walks over to Art without answering and Art hands him a pair of gloves and starts putting another pair on Okie.

"Would you put these on me?" The Kid asks.

"You sure you want to do this?" I ask, wondering why Art would let him box when he's never even punched the bags.

"I like the way you put away that little Dago."

"Yeah, but—" I say and stop. I don't want to get in trouble for butting-in again. One fight over that in one day is enough. I'm glad Blue Beard's in back, taking a shower. But I am worried about The Kid, especially if he's doing it for me.

"Got a mouthpiece?" I ask, after I put my sweaty headgear on him.

"Borrowed this," he says and points with his glove at a cheap model on the table that could fit anybody. I wash it off and put it in his mouth, then watch him go up the steps, through the ropes, and into the ring, where he turns and looks at me with a scared face, then turns away.

I look at him up there in his swimming suit, bare-legged clear to the balls, and feel responsible. I look at this pale legs and his pale face and try to look into his eyes, but he keeps his face turned and moves slowly out into the ring when the bell sounds.

Sure enough, as soon as Okie gets in range, he starts wind-milling like a six-year old kid, sloppy but hits Okie a couple of times and keeps him off. He even backs him around the ring, until he starts puffing and slows down and drops his arms, his face white like he's really winded. Then Okie walks in swinging, catches him with three smashes to the face, makes me wince, they're so hard, and I'm even glad when he drops down and grabs Okie's legs. At least, he made Okie stop, though everybody in the gym starts laughing.

He lets go of Okie's legs and stands up, but Okie doesn't even step back, steps right in without giving him a chance, and The Kid starts swinging wild with looping punches again, hits Okie on the cheek with the first one, and makes him step back and shake his head like it stunned him.

But Okie charges in again, slugging with both hands, knocks The Kid back against the ropes and starts pounding on him so bad, The Kid drops into a ball and grabs his legs again. But Okie keeps punching on his head and when I glance over at Art to say something, The Kid lifts Okie off his feet.

Everybody laughs again.

But when The Kid puts him down, Okie leaps on him with two roundhouse punches to the head and knocks him back a couple of steps, makes him duck down into a ball again, and keeps punching on him instead of letting him up, keeping his legs back so The Kid can't grab them.

I keep waiting for Art to jump up there and make Okie step back, but Art doesn't move and nobody else says a word either, and I finally yell, "Stop!"

But when Okie keeps punching and The Kid's rocking back and forth in his ball like he's going to topple over, taking all those head shots blood streaked across his face, I jump up onto the ring apron and say "Okie! You're supposed to step back."

But Okie keeps punching on him without even looking at me, and I slip through the ropes and grab his arms and pull him off, shove him toward Art, who's finally come into the ring, grinning.

I feel really bad. The Kid's nose is bleeding and his eyes are glassy.

"Come on," I say. "Let me get that headgear and gloves off."

I take them off and put them on the table by the ring, then put my arm around him and walk him back to the locker room, saying, "It's okay man. Everything's okay."

I feel responsible. He did it to imitate me. But I have skill, if not much experience, and he doesn't have either. I stay back there with him until he gets his clothes off and gets in the shower, where the water can refresh him. I see he's soft, without muscular definition, though he's not fat.

I walk out in front, snub Art for not stopping it, and sit down on the bench by the ring, wondering what I'm doing in a pro gym where all the guys are out for blood, not for the sport like me. They're in an entirely different league. I wonder if it's worth it. I almost got my ass beat by that little beast trying to save Okie and now Art lets Okie beat up on The Kid. I make up my mind right then to take my shower and pack my gym bag and get out of there for good, go back to my alma mater gym, where it's all about proving yourself, not killing the other guy. I pull my locker key out of my pocket to leave for good when The Kid comes walking out of the locker room with his felt hat on, gabardine slacks creased, polyester shirt rippling with shiny highlights and his shoes glimmering.

I stand up, wondering what I can say to make him feel better, and hold my breath when he crosses over to Okie on a big bag.

He smiles with tight lips like he's trying to be brave, then bows from the waist and shakes the tip of Okie's bag glove with his fingers, then shakes Art's hand, smiles and bows, and starts toward me.

"Hey, look, man," I say. "You keep coming around and I'll train you. I'll teach you how to throw a good jab and a one-two that will stop Okie in his tracks. I'm really sorry I—"

But The Kid holds up his hand like an Indian signifying peace and says, "Don't worry about it, Old Man," and turns and, instead of slinking out the door, defeated, like I feared, he starts strutting out like he had just won his fight, hopping up on one toe with every other step like street kids do, swinging his arms, his head up high, tall as his hat and just as proud, with that beatific smile on his lips.

"Well, I'll be goddamned!" I say, shaking my head, then look at my key, toss it up, catch it in my hand and stick it back in my pocket.

Writings

Novels: Tatoo the Wicked Cross, Grove, 1967. *What Now My Love,* Grove, 1970; Arte Público Press, 1994. *Lay My Body on the Line,* Y'Bird Press, 1978. *State of Emergency,* Arte Público Press, 1996. **Memoir:** *Buffalo Nickel,* Arte Público Press, 1992. **Poems:** *To My Wife to Tell Her Boss What I Do All Day,* Crosscut Saw, n.d. *Color of My Living Heart* (poems), Arte Público Press, 1996. **Editor/Contributor:** *I Write What I Want,* San Francisco State University, 1974. *Word Hustlers,* Word Hustlers Press, 1976. *To Build a Fire,* Mark Ross Publishers, 1977. *Stories & Poems from Close to Home,* Ortalda & Associates, 1986. **Poems, Articles, Reviews:** In periodicals including *Writer, Transfer,* and *Hyperion.*

Luis Omar Salinas

Luis Omar Salinas is one of the most beloved and enduring poets to emerge from the Chicano literary movement. His productivity has spanned the entire contemporary movement, with his first poems appearing in newspapers, magazines, and anthologies in the late 1960s, about the time when the first Chicano literary magazines and presses were being founded. Rather than solely basing his works in the socio-political reality of the ethnic minority struggle, his works have provided a broadly romantic and highly lyric inspiration to Chicanos in search of roots. Highly influenced by Spain's Federico García Lorca and Chile's Pablo Neruda, Salinas has created a somewhat surreal, thoughtful, and very personal ongoing text in what otherwise has been an epic and com-munal literature. Salinas has said that his poetic ideal is to "somehow come to terms with the tragic and through the tragic gain a vision which transcends this world in some way."

Born in Robstown, Texas, close to the Mexican border, on June 27, 1937, Salinas spent some of his early years in Mexico and by age nine had moved to live with an aunt and uncle in California. He attended public schools and began college at Fresno State University, where he edited the literary magazine, *Backwash,* but never received his diploma. At Fresno State in 1966, Salinas took a creative writing course, but his writing education ended when he moved with his family to Sanger, California. During the 1960s, Salinas was hospitalized on various occasions for nervous breakdowns, and these breakdowns have recurred periodically since. His first breakdowns were the result of the combined pressures of his involvement in the Chicano Civil Rights Movement and his teaching Chicano Studies.

In 1970 he published his first book of poetry, *Crazy Gypsy,* a highly artistic work that became an anthem for Chicano activists. Many of the poems were included in the first anthologies of Chicano literature and have become canonized in U.S. Hispanic literature: "Crazy Gypsy," "Aztec Angel," "Nights and Days," "Mexico, Age Four," and others. In *Crazy Gypsy* Salinas introduces themes that are evident in all of his works: alienation and loneliness, death, and the defamiliarization of the world around us. Salinas offers a wealth of images in which the stark beauty of language, fed from the grand traditions of both Hispanic and Anglo-American lyric poetry, convinces the reader of the possibilities offered by a synthesis gained from a complete understanding of two or more cultures.

In *Darkness under the Trees: Walking behind the Spanish* (1982), and in the works that follow, Salinas heightens the note of sorrow and melancholy as he attempts to rationalize his unjust fate. The themes of love, death, and madness dominate. The second part of the book pays homage to the Spanish Civil War poets who have served as his models, including García Lorca.

Salinas is the most lyric, most imaginative, deepest, and most humane Chicano/Latino poet. He is, nevertheless, generally overlooked by the academy, often passed by not only be readers but by other Hispanic writers—perhaps because his illnesses have not permitted him to tour and engage in exchanges with editors and other writers, or perhaps because he is shy and has not done anything to promote himself in a field that today quite often demands stellar oral performances and promotional campaigns.

> *"For Salinas the common or 'normal' dulls our senses and deadens our response to the tyranny of the mechanical habits of daily living. By creating 'the fullness of the unreal,' he defamiliarizes the world for us and . . . forces us to confront the 'true' nature of the society that surrounds us."*
>
> **from Chicano Literature**

Personal Stats

Chicano poet, editor, and interpreter.   **Born:** June 27, 1937, in Robstown, Texas. **Education:** A.A., Bakersfield Junior College, 1958; attended Fresno State University, 1967–72.   **Career:** He has supported himself through a variety of blue-color jobs. **Awards/Honors:** California English Teachers citation, 1973; Stanley Kunitz Poetry Prize (for *Afternoon of the Unreal*), 1980; Earl Lyon Award, 1980; General Electric Foundation Award, 1983.   **Address:** 2009 Ninth Street, Sanger, CA 93652

For Armenia

from *The Sadness of Days: Selected and New Poems*, Arte Público Press, 1987, p. 33

I feel enchantment every time
I enter an Armenian household.
Their daughters, you know . . .
I am the kibitzer of chatter
in the kitchen, companion
to the baying of firepans
and doors.
Here I am. Poet and vagabond
eating tacos in Armenia,
in the house of Shish-Kabob
and Kings. I tell them
I am the descendant of
Cuauhtemoc and the evening
gathers like knives in the moonlight.
I drink coffee, eat baklava
and the night air comes in
singing to the tune of dusted
stars, hovering above
like mad gypsies.
I want to tell them
I'm off on a gretchen
mission of immortality
as I abandon rainbows,
universities and dictionaries.
But I falter like a fatal Aztec
ghost, and condemn dreams.
I leave, rousted off to the
mountain of languages
stuffed with life and secrets.
And what awaits me is the future—
blue ringing of flesh—
as I waltz,
a man like any other,
watching everything emerge
like a crazy wake.

Ode to the Mexican Experience

from *The Sadness of Days: Selected and New Poems,* Arte Público Press, 1987, pp. 35—36

The nervous poet sings again
in his childhood voice, happy,
a lifetime of Mexican girls
in his belly, voice
of the midnoon bells
and excited mariachis
in those avenues persuaded out
of despair.

He talks of his Aztec mind,
the little triumphs and schizoid trips,
the many failures
and his defeated chums
dogs and shadows,
the popularity of swans in his neighborhood
and the toothaches of rabbits
in the maize fields.

I know you in bars
in merchant shops,
in the roving gladiators,
in the boats of Mazatlan that never anchor,
in the smile of her eyes,
in the tattered clothes of school children,
in the never-ending human burials;
those lives lost in the stars
and those lost in the stars
and those lost in the wreckage
of fingernails,
the absurd sophistry of loneliness
in markets, in hardware stores,
in brothels.

The happy poet talks in his sleep,
the eyes of his loved one
pressing against him—

her lips have the softness
of olives crushed by rain.

I think of the quiet nights
in Monterrey
and of my sister who woke me up
in the mornings.

The soft aggressive spiders
came out to play in the sunlight,
and suffering violins in pawn shops,
hell and heaven and murdered angels
and all the incense of the living
in poisoned rivers
wandering aimlessly amid dead fish,
dead dreams, dead songs.
I was an altar boy,
a shoeshine boy,
an interventionist in family affairs,
a ruthless connoisseur of vegetables,
a football player.
To all the living things I sing
the most terrible and magnificent
ode to my ancestry.

My Father Is a Simple Man

from *The Sadness of Days: Selected and New Poems,* Arte Público Press, 1987, p. 141

I walk to town with my father
to buy a newspaper. He walks slower
than I do so I must slow up.
The street is filled with children.
We argue about the price
of pomegranates, I convince
him it is the fruit of scholars.
He has taken me on this journey
and it's been lifelong.
He's sure I'll be healthy
so long as I eat more oranges,

and tells me the orange
has seeds and so is perpetual;
and we too will come back
like the orange trees.
I ask him what he thinks
about death and he says
he will gladly face it when
it comes but won't jump
out in front of a car.
I'd gladly give my life
for this man with a sixth
grade education, whose kindness
and patience are true . . .
The truth of it is, he's the scholar,
and when the bitter-hard reality
comes at me like a punishing
evil stranger, I can always
remember that here was a man
who was a worker and provider,
who learned the simple facts
in life and lived by them,
who held no pretense.
And when he leaves without
benefit of fanfare or applause
I shall have learned what little
there is about greatness.

Writings

Poetry Books: *Crazy Gypsy: Poems,* Origines Publications, 1970. *Entrance: Four Chicano Poets: Leonard Adame, Luis Omar Salinas, Gary Soto, Ernesto Trejo* (anthology), Greenfield Review Press, 1975. *I Go Dreaming Serenades,* Mango, 1979. *Afternoon of the Unreal,* Abramás Publications, 1980. *Prelude to Darkness,* Mango, 1981. *Darkness under the Trees: Walking behind the Spanish,* University of California Chicano Studies Library, University of California, 1982. *The Sadness of Days: Selected and New Poems,* Arte Público Press, 1987. **Poems:** In *The Americas Review, El grito, Voices of Aztlán: Chicano Literature Today, Festival Flor y Canto, We Are Chicanos, Mexican American Authors,* and numerous other anthologies, magazines and textbooks. **Other:** *From the Barrio: A Chicano Anthology,* edited with Lillian Faderman, Canfield Press, 1973.

Ricardo Sánchez

As one of the most prolific Chicano poets, Ricardo Sánchez was one of the first creators of a bilingual literary style and one of the first to be identified as part of the Chicano Movement. He was a tireless and popular oral performer and social activist whose creative power expressed itself in his poetry through the innovative use of Spanish and English, frequently through the creation of interlingual neologisms and abrupt linguistic contrasts. His verse is as overwhelming in sheer power as was his strong and aggressive personality, which was forged in hard prison labor.

Ricardo Sánchez was the last of thirteen children born to Pedro Lucero and Adelina Gallegos Sánchez in the notorious Barrio del Diablo (Devil's Neighborhood) in El Paso, Texas. He received his early education there but later dropped out of high school. He enlisted in the Army but in the early 1960s was incarcerated in California state prisons including Soledad Prison and he spent 1965–69 at the Ramsey Prison Farm Number One in Texas. It was at these institutions that he began his literary career.

Sánchez's poetry chronicles much of his early life experiences of oppressive poverty, overwhelming racism, the suffering he endured while imprisoned, his self-education, and his subsequent rise to a level of political and social consciousness. His works, though very lyrical, are perhaps the most autobiographical of all the Hispanic poets. Sánchez always envisioned himself participating in, and in fact leading, a socio-political consciousness-raising movement. Through his many trav-

els and itinerant lifestyle (he was always in search of a permanent job in academia), he became a troubadour for the developing Chicano literary movement. His poetry announced an authentic bilingual writing style rooted in oral tradition and community issues.

Once his writing career was established and Sánchez began publishing his works with both mainstream and alternative literary presses, he assumed various visiting appointments as a professor or writer-in-residence at universities. He was a founder of the short-lived Mictla Publications in El Paso, edited special issues of literary magazines such as *De Colores* (Of Colors) and *Wood/Ibis,* was a columnist for the *San Antonio Express,* as well as a bookseller, migrant worker counselor, and an active performer of his poetry in the United States and abroad. In 1991, Sánchez finally secured a permanent teaching position, in the Chicano Studies Program at Washington State University in Bellingham. While there, it was found that he had cancer, which resulted in his death in 1995.

Sánchez's poetry is characterized by an unbridled linguistic inventiveness that not only calls upon both the English and Spanish lexicons, but also is a source of neologisms and surprising combinations of sounds and symbols from both languages. His work can be virile and violent at one moment and delicate and sentimental at the next, as he follows the formulas and dictates of a poetry written for oral performance. His is often the exaggerated gesture and emotion of the *declamador,* or poetic orator, whose works are performed to inspire a protest rally, inaugurate a mural, celebrate a patriotic holiday, or eulogize the dead. Most of all, Sánchez is the autobiographical poet who casts himself as a Chicano Everyman, participating in the epic history of his people through his poetry. His bilingual facility and immense vocabulary and inventiveness are legendary in Chicano literature. Besides publishing hundreds of poems in magazines and anthologies, Sánchez has authored several collections including *Canto y grito mi liberación (y lloro mis desmadrazgos)* (I Sing and Shout for My Liberation [and Cry for My Insults]), *Hechizospells: Poetry/Stories/Vignettes/Articles/Notes on the Human Condition of Chicanos & Pícaros, Words & Hopes within Soulmind, Milhuas Blues and Gritos Norteños* (Milwaukee Blues and Northern Cries), *Amsterdam Cantos y Poemas Pistos* (Amsterdam Songs and Drinking Poems), and *Selected Poems.*

Personal Stats

Chicano poet, teacher. ***Born:*** March 29, 1941, in El Paso, Texas. ***Died:*** In 1995, in Bellingham, Washington. ***Education:*** Extension courses while in prison, Alvin Junior College, 1965–69; Ph.D., Union Graduate School, Ph.D., 1975. ***Career:*** Incarcerated in California and Texas state prisons in the early 1960s and 1965–69; correspondent, *Richmond Afro-American newspaper,* Richmond, Virginia, 1969; research assistant and instructor, University of Massachusetts, School of Education, Amherst, 1970; director, Itinerant Migrant Health Council, Denver, Colorado, 1970–71; part-time lecturer-consultant, Chicano Affairs Program, University of Texas at El Paso, 1971–72; part-time lecturer-consultant, New Mexico State University at Las Cruces, 1972–73; professor of poetry, literature, and critical theory, El Paso Community College, 1975; National Endowment for the Arts poet in resident, 1975–76; visiting professor, University of Wisconsin–Milwaukee, 1977; assistant professor of Chicano Studies, University of Utah, 1977–80; book store owner and manager (Paperbacks y mas), San Antonio, 1983–85; free-lance writer, 1985–90; assistant professor of Chicano Studies, Washington State University–Bellingham, 1990–95 ***Memberships:*** International PEN, Poets and Writers, Inc. (New York City). ***Awards/Honors:*** Frederick Douglass Fellowship in journalism, 1969; Ford Foundation fellow, Union Graduate School, 1973–75; outstanding professor award from the Chicano Student Association, University of Utah, 1979.

Soledad Was a Girl's Name

from *Selected Poems,* Arte Público Press, 1985, pp. 27—29

Soledad, June 10, 1963

Soledad was a girl's name,
years ago
at jefferson high,
and she was soft and brown
and beautiful.
i used to watch her,
and think her name
was ironic
and poetic,
for she was Soledad Guerra,
                    solitude and war,
and she used to always smile
con ternura morena
como su piel,
and now in this soledad
that i am leaving soon,
this callous nation
of bars and cement and barbarity,
it seems strange
that a name can call out to me
and mesmerize me,
yet repel me,
one a girl, now a woman,
and the other
a jagged prison world
            where hate
            is a common expletive,
            seems everyone hates,
            seems everyone is a convict,
            even the guards and counselors
                 do time here
                 everyday trudging into
                 this abysmal human warehouse.

Ricardo Sánchez

am leaving
and it hurts,
funny that it hurts;
i see the faces of my friends,
we joke about my getting out,

and they ask pleading things,
"DO IT ONE TIME FOR ME, ESE!"

just one time, carnal,
nomás una vez.
hell, bato, i'll go all over
and do it a million times
recalling all the sadness
that hides
within this place;
i'll do it a jillion times
for me, for you, for all of us,
and maybe the next soledad i see
is a morenita from el chuco
i had been too timid
to ask out . . . it's strange
that i recall her,
but then la pinta
makes you think/regret.
but huáchenle, batos,
when i'm doing it for us
i'll probably burst out laughing,
not at you or me or even at some ruca,
but at all the pendejadas,
at all the crazy lies
that say that we are savage;
i'll laugh at mean-ass convicts
who terrify the world
yet love to eat ice cream,
i'll laugh at convicts scurrying
from cell block to the canteen
with books of scripted money
to purchase cokes and cookies
and candy bars as well;
i'll laugh at contradictions
and yet within i'll hurt
remembering xmas packages
and letters full of pain,

recalling those sad moments
when night became the coverlet
and darkness filtered songs,
when all alone i'd die
realizing just how sordid
a prison life can be . . .

yes, i'll laugh, carnales,
just like we all want to laugh,
not to mock us nor to spite you,
just to say i understand,

pero eso si, compiras,
no quiero regresar.

Letter to My Ex-Texas Sanity

from *Selected Poems,* Arte Público Press, 1985, pp. 68—70

new pancreas abound,
 new promises of paradise,
new to me and oddly old
            to others, Utah
sours dream and it should
begin with a P for its
perversity and putismo . . .
been here over a week, damn,
but it seems forever . . .
Saltyville of a Lakeburg
            September 30, 1977

left you, Tejas,
over a week ago,
had to,
for work
is here and not there,
home
resides wherein one lives,
and i live (almost do)
in salt lake city.
it hurls its salty dust
at your soul's eyes,

burns its vapid senselessness
into the furrows
of your thoughts,
it urges you to give up
life, liberty and the
real pursuit of selfdom,
clothes, everything,
with missionary zeal,
demands
your capitulation,
bicycles you to death,
and then intones
that heaven
merely is for those
who have renounced
all semblance of having been
salient/lively creatures
who lived to love
while loving to live.
ay, utah brutalizes
hope
with its spineless
and amorphous
gelatinous mentality.
perverse and anti-human,
your temple
manufactures
complacent/placid smiles
to keep all niggers out,
your westside of salt lake,
awash with fetid meskin smells,
it creaks and groans
with fear
that we might multiply,
your fear of loathsome Laman
defines the way you see us,
for Lamanites you think us,
a mass of swarthy people
who revel in their evil.
ay, brutah, putah, utah,
whose land is so majestic,

with deserts y montañas
and nature's pungency,
you fear
those who are darker,
and claim to be so saintly,
enslaver of the frail
and dementer of the fragile,
your sacrosantimonious
attempts at being holy
are ludicrous at best,
at worst imperialistic
and ever missionizing.
you flail, hither-thither,
the differences you fear,
and though you feel superior
and smug in your behest,
you strive like hungered zealots
to make us look your best,
oh, poor and foolish bigots,
you have no need to fear us,
for you have nothing worthy
to send us on in quest.
you see,
this land belongs
to all who wish to love it
and within it reside.
we'll be ourselves, ay, utah,
and celebrate our difference,
we'll look at you and smile
and continue on our way
to live within your valleys
while we project our name . . .

Writings

Poetry Books: *Canto y grito mi liberación/The Liberation of a Chicano Mind,* Mictla, 1971; Doubleday-Anchor, 1973; Cinco Puntos Press, 1996. *Obras,* Quetzal-Vihio Press, 1971. *Hechizospells,* Chicano Studies Center, University of California, Los Angeles, 1976. *Milhuas blues y gritos norteños* (Milwaukee Blues and Northern Cries), Spanish-Speaking Outreach Institute, University of Wisconsin-Milwaukee, 1980. *Brown Bear Honey Madness: Alaskan Cruising Poems,* Slough Press, 1982. *Amsterdam cantos y poemas pistos* (Amsterdam Songs and Drinking Poems), Place of the Herons Press, 1983. *Selected Poems,* Arte Público Press, 1985. **Film Script:** *Entelequía,* Stazar (Denver), 1979. **Poems:** In *The Americas Review/Revista Chicano-Riqueña, Points of Departure, We Are Chicanos, Festival de Flor y Canto, Canto al Pueblo: An Anthology of Experiences,* and numerous other magazines, anthologies, and textbooks.

Virgil Suárez

Crossing borders has been a way of life for Virgil Suárez: he spent his early years in Havana, Cuba; experienced culture shock from his new-found freedom when his family immigrated to Madrid, Spain, in 1970; and, after his family came to the United States in 1974, he knew the trials of traveling the bicultural highway in pursuit of the American Dream.

The only son of a pattern-cutter and a piecemeal seamstress working the sweatshops, Suárez was born in Cuba in 1962 and raised in the United States since 1974. Suárez is the holder of an MFA in Creative Writing (1987) from Louisiana State University, where he studied with Vance Bourjaily. He is currently an assistant professor of creative writing at Florida State University in Tallahassee. Although educated in the United States from age eight, Suárez has been preoccupied with the themes of immigration and acclimatization to life and culture in the United States. He arrived in this country as a refugee from communist Cuba; before settling here with his parents, however, they spent four years in Spain in a refugee community.

Suárez is the author of five successful novels and numerous stories, essays, and poems, which have been published in literary magazines. He is also an active book reviewer for newspapers around the country, as well as an editor of anthologies of Latino literature. His first novel, *Latin Jazz* (1989), chronicles the experiences of a Cuban immigrant family in Los Angeles by adopting the narrative perspectives of each of the family members. New York's *Newsday* hailed the novel as "a striking debut. A well crafted and sensitive novel. An engrossing, honest book by a writer who cares deeply about preserving ties within the family unit and, by extension, within the Hispanic community and America. Suárez is marvelous."

His second novel, *The Cutter* (1991), deals with the desperate attempts of a young sugar-cane cutter to leave Cuba and join his family in the United States. *Publishers Weekly* said that "Suárez's powerful novel about one individual's response to the abuses and arbitrariness of totalitarianism shows us how ordinary people can be driven to take extraordinary risks."

Suárez's collection of short fiction, *Welcome to the Oasis* (1992) portrays a new generation of young Hispanics who struggle to integrate themselves into American culture while preserving pieces of their heritage. *Kirkus Reviews* baptized Suárez as a leading spokesperson for his generation of Cuban-Americans:

> *Welcome to the Oasis* is "a tightly controlled but affecting exploration of funda-
> mental tensions in a community for whom Suárez is becoming an eloquent and promis-
> ing voice.

Havana Thursdays (1995) and *Going Under* (1996) are mature novels in which Suárez casts a critical eye at middle-class Cuban American life in Miami. *Havana Thursdays* brings together a family of exceptional women who are attending a funeral and are in the process of adjusting to their loss. The funeral becomes an occasion for a painful assessment of their lives. Virgil Suárez had this to say about the women: "I wanted to create a garland—a necklace of voices beautiful and lasting. After I finished the book, I spent almost a year being haunted by the voices of these great women." *Newsday* stated, "You can feel the author rooting for his women characters as they attempt to break the double-binds they are caught in and struggle to balance the need for privacy and independence—American values—with Cuban traditions of family solidarity."

Going Under is the chronicle of a Cuban American yuppy who is sold on the American Dream: He is nervous and energetic and blind to the consequences of his feverish chase up the ladder of success. He loses sight of and control over things of value—family, friends, identity.

The New York Times sized up Suárez's style and literary accomplishments: "Mr. Suárez writes in a cold, unornamental, Hemingwayesque style, always straight forward and cinematic." *The Village Voice* echoed praise: "Like Hijuelos, Suárez has taken pains with his craft, orchestrating points of view and narrative time. His forte is directness of description and action."

"Mr. Suárez writes in a cold, unornamental, Hemingwayesque style."

The New York Times

Personal Stats

Cuban American writer, professor. **Born:** January 29, 1962, in Havana, Cuba. **Education:** B.A. in Creative Writing, California State University at Long Beach, 1984; MFA in Creative Writing, Louisiana state University, 1987. **Career:** adjunct instructor, Miami Dade Community College, 1988–89; adjunct instructor, Florida International University and the University of Miami, 1989–91; instructor, Louisiana State University, 1991–92; assistant professor, Creative Writing, Florida State University, Tallahassee, 1992–present. **Memberships:** PEN International, Poets & Writers, Associated Writers' Program. **Address:** English Department, Florida State University, Tallahassee, FL 32306

Jicotea/Turtle

unpublished, n.d., Arte Público Press

They arrived in yute sacks. Their carapaces forming lumps as they pushed against the weaved string of the brown sacks. Once my father had put down the sack on the cemented patio of the house in Havana, I walked around the lumpy pile, intrigued. I was still at the age of endless questions. My father said he'd gotten lucky this time at La Ciénega de Zapata, a pocket of the province of Las Villas. My father was from this swampy area of the island of Cuba. "What is it?" I asked. "*Jicoteas,*" he said and smiled, then reached into his shirt pocket for a cigarette. This was the time when my father still smoked, despite his bouts with asthma. *Jico* . . . I began but my tongue stumbled over the word . . . *teas?*" *Tortuguitas,*" he said. Let me show you one." He opened the mouth of the sack and reached into it the way a magician might into his hat to pull out a fluttering white dove. It appeared: a turtle. Startled, waving its claws? Feet? Legs? in the air as if making a futile attempt at swimming or escaping. "See?" My father asked. "Surely you've been shown pictures at school." (At school we'd only been shown pictures of Camilo Cienfuegos, Che Guevara, Jose Martí, Karl Marx, Máximo Gómez, Vladimir Lenin, etc . . . .) "Give me a hand," he said. At first I was reluctant, but then my father turned the sack upside down and let about thirty of these turtles free. "But they'll get away," I told him. And again, he smiled, then blew smoke out of his nostrils. "No, no, no," he said. "See how they move? They are slow. They can't get away fast enough." Get away from what, I thought. Indeed, these slowpoke creatures tried to make a path on the cemented patio and, I swear, made little scratch sounds with their nails against the surface. My father crushed the cigarette under his shoe, reached to the sheath tied to the side of his right thigh and pulled out his sharp machete. "This is what I want you to do, son," he said and showed me. He grabbed one of the turtles, stepped on it so that it could not move, then with his free hand he pulled and extended the neck of the turtle. "Like this, see?" He stretched. I looked, not catching on yet. Then, to my surprise, he swung the machete downward fast. There was a loud crushing sound.

There was a spark as the machete sliced through the turtle's neck and hit the hard concrete underneath. The stub of the creature's neck lay on the floor like a piece of rotted plantain. It was still twitching as I looked up at my father who was saying, "It's that simple: you grab and pull and I chop."

As reluctant as I was, I did as I was told. I grabbed every one of those thirty turtles' necks, pulled without looking into their eyes, and closed mine each of the thirty times the machete came down. Turtle, after turtle, after turtle. All thirty. "After this you help me clean up, no?" my father was saying. "We need to remove the shells so that your mother can clean the meat and cook it." Yes, we were going to eat these turtles, these *jicoteas* (the sound of the word now comes naturally). There was nothing I could say on behalf of the creatures I had helped my father slaughter. And so the idea of death had been inflicted upon me quickly, almost painlessly, with the sacrifice of thirty *jicoteas.*

Bitterness

from *Little Havana Blues,* Arte Público Press, 1997

My father brings home the blood of horses on his hands, his rough, calloused, thick-fingered hands. He comes home from the slaughter house where the government pays him to kill old useless horses that arrive from all over the island. The blood becomes encrusted and etched on the prints and wrinkles of his fingers, under his nails, dark with the dirt too, the filth and grime, the moons of his fingers pinked by the residue, his knuckles skinned from the endless work. Sticky and sweet-scented is the blood of these horses, horses to feed the lions in the new zoo which is moving from Havana to Lenin's Park, near where we live. Dark blood, this blood of the horses my father slaughters daily to feed zoo lions. I ask how many horses it takes to feed a single lion. This makes my father laugh. I watch as he washes and rinses the dried-up blood from his forearms and hands, those hands that kill the horses, the hands that sever through skin and flesh and crush through bone. My father, the dissident, the *gusano,* the Yankee-lover, walks to and from work on tired feet, on an aching body. He no longer talks to anybody, and less to us, his family. My mother and my grandmother, his mother. But they leave him alone, to his moods, for they know what he is being put through. A test of will. Determination. Salvation and survival. My father, under the tent on the grounds of the new zoo, doesn't say much. He has learned how to speak with his hands. Sharp are the cuts he makes on the flesh. The horses are shot in the open fields, a bullet through the head, and are then carted to where my father, along with other men, do the butchering. He is thirty (the age I am now) and tired, and when he comes home his hands are numb from all the chopping and cutting. This takes place in 1969.

Years later when we are allowed to leave Cuba and travel to Madrid, to the cold winter of Spain, we find ourselves living in a hospice. The three of us, my father, my mother and me, in a small room. (My grandmother died and was buried in Havana.) Next door is a man named Izquierdo, who keeps us awake with his phlegmy coughs. From the other side of the walls, his coughing sounds like thunder. We try to sleep; I try harder but the coughing seeps through and my father curses under his breath. I listen to the heat as it tic-tacs coming through the furnace. My father tries to make love to my mother. I try not to listen. The mattress springs sound like bones crushing. My mother refuses without saying a word. This is the final time she does so tonight. There is what seems like an interminable silence, then my father breaks it by saying to my mother, "If you don't, I'll look for a Spanish woman who will." Silence again, then I think I hear my mother crying. "Someone," my father says, "will want to, to . . . ." And I lay there on my edge of the mattress, sweat coming on from the heat. My eyes are closed and I listen hard, and then the sound of everything stops. This, I think, is the way death must sound. Then my father begins all over again. The room fills with the small sounds . . . the cleaver falls and cuts through the skin, tears through the flesh, crushes the bone, and then there is the blood. All that blood. It emerges and collects on the slaughter tables, the blood of countless horses.

Sleep upon me, I see my father stand by the sink in the patio of the house in Havana. He scrubs and rinses his hands. The blood dissolves slowly in the water. Once again I build up the courage to go ahead and ask him how much horse meat it takes to appease the hunger of a single lion.

Writings

Novels: Latin Jazz, William Morrow, 1989. *The Cutter,* Ballantine Books, 1991. *Welcome to the Oasis,* Arte Público Press, 1992. *Havana Thursdays,* Arte Público Press, 1995. *Going Under,* Arte Público Press, 1996.   **Anthologies:** *Iguana Dreams: New Latino Fiction,* co-edited with Delia Poey, HarperCollins, 1994. *Paper Dance: 55 Latino Poets,* co-edited with Victor Hernández Cruz and Leroy V. Quintana, Persea Books, 1995. *Little Havana Blues,* co-edited with Delia Poey, Arte Público Press, 1996.   **Short Fiction:** In *Colorado Review, Michigan Quarterly, Borderlands,* and *The Americas Review.*   **Book Reviews:** For *Philadelphia Inquirer, Miami Herald, Los Angeles Times, Spontaneous,* and *Vista.*

Piri Thomas

Piri Thomas's on-going, passionately poetic autobiography, has been the first to address the question of race and racial prejudice among Latinos. His Down These Mean Streets *(1967) was also the first tale of the agonizing search for identity among the conflicting cultural, racial, ethnic, and linguistic alternatives presented to Latinos as well as to Afro-Hispanic peoples in the United States.* Down These Mean Streets *was such a milestone that the Nuyorican and Latino literature that followed it either continued its themes or totally rejected its poetic melange of street language and psychodrama as a naive and unsophisticated cry arising out of the culture of poverty.*

Piri Thomas was born John Peter Thomas on September 30, 1928, in New York City's Harlem Hospital, to a white Puerto Rican mother and an Afro-Cuban father of the working class. In his upbringing he experienced racism in the most intimate of settings—his home. His siblings were lighter-skinned than was he with his obviously dark African inheritance—which, of course, presented one of the principal causes for anguish in his life and in his books. When his family attempted to escape the ills of the city by moving to Babylon, Long Island, again he faced rejection at school and in the neighborhood because of his skin color. In part, this is the subject of *Savior, Savior Hold My Hand* (1972), which also deals with the hypocrisy he faced while working with a Christian church after he was released from prison.

Thomas grew up on the streets of Spanish Harlem, where he became involved in gang activity and criminality. In 1950, he participated in an armed robbery at a nightclub, which left him and a policeman wounded; he was sentenced to and served seven years in jail, the subject of *Seven Long Times* (1974). While in prison, Thomas became part of the black pride movement, converted to Islam, earned a G.E.D., and began writing. As an ex-convict in 1962, he was befriended by an editor from Knopf and was supported by a grant for five years from the Louis M. Rabinowitz Foundation. These circumstances enabled him to produce the modern classic, *Down These Mean Streets,* which forever changed his life and the direction of Latino and ethnic literatures in the United States. *The New York Times* raved that *Down These Mean Streets* is a linguistic milestone:

> It claims our attention and emotional response because of the honesty and pain of a life led in outlaw, fringe status, where the dream is always to escape. . . . It is something of a linguistic event. Gutter language, Spanish imagery and personal poetics . . . mingle into a kind of individual statement that has very much its own sound.

And of *Seven Long Times* the *Times* stated, "Thomas has written an intensely human document of one man's will for survival . . . . Thomas follows in a long tradition of prison writers: Jean Genet, Malcolm X, Eldridge Cleaver, and George Jackson."

Despite his agonized and violent beginning, Thomas has achieved remarkable success. The same force of will that made Thomas a gang leader, also made him a writer: he willed himself into that existence, and his life became the work of art that he envisioned through literature. The thrice married and father of five said, "I'm happy in the sense of assuredness that my life is not a failure, that I am not considered an ex-junkie or an ex-con . . . . I learned how to deal with my harsh reality objectively and redirect my energy for creative flow. It came very natural. I promised God that if he didn't let me die in prison, I would use the Flow."

Personal Stats

Afro-Cuban/Puerto Rican writer. **Born:** on September 30, 1928, in New York City. **Education:** G.E.D. in prison and thereafter obtained an informal education. **Career:** staff associate, Center for Urban Education, New York City, 1967–? **Memberships:** Authors Guild, Community Film Workshop Council, American Film Institute. **Awards/Honors:** Louis M. Rabinowitz Foundation Grant, 1962; Lever Brothers Community Service Award, 1967. **Address:** c/o Suzanne Dod Thomas, 964 Shattuck Ave., Berkeley, CA 94707

Those With Less Shared More

from *Stories from El Barrio*, Arte Público Press, (reprint) 1997

Las Navidades de mi niñez eran más que Kris Kringle, alias Santa Claus, alias Mami y Papi, o quién sea. Para mi las Navidades eran la alegria de ester con la familia—pobres de bolsillo, pero ricos de corazón.

Las calles del barrio se llenaban de alegria. Villancicos salian de las vitrolas y radios, de las esquinas y las iglesias y las casas—cantados en muchas lenguas, pues nuestro barrio no era sólo puertorriqueño. En Nochebuena nos olvidábamos de que éramos pobres. La mesa rebosaba con la cena tradicional; todo sabia tan delicioso que nadie pensaba en el costo.

Sí, recuerdo las Navidades y los Días de Reyes de antaño, pero más que nada recuerdo las sonrisas de cariño que nos regalábamos unos a otros.

Christmas to me, from childhood on, has been a kaleidoscope of things. Christmas was, as I remember it, Momma's version of Seventh Day Adventist Christ and having to deal with hopped-up prices. Poppa was always the kind of pops that strained his brains digging up ways on the WPA to make the extra pesos needed at Christmas times.

It wasn't that moms and pops didn't know how to save. But in order to save, there had to be some moneys left after pop's emaciated paychecks got through taking care of rent, food, clothing, etc. Mostly there were but few pennies, quarters, dimes, nickels left. The big glass jar set in its closet shrine would celebrate a rare holiday when a crumpled, count-worn dollar bill sulkily floated down through its slot and came to rest on coppers and silvers. Unfortunately, the bottle would never fill and most times would become very empty, because of emergencies like no *leche*, no *pan,* no carfare, no breakfast, no lunch, no dinner. Middle-class kids and on up the class ladder weren't the only ones with appetites. Poor *barrio* children were often accused of having hollow legs and two stomachs, like camels.

Anyway, economics was the main reason many of us got to Christmas time broke, and that, pardon the rhyme, was no joke. To force Christmas cheer and joy for the kids was to accept that Christmas was going to meet you broke and leave you even broker.

But "what the hell" was the jolly wartime cry in 1942. Enjoy while you can. You're a long time dead. So deck the halls with boughs of holly, falalalala and *p'alante* for the credit line—that is, if you can apply. Somehow, someway, the money was found. It seemed that those who had more shared less, and those who had less shared more.

Moms and pops were always that way and, diggit, they weren't alone. *Muchos* were of the same *corazón.* And to many of us of all colors and all creeds, Christmas was more than shopping sprees to *La Marqueta* or Kresge's Five and Dime or, for the elite among us, to Macy's,

Bloomingdale's or even Klein's, which was the store for the poor who had a millionaire's taste for champagne with a Pepsi Cola pocket.

As a Puerto Rican, I saw how other ethnic groups in all class levels celebrated Christmas. As a child, I was always pleased that they had only one Christmas on December 25th and that we Puerto Ricans had another on January 6th, *El Dia de los Tres Reyes*. Both days were for sharing and exchanging gifts. We celebrated not only the birth of Christ but also the three kings who followed the bright star to Bethlehem and found Jesus born in a stable, worshipped him and offered him fine gifts. In my home, Christmas presents were given out on Christmas morning, the idea being, of course, that Santa Claus had done his thing down a nonexistent chimney and out a nonexistent fireplace. So as not to hurt our parents' feelings, we went along with labored letters in English to a cold North Pole, asking an overweight Santa Claus for a list of never-to-come toys, while suspecting him of overindulging in 150 proof Ron Rico because his nose was too tomato red.

But anyway, Christmas to me was more than Kris Kringle, alias Santa Claus, alias my moms and pops, or whoever gave. To me Christmas was the joy of being with my family, poor in pocket and rich in a whole lot of love and understanding. It is true that the cruelties of forced poverty got in the way, but that was purely physical. Spiritually, it wouldn't relate.

The *barrio's* streets would be alive with Christmas carols sung from juke boxes and radios and street corners and churches, especially in the homes, all in *muchas lenguas*, of course. For our *barrio* was not just made up of Puerto Ricans. It was mixed with almost all the nationalities represented on the branches of ghetto Christmas trees.

In my home in those never-to-be-forgotten days, the preparation of Christmas food was underway, giving promises of delight. Food that was seen not too many times a year was in the making, and the dishes had exotic names that often brought blank stares from those unable to understand that the food tasted even better as *lechón* asado, prepared with spices and roasted slowly until crunchy beyond compare. This melted in your mouth to your heart's content, and you forgot its cost. *Arroz con gandules, pasteles* (wrapped in banana leaves or boiling paper, which gently held the blending plátanos, potato, yuca and spiced meats), *arroz con dulce* (teasing the tongue with coconut, cinnamon and raisins), flan, and on and on. And of course, Christmas cheer from *ron* and milk, eggs and spice which is called *"coquito,"* a creamy delight that goes down smoothly, but, if you're not careful, can blow your mind.

Christmas to me as a child was this and more. For it brought many large families together. Guitars would appear, and songs of Puerto Rico would be sung, with most people leaving the room if anyone was uncouth enough to play *I'm Dreaming of a White Christmas*. Considering the constant lack of heat in apartments in winter time, you could hardly expect the singing of "White Christmas" to be a big hit.

Religion played big on Christmas—all religions. Momma was Seventh Day Adventist; aunts and uncles were Pentecostal; poppa was a death-bed Catholic who would only see a priest long after he was dead. The church we went to on 116th Street and Madison Avenue was on the second floor, above a bank. In churches all over, plays were being enacted, *La Santa Cena, La Crucificción, La Natividad. Caramba!!* I even played Tiny Tim in *A Christmas Carol,* by Charles Dickens. Tiny Tim, who was crippled, walked fine compared to me. For I hammed it so much, it took what seemed hours for me to dramatically drag my "crippled" body six inches across the stage into the arms of my stage father as played by Reverend Samuels.

The dancing was beautiful in our Christmas lives as well as on Three Kings' Day. As a matter of fact, songs and dances were every day, for it is a matter of our culture—*a nuestra manera.* Slow romantic boleros, fast mambos, smooth island *danzas* full of love and grace. And Three Kings' Day brought *asalto* time. People came singing at your door with music and instruments galore. They would be invited in, served food and drink. Then the whole family would join them, and all went singing and dancing on to the next house—and on and on far into the night and early morning light.

The hardships of reality were set aside in the warmth of the Christmas illusions. But who cared? Reality returned soon enough. We knew when Christmas was over. It was over as soon as they came to collect the rent, the light bill, the gas bill, the furniture bill, the Household Finance, the *bodega* bills and all the rest of the little hells . . .   But what the heck! Later!

I remember Christmas and *Día de los Reyes* in the *barrios* of long ago, and, of all, I remember best the smiles of love we gave to each other. To me they were better than all the rest. They weren't wasted smiles.

Writings

Autobiographies: *Down These Mean Streets,* Knopf, 1967; Vintage, 1991. *Savior, Savior, Hold My Hand,* Doubleday, 1972; Arte Público Press, 1997. *Seven Long Times,* Praeger, 1974; Arte Público Press, 1995. **Young Adult:** *Stories from El Barrio,* Knopf Books for Young Readers, 1992. **Produced Play:** *The Golden Streets* (1970). **Films:** *Petey and Johnny* (1961). *The World of Piri Thomas* (1970). **Short Stories, Poems, and Essays:** In *The Saturday Review of Literature, The Times Sunday Magazine, Social Justice, The Rican,* and many other magazines, textbooks, and anthologies.

Luis Valdez

As the instigator of the contemporary Chicano theatrical movement and its most outstanding playwright, Luis Valdez is considered the father of Chicano theater. Valdez has distinguished himself as an actor, director, playwright, and filmmaker. However, it is in his role as the founding director of El Teatro Campesino, a theater of farm workers in California, that he has inspired young Chicano activists across the country to use theater as a way to organize students, communities, and labor unions around a cause.

Luis Valdez was born on June 26, 1940, into a family of migrant farm workers in Delano, California. The second of ten children, at age six he began working the fields, and with his family, followed the crops. Consequently his education was frequently interrupted. Nevertheless, he finished high school and went on to San Jose State College, where he majored in English and pursued his interest in theater. While there he won a playwriting contest with his one-act, *The Theft* (1961) and in 1963 the Drama Department produced his play, *The Shrunken Head of Pancho Villa.* After graduating in 1964, Valdez joined the San Francisco Mime Troupe and learned the techniques of agitprop (agitation and propaganda) theater and Italian *commedia dell'arte,* both of which influenced Valdez's development of the basic format of Chicano theater: the one, presentional *acto* or "act." In 1965 Valdez joined César Chávez's mission to organize farm workers into a union. It was in Delano that Valdez brought together farm workers and students in El Teatro

Campesino to dramatize the plight of the farm workers. The publicity and success gained by the troupe prompted a national Chicano theater movement.

In 1967 Valdez and El Teatro Campesino left the unionizing effort to expand their theater beyond agitprop and farm worker concerns. Valdez and the theater have explored most of the theatrical genres that have been important to Mexicans in the United States, including religious pageants, vaudeville (with the down-and-out *pelado,* or underdog figure), and dramatized *corridos* (ballads). The new type of socially engaged theater that El Teatro Campesino pioneered led to the creation of a full-blown theatrical movement in fields and barrios across the country. For nearly three decades, El Teatro Campesino and Valdez have dramatized through stage, television, and film the political and cultural concerns of Hispanics, initially among workers and their supporters, but later among students in universities and the general public. In establishing the canon of what *teatro chicano* should be, Valdez and El Teatro Campesino published their *actos* (short, one-act agitprop pieces) in 1971 with a preface in which Valdez outlines their theatrical principals:

> (1) Chicanos must be seen as a nation with geographic, religious, cultural and racial roots in the Southwest; teatros must further the idea of nationalism and create a national theater based on identification with the Amerindian past; (2) the organizational support of the national theater must be from within and totally independent; (3) "Teatros must never get away from La Raza. . . . If the Raza will not come to the theater, then the theater must go to the Raza. This, in the long run, will determine the shape, style, content, spirit and form of *el teatro chicano.*"

Whether or not Valdez and El Teatro Campesino have strayed from the spirit of this declaration will be judged by future generations. But there is no disputing the fact that Valdez and his theater have expanded horizons by taking Chicano theater to Broadway and other commercial venues and by moving it onto cinema and television screens.

During the late 1960s and the 1970s, El Teatro Campesino produced many of Valdez's plays, including *Los vendidos* (1967, The Sell-Outs), *The Shrunken Head of Pancho Villa* (1968), *Bernabé* (1970), *Dark Root of a Scream* (1971), *La Carpa de los Rascuachis* (1974), and *El Fin del Mundo* (1976). In 1978, Valdez broke into mainstream theater in Los Angeles, with the Mark Taper Forum's production of *Zoot Suit* and, in 1979, with the Broadway production of the same play. In 1986 he had a successful run of his play *I Don't Have to Show You No Stinking Badges* at the Los Angeles Theater Center. *Bernabé,* included in this anthology, is one of Valdez's most poetic plays. It is the story of a young village idiot who is transformed into a natural man by his marriage to La Tierra (The Earth) and his subsequent death. Employing Aztec mythology and symbols in a tale about contemporary barrio characters, the play explores the pre-Colombian heritage of Chicano society. Here

"The term Hispanic refers to the entire process of the Americas, and not just to another wave of immigrants. Without Hispanics there is no America; without America, there are no Hispanics. It is as simple and as complex as that. How do you extricate the essence of the word from its continental significance?"

Luis Valdez, from the foreword to The Hispanic Almanac: From Columbus to Corporate America

Valdez develops the Mayan theme of death-is-life and life-is-death, which appears again in this later works. *Bernabé* marks the beginning of Valdez's search for the meaning of Aztec and Mayan legends, history, and philosophy, and also reveals the influence of Spanish playwright Federico García Lorca, who also strove to elevate country folk to a heroic and mythic stature.

Valdez's screenwriting career began with early film and television versions of the Corky González's poem *I Am Joaquín* (1969) and *Los Vendidos,* and later with a film version of *Zoot Suit* (1982). His real incursion into major Hollywood productions and success came when he wrote and directed *La Bamba* (the name of a dance from Veracruz), the screen biography of Chicano rock and roll star Ritchie Valens. With successes on screen and on stage, Valdez has established himself as a key figure in the world of performance arts.

Personal Stats

Chicano filmmaker, playwright, actor. **Born:** June 26, 1940, in Delano, California, into a family of farm workers. *Education:* B.A. in English from San Jose State College (University). *Career:* Actor, San Francisco Mime Troupe, 1964–65; founder/director, El Teatro Campesino, 1965 to present; film director, 1987–present. *Memberships:* Directors Guild of America, Writers Guild of America, Society of Stage Directors and Choreographers. *Awards/Honors:* Obie, 1968; Los Angeles Drama Critics Awards, 1969, 1972 and 1978; Emmy, 1973; San Francisco Bay Critics Circle Award, 1983; National Medal for the Arts, 1983; honorary doctorate degrees from Columbia College, San Jose State University, and the California Institute for the Arts. *Address:* El Teatro Campesino, P.O. Box 1240, San Juan Bautista, CA 95045

Bernabé

from *Luis Valdez—Early Works: Actos, Bernabe and Pensamiento Serpentino,* edited by Luis Valdez and El Teatro Campesino, Arte Público Press, 1990, pp. 134–67

Characters:

> *Bernabé*
>
> *Madre*
>
> *El Primo*

El Tío/El Sol

Torres/La Luna

Consuelo/La Tierra

The action takes place in a rural town in the San Joaquin Valley of California. The time is the early 1960s. It is summer—not a cloud in the sky, not a breeze in the air. The crops lie majestically over the landscape, over the immensity of the fecund earth. The valley is sweltering under the heat. The sun is lord and master.

Rising abruptly on the flatness of the land is Burlap, California—a small squat town not picturesque enough to be called a village, too large to be a labor camp—population 2,100, one of hundreds of similar tank towns that dot the long flat immensity of the valley, covered with dust and crankcase oil. The town has a Main Street, the commercial center of town, consisting of a gas station, general store, bank, hardware, cafe, Mexican show, and Torres Bar & Hotel. Amid these business establishments are empty lots littered with debris.

This is the world of Bernabé, a mentally-retarded farm worker in his early thirties touched with cosmic madness. The world of man he inhabits judges him insane but harmless—a source of amusement and easy stoop labor. In his own world, however—a world of profoundly elemental perceptions—he is a human being living in direct relationship to earth, moon, sun, and stars.

The set, then, is necessarily abstract—a design that blends myth and reality—the paradoxical vision of a cosmic idiot simply known as Bernabé. For he is a man who draws his full human worth not from the tragicomic daily reality of men, but from the collective, mythical universality of Mankind.

One

Midday: a scorcher in the San Joaquin Valley. Under an infinite pale blue sky, the dusty streets of Burlap, California are empty. No signs of life. Near Torres Bar & Hotel, BERNABÉ comes walking down the hot sidewalk at a steady clip. He is followed at some distance by his MADRE. Holding a transistor radio to his ear, BERNABÉ is listening to Tex-Mex music, oblivious to the heat.

MADRE: *(Stopping.)* Bernabé . . . (BERNABÉ *keeps going.)* Berna-BEH! (BERNABÉ *stops with a sly grin.)*

BERNABÉ: What?

MADRE: Wait . . . ¡Ay, Dios—this heat! (MADRE *waddles forward, sweating and gasping for air—a wizened vision of old age in black with a shawl wrapped tightly around her head.)*

BERNABÉ: *(Rudely.)* What do you want?

MADRE: Don't go so fast, hijo. You leave me behind.

BERNABÉ: Well, step on it, you old bag.

MADRE: *(Angered.)* Don't be ill-bred, hombre! I don't know why you have to get so far ahead of me. What if I fall down, eh? Is that what you want—to see me dead in the streets?

BERNABÉ: *(Grumbling.)* . . . always dying of something.

MADRE: *(Sharply.)* ¿Qué?

BERNABÉ: Nothing.

MADRE: *(Fiercely.)* Be careful how you speak to me, eh? I'm your madre! Do you want the ground to open up and swallow you? That's what happens to sons who don't respect their mothers. The earth opens up and swallows them alive, screaming to the heavens!

BERNABÉ: *(Looking down.)* La tierra? . . . Chale, not me. *(We hear a distant drone high above. Distracted, BERNABÉ looks up at the sky. Smiling.)* Look . . . an airplane. It's a crop duster.

MADRE: *(Hitting him.)* Aren't you listening to me, hombre? I'm getting too old to be out chasing you in the streets—and in this hot sun! Dios mío, you should feel this headache I'm suffering. ¿Sabes qué? You better go on to the store without me. Here. *(She pulls out a small money purse and turns away, digging out coins. BERNABÉ peeks over her shoulder.)* Get back. *(BERNABÉ backs off. MADRE unfolds a ten dollar bill and hands it to him preciously.)* Take this. Buy some eggs, a pound of coffee, and a dozen tortillas. Do you think you can remember that?

BERNABÉ: *(Nodding.)* Eggs . . . coffee . . . tortillas. *(Pause.)* No pan dulce?

MADRE: No! And be careful with the change, eh? Don't let them cheat you. God knows what we're going to do till you find work. *(CONSUELO comes down the sidewalk, heading for the bar. BERNABÉ ogles her the moment she appears. MADRE scandalized.)* ¡Válgame Dios! Bernabé, turn around!

BERNABÉ: *(Grinning.)* ¿Por qué?

MADRE: ¡Qué importa! *(She turns him around. CONSUELO pauses for a second, smiling cynically, then exits into Torres Bar.)* Shameless viejas! ¡Descaradas! Don't ever let me catch you going into the cantinas, Bernabé—the shame would kill me! Andale, pues, get to the store. Go on . . . *(MADRE starts to exit. BERNABÉ pauses and picks up an empty beer can on the street.)*

BERNABÉ: Oiga, can I buy me . . . *(Looks at the beer can and hides it.)* . . . an ice cream?

MADRE: *(Turning.)* No, no, no! Qué ice cream ni qué mugre! There's no money for sweets. And if you see Señor Torres, the labor contractor, ask him for work. Tell him your leg is fine now. Get going! *(BERNABÉ starts to go, and MADRE exits in the opposite direction. BERNABÉ stops, once she is out of sight, and comes back to the bar. He crouches in the doorway looking in, as EL PRIMO and TORRES come down the sidewalk from the other side.)*

TORRES: So how was Tijuana?

PRIMO: A toda eme, boss.

TORRES: No problems, eh?

PRIMO: *(Cool and secretive.)* Chale. They had the carga waiting, I slipped them la lane, and I came back de volada. I got the stuff with me . . . fine shit, boss. The girls'll dig it.

TORRES: Let's go inside.

PRIMO: Orale.

TORRES: (Spotting BERNABÉ.) Well, well-look who's here. Your cousin! *(He kicks* BERNABÉ *playfully.)*

BERNABÉ: (Jumping.) ¡Ay! Baboso, hijo de la . . .

TORRES: (Laughing.) Don't get mad, loco.

PRIMO: (Feeling bad.) He's only playing with you, primo.

TORRES: ¿Qué pues? Aren't you going to say hello?

BERNABÉ: (Uneasy.) Hello, Torres.

TORRES: (In a joking mood.) Say, Eddie, did you know Bernabé has himself an old lady?

PRIMO: (Humoring him.) No, really, cousin?

BERNABÉ: (Surprised.) How do you know?

TORRES: The whole town knows. You've been sleeping with her.

PRIMO: No, really? (BERNABÉ *smiles mysteriously.)* Who is it, cousin? La Betty?

BERNABÉ: No.

PRIMO: La fat Mary?

BERNABÉ: (Laughing.) Chale.

PRIMO: Who, pues?

TORRES: Who else? The old lady who still gives him chi-chi. His mamá! (TORRES *laughs bois- terously.)*

PRIMO: (Offended.) Orale, boss, you're laughing at my tía, man.

TORRES: Just kidding, hombre. ¿Qué traes? *(Getting back to business.)* Bueno, Bernabé, we got work to do. Let's go, Eddie.

PRIMO: Ahi te watcho, cousin. (TORRES *and* PRIMO *start to go into the bar.)*

TORRES: Está más loco . . .

BERNABÉ: (Boldly.) Hey, Torres!

TORRES: (Stopping.) What? *(Long pause.* BERNABÉ *searches for words.)*

PRIMO: What is it, primo?

BERNABÉ: (Smiling slyly.) I wanna be with my ruca.

PRIMO: Your ruca? What ruca?

BERNABÉ: The one that's right here.

TORRES: Here in my cantina?

BERNABÉ: No, here outside.

PRIMO: The sidewalk's empty, ese.

BERNABÉ: (Insanely vague.) The sidewalk's cement. She's over here . . . where the ground is . . . and out in the fields . . . and in the hills. *(Looking up.)* She loves the rain.

TORRES: (Laughing.) ¿Sabes qué? Something tells me this idiot wants to go upstairs.

PRIMO: (Smiling.) You mean—to visit Connie?

TORRES: He's got the itch. Isn't that it, Bernabé? You want one of my chamacas?

BERNABÉ: No!

TORRES: ¿Cómo que no? Your tongue's hanging out, loco. Look, if you tell me what you want, I'll get it for you. Compliments of the house.

BERNABÉ: With my ruca?

TORRES: The one you like.

BERNABÉ: (Pause.) I want a job.

TORRES: (Puzzled.) Job?

BERNABÉ: In the fields.

PRIMO: (Laughs.) He's got you now, Torres! You're gonna have to give him a chamba. The cousin's not as crazy as you think!

BERNABÉ: (Laughs.) Simón, I ain't crazy.

TORRES: (Scoffing.) You can't work with that crooked leg of yours.

BERNABÉ: It's okay now.

TORRES: And what about your head, loco? I can't have you throwing another fit and falling off the truck. Five men couldn't handle you.

PRIMO: Aliviánate, boss—it was only a heat stroke. Besides, Bernabé's the best swamper you ever had. How many potato sacks did you load last year, cousin? Two hundred, five hundred, mil?

BERNABÉ: Vale madre, mil!

PRIMO: A thousand sacos a day, man!

BERNABÉ: How about it, Torres?

TORRES: (Shaking his head.) Ni modo, Quasimodo. Tell your mother to try the Welfare.

BERNABÉ: I need money to buy la tierra.

TORRES: What tierra?

BERNABÉ: This one. Here and there and all over.

PRIMO: (Humoring him.) You wanna buy a ranchito?

BERNABÉ: (Emphatically.) No, a big rancho—with lots of tierra! All the tierra on earth. She's all mine.

TORRES: Yours?

BERNABÉ: My woman. We're gonna get married.

TORRES: (Bursting out laughing.) Pinche loco! Vámonos, Eddie. His woman! What this idiot needs is a vieja. *(He exits laughing.)*

PRIMO: Llévatela suave, primo. (PRIMO *exits. Long pause.* BERNABÉ *kneels on the earth.)*

BERNABÉ: (Slyly.) Tierra, they think I'm crazy. But you know I love you. *(Looks around.)* See you tonight, eh? . . . like always. *(He kisses the ground and exits.)*

Two

> The scene is above and below the earth. Above, BERNABÉ's *house, a small unpainted shack sits back from the street on a narrow lot. Below,* BERNABÉ *sits in a hole in the ground covered with planks, lighting candles to a sexy Aztec goddess pictured on a calendar from Wong's Market.* MADRE *emerges from the house. It is sundown.*

MADRE: (Calling.) Bernabé? Bernabé, come and eat! Válgame Dios, where is this hombre? BER-NA-BE! (BERNABÉ *ignores her.* EL PRIMO *enters on the street.)*

PRIMO: Buenas tardes, tía. What's wrong? Lose Bernabé again?

MADRE: No, qué lose! He hides just to make me suffer. Have you seen him, hijo?

PRIMO: This morning, outside the cantina.

MADRE: *(Alarmed.)* La cantina?

PRIMO: I mean, the store, tía. The Chinaman's supermarket.

MADRE: *(Relieved.)* Pues, sí. I sent him to buy a few things for me. I have a week now with a headache that won't go away. If you only knew, hijo—how much I suffer and worry. Our rent is almost up, and Bernabé without work. *(Pause.)* You do have a job, no m'ijo?

PRIMO: *(Nods.)* I'm working with Torres.

MADRE: Ay, pos sí, ¿no? They say that Señor Torres is rich. He always has money.

PRIMO: Almost all the men in town are unemployed, tía. There won't be anything till the picking starts. Look, let me lend you ten bucks.

MADRE: *(Self-righteous.)* No, Eduardo. What would your mother say? May God forbid it. I know my sister only too well. When it's about money, she's an owl. No, no, no!

PRIMO: *(Holding out a ten spot.)* Here, tía.

MADRE: No, hijo, gracias.

PRIMO: Andele. Take it. *(He tries to put the money in her hand.)*

MADRE: *(Folding her arms.)* No, no—y no!

PRIMO: *(Shrugging.)* Well . . .

MADRE: *(Quickly.)* Well, okay, pues! (MADRE *snatches the ten dollars with lightning reflexes and stuffs it in her bosom hypocritically.)* And how is your madrecita?

PRIMO: Fine, like always.

MADRE: Gracias a Dios. Bueno, if you see m'ijo, send him straight home, eh? I don't know what will become of him. One of these days they'll put him in the crazy house, then what will I do?

PRIMO: Try not to worry, tía. Adiós. (MADRE *exits into her house.* PRIMO *starts to move on.* EL TÍO *enters down the street.)*

TÍO: ¡Oye, sobrino! Eddie!

PRIMO: Orale, tío—how you been?

TÍO: Pos, ¿cómo? Hung-over. Oye, you wouldn't happen to have two bits? Un tostón—for the cure, you know? With 35 cents I can buy me a mickey y ya 'stuvo. (PRIMO *gives him the money.)* N'ombre! That's a real nephew. Say, I couldn't help notice you slipped some money to my little sister, eh?

PRIMO: A few bolas. So what?

TÍO: *(Scratching his head.)* No, nothing, but I bet you she didn't even say gracias, right? Sure, don't deny it! Don't be a sucker, Guaro—haven't I told you? That old dried prune don't appreciate nothing. Look at me. How many years did I bust my ass in the fields to support her, her idiot son, and your own sweet mother who I love more than anybody? You know, when I go over to your house, your 'amá never fails to offer me a cup of coffee, a plate of beans—vaya, whatever, no? But this other miserable sister I got won't even give me a glass of water. Instead she tells me to get the hell on my way, because she has to feed Bernabé, and she don't like nobody to watch him eat! (PRIMO *laughs.*) isn't that so? That's how she is.

PRIMO: Orale, pues, tío. And speaking of the primo, you seen him?

TÍO: (*Suspiciously.*) ¿Por qué? Is that old coyote looking for him? ¡Qué caray! (*Pause.*) Look, you know where the poor loco is?—but don't tell his madre, eh? . . . he's right there, in the field by his house.

PRIMO: The empty lot?

TÍO: Si, hombre, the little llano where the kids play. He's got a hole there he dug into the ground, see? That's where he crawls in and hides. At first he used to get into rock fights with the snot-noses, but lately he's been waiting till dark to go down there, so nobody bothers him.

PRIMO: (*Puzzled.*) How do you know all this, tío?

TÍO: I've seen him. He disappears like a gopher and don't come out for two or three hours.

PRIMO: What does he do?

TÍO: ¡Sabrá Judas! I even went and got into the hole myself once—when he was downtown with his madre, but I didn't see nothing . . . except for the dirt, soft and warm—like he crawls in and squirms around it.

PRIMO: In the dirt?

TÍO: : What else is there?

PRIMO: (*Pause.*) Chale. It can't be.

TÍO: ¿Qué?

PRIMO: Forget it. He's not that crazy.

TÍO: Sure he's crazy. Completely nuts.

PRIMO: Can he be that far gone?

TÍO: Cracked and eaten by burros! What's on your mind?

PRIMO: Just something he told me and Torres this morning.

TÍO: (*Pause.*) What?

PRIMO: Nothing much. It's impossible.

TÍO: (*Exasperated.*) Well, what is it, hombre? You got me standing on my toenails!

PRIMO: (*Pause.*) He said he has a girlfriend.

TÍO: Girlfriend?

PRIMO: La Tierra.

TÍO: You mean the dirt?

PRIMO: (*Nods.*) And that they're gonna get married.

TÍO: (*Pause.*) And you think he . . . ? No, hombre! He can't be that crazy!

PRIMO: Didn't I tell you?

TÍO: (*Pause.*) A hole in the ground? (*Angered.*) Pos, mire qué loco tan cochino, hombre! How can he be doing such a dirty thing? Fucking idiot!

PRIMO: Easy, tío.

TÍO: It's disgusting, Guaro. He's not your nephew.

PRIMO: He's a cousin.

TÍO: Pos, ¡ahi 'ta! He's disgracing the whole family. We got the same blood, hombre. Chihuahua! What's his madre going to say if she finds him out? I bet you she suspects something already.

PRIMO: Chale.

TÍO: Sí, señor. You think I don't know my own sister?

MADRE: (Offstage.) Berna-beh!

TÍO: Listen! Here she comes again. (PRIMO and TÍO *hide in the shadows, as* MADRE *re-enters. She spots* BERNABÉ's *hole in the ground and approaches it suspiciously. Lifting a plank she suddenly spots him.*)

MADRE: (Gasping.) Bernabé? Por Dios, come out of there!

PRIMO: She's got him.

TÍO: ¡Pobre loco! He's going to get it now. (MADRE *starts tearing off the planks, as* BERNABÉ *cowers in his hole.*)

MADRE: ¡Ave María Purísima! ¡Virgencita pure, ayúdame! (PRIMO and TÍO *rush to the hole.*)

TÍO: Quihubo pues, sister? What's the matter?

MADRE: Don't bother me now, Teodoro! I've got too many troubles.

TÍO: Huy, pos—what's new?

MADRE: Don't even talk to me, hombre! You can be a disgraceful wino if you want, but I have to look out for m'ijo!

PRIMO: Did you find Bernabé, tía?

MADRE: Si, hijo! Look where he is—in a filthy hole! Come out of there, Bernabé!

BERNABÉ: (Refusing to come out.) CHALE!

MADRE: ¡Sal de ahi te digo!

BERNABÉ: (Cursing.) ¡Vieja cabrona, píntese!

MADRE: (Shocked.) What? ¡Bendito sea Dios! Did you hear what he called me?

TÍO: (Smiling.) What's he doing?

MADRE: (Pushing him back.) None of your business! You up here—staggering in the streets, and my son down there risking death, verdad?

TÍO: What death? Stop exaggerating.

MADRE: (Fuming.) Exaggerating? Exaggerating! And if the ground falls on top of him, what can happen, eh? Dios mío, he'll suffocate! Do you hear me, Bernabé? Come out of that dark, ugly hole!

PRIMO: The tía's right, primo. Come on out.

MADRE: Talk to him, Eduardo. Please! Before I die of the . . .

TÍO: Exaggeration.

MADRE: (Lashing at him.) ¡Cállate el hocico! Just get out of here, sabes? Leave!

TÍO: You leave! Pos, mire, qué chirrión.

MADRE: Come out, Bernabé! ¡Ahorita mismo!

PRIMO: (Reaching in.) Come on, primo.

BERNABÉ: (Shaking his head.) What are you going to do to me?

MADRE: Nothing. Just come out.

PRIMO: Grab my hand, ese. (BERNABÉ *grabs* PRIMO's *hand and slowly emerges from the pit.*)

BERNABÉ: (Fearful.) Are you going to hit me, oiga?

MADRE: Come on, Bernabé!

BERNABÉ: (Coming out.) If you lay a finger on me, I'll kick your ass.

MADRE: (Gasps.) ¡Válgame Dios, Bernabé! *(She grabs him.)* Now I am going to hit you, for your filthy mouth! ¡Malcriado! *(She beats him.)*

BERNABÉ: (Cowering.) ¡Ay! ¡No! ¡No, mamá!

TÍO: That's enough, let him alone!

PRIMO: Don't hit him, tía.

MADRE: (Incensed.) Stay out of this—both of you! Bernabé's my son and I have the right to punish him. *(She hits him again.)*

TÍO: But he's a man. Not a kid! *(Stopping her.)*

MADRE: I don't care! I'm his madre. And so long as God gives me life, I'll go on punishing him when he does wrong! Let go of me!

BERNABÉ: (Weeping like a child.) I didn't do nothing!

MADRE: Sí, nothing! You think I'm blind, eh? What were you doing in that hole? You think I don't know what dirty things you do in there? I can just imagine! But one of these nights the moon is going to come down and swallow you alive—¡por cochino!

BERNABÉ: (With fear.) No, 'amá, la luna no.

MADRE: Yes, you'll see! ¡Vamos, ándale! Into the house! ¡Ave María Santísima! (MADRE *exits with* BERNABÉ, *pulling him by the hair.* PRIMO *and* TÍO *look at each other sorrowfully.*)

TÍO: Pobre loco.

PRIMO: She treats him like a kid.

TÍO: That's what he is. You saw him—he really believes the moon can come down and swallow him. But I know what you mean. In a few weeks, he'll be in the fields, working and sweating like an animal. And do you think my sister appreciates it? No, hombre, she rents him like a burro!

PRIMO: Say, tío—how old is Bernabé?

TÍO: Pos, lemme see . . . thirty four? No, wait . . . thirty seven! *PRIMO:* And how many girl-friends has he had?

TÍO: Are you serious?

PRIMO: Simón. *(Pause.)* None, am I right?

TÍO: Ninguna.

PRIMO: ¡Orale! Then it's not craziness.

TÍO: What?

PRIMO: All the funny stuff about la tierra and the hole and everything, tío. Figure it out. *(Pause.)* Look, will you help me do the cousin a favor?

TÍO: Like what?

PRIMO: Pos, ya sabe. You know Consuelo, the hot momma that works over in Torres Club?

TÍO: ¿La p . . .?

PRIMO: ¡Simón, la chavalona!

TÍO: No, Guaro, I don't get into those things no more.

PRIMO: So what? Look, go to the club and tell her to wait for me in one hour. Tell her Eddie wants to talk to her. Understand?

TÍO: And why don't you go?

PRIMO: Because I'm bringing the primo.

TÍO: *(Scoffing.)* Oh, sure. His madre's gonna let him go straight to the cantina! Forget it, sobrino. You're a bigger fool than I thought.

PRIMO: *(Smiling.)* You just leave the tía to me. She and I get along fine. If I tell her I'm taking Bernabé to see Torres about a job, no hay pedo. I'll have him there. ¿Juega?

TÍO: Pos, qué caray, okay pues. ¡Juega!

PRIMO: *(Taking out money.)* Then here—have a few cold beers while you wait for us.

TÍO: *(Taking the money eagerly.)* ¡Ay, chirrión! You mean I have to wait?

PRIMO: Don't you want to see your nephew happy?

TÍO: What nephew? That pitiful idiot?

PRIMO: He's not such an idiot, tío. You'll see. Bueno, trucha pues. Torres Club, eh? Around nine. (PRIMO and T Í O *start to go in opposite directions.)*

TÍO: *(Stopping.)* ¡Epa! And what's the name of the . . . ?

PRIMO: Consuelo. She's got the big chamorrotes (thighs).

TÍO: Pos, you ought to know. I don't.

PRIMO: *(Laughing.)* Orale, pues, ahi nos watchamos later. I'm going to eat with the tía. *(Starts to go again.)*

TÍO: *(Stopping again.)* ¡Oye! And if Bernabé doesn't want to . . . tú sabes . . .

PRIMO: Then the favor's for you, tío. *(Exits.)*

TÍO: *(Starts to exit.)* Ha! For me . . . *(Stops. Reconsiders, tilts head, smiles.)* Consuelo, eh? *(He exits.)*

Three

> Torres Club. Outside in the back alley. BERNABÉ *comes out of the cantina with a beer can. The moon is bright.*

BERNABÉ: *(Looking down.)* Tierra? It's me . . . out here in this alley. See, that's Torres' cantina . . . Look—a cerveza. You know what? My primo went and covered the hole where we get together. Mi 'amá sent him. But who cares, huh? It's just some boards. Tomorrow I'll take 'em off! Anyway, you're here, and over there, and way over there. And right, right here. We're always together! *(Laughs and kisses the earth.* TORRES *enters. Sees* BERNABÉ, *laughs to himself, shaking his head.* BERNABÉ *scoops up a handful of dirt.)*

TORRES: Oye, oye, stop feeling her up!

BERNABÉ: *(Startled.)* Uh?

TORRES: *(Laughs.)* Don't get scared, loco. It's me. How's the girlfriend, okay?

BERNABÉ: Simón, okay. *(He rises.)*

TORRES: Nice and cool, eh? Pos, qué suave. Chihuahua, it's hot, hombre! The sun went down and the night stayed hot. What are you doing here so late?

BERNABÉ: Nothing. *(Hiding his handful of dirt.)*

TORRES: And that beer?

BERNABÉ: My primo bought it for me. We came to look for work.

TORRES: So where's Eddie? Inside?

BERNABÉ: *(Nodding.)* Talking to Torres.

TORRES: Oh sí, eh? And who am I? La Luna?

BERNABÉ: *(Startled.)* Chale.

TORRES: *(Laughs.)* No, ¿verdad? There's the moon up there. Look how big she is! I wonder if she's jealous? The moon's a woman too, eh? Or maybe not. Maybe he's the brother of your ruca. Watch it, Bernabé, he's gonna take her away!

BERNABÉ: ¡Pura madre! Nobody can take her away!

TORRES: Well, don't get pissed.

BERNABÉ: She's mine. *(Looks at his handful.)*

TORRES: *(Tongue in cheek.)* Then tell that to the gabachos. See if they give her back.

BERNABÉ: What gabachos?

TORRES: The landowners, manito. Banks, corporations.

BERNABÉ: They ain't nobody.

TORRES: *(Pause.)* Hey—and if I wanted the land too, Bernabé? What do I do?

BERNABÉ: *(Laughs.)* Aguántate. You just wait!

TORRES: But she's my mamá.

BERNABÉ: ¿La tierra?

TORRES: Sure. She's your momma too.

BERNABÉ: Up yours! She's not my mother.

TORRES: Bueno, your hot momma, then. But look how the ranchers treat her, hombre. They sell her whenever they feel like it—to the highest bidder! See those fields over there? I just bought 'em yesterday. I own the ground under your feet too. All the lots on this street. And I got more on the other side of the *barrio*. Check it out. But you know what, loco? I'll rent her to you. *(Laughs.)* Give me a few bucks, and I'll let you have her—for the night! (BERNABÉ *is genuinely puzzled. He finds* TORRES's *reasoning totally nonsensical.*)

BERNABÉ: Say, Torres, you're even crazier than me! *(Laughs.)* ¡Ah, qué Torres!

TÍO: *(Entering.)* ¡Oye tú! Where you been?

BERNABÉ: Right here.

TÍO: What are you up to, hombre? Why did you leave the bar? *(Spots* TORRES.) Oh, buenas noches, Señor Torres.

TORRES: Buenas . . . *(Suspicious.)* What's up, Teodoro?

TÍO: *(Nervous.)* No, nothing, this burro . . . I don't know why I got into this! Eddie brought him here . . . to do him a favor . . . *(Barking at* BERNABÉ.) Let's go inside, ándale! Your cousin already went up with the vieja. He said to get ready.

TORRES: No, hombre! He's going in with Connie?

TÍO: Pos sí, if she lets him in.

TORRES: (*Smiles.*) Sure she'll let him. She does what I tell her.

TÍO: My nephew's already talking her into it.

TORRES: So you're going to get laid, eh Bernabé?

BERNABÉ: (*Getting scared.*) I want another beer.

TÍO: There's no more. Go do your duty!

TORRES: Don't rush him, hombre. This is an occasion. Come on in. So you're finally going to get married, eh loco?

TÍO: ¡Qué pinche vergüenza! (*Exits.*)

Four

> Torres Club—interior. The upstairs hallway of a cheap hotel. PRIMO enters, his arm
around CONSUELO.

PRIMO: Orale, Connie, gracias for doing me this favor, eh?

CONSUELO: It's no favor, man. You gotta pay me.

PRIMO: Simón, but the veto's muy especial, you know?

CONSUELO: Who is this jerk?

PRIMO: My cousin.

CONSUELO: Who?

PRIMO: Bernabé.

CONSUELO: (*Nonplussed.*) You mean . . . el loquito del pueblo? Sorry, Eddie, I'm sorry, but no dice.

PRIMO: ¿Por qué no?

CONSUELO: Because, porque no. How do I know what he's gonna do? Because he's crazy, that's why!

PRIMO: He's not that loco, chula. He just needs a little break.

CONSUELO: Well, it's not me, man.

PRIMO: Look, it's no big deal. I'm asking you to do the veto a favor. He's my primo—sure he's missing a few marbles, but so what? He's got everything else. Andale, chula—just for a little bit. I promised him—it's his birthday.

CONSUELO: (*Pause.*) Give me fifteen bucks and he's on.

PRIMO: Fifteen bolas? What are you—gold-plated down there? (CONNIE *starts to go.*) No, look, Connie—don't be that way. Besides, all I got are nine bills, see? Here. (*Gives her the money.*)

CONSUELO: (*Takes it reluctantly.*) Bueno, okay. But just one turn on the merry-go-round and that's it. Where's the loco at?

PRIMO: He's coming with el tío—they had a beer first.

CONSUELO: Tío?

PRIMO: Teodoro.

CONSUELO: That winito's your tío?

PRIMO: Simón, and also Bernabé's.

CONSUELO: And is his mamá here too?

PRIMO: Chale, what's with you?

CONSUELO: Naranjas, corazón. Okay, send him in, pues. (CONSUELO *exits into her room.*)

TÍO: (Offstage.) Guaro?

PRIMO: Orale, tío—up here.

TÍO: (Offstage.) Here comes Lover Boy . . . shorts! Is she ready?

PRIMO: And set to go.

TÍO: (Enters puffing.) Hijole, la chicharra, hombre! It took long enough to get up here. Where's the bride?

PRIMO: In her room.

TÍO: (Looking.) Ah, pos sí, I recognize the place.

PRIMO: Just like old times, eh tío?

TÍO: Huy, what can I say, sobrino? I personally broke in this hotel. Every payday, I couldn't keep my nose out of here. They had some big fine things up here in those days.

PRIMO: And Bernabé?

TÍO: (Turning.) He was right behind . . . Adiós, where did he go? There he is! See? ¡Andale, oyes! Don't hide. Come on up.

BERNABÉ: (Offstage.) For what?

TÍO: For what? Pos—what do you think? It's payday. Are you scared?

BERNABÉ: (Offstage.) NO!

PRIMO: All right, ese, the ruca's waiting for you.

BERNABÉ: (Entering.) Where?

PRIMO: In there. It's la Connie, the one who was at the bar? La watchates? The fine buns and the big legs? (BERNABÉ *laughs.*) Simón qué yes, verdad? She's ready, she's willing, and she's able, carnal. So get in there. Go get it!

BERNABÉ: (Playing dumb.) What?

PRIMO: You know, loco. (BERNABÉ *laughs lasciviously. He looks at his* PRIMO *and* TÍO, *then hesitantly starts toward* CONSUELO's *room. He reaches the door and is about to go in, when he stops suddenly and turns grinning idiotically.*)

BERNABÉ: (Backing off.) Chale.

PRIMO: Nel, primo—don't chicken out, man. She's all set. Andale!

BERNABÉ: (Shaking his head.) No, she'll swallow me.

TÍO: Swallow you!

BERNABÉ: La Luna. For being dirty.

PRIMO: That's bullshit, primo. Come on, you saw Connie. You liked what you saw, right?

BERNABÉ: Yeah.

PRIMO: Well then? Go see it all.

BERNABÉ: Not now.

PRIMO: Why not?

BERNABÉ: I don't feel like it.

TÍO: You felt like it downstairs.

BERNABÉ: (Turning.) I want another beer first.

TÍO: Later—afterward.

PRIMO: You have to go in now, primo. She's waiting for you. Besides, I already paid her . . . twenty bucks. Okay?

BERNABÉ: I don't think so.

TÍO: But didn't you hear, hombre. He already paid the vieja!

BERNABÉ: I don't give a shit. I don't want that vieja!

TÍO: Bueno, if he's not going in . . . *(Pause.)* He's not going in. Take the idiot home, and that's it.

CONSUELO: (At her door.) Eddie? Oye, Eddie? ¿Qué pasó, pues?

PRIMO: Hold it a second.

CONSUELO: Hold it yourself! Tell him to hurry. *(She retreats into her room.)*

PRIMO: You see? She wants you to go in.

TÍO: And to hurry.

PRIMO: Come on, ese. I know you want to.

TÍO: Sure, he wants to. ¡Está buenota, hombre! I wouldn't hold back.

BERNABÉ: Then, you get in there.

TÍO: Don't be an idiot! Qué caray, I would if I could, but I can't no more. She's more than I can handle. Here, have a drink—to give you strength. *(Gives him a swig of his beer.)*

PRIMO: Okay, pues, get in there, cuz!

TÍO: Be a man, m'ijo. (BERNABÉ *starts to move toward* CONSUELO's *door again. Cautiously, he is about to enter, but he stops and beats a retreat.)*

BERNABÉ: (Backing off again.) Chale, I can't!

TÍO: (Cursing.) ¡Me lleva la . . . que me trajo! This is a jackass without a rope, hombre.

PRIMO: (Giving up.) Simón, let's go, pues.

BERNABÉ: Where we going?

PRIMO: Home to your chante.

BERNABÉ: Nel, I wanna booze it up.

TÍO: We already boozed it up.

BERNABÉ: Just one.

TÍO: (Exasperated.) N'ombre! This fool don't want a puta, he wants a peda. Better take him home, Guaro. Before he gets drunk.

BERNABÉ: I'm not going to get drunk, oiga!

PRIMO: Let's go, Bernabé.

BERNABÉ: No! I wanna stay here.

TÍO: Your madre's waiting for you.

BERNABÉ: ¡Me importa madre! They're waiting for me here too.

TÍO: (Shoving him toward the door.) Then, get in there!

BERNABÉ: (Pause.) No . . . she'll swallow me.

PRIMO: *(Tries to pull him.)* Let's go, ese.

BERNABÉ: No!

TÍO: ¡Andale! Grab him! (PRIMO *and* TÍO *grab* BERNABÉ.)

BERNABÉ: *(Resisting.)* No! Nooo! I wanna drink! I wanna viejaaa! I want la tierraaa! (CONSUELO *comes out of her room in a nightgown.*)

CONSUELO: Oye, oye, what's happening, Eddie?

PRIMO: Nothing. We're going.

CONSUELO: ¿Qué pasó? Isn't he coming in?

PRIMO: Chale.

TÍO: He's crazy. (CONSUELO *comes up to* BERNABÉ, *mockingly wanton, sultrily flaunting her body before his gaping eyes.*)

CONSUELO: ¿Qué pasó, Bernabé? You don't want to come with me? You know me, ¿qué no? I'm Consuelo—la Connie. Come on, gimme a little hug. (BERNABÉ *retreats.*) Andale, hombre—don't back away! Eddie tells me you like las chavalonas. Is that true, eh? Mira—gimme your hand like this . . . and now we put it here. *(She wraps his arm around her* BERNABÉ *opens his fist—the handful of earth falls to the floor.)* Like novios, see? Do you want to dance? I have a record player in my room. Come on, let's go to the baile . . . *(She takes him to the door of her room.)* ¿Y ustedes? What are you gawking at? Get lost! Can't you see we're going on our honeymoon? (CONSUELO *laughs and closes the door, pulling in* BERNABÉ *with her.* PRIMO *approaches the dirt on the floor.*)

TÍO: ¿Qué es eso? What did he drop?

PRIMO: Tierra . . . *(They look at each other.)* Come on, tío. I'll buy you a beer.

TÍO: Let's go. This idiot nephew's driving me crazy! *(They exit.)*

Five

CONSUELO's *room: darkness. A brief erotic silence, slowly punctuated by* CONSUELO's *moans and the pounding of* BERNABÉ's *heartbeat.*

CONSUELO: *(In the dark.)* Ay, papasito . . . Ay, ay, ¡AY!

BERNABÉ: *(Screaming.)* ¡AYYY!

CONSUELO: *(Pause.)* Bernabé?

BERNABÉ: ¡Quítate! ¡AYYYY!

CONSUELO: Shut up, hombre! ¿Qué tienes?

BERNABÉ: No, mamá, yo no hice nadaaaa!

CONSUELO: Are you going nuts on me?

BERNABÉ: Mamá! Mamááááá! *(Strobe light effect, slow to fast.* BERNABÉ *is backing away from* CONSUELO—*or at least the* MADRE *dressed in* CONSUELO's *clothes. The effect is nightmarish.)*

MADRE: *(As* CONSUELO.) ¿Qué tienes, papasito?

BERNABÉ: *(Backing off.)* No, nooooo!

MADRE: Naranjas, corazón. Don't you want to be with me? I'm your girlfriend . . . tu novia.

(Changing into MADRE.) ¡Pero también soy madre y te voy a pegar! ¡Por cochino! ¡Vente! ¡Vámonos pa' la casa! *(She grabs him by the hair.)*

BERNABÉ: *(Like a child.)* No, mami, noooo! (MADRE *changes into* CONSUELO *and strokes* BERNABÉ's *head and face, calming him down.)*

MADRE: *(As* CONSUELO.) Pero, ¿por qué no, bonito? You know me, que no? I'm Consuelo, La Connie. Eddie tells me you like las chavalonas. Don't you want me? Soy tu novia . . . *(Back to* MADRE.) ¡Y por eso te voy a pegar! Soy tu madre, y tengo derecho de castigarte mientras Dios me preste vida. You want la tierra to swallow you alive? Come with me!

BERNABÉ: *(Shoving her back.)* No, noo, no quierooo! Tierraaaa! (BERNABÉ *runs out into the hallway. Lights up. Strobe effect disappears.* PRIMO, TORRES, *and* TÍO *come running.)*

PRIMO: What's the matter, primo?

TORRES: ¡Oye, Connie! What the hell's going on, pues? (CONSUELO *comes out of her room, as herself.* BERNABÉ *screams.)*

CONSUELO: Torres! Get this baboso out of here! ¡Sáquenlo!

PRIMO: What happen, chula?

CONSUELO: I don't know what happen. Está loco, ¿qué no ves?

BERNABÉ: *(Terrified.)* ¡Yo no hice nada!

TORRES: Did he go in at least?

PRIMO: Sure he went in.

TÍO: Se metió bien contento.

CONSUELO: I told you, Eddie! ¡Te dije!

PRIMO: Come on, primo. Let's go home.

BERNABÉ: *(Cries out in horror.)* No! Nooo! ¡Me pega! She'll hit me!

PRIMO: Who'll hit you?

BERNABÉ: *(Points at* CONSUELO.) ¡Mi 'amáááá!

TÍO: This isn't your mother, suato!

CONSUELO: See what I mean. (BERNABÉ *screams.)*

TORRES: *(To* CONSUELO.) Don't talk to him, stupid! Keep your mouth shut!

CONSUELO: You bastard. This is all your fault! You think I like to do this?

TORRES: ¡Cállate el hocico!

CONSUELO: And you keep the money!

TORRES: Get into your room! *(He pushes her.)*

CONSUELO: *(Defiantly.)* Tell them! Tell 'em how you use the girls! And for what? Your pinche drugs?

TORRES: *(Slapping her around.)* I said shut your fucking mouth!

BERNABÉ: *(Reacting.)* No, nooo! MAMA! *(Rushes* TORRES.)

PRIMO: ¡Bernabé, cálmala!

TÍO: Settle down, hombre!

TORRES: (BERNABÉ *on his back.)* Get him out of here!

PRIMO: We're trying, boss!

CONSUELO: Kick his ass, Bernabé!

TORRES: *(Pushing CONSUELO.)* I'm gonna get you!

BERNABÉ: *(Pounding on him.)* No, ¡déjala! Leave her alone! (PRIMO *and* TÍO *struggle to take* BERNABÉ *off* TORRES.)

PRIMO: Primo!

TÍO: Bernabé!

BERNABÉ: She's mine! My woman is mine!

TORRES: ¡Quítenlo! Get him OFF OF ME! *(He falls.* CONSUELO *laughs.* BERNABÉ *is hysterical, totally out of it.* PRIMO *and* TÍO *succeed in pulling him off* TORRES.)

BERNABÉ: ¡Lo maté! ¡LO MATE! I KILLED TORRES! (BERNABÉ *runs out.* TÍO *starts to run after him.* PRIMO *helps* TORRES *on his feet.* CONSUELO *is still laughing.)*

TÍO: *(Calling.)* Bernabé! Come back here, you idiot!

PRIMO: You okay, boss?

TORRES: ¿Pos, luego? Let me go.

TÍO: ¡Oye, Guaro! The loco ran outside! What if he goes and tells his madre?

PRIMO: I don't understand what happened to him. What did you do?

CONSUELO: Don't ask me, man! It's not my fault if he thinks I'm his pinche madre!

TÍO: *(To* PRIMO.) ¡Vámonos, hombre! We're gonna lose him!

PRIMO: Orale, let's go. Sorry, Torres. *(They exit.* CONSUELO *and* TORRES *are left behind.* CONSUELO *looks at* TORRES *and starts laughing. A deep bitter laugh, not without a certain satisfaction. She exits into her room.)*

TORRES: Goddamn whore! *(He exits.)*

Six

      El llano: night. There is a full moon, unseen, but casting an eery light on the earth. BERNABÉ *is at his hole, pulling off the boards. Suddenly, from the sky comes music.*

BERNABÉ: *(Crying out.)* ¡Tierraaa! I killed Torres! ¡Hijo 'e su tiznada madre! ¡LO MATE! *(Pause. He hears the danzón music.)* What's that? *(Stops. Fearfully looks at sky, sees moon.)* ¡La Luna! It's coming down! ¡Mamá, la lunaaa! *(Sobs like a child. Moonlight gathers into a spot focussed on him.* LA LUNA *enters, dressed like a Pachuco, 1942 style: Zoot suit, drapes, calcos, hat with feather, small chain, etc.)*

LUNA: Orale, pues, ese vato. No te escames. Soy yo, la Luna.

BERNABÉ: *(Wrapping himself into a ball.)* ¡No, chalOe!

LUNA: Control, ese. Ain't you Chicano? You're a vato loco.

BERNABÉ: *(Looks up slowly.)* I ain't loco.

LUNA: Oh, simón. I didn't mean it like that, carnal. Te estaba cabuliando. Watcha. If they don't like you the way you are, pos que tengan que, ¡pa' que se mantengan! ¡Con safos, putos! Shine 'em on, ese. Inside you know who you are. Can you dig it?

BERNABÉ: *(Feeling better.)* Simón.

LUNA: Pos a toda madre. *(Pause. Reaches into his pocket.)* Oye, like to do a little grifa? A good reefer will set you straight. You got any trolas? *(Finds match, lights joint for* BERNABÉ.)

The Hispanic Literary Companion

Alivian el esqueleto, carnal. Me and you are going to get bien locos tonight. Ahi te llevo. *(Grabs joint from* BERNABÉ.) No le aflojes. (BERNABÉ *gets joint again.)* Ese, you see them stars way up there?—some of them got some fine asses . . . (BERNABÉ *laughs.)* Say, I saw you go into Torres Club tonight. How was it?

BERNABÉ: *(Guilty.)* Okay.

LUNA: Simón, that Connie's a real mamasota, carnal. But tell me—a la bravota—why didn't you put it to her? Chicken? (BERNABÉ *throws the joint down.)* No, chale, don't tell me, pues. None of my beeswax. Here, no te agüites. *(Gives him back the joint.)* Oye, Bernabé, ¿sabes qué? I got a boner to pick with you, man. It's about my carnala.

BERNABÉ: Your carnala?

LUNA: Mi sister, loco. What you up to?

BERNABÉ: Nothing.

LUNA: Don't act pendejo, ese! I've been watching you get together almost every night. You dig me? She asked me to come down and see what's cooking. You just wanna get laid or what? She wants to make it forever, loco.

BERNABÉ: Forever?

LUNA: With you. Me la rayo. Watcha, let me call her. *(Calls.)* Oye, sister, come on! Somebody's waiting for you. *(Music accompanies the entrance of* LA TIERRA. *She emerges from the hole dressed as a soldadera [soldier woman of the Mexican Revolution, 1910] with a sombrero and cartridge belts.* BERNABÉ *is spellbound the moment he sees her. She stares at* BERNABÉ, *amazon and earth mother.)*

TIERRA: ¿Quién es?

LUNA: Pos, who? Your vato loco. Bernabé, this is my carnala. La Tierra.

TIERRA: Buenas noches, Bernabé. (BERNABÉ *makes a slight grunt, smiling idiotically.)* You don't know me? (BERNABÉ *is speechless and embarrassed.)*

LUNA: Orale, pues, carnal, say something. Don't tell me you're scared of her? (BERNABÉ *struggles to say something. His mind tries to form words. He ends up starting to laugh moronically, from helplessness.)*

TIERRA: *(Sharply.)* No, hombre, don't laugh! Speak to me seriously. Soy la tierra. (BERNABÉ *stares at her. A sudden realization strikes him and turns into fear. He screams and runs.)*

LUNA: ¡Epale! Where you going, loco? *(Stops* BERNABÉ *with a wave of his arm.)* Cálmala—be cool! There's nothing to be scared of. *(Pulls him toward* TIERRA.) Look at my carnala, see how a toda madre she looks in the moonlight . . . She loves you, man. Verdad, sister?

TIERRA: If he is a man. (BERNABÉ *is caught in a strange spell. He and* LA TIERRA *look at each other for a long moment.* LA LUNA *gets restless.)*

LUNA: Bueno, le dijo la mula al freno. You know what? I'm going to take a little spin around the stars—check up on the latest chisme. Oye, Bernabé, watch it with my sister, eh? Llévensela suave, pues. *(Exits.)*

TIERRA: *(Softly.)* What are you thinking, Bernabé?

BERNABÉ: *(Struggling to say something.)* I killed Torres.

TIERRA: *(Pushing him down.)* H'm, ¡qué pelado este! Weren't you thinking about me? Don't pride yourself. Torres isn't dead.

BERNABÉ: He's still alive?

TIERRA: Pos, luego. How were you going to kill him? With your bare hands? Right now, he's in his bar laughing at you!

BERNABÉ: ¿Por qué?

TIERRA: Because he knows I belong to him. Not to you.

BERNABÉ: (Incensed.) Chale, you're mine!

TIERRA: And how am I yours, Bernabé? Where and when have you stood up for me? All your life you've worked in the fields like a dog—and for what? So others can get rich on your sweat, while other men lay claim to me? Torres says he owns me, Bernabé—what do you own? Nothing. (Pause BERNABÉ's head is down.) Look at me, hombre! Soy la Tierra! Do you love me? Because if your love is true, then I want to be yours. (BERNABÉ reaches out to embrace her.) But not so fast, pelado! I'm not Consuelo, sabes? If you truly love me, you'll have to respect me for what I am, and then fight for me—¡como los machos! Don't you know anything? Many men have died just to have me. Are you capable of killing those who have me . . . and do not love me, Bernabé?

BERNABÉ: You want me to kill?

TIERRA: To set me free. For I was never meant to be the property of any man—not even you . . . though it is your destiny to lie with me. (She extends her hand. BERNABÉ goes to her. She pulls him down, and they lay down. He is almost going to embrace her, when LA LUNA comes back.)

LUNA: Orale, stop right there! (BERNABÉ sits up.) ¿Qué, pues, nuez? Didn't I tell you to watch it with my sister? What were you doing, eh?

BERNABÉ: (Rises.) ¿Qué te importa, buey? (LA TIERRA rises and stands to one side, observing silently but with strength. BERNABÉ seems more self-possessed.)

LUNA: Oye, so bravo all of a sudden?

BERNABÉ: You'd better leave, Luna!

LUNA: I'd better not, carnal!

BERNABÉ: Get out of here!

LUNA: Look at him, will you? Muy machote. What did you do to him, sis?

BERNABÉ: ¡Lárgate! (Pushes LUNA.)

LUNA: Hey, man, watch the suit. I'm your camarada, remember? Almost your brother-in-law.

TIERRA: (With power.) Luna! Leave us in peace. He means me no harm.

LUNA: Pura madre, how do you know?

TIERRA: Because I know him. Since the very day of his birth, he has been innocent, and good. Others have laughed at him. But he has always come to my arms seeking my warmth. He loves me with an intensity most men cannot even imagine . . . for in his eyes I am woman . . . I am Madre . . .

LUNA: Simón—¡pura madre!

TIERRA: Yet I'm forever Virgin. So leave us alone!

LUNA: Nel, sister. Qué virgen ni que madre. I know what you two are up to. Are you going to get married or what? Is this a one night stand?

TIERRA: That's up to Bernabé.

LUNA: What do you say, loco? Is this forever?

BERNABÉ: (Pause.) Simón.

LUNA: Pendejo.

TIERRA: Satisfied?

LUNA: Chale. You still need Jefe's blessing.

TIERRA: He'll grant it.

LUNA: Pos, you hope. First he's gotta meet Bernabé. You ready for Him, ese?

BERNABÉ: Who?

LUNA: El Mero Mero, loco. Su Papá. Mi Jefito. ¡EL SOL!

BERNABÉ: ¡¿Sol?!

LUNA: (Turning.) He's coming—watcha. It's almost dawn. ¿Sabes qué, ese? You better let me do the talking first. Me and the Jefe get along real suave. I'll tell Him you're Chicano, my camarada.

TIERRA: No, Luna.

LUNA: What?

TIERRA: He has a voice. Let him speak for himself.

LUNA: (Shrugging.) Orale, no hay pedo. But you know the Jefito.

TIERRA: You will have to face him, Bernabé. If you truly love me, then you should have no fear of my father. Speak to him with respect, but with courage. He has no patience with cowardly humans.

LUNA: ¡Al alba! Here he comes! Don't stare at his face too long, ese! He'll blind you! (LA TIERRA *and* LA LUNA *kneel before the place where the sun is rising. Indígena music: majestic flutes and drums.* EL SOL *rises in the guise of Tonatiuh, the Aztec Sun God. He speaks in a resounding voice.)*

SOL: Buenos días, mis hijos.

TIERRA: Buenos días, Papá.

LUNA: Buenos días, Jefe.

SOL: Luna! How goes my eternal war with the stars? ¿Cuidaste mi cielo por toda la noche?

LUNA: Simón, Jefe, the heavens are fine.

SOL: ¿Y tu hermana? Did you watch over her?

LUNA: Sí, señor. ¡Cómo no!

SOL: ¿Pues cómo? . . . ¡CALLATE!

TIERRA: ¿Apá?

SOL: (Gently.) Sí, m'ija, ¿cómo estás?

TIERRA: Bien, Papá.

SOL: And all your humanity, that plague of miserable mortals you call your children? Do they still persist in their petty greed and hatred and fear of death?

TIERRA: Sí, Tata. (To BERNABÉ.) Go.

BERNABÉ: ¿Señor? *(Pause.)* ¿Señor de los cielos?

SOL: ¿Quién me llama?

BERNABÉ: It's me, Señor. Down here.

SOL: ¿Quién eres tú?

BERNABÉ: Bernabé.

SOL: ¿Qué? ¡LOOK AT ME!

BERNABÉ: *(Shielding his eyes.)* Bernabé . . . I come to tell you something, Señor . . . de mi amor . . .

SOL: *(Disdainfully.)* ¿Amor?

BERNABÉ: Por la Tierra.

SOL: ¡¿M'ija!?

BERNABÉ: *(Humbly.)* Con todo respeto, señor.

SOL: *(Pause.)* Many centuries have passed, Bernabé, since men remembered who is el padre de la tierra. En verdad, very few have ever had the courage to face me, como es debido. Why have you come?

BERNABÉ: I am a man, Señor.

SOL: ¿Y eso qué me importa a mí?

BERNABÉ: I love her.

SOL: *(Scoffing majestically.)* Ha! Billions of men have loved her. Do you think you are the first? Look at her, Bernabé, this is la Tierra who has been all things to all men. Madre, prostituta, mujer. Aren't you afraid?

BERNABÉ: *(Bravely.)* No, Señor, of what?

SOL: ¡De su PADRE, desgraciado! ¡¡¡EL SOL!!! *(There is a terrifying flash of light and thunder.* BERNABÉ *runs and hides.)* Look at him running like a coward! ¡MALHORA! I should kill you for what your kind has done to m'ija!

BERNABÉ: It wasn't me, Señor!

TIERRA: *(Stepping forward.)* ¡Por favor, Tata! ¡Es inocente!

LUNA: Es cierto, Jefe. The vato's a Chicano. He's never had any tierra!

SOL: *(Pause, calms down.)* What is your work, Bernabé?

BERNABÉ: I work in the fields.

SOL: You are dirt poor, then?

BERNABÉ: Sí, Señor.

SOL: Then, how do you intend to take care of my daughter? You have no money! You have no POWER!

BERNABÉ: *(Pause.)* Señor, I am nobody, that's true. In town people say I'm only a loco. But I know one thing, that the rich people are more locos than me. They sell la Tierra all the time, in little pedacitos here and there, but I know she should never be sold like that . . . because she doesn't belong to anyone. Like a woman should never be sold, ¿qué no? Eso es lo que pienso, Señor. If anybody has hurt la Tierra, it's not the pobres, it's the men with money and power. I can only love her.

LUNA: *(Sotto voce.)* ¡Orale, te aventates, ese! (EL SOL *silences* LUNA *with a powerful glance.)*

SOL: Dices bien. *(Pause.)* Now I know who you are, Bernabé. Eres el último y el primero . . . The last of a great noble lineage of men I once knew in ancient times, and the first of a new raza cósmica that shall inherit the earth. Your face is a cosmic memory, Bernabé. It reminds me of an entire humanity, de tus mismos ojos, tu piel, tu sangre. They too loved la Tierra and honored su padre above all else. They too were my children. They pierced the human brain and penetrated the distant stars and found the hungry fire that eats of itself. They discovered what today only a loco can understand—that life is death, and that death is life. Que la vida no vale nada porque vale todo. That you are one, so you can be two, two so you can be four, and then eight, and then sixteen, and on and on until you are millions, billions!—only to return once again to the center and discover . . . nada, so you fill up the space with one again. ¿Me comprendes, Bernabé? What power was that?

BERNABÉ: El poder del Sol, Señor?

SOL: *(Pauses.)* Tienes razón . . . and that's why if you unite with m'ija, you shall have that poder. And you shall be my Son! Tierra, do you love this man?

TIERRA: Sí, Papá.

SOL: Bernabé, ¿de veras quieres a la Tierra?

BERNABÉ: Con todo el corazón.

SOL: *(Ironically.)* ¿Corazón? No, hijo, not with your corazón. You may love her with your body, your blood, your seed, but your heart belongs to me. ¿Estás listo pare morir?

BERNABÉ: ¡Morir!

SOL: ¡Pare vivir! (BERNABÉ *is momentarily stunned and confused. He looks at* LA LUNA *and* LA TIERRA. *They say nothing.)*

BERNABÉ: Señor, I don't want to die.

SOL: Hijo, I offer you the power of the Sun. You have been nothing, now you shall be everything. Yo soy el comienzo y el fin de sodas las cosas. Believe in me and you shall never die. Will you give me your corazón?

BERNABÉ: *(Pause.)* Sí, Señor.

SOL: ¡Que sea así! *(Drums and flutes.* BERNABÉ *is sacrificed.* LA TIERRA *and* LA LUNA *lay his body out.)*

SOL: ¡Bernabé, levántate! (BERNABÉ *rises—a complete man.)* For here on you shall be un hombre nuevo and you shall help me to conquer the stars! (BERNABÉ *walks erect.)* Bernabé, la Tierra es virgen y tuya. Sean felices.

TIERRA: ¡Bernabé! (BERNABÉ *and* LA TIERRA *embrace.)*

LUNA: ¡Orale! Congratulations, loco—I mean, ese. ¡A toda madre!

SOL: ¡SILENCIO PUES! *(Pause.)* The day is dying. The hour has come for me to go. Mis hijos, I leave you with my blessings. *(Blesses them.)* Luna, stand vigil over my cielo through the darkest night, and give light to your hermana, eh?

LUNA: Sí, Jefe, like always.

SOL: Bueno, me voy pues. Bernabé, Tierra, tengan hijos . . . muchos hijos. *(Starts to sink.)*

TIERRA: Buenas noches, Papá.

LUNA: Buenas noches, Jefe.

BERNABÉ: Buenas noches, Señor.

SOL: *(Sinking fast.)* Buenas noches . . . Bernabé! (SOL *is gone. There is a silence.* LA TIERRA *shivers, then* BERNABÉ *and* LA LUNA.)

TIERRA: It's cold.

LUNA: Simón, the Jefito's gone. *(Looks up at the sky.)* Well, I better get up to my chante también. Orale, novios—what kind of moonlight would you like? Something muy romantic y de aquellas?

TIERRA: Never mind. Just leave.

LUNA: Mírala, mírala—just because you got married again! For the zillionth time.

BERNABÉ: *(With a powerful calm.)* Mira, hermano, the time for insults is over. If once I was a loco, now I am a man—and I belong to la Tierra, as she belongs to me. So, good night.

LUNA: Okay, 'ta bien, pues. I gotta get to work anyway. *(Looks up.)* Fat-assed stars! I bet you they're just itching to horn in on Jefe's territory. I better go keep 'em in line. Buenas noches, pues, y don't be afraid to get down and dirty, eh? ¡Orale! (LA LUNA *exits.* LA TIERRA *turns her back on* BERNABÉ.)

TIERRA: ¿Bernabé?

BERNABÉ: ¿Qué?

TIERRA: Will you love me—¿pare siempre?

BERNABÉ: Siempre.

TIERRA: ¡Haste la muerte? *(She turns. Her face is a death mask.)*

BERNABÉ: Hasta la muerte. *(They embrace.)*

Seven

BERNABÉ's *house.* EL TÍO *comes in quickly, looking over his shoulder.* MADRE *is at the door of her house.*

MADRE: Teodoro, ¿qué paso? Did you find m'ijo?

TÍO: What are you doing in the street, hermanita? Get into the house, ándale!

MADRE: ¿Pa' qué? To worry even more?

TÍO: ¡El sol está muy caliente!

MADRE: I don't care if it's hot! What happen with m'ijo?

(Pause.) ¿Qué pasó, pues, hombre? Did they find him? Miserable wino, what good are you? Bernabé's your nephew, but nothing worries you, verdad? Did I tell you to go look in the pozo he made? *(Pause.)* You went, verdad? You know something! ¿Qué pasó, hombre? *(She looks down the street.)* Ay, Teodoro, some men are coming. Eduardo is with them! They're bringing a body. ¡Válgame Dios! (MADRE *starts to run forward.* TÍO *stops her.)*

TÍO: Stay here, hermanita!

MADRE: *(Starting to get hysterical.)* NO, ¡déjame ir! ¡Déjame ir! It's m'ijo. You know it is, ¿verdad? ¿Qué pasó? ¿Qué pasó?

TÍO: Está muerto.

MADR€: ¡Ay! *(Gasps. Can't get breath.)*

TÍO: We found him—buried in the earth. *(TORRES and PRIMO bring in BERNABÉ's body. They lay him down, covered with a canvas. Now MADRE releases a long, sorrowful cry as she leans over the body.)*

MADR€: M'ijo! M'IJITO!

PRIMO: It's all my fault, tío. Fue toda mi culpa.

TÍO: No, hijo, don't blame yourself. You only wanted to help him. This was God's will. Fue por la voluntad de Dios. *(Drums and flutes. In the sky above and behind them, BERNABÉ and LA TIERRA appear in a cosmic embrace. He is naked, wearing only a loincloth. She is Coatlicue, Mother Earth, the Aztec Goddess of Life, Death, and Rebirth.)*

Writings:

Published Plays: *Dark Root of a Scream,* in *From the Barrio: A Chicano Anthology,* edited by Lillian Faderman and Luis Omar Salinas, Canfield Press, 1973. *Bernabé: A Drama of Modern Chicano Mythology,* in *Contemporary Chicano Theatre,* edited by Roberto J. Garza, University of Notre Dame Press, 1975. *The Shrunken Head of Pancho Villa,* in *Necessary Theater: Six Plays about the Chicano Experience,* edited by Jorge Huerta, Arte Público Press, 1989. Individual *actos* in numerous anthologies and textbooks.   **Play Collections:** *Actos by Luis Valdez y El Teatro Campesino,* Cucaracha Press (El Teatro Campesino), 1971. *Luis Valdez and El Teatro Campesino—The Early Works,* Arte Público Press, 1990. *Zoot Suit and Other Plays,* Arte Público Press, 1992.   **Produced Plays (and year first produced):** *The Shrunken Head of Pancho Villa* (1964). *Los vendidos* (one-act; 1967). *Vietnam Campesino* (one-act; 1969). *Soldado Razo* (one-act; 1969); *Actos* (one-act works; 1969–70). *Bernabé* (one-act; 1970). *La virgen del Tepeyac* (musical; 1971). *The Dark Root of a Scream* (one-act; 1971). *La carpa de los Rasquachis* (1974). *El fin del mundo* (1976). *Zoot Suit* (1978). *Bandito: The American Melodrama of Tiburcio Vasquez* (1980). *I Don't Have to Show You No Stinking Badges* (1986).   **Poetry:** *Pensamiento serpentino,* Menyah Publications (El Teatro Campesino), 1973. **Screenplays:** *I Am Joaquín* (1969). *Los Vendidos* (1972). *Zoot Suit* (1981). *Corridos* (1982). *La Bamba* (1987). *La Pastorela* (1991). *The Cisco Kid* (1994).   **Other Selected Writings:** *Aztlán: An Anthology of Mexican-American Literature,* edited with Stan Steiner, Vintage Books, 1972. "The Actos," in *Guerilla Street Theater,* edited by Henry Lesnick, Avon Books, 1973. "From a Pamphlet to a Play," *Performing Arts* (April 1978). "Notes on Chicano Theater," in *People's Theater in Amerika,* edited by Karen Malpede Taylor, Drama Book Specialists, 1972; *Latin American Theatre Review* 4/2 (Spring 1973): 83–87. *El Teatro Campesino: The Evolution of America's First Chicano Theatre Company 1965–1985,* edited by Luis Valdez and El Teatro Campesino, El Teatro Campesino, 1985.

Evangelina Vigil-Piñón

Of all the Chicano poets, Evangelina Vigil-Piñón is the one who has most sensitively portrayed and celebrated working-class culture. She is also one of the leading exponents of bilingual code-switching in poetry (transferring from English to Spanish and back again) which for Vigil-Piñón is as natural as conversation at the kitchen table. Working at the center of U.S. Hispanic literature as the poetry editor for the leading Hispanic literary magazine, The Americas Review, *and as an anthologizer and speaker, Vigil-Piñón is a leader in the Hispanic women's movement.*

Born in San Antonio, Texas, on November 19, 1949, Vigil-Piñón was the second of ten children of a very poor family that lived in public housing for many years. Later in her childhood, Vigil-Piñón lived with her maternal grandmother and uncle, from whom she learned much of the oral lore that became an important basis for her poetry. Vigil-Piñón's mother was also an avid reader who instilled in her daughter a love of books. From her grandmother, she learned "to observe and listen for words of wisdom which come only with experience." And, indeed, the predominant voice in Vigil-Piñón's first full-length book, *Thirty an' Seen a Lot* (1982), is that of the acute but anonymous observer—the observer of the life of working-class people in her beloved West Side barrio of San Antonio, the recorder of their language and diction, their proverbs and music, their joys and sorrows. Despite the apparently natural vernacular of her writing, Vigil-Piñón's poetry is the product of great craftsmanship, which she has achieved through extensive reading and self-education as well as through formal study: Vigil-Piñón earned her B.A. in English from the University of Houston in 1974, and took post-graduate courses at various institutions. She has served as an adjunct faculty member for the University of Houston since the mid 1980s.

Vigil-Piñón is also a talented singer and guitarist whose definition of poetry always includes music:

> To me poetry is music. It is that song in our hearts. Life is the dance to that music.

In addition to that inner song, Vigil-Piñón is a connoisseur of folk and popular music, both of which have influenced her work. But it is the Tejano polka, which often serves as the vehicle for a *corrido* (folk ballad), that has left its indelible mark on her verse.

The Computer Is Down (1987), Vigil-Piñón's second full-length collection, is a departure from her short, sensitive poems depicting the Mexican American barrio in San Antonio. *The Computer Is Down* is dedicated to the fast-paced, high-tech life of Houston, but again from a perspective not far-removed from the working class—and not just of Mexican Americans but of all urban groups. The book represents another important departure for Vigil-Piñón in its experimentation with long, narrative poems, which she uses to portray the dehumanization and oppression that result from life in the urban machine.

Vigil-Piñón's direction has changed once again with poems she recently published in magazines around the country: In part she has returned to her more vernacular voice, but now, within the context of epic narration in verse that tells of the evolution of her people. Since her marriage to artist Mark Piñón in 1985 and the birth of her son Mark Anthony in 1986, Piñón has also been experimenting with children's literature.

> *The predominant voice in* Thirty an' Seen a Lot *is that of an acute but anonymous observer—the observer of the life of working-class people in her beloved West Side barrio of San Antonio, the recorder of their language and diction, their proverbs and music, their joys and sorrows.*

Personal Stats

Chicana television executive, writer. ***Born:*** November 24, 1949, in San Antonio, Texas. ***Education:*** Studied Business Administration, Prairie View A & M University, 1968–70; B.A. in English, University of Houston, 1974. ***Career:*** Variety of employment in arts administration, teaching and community services, 1974–82; counselor, Harris County Courts Victim Assistance Program, 1982–88; public affairs officer, Cultural Arts Council of Houston, 1988–95; community affairs director, ABC network affiliate (KTRK-TV) in Houston, 1995–present. ***Memberships:*** National Association of Hispanic Journalists, National Broadcast Association for Community Affairs. ***Honors/Awards:*** First Place, National Literary Contest, Coordinating Council of Literary Magazines, 1977; National Endowment for the Arts Fellowship, 1979; American Book Award from the Before Columbus Foundation for *Thirty an'*

Seen a Lot, 1983; State Award for Literature, Tribute to Hispanic Women in the Arts, Centro Aztlán, San Antonio, 1984. **Address:** KTRK-TV, Channel 13, PO Box 13, Houston, TX 77001-0013

was fun running 'round descalza

from *Thirty an' Seen a Lot,* Arte Público Press, 1985, pp. 62–63

barefoot is how I always used to be
running barefoot
like on that hot summer

in the San Juan Projects
they spray-painted all the buildings
pastel pink, blue, green, pale yellow, gray
and in cauldrons tar bubbling, steaming
(time to repair the roofs)
its white smoke filling summer air with aromas of nostalgia
for the future
and you, barefoot,
tender feet jumping with precision
careful not to land on nest of burrs or stickers
careful not to tread too long on sidewalks
converted by the scorching sun into comales
"¡se puede freír haste un huevo en esas banquetas!"
exclamaba la gente
ese verano tan caliente
no sooner than had the building wall/canvasses been painted clean did barrio kids take to carv-
    ing new inspirations
and chuco hieroglyphics
and new figure drawings of naked women
and their parts
and messages for all
"la Diana es puta"
"el Lalo es joto"
y que "la Chelo se deja"
decorated by hearts and crosses
and war communications
among rivaling gangs
El Circle
La India
pretty soon kids took to just plain peeling plastic pastel paint
to unveil historical murals
of immediate past well-remembered:
más monas encueradas
and "Lupe loves Tony"
"always and forever"
"Con Safos"
y "Sin Safos"
y que "El Chuy es relaje"
and other innocent desmadres de la juventud
secret fear in every child

que su nombre apareciera allí
y la música de los radios
animando

> "Do you wanna dance under the moonlight?
> Kiss me Baby, all through the night
> Oh, Baby, do you wanna dance?"

was fun running 'round descalza
playing hopscotch
correr sin pisar la líneas—
te vas con el diablo

was fun running 'round descalza
shiny brown legs leaping with precision
to avoid nido de cadillos crowned with tiny blossoms pink
to tread but ever so lightly on scorching cement
to cut across street glistening with freshly laid tar
its steam creating a horizon of mirages
rubber thongs sticking, smelting
to land on cool dark clover carpet green
in your child's joyful mind
"Got to get to la tiendita, buy us
some popsicles and Momma's Tuesday Light!"

was fun running 'round descalza

ser conforme

from *Thirty an' Seen a Lot,* Arte Público Press, 1985, p. 40

my mother made me a beaded necklace
a beaded ring
and also a bracelet
gypsy colors
were the ones she used
indio colors but
fluorescent

and I think to myself
why is it that mothers always know
what kinds of things their daughters like
like when you were small and

she'd come home with two new dresses
one that you just loved
but expensive and
one that didn't strike
your fancy but was
cheaper

Writings

Poetry Books: *Nade y nade,* M & A Editions, 1978. *Thirty an' Seen a Lot,* Arte Público Press, 1982. *The Computer Is Down,* Arte Público Press, 1987. **Poems:** In *Caracol, Hembra: An Anthology of Writings by Chicanas, Canto al Pueblo, The Ethnic American Woman, Imagine, The Americas Review/Revista Chicano-Riqueña,* and numerous other magazines, textbooks, and anthologies. **Other:** Editor, *Woman of Her Word: Hispanic Women Write,* Arte Público Press, 1983. Co-Editor, *The Americas Review.* Writer/director, *Night Vigil* (film), De Colores Productions, 1984. Translator, *. . . y no se lo tragó la tierra,* by Tomás Rivera, Arte Público Press, 1987.

Victor Villaseñor

Through his novel of immigration, Macho!, *which was published in 1973 by the world's largest paperback publisher, Victor Edmundo Villaseñor brought Chicano literature to the widest audience of the American reading public. Villaseñor has continued to reach wide audiences through the television screenplay of* The Ballad of Gregorio Cortez *and through the 1991 publication of the epic saga of his own family in* Rain of Gold.

Born on May 11, 1940, in Carlsbad, California, the son of Mexican immigrants, Villaseñor was raised on a ranch in Oceanside, where he experienced great difficulty in school, having started as a Spanish-speaker and, unknown to his family and teachers, was also dyslexic.

Both my parents are from Mexico and I grew up in a house were there were no books. When I started school, I spoke more Spanish than English. I was a D-student and every year of school made me feel more stupid and confused—many of these feelings had to do with being Chicano. In my junior year of high school, I told my parents I had to quit school or go crazy.

He dropped out of high school and worked on his family's ranch, in other agricultural fields as a farm worker, and as a construction laborer. After attempting college at the University of San Diego for a brief period, he again dropped out and went to live in Mexico, where he discovered the world of books and learned to take pride in his identity and cultural heritage.

I felt good about myself. I wanted to stay in Mexico and never return to the United States where I felt ashamed of being Mexican. But my parents came for me and after weeks of arguments I agreed to go back home for awhile.

Villaseñor did return to southern California, but he found himself "feeling like a bombshell, ready to explode and kill anyone who made me feel ashamed." Back in California, Villaseñor was overcome by a classic conversion to overcompensate precisely for what was most difficult for him, reading and writing:

I would write. Instead of killing or bashing people's brains out, I would change their minds. I would write good books that reach out and touch people and I would influence the world.

In ten years time, during which he supported himself as a construction worker, Villaseñor completed nine novels and sixty-five short stories. After making some 260 submissions to publishing houses, *Macho!* was accepted for publication in 1973 and his career as a professional writer was launched. The next thing he published was *Jury: The People vs. Juan Corona,* (1977) a non-fiction narrative of the life and trial of a serial killer. Villaseñor, aware of the sensationalism and negative stereotypes used to characterize Mexicans in the media, was drawn to the case of Juan Coronoa and he pursued it like an investigative reporter: Villaseñor set out to find out the truth about Juan Corona, to document the trial by jury, and to follow-up with the jurors after the case. But Villaseñor's most important work would come much later, for it took years of research to produce his own family's biography, *Rain of Gold* (1991), which became the very first Chicano best seller.

Rain of Gold was so powerful and important a story that it occupied the next years of literary production for Villaseñor. His collection of stories, *Walking Stars* (1994), was a compilation of additional stories from his family saga, and *Wild Steps of Heaven* (1995) was a "prequel" to *Rain of Gold.*

Macho! follows the classic lines of the immigration novel, but departs from the model in that, upon return to his hometown in central Mexico, the protagonist finds he has been forever changed and is therefore unable to accept the social code in his homeland. The novel tells the tale of one year in the life of Roberto García, a Tarascan Indian teenager from the state of Michoacán, Mexico, who comes to work in the United States without legal documentation. García finds employment in the agricultural fields of California and becomes caught up in the farm-labor organizing movement headed by César Chávez. When García becomes the victim of culture shock, discrimination, and exploitation, he decides to go back to his village, but he returns there a mature and wiser man, unable to accept traditional roles such as that of the *macho.* Specifically, he refuses to take blood vengeance on the man who killed his father. In *Macho!,* Villaseñor was able to take advantage of

"I got a dictionary and a high school English grammar book and I built a desk and I began to read books eight months out of the year. I'd go to book-stores and buy ten books at a time, read them, dissect them, and then reassemble them. Then for four months of the year I'd support myself in construction."

Victor Villaseñor

his first-hand experience with field work and the ever-present conflicts of biculturalism.

Most of the critical appraisal of Rain of Gold *focused on the epic sweep of the story, another chapter in the ongoing saga of the American Dream.*

The critics received *Macho!* exceptionally well, especially given that it was a first novel by a minority writer. The *Los Angeles Times* compared *Macho!* to the best work of John Steinbeck, saying the novel is "poetic in its devotion to realistic detail and classic spareness of style. . . . The relentless, spare detail is stunning, the descriptions of violent encounters among men trying to get across the border in any way possible are terrifying." Jerry Belcher in the *San Francisco Examiner* said, "It rings true. His sentences and his characters have the smell of rich earth and honest sweat about them. His story, too, is direct and exciting."

In his second book, Villaseñor began experimenting with and honing the techniques and research necessary for writing non-fiction. *Jury: The People vs. Juan Corona* is a well-written investigative report on the Corona trial, paying particular attention to the jury deliberations. In 1973, Corona, a labor contractor, was convicted of murdering twenty-five derelicts and drifters. In his narrative, Villaseñor was successful in reconstructing the agonizing and painstaking process the members of the jury underwent to arrive at a verdict. To accomplish a seamless recreation of the events surrounding the trial, Villaseñor conducted months of interviews, which were followed by months of writing—a process that took three years. It was a process that Villaseñor took on because of his concern over the sensationalism surrounding "another Mexican being arrested," and his concern that Corona be treated fairly. Once again, the theme of social justice and the fight against discrimination were paramount in Villaseñor's motives for writing. The *San Diego Union* declared the *Jury* provides "one of the finest insights into the conflicts and emotions of twelve ordinary people deciding the fate of one of their peers that has probably ever been published." *The Sacramento Bee* echoed the comment that is often heard about Villaseñor's non-fiction: "Villaseñor's book is based on fact but reads like a fast-paced suspense novel." The Portland *Oregonian* concluded that *Jury* is "one of the most thorough and authoritative reports on just what a juror in a major case is called upon to do and the great importance of what the jury does."

Rain of Gold chronicles how the Villaseñor family survived the Mexican Revolution and eventually immigrated to establish themselves in California. The style is influenced by myths and oral tradition, derived no doubt from Villaseñor's rearing in the bosom of his extended working-class family, where he heard many stories. The saga of *Rain of Gold* is based on the Villaseñor family lore, but he conducted years of interviews and research in order to write the book.

Rain of Gold follows the maternal and paternal lines of Victor Villaseñor's family until they become unified when his parents meet, court, and marry. The book begins in 1911 in mountainous northwest Mexico in a secluded box canyon where the goldmine named *Lluvia de Oro* (Rain of Gold) indirectly provides a meager living for Villaseñor's maternal grandmother Lupe Gómez and her family. This hard life amid a beautiful, almost magically lush, setting is periodically interrupted by seasonal floods and the surprise raids by marauding soldiers, which have become more frequent as the Mexican Revolution has grown. The main force behind the family's strength is Lupe's mother, Doña Guadalupe, who, through her intelligence and cunning, manages to keep her children together, see her older daughters marry, save her son from execution, and accept her husband back into the family after years of forced absence. At age eleven, a now-mature Lupe and her family are able to leave the canyon and the war-torn goldmine on an arduous journey to the United States.

Part II of *Rain of Gold* begins as an eleven-year-old Juan Villaseñor, his mother, and sisters make their way north to cross the Rio Grande into the United States. They journey on foot and in box cars that are crowded with thousands of other starving refugees of the Revolution. Doña Margarita, Juan's mother, never despairs and despite her temporary blindness and Juan's wild (and occasionally dangerous) antics, keeps the family together and manages to lead them to the border. Once there, the situation is so desperate that Doña Margarita, the grand dame educated in Mexico City, is forced to beg on the streets so that her family can survive. The family finally crosses the border only to become separated on the other side: Juan serves time in prison and escapes to Montana, where he becomes a gambler and adventurer. When he rejoins the family in California, Juan becomes aware of the widespread exploitation of and discrimination against Mexicans. He finds it impossible to work for others under such circumstances and sets on a path to create his own businesses, first as a bootlegger during Prohibition, later in more legitimate enterprises.

Lupe's family, on the other hand, has entered the migrant farmworkers stream up and down the length of California. Lupe has grown into a breathtaking beauty who captures Juan's attention and heart. She, however, is somewhat repelled by the tough and marginally criminal Juan. Lupe vows that she will never marry a man who has anything to do with liquor, violence, or cards. It takes Juan months to work out his courting strategy to win Lupe over, while he hides his illicit bootlegging business—the very enterprise that will allow him to build a grand house like the one the family left behind in Mexico. Despite many reversals and barriers, Juan and his family eventually win Lupe and her family over. It is the women who make the decisions and bring their strength together to forge the new Villaseñor clan. The book ends in an epiphany as Juan and Lupe have the largest and most expensive wedding the barrio has ever seen—a celebration of both their mothers, great women who have survived so much through war and starvation and dislocation.

Over the course of years, most critics have agreed that Villaseñor is a splendid storyteller and that his works reveal real-life experiences and first-hand knowledge. But *Rain of Gold* was greeted with scores of overwhelmingly positive and celebratory reviews in all of the major print and secondary media. *Publishers Weekly* called Villaseñor "a born storyteller, and this, the Latino *Roots*, ". . . a gripping inspirational epic full of wild adventure, bootlegging, young love, tragedies, murder and triumph over cultural barriers." *Kirkus Reviews* stated that the book was "an inspiring, fast-paced tale with a simple, fable-like quality that's often surprisingly moving." *The New York Times* called it "a grand and vivid history." *The Washington Post* called its a "story that deserves to be told, bringing to life a cultural heritage of all Americans." And the *San Francisco Chronicle,* described it as "a bighearted, ambitious book."

Most of the critical appraisal of *Rain of Gold* focused on the epic sweep of the story, another chapter in the ongoing saga of the American Dream. Many a critic also pointed out the narration's indebtedness to the oral tradition of the family. The style owes a great deal to the culture and worldview of working-class people. And the spirituality and faith that undergird the story of survival are derived from a folk culture that is connected to the earth and to both pre-Colombian and Catholic conceptions of God and creation.

For millions of American readers, *Rain of Gold* has brought to life the social, economic, and political struggles that are catalysts for Mexican immigration into the United States. Once here, the epic of Mexican-American life is made up of new stories of racism and discrimination, and the triumph over these barriers.

In *Walking Stars,* his collection of stories for young adult readers, Villaseñor revisits the spirituality of the magical world his parents lived in as children in a very dangerous, revolutionary Mexico. Full of wisdom handed down in the oral tradition, *Walking Stars* engrosses readers in stories about death, dogs' uncanny ability to know when their masters die, his father's indomitable spirit, the power of witches, and how two children set out to kill a tyrant.

"Both original and moving," concluded *Publishers Weekly. Booklist* called *Walking Stars* "an exquisite example of quality literature that helps explain diverse cultures and beliefs while unifying us all within the human family." *The San Diego Union* added, "Villaseñor's vigor is infectious. If at the end the readers come away thinking they can overcome obstacles, then they will feel they will have the magic and power to walk across the stars."

In *Wild Steps of Heaven* Villaseñor goes back in time to follow the development of his father's family during the days just before the Mexican Revolution, when dictator Porfirio Díaz attempted to Europeanize Mexican culture, scorning his country's (and his own) indigenous past and its pastoral society. The family's story illustrates the making of mestizo heritage in Mexico: the struggles of

Villaseñor's grandfather, a pure-blooded Spaniard, and his grandmother, an Indian woman, reflect the struggles bewtween the two heritages. But Villaseñor states that "the book is really about unconditional love and hate. Here's my grandfather with all his arrogance and all his hate, and it's killing him. And here's the woman he married, with all her love for her children, unconditional love and adaptability."

While it was received warmly by the critics and the public at large, *Wild Steps of Heaven* attained neither the outstanding reviews nor public acclaim of *Rain of Gold*.

Personal Stats

Mexican American writer. **Born:** May 11, 1940, in Carlsbad, California. **Education:** Attended University of San Diego and Santa Clara University. **Career:** Construction worker, 1965–70; writer, 1970–present. **Address:** Margaret McBride Agency, 7744 Fay Ave., Ste. 201, La Jolla, CA, 92037

Death of an Assassin

from *Walking Stars: Stories of Magic and Power,* Piñata Books, 1994, pp. 153–78

"The colonel is coming! The colonel is coming!" shouted a young, barefooted boy, running up the cobblestone street of the little settlement.

It was almost dark, and quickly Juan ran into his home, yelling, "Hurry, Mamá! Here comes el coronel!"

Emilia started screaming with terror. The last time the colonel and his men had caught them, they'd raped and beaten Emilia in front of Doña Margarita's very own eyes so that they, the Villaseñors, could see what became of anyone who refused to bow down to authority. But the great woman, Doña Margarita, had not shied away from her responsibilities. No, she'd knelt down and began to pray, refusing to close her eyes to the horrors that these abusive, federal troops put her daughter through. And she had watched them with her eyes wide open and prayed with her rosary in hand, asking God to forgive them and to not blame their mothers whose loins they came from.

Hearing Doña Margarita's words, one soldier had lost his ability to rape Emilia, and he'd become so enraged with the old woman's praying that he'd pulled up his pants and rushed across the room to beat Doña Margarita. But another soldier had knocked him down. Then, in a fit of rage, the federal troops had begun to fight amongst themselves until the colonel had come in and separated them, calling them a bunch of weak fools because they didn't know how to properly treat a woman. The colonel had then yanked Doña Margarita's rosary from her hand and slapped her, calling her "a stupid Indian." And then he tore the rosary to pieces, scattering the well-worn beads to the wind.

Now Luisa and Doña Margarita quickly tried to get Emilia to stop screaming and ushered her out the back door of their home so they could hide in the bushes underneath the wall of the ramada. It was almost dark; there was just a little pink and pale yellow in the western sky painted across the heavens in soft, long horizontal brush strokes. The colonel and his men could be heard entering the village, their horses' hooves echoing on the rock smooth cobblestones. Emilia began to cry again, whimpering like a lost little child. She wanted her doll. Ever since her last beating, nothing could pacify her except her dirty, little, ragged doll. It was a doll that she'd gotten as a child, ordered all the way from Spain, and at one time had been a wondrous Flamenco dancing woman with fine clothes and real blond hair.

"I'll run back inside and get it for her," said Salvador, his heart pounding in deadly fear.

"Oh, no, you don't!" said his mother. "They so much as see one little movement and they'll start shooting! You know how much they still fear us and hate us! No, you stay put!"

"But, Mamá," said Luisa, who was big with child, "if he doesn't go and get her dirty little doll, they'll find us all and maybe even kill us this time. Please, let him go quickly before they get any closer and hear her."

Emilia was crying and whimpering, and the colonel and his troops were halfway up the street now. They were walking slowly, confidently, each horse stepping deliberately—well-shod horses and well-armed men coming down the cobblestones, watching every house, every shadow, as they came. They'd killed almost every male human down to the age of twelve in all the area, and so they figured that they had no one left to fear, fully realizing that the old men and little boys who were left had seen so much bloodshed in the last few years that their hearts were gone out of them.

"Mamá, Luisa is right," said Juan. He was ten years old and he'd been running and hiding and dodging bullets for the last three years of his life. "I've got to do it, and now!"

Quickly, he jumped up and sped out of the bushes, up over the wall, and across the *ramada.* The colonel and his men were only three houses up the street. He had to find his sister's doll and get back into hiding instantly or all would be lost. My God, he was so scared that his little heart was pounding a million miles an hour.

Going inside the house, he glanced all around the kitchen, but didn't see the doll. He rushed to the back, looking through the bed where Emilia and Luisa slept together. Ever since José–Luis' death, Luisa slept with Emilia. That way they could give each other comfort in the quiet of the night.

He found nothing. He rushed into the room where he and his mother slept on another straw mat on the floor. The last time the soldiers had come, they'd taken all their bedding and furniture and set it on fire in the street in front of their home. Oh, these soldiers were determined to show them what became of people who raised sons who dared feast their eyes on the Heavens and think of themselves as having value.

Searching desperately, Juan didn't find the doll there, either. Then he heard his sister's cries and the horses dancing, echoing, their well-shod hooves getting closer and closer. He just knew that they were going to be found. He rushed into the kitchen to get a pan or a knife to throw at the horseman, so that they'd give him chase and not find his mother and sisters. That's when he saw Emilia's doll. Why, it was sitting there on the ledge of the broken kitchen window with the last of the going sunlight reflecting off the doll's fine, smooth face.

Juan snatched up the doll and dashed out to the *ramada,* coming within a few feet of the well-shod horses' hooves. He dropped, crawling alongside the twisted vines of the *ramada,* his chest pounding against the good Earth. And he was just going to drop the doll over the rock wall to his mother and sisters when a soldier heard him and reined in his mount.

"What's that?" shouted the soldier, drawing his pistol and shooting once, twice, three times into the vines of the dark twisting *ramada.*

Hearing the shots, Doña Margarita and her daughters glanced up and saw Juan's hand hanging over the top of the wall above them. His hand opened, letting go of the doll, and then went limp. The old ragged dancing Flamenco woman came tumbling down through the leaves and branches of the bushes into Emilia's starving hands. Immediately, Emilia calmed down as if she'd been given a gift from Heaven. It took every ounce of power for Doña Margarita to not scream out in HORROR! Juan was dead. His hand had gone limp. They could now hear the colonel's huge, bellowing voice.

"Stop wasting your bullets, you fool!" snapped el *coronel*. "This village has nothing worth shooting anymore with our guns!"

The colonel's men laughed and continued down the cobblestone street, shooting now and then and laughing as they went. They'd won; the colonel figured that they'd killed each and every man, woman and child who'd seen him run down the road that night with his fat ass wiggling in awful fear. And anyone who might still be living, the colonel was sure that they wished that they were dead.

■ ■ ■

Late that night, little Pelón, Mateo's youngest brother, who'd given Juan his smooth, good-luck rock on the night of the witch, came to see Juan. The word was out that the federal troops had put three good bullet holes through Juan's body but that his mother, Doña Margarita, the great *curandera,* healer, had slipped the bullet holes from his body to his loose clothing and saved his life. Little Pelón found Juan and his family in the thick trees just down the hill from the town. They were going to sleep outside for a few nights in case the soldiers returned.

After inspecting the three bullet holes in Juan's clothing, just inches away from his neck and left side, Pelón informed Juan that the last of his brothers had been assassinated two days before "They came late in the day as we were eating, but we didn't run," said Pelón, tears coming to his eyes, "because I'm ten and Alfonso was only twelve, and they'd already killed Mateo and all my older brothers. So, well, my mother said, 'Don't run! Just keep eating and they'll leave us alone.' But they didn't. They shot Alfonso as he sat there eating his *taco de frijoles.*"

No one knew what to say. There'd been so much killing in the last couple of years that, my God, there seemed to be no end to it. As soon as a boy began to just show any little sign of manhood, he was executed on the spot. And the word was out that these killings would continue until every man, woman or child with any bad Indian blood was eradicated so that Mexico could then take its proper place among the modern nations of the world.

"Look," Pelón whispered to Juan once the women were asleep, "I've figured out a way to kill the colonel, but I need your help."

Juan glanced around, not wanting his mother and sisters to hear. He got up, and he and Pelón went out to the meadows beyond the trees. The moon was out and the sky was filled with thousands and thousands of stars. Facing each other, they sat down like two little dark stones, and Pelón explained the whole thing to Juan.

"You see, Juan, this is our only chance to do it," said Pelón, "now that *el colonel* figures that he's killed all of us and he's starting to use the same trails each time to come up here."

Juan nodded. He could see that it was a good plan and the right time to do it, now that the colonel was so confident that he was leisurely coming up each time on the easy main trails. But, still, there was the problem of a weapon. Every pistol and rifle had long ago been confiscated by the Federales. There wasn't a weapon to be had in all the mountains.

"No, that's not true," said Pelón. "I saw where my brothers buried a couple of good rifles before, they were killed." He stood up. "Are you in?"

Juan sat there on the ground, looking up at his childhood friend whom he had known since they'd begun to walk. "Yes," said Juan, standing up and taking hold of his friend's hand. "I'm in a *lo macho*!

"*A lo macho*!" repeated Pelón, and he took Juan into his arms, hugging him. Two little boys, each ten years old, and each so scared and torn and worn that they didn't know what else to do.

"Look," added Pelón, wiping his eyes, "with you at my side, Juan, what can possibly go wrong? You're the one who faced La Bruja single-handedly and took three of the colonel's best bullets and didn't even lose a drop of blood! Nothing can go wrong, I tell you. It's done! Day after tomorrow, before the sun is chest high, *el coronel* will be dead, and this land will be free once again!"

And they held each other in a long *abrazo,* both knowing fully well that they really had not one chance in hell of pulling this off. But there was nothing else that they could do, for tomorrow they'd get a little hair on their upper lip or just a little bit taller, and then it would be their turn to be executed. Now, only while they were still children, did they have any chance whatsoever of succeeding.

■ ■ ■

Two days later, Juan met Pelón down in the deep gulleys north of town. It was late afternoon; they only had a couple more hours of good daylight. "Did you tell anyone?" asked Pelón. Pelón, meaning "bald-headed," had such a big, thick mane of wild hair that everyone had teased him about his hair ever since he could remember, saying that all the forests of the world would be gone before Pelón went bald.

"No," said Juan. "I told no one."

"Not even your mother?" asked Pelón.

Juan resented this question. "Especially not my mother!" he snapped. "My God, she'd be out of her head with worry if I'd told her what we were about!"

"All right, calm down," said Pelón. "Calm down. I was just checking. We can't be too careful with what we're about to do."

"Did you get the rifle?" asked Juan.

"Sure. I got it over there in those rocks, wrapped in a serape and covered with leaves."

Juan glanced over to the pile of large boulders and could see nothing. He was glad that Pelón had hidden the weapon well. After all, they didn't want to be seen lugging a rifle around the countryside. He glanced back at Pelón. There was something different about this childhood friend of his; his eyes were not the eyes of a young boy anymore.

"Come," said Pelón, "we'll go over my plan once more. You have Don Pío's blood in your veins, just like your brother José, so you should have a head for strategy. Oh, my brothers would marvel at José's strategy of battle. Our brothers, they were great, weren't they?" he added.

"Yes," said Juan. And he almost added, "If only they had lived." But he didn't say this. He held. They went over to the boulders and hunched down out of sight, warmed a couple of *taquitos,* and ate as they spoke. The sun was finally going down, and they could soon travel without being seen.

Pelón's plan was simple. He'd been watching the federal troops for days now, and he'd come to realize that the colonel and his men were coming up from the lowlands on the same trail. And, every time, they'd rest their horses three-fourths of the way up the mountain in a little basin where there was water and grass. The colonel had also gotten in the habit of walking a little way away from his men to take a crap over a large, fallen log, from where he could keep watch on the trail above and below him.

"So, you see," Pelón had explained to Juan, "all we got to do is get there the night before and bury me in the dirt and cover me with leaves and broken branches. Then, in the morning, when he has his pants down and he's shifting, I'll just rise up and shoot him dead from a distance of about ten feet, so I'll be sure not to miss."

The plan could work, Juan was sure of it, if only he covered Pelón up correctly with the leaves and branches and the colonel came the same way and took his same crap and Pelón didn't lose his nerve.

"Look," said Juan, "I've been thinking your plan over very carefully, and I really do think that it can work. But, well, it's going to take a lot of nerve for you to stay there quietly all night and then to not panic or make a single move when the colonel and his men ride up, making so much noise and trampling all around you with their horses."

"I got the nerve," said Pelón. "Believe me, I got the nerve. After they killed Mateo and all my brothers, I've been thinking of nothing else but this!

"You know," he said, a strange calmness coming to his eyes, "*el coronel* is right. There isn't ever going to be peace in Mexico until they kill every one of us, damn their wretched souls!"

Juan was taken aback. He hadn't expected this hate, this power, this conviction, to come from one of his own playmates who was so young. But he could now see that he'd been kidding himself. For he, too, was raging mad inside, wanting to kill, to destroy this damned colonel and all his men. Oh, the abuses, the absolute horrors that these men had committed in the name of law and order were monstrous!

"All right," said Juan, "I agree with you that there isn't going to be peace in Mexico until somebody is killed, but it's not going to be us. It's them who must die. They don't work the fields, they don't protect their homes and families, so it's them who must go. We have to live as my brother José said. We, the meek, who give heart and soul and the sweat off our backs to our sacred piece of Earth."

"You're right," said Pelón. "And that's why we must do this. Let's go."

"Just wait," said Juan. "I want to see the rifle. Also, after I bury you, how will you know when to raise up and start shooting, especially if I bury you so well that you can't see and you can't be seen, either?"

Pelón was stumped. But not for long. "I guess I'll know to come up shooting when I hear his first shits and farts."

Both boys started laughing.

"Then, let's hope he eats well tonight and drinks a lot so he'll be shifting and farting big and loud tomorrow," added Juan, laughing all the more.

And so there they went, two little boys, lugging an old *retrocarga,* homemade shotgun, that hadn't been fired in years, to do in the most famous bad men of all the region. The sun was down now and the western sky was painted in long streaks of pink and rose and yellow and gold. The clouds were banked up against the distant mountain called El Serro Gordo, The Fat Mountain, and all the rolling little hills and valleys between that distant mountain and their own great mountain called El Serro Grande, The Big Mountain, were green and lush, looking so beautiful and peaceful.

The two little boys began to whistle as they went. They were absolutely stout-hearted in their belief that they would succeed, and so they were happy.

Overhead, the last of the great flocks of fork tailed blackbirds came swooping by on their way to roost in the tall grasses by the shallow mountain lakes. It had been another good day on God's sacred Earth, and she, the Night, was now approaching in all her splendor and magic. The first few stars were beginning to make themselves known, shining brightly in the heavens. Oh, it was good to be alive, holding your head high and feasting your eyes upon the wondrous evening sky with your heart full of hope and glory.

■ ■ ■

No one knew where Juan was, and Doña Margarita was becoming very anxious. She wondered if her little son's disappearance had anything to do with Pelón having come by the night before. She decided to call Luisa back from looking for Juan. She just had this little quiet feeling deep inside herself that the two boys were up to something, and so maybe it was best not to draw anymore attention to the fact that Juan was missing.

Doña Margarita took in hand what was left of her father's once-fine handmade rosary and went outside to pray. The sun was gone and the night was coming, and soon it would be dark. Doña Margarita began to pray, releasing her soul to God and knowing deep inside of herself that all would turn out for the Sacred Good, if only she kept faith and allowed God to do His work, and let herself bend with the turns and twists of life, and not take too seriously those fears that kept coming up inside her weak, human mind. For she well knew that the turns and twists of life could never be understood with the head, but had to be felt by the heart and allowed to blossom with the wisdom of one's God given soul.

Oh, if it weren't for her complete faith in God, she was sure that she never could've survived that terrible day that the colonel and his men had abused Emilia. But, with her feet well-planted in the rich soil of the Mother Earth, she had endured and she'd been able to go on, just as she was going to go on now. This was the power of living; this was the power of bringing in God's light with every breath one took. To fill one's being with so much light that no little, dark, sneaky thought of fear or doubt could reside in one's entire being.

Doña Margarita now continued praying, eyes focused on the Father Sky and feet planted in the Mother Earth, not really knowing where her little boy was, but fully realizing that her soul was gone from her body, having been released to God's infinite powers, and her soul would somehow find the means with which to help her son. She prayed and the Universe listened and the stars brightened.

■ ■ ■

Going down through the trees, the two boys dropped into the little basin. It was dark now, and they needed to move slowly, carefully, and not leave any signs of having passed through there. Grass was in the open places and leaves and broken branches were under the trees. Then, they heard a sound. They froze, not moving a muscle, and glanced around, but only with their eyes—barely moving their heads or bodies.

Two eyes were watching them from over there by two trees. They couldn't quite make out what the two eyes were until they saw the flicker of the ears. Then they knew that it was a deer. In fact, they could now make out that it was a doe and her fawn, which had stepped out from behind her.

"*Mira, mira,*" said Pelón, blowing out with relief. Both boys had been holding their breath in deadly fear. "I thought maybe it was a tiger, or maybe even a soldier. You know, if the colonel was smart," continued Pelón, "he would leave a group of soldiers behind to keep track of their trails. That's what I'll do when I join Villa," he added with *gusto.*

"You're going to join Pancho Villa?" asked Juan, also feeling relieved that it had turned out to be only a deer.

"Sure, of course. It's either join the rebels or continue to stay up here all alone in these God-forsaken mountains until they hunt us all down. It's not going to stop with us killing the colonel, you know. They'll be sending others."

"Well, then, why are we doing this?" asked Juan. He'd assumed that once they'd gotten rid of *el coronel* it would all be over.

"Because the BAS . . ." Pelón began shouting in anger.

Just then, the doe leaped, looking behind her, and was off in large, graceful bounds. Her fawn went right after her in small, tight prancing leaps. Both boys crouched down, holding deadly still. They couldn't see what had startled the doe, but they were terrified once again. Pelon signaled Juan to follow him, and they moved quietly along the ground, their little hearts beating wildly.

Crawling into the brush, they lay down, chests against the good Earth. Juan drew close to Pelón's right ear and whispered, "Look, maybe we shouldn't bury you right now. I think maybe we should wait until daybreak, when we can see better. That doe was really frightened."

"Maybe it was just because I raised my voice," said Pelón.

"Maybe," said Juan, "but maybe not. I think we should wait."

"I don't know," whispered Pelón. "They've been coming by here pretty early."

"Yes, but what if the situation doesn't look right in the morning? Once you're buried, Pelón, that's it. We can't just uncover you. I think we better wait until daylight so we can see. Then I can bury you carefully and fix up the area so it looks like nobody has been here."

Pelón glanced around, thinking over the situation, then said, "Okay, I'll trust your judgment, Juan, but I just hope he doesn't come by too early and catch us sleeping."

"He won't," said Juan. "Remember, he's going to eat and drink a lot tonight, so he'll fart big and loud for us tomorrow!"

Both boys laughed quietly, trying hard to keep their voices down. They still didn't know what had startled the doe, and they wanted to be very careful.

"You know," said Juan, glancing up at the star-studded heavens, "I think we should maybe pray."

"You still pray," asked Pelón, "after all that's happened to our families?"

At first Juan was taken aback by Pelón's question, but then he recovered and said, "Yes, of course. In fact, at home we probably pray more now than ever before." And so Juan knelt there in the brush where they were hiding and began to pray, with Pelón only watching. Overhead the stars continued blinking, winking, giving wonderment and beauty.

"Come on," said Juan to Pelón, "join me. In the morning, we'll have plenty of time to do everything."

"All right," said Pelón. "I hope you're right."

And so now, both boys were praying together. The doe came back down into the grassy meadow and began to graze once again. Whatever had frightened her was gone now. Upon seeing the doe and her fawn return, the boys felt better and finished up their prayers, feeling good and confident once again.

"And so, *buenas noches,* dear God," said Juan, finishing his prayer, "and let us sleep in peace and keep us well throughout the night."

"And help us tomorrow," added Pelón, "that we not fail, for we are pure of heart and only wish to protect our homes and families."

Making the sign of the cross over themselves, the two boys came out from the brush and stood up in the clearing by the doe and her little fawn. It was a magnificent night, filled with thousands of bright stars and not a single cloud. The doe and her fawn looked at the two small boys, but didn't bolt. The two animals seemed very much at peace once again.

"I wonder," said Juan, "if animals pray, too. Look how relaxed and happy they are now."

"Animals don't pray," said Pelón, laughing. "What are you, *loco?*"

"No," said Juan, "my mother has always told us that praying calms the heart, and look how peaceful those deer are now."

Pelón glanced at the deer and then back at Juan. "Did your mother really move those bullet holes from your body to your clothes? You know, everyone is starting to say that your mother is the real *bruja* of our region, but that she's a good witch because she goes to church every day."

"My mother is no *bruja!*" snapped Juan.

"Look, I didn't mean to offend you," said Pelón. "It's just that, well, did she move those bullets from your body to your clothes?"

Juan didn't want to answer. He'd been out cold when they'd taken him inside. "I don't know," he said. "I was told that the one bullet hit so close to my head that I was knocked out. But, yes, that's what they were saying when I came to. They said that they'd seen the other two bullets in my body, and I was dead until my mother lit the candles and put her hands on me and started praying."

"Then your mother really is a witch," said Pelón, making the sign of the cross over himself, eyes large with wonder.

"No, she isn't!" said Juan. "Women just come from the moon—you know that. And, well, when they show their power, and the men see that they can't move them, people start calling them witches. But they're not. They're just women, damn it! My mother is no witch! Not any more than yours!"

"Don't call my mother a witch!" yelled Pelón.

"Well, then, don't call mine one, either. Hell, your mother has done wonders, too. No one can figure out how she keeps your corn growing, even after the soldiers trample and burn it."

Pelón calmed down. "All right," he said, "you're right. My mother does wonders, too, so I won't call your mother, well, a *bruja* anymore. But tell me, Juan, how come you know so much about all this?" asked the boy, his eyes still huge with fear. "You aren't a brujo, are you?"

"Of course not," said Juan, getting really tired of the whole subject. "It's just that each night when my mother puts us to bed, she tells us stories."

"What kind of stories?"

"Well, stories about the magic of life. Stories that give us hope and strength, wings of understanding, so no matter how awful the world gets all around us, we'll always still feel the power of God's breath . . . giving us light, just like those stars and moon give light to the darkness."

"I see," said Pelón. "I see. Just like those stars and moon, eh?"

"Yes," said Juan. "Just like those stars and moon."

The fawn had come closer to the two boys. It was obvious that Pelón still wasn't too sure about Juan and had a thousand more questions, but Juan wanted no more of this. He was exhausted. Ever since that soldier had shot at him, everyone had been asking him what his mother had done to him and if it was true that she'd brought him back from the dead.

"I'm tired," said Juan. "I think we better find a place to bed down for the night so we can go to sleep.

"Look, the little fawn wants to smell us," added Juan, smiling and putting his hand out to the little deer. The fawn stretched out his neck, sniffing Juan's fingertips. "You know, I bet animals really do pray in their own way," said Juan. "That's how they're able to live surrounded by lions and all these other dangers but still live in such peace and happiness."

"Maybe you're right," said Pelón, feeling that no deer would come this close to a real witch because wild animals—it was well-known—could see what lurked inside a human's heart. "Come on, I'm tired, too. Let's go over to that huge tree by the fallen log where the colonel does his *caca* and find a place to sleep."

"Okay," said Juan, getting to his feet slowly. He didn't want to startle the little deer.

Both boys now went over to the huge tree by the fallen log where the colonel had been relieving himself each time he came up the mountain. They got down between the thick, bare roots of the tree that some pigs had uprooted, creating a little hollow. They wanted to get out of the wind and cold so that they could get a good night's rest.

The fawn, who'd been watching them, saw them disappear into the hollow and came over to see what had happened to them. The doe followed her fawn and saw the two boys going to sleep. She took up ground, standing over the boys and her fawn like a sentry.

Juan remembered opening his eyes once and seeing the mother deer standing over them, and he just knew that his mother had come to protect them in the form of a mother deer. But he didn't say anything about this to Pelón. He didn't want to confuse things any more than they already were. High overhead, the stars were blinking, winking by the thousands, and the moon gave her magic light, too. It had been another good day and now it was becoming a good night. There were no witches or other evils on the other side. No, there was just the fear and jealousy that people took with them in their souls.

"*Buenas noches*," said Juan to the miracle of the heavens. "And thank you, Mamá," he said to the mother deer. He breathed more easily and went back to sleep, feeling safe, and dreamed of green meadows and happy deer praying to the Almighty.

■ ■ ■

The two boys were fast asleep when they first heard the snorts of the colonel's horses coming up the steep grade. Quickly, they opened their eyes, not knowing what to do. Oh, my God, they'd been caught with their pants down. And now they couldn't just jump up and take off running or they'd be spotted and shot down for sure. They glanced at each other, then raised up their heads as much as they dared and looked between the displaced tree roots. They saw that the soldiers were already in the basin. Some were already off their horses and putting them to graze. Others were taking their mounts down to the water to drink. Then, they heard the colonel's big, powerful voice and realized that he was directly behind them. But they didn't dare turn around to look.

"Take my horse!" shouted *el coronel,* belching loudly. He sounded like a man with a bad stomach. "Over there, over there. Get the hell away from me!"

They could hear the soldier doing as he was told, grabbing the reins of the colonel's horse and quickly leading him off, coming so close to them that they could see the horse's hooves passing by as they looked from under the big roots of the huge tree. Then, here came the colonel himself, passing by them even closer, his tall, leather boots glistening in the early morning light. He was grabbing tree branches as he passed, causing leaves to fall, and belching with every step. Oh, he was in terrible shape. They could smell the sour odor coming off of him.

Juan and Pelón glanced at each other and, if they hadn't been so terrified, they would've burst out laughing. This was exactly what they'd wanted. They couldn't have asked for it any better. Then, there was the colonel, only fifteen feet away from them, unbuckling his gun belt and dropping his pants. He turned away from them and barely got his big white ass over the fallen log before he began to shit with enormous-sounding explosions.

Quickly, Pelón reached under himself, bringing up the rifle, which was still wrapped in the serape. He tried to unwrap the weapon as quickly and quietly as he could, but he was having trouble working within the small confines of the little hollow.

Juan kept glancing at the colonel, praying to God, "Oh, please, dear God," he said to himself, "let him be so full of farts and caca that he doesn't stop shifting and can't hear us!"

Finally, Pelón had the weapon uncovered, but it was pointing in the wrong direction. Quickly, he tried turning it around, hitting Juan in the face with the barrel.

Seeing the huge barrel of the homemade retrocarga, Juan blurted out, "That's it? That's our weapon?"

"Quiet!" whispered Pelón under his breath as he shoved the huge weapon between the roots, pointing it at the colonel's back side.

"But it won't shoot!" said Juan. "I thought we had a real rifle!"

But Pelón wasn't paying attention to Juan anymore, and he now cocked back the two big hammers and spoke out loud. "*Coronel*," he said in a clear, good voice, "I'm Mateo's little brother!"

And, as the colonel turned to see who had the audacity to come up behind him and bother him while he relieved himself, Pelón pulled both triggers. But nothing happened; the hammers just didn't move.

Instantly, the colonel saw the situation: two little boys with an old retrocarga from the days of Benito Juárez, hunched down under a bunch of big tree roots, trying to kill him. Quick as a cat, he pulled up his pants and reached for his gun belt. But, at that very instant, Juan hit the two hammers with a stone, and the old weapon EXPLODED, pipe-barrel splitting in two and a fountain of rock and used little pieces of iron shooting towards the colonel. The two boys were thrown back with the explosion of the weapon, smashing Pelón against the dirt across the hollow. The colonel was thrown over backwards across the log. Instantly, his men were shouting and taking cover, returning fire.

Crawling out of the hollow, Juan was up and trying to clear his head so they could take off running. But what he saw Pelón do next was something he'd never forget. Pelon didn't run. No, he cleared his head and ran over to the colonel, who was squirming about in terrible pain, took the colonel's gun from his gun belt and emptied the pistol into his naked, bloated belly. The soldiers' bullets sang all around Pelón's head, but he never gave them any importance. Only when he saw that the great bad man was dead did Pelón throw down the gun and come running towards Juan. Then they were off like deer, running down through the brush and trees as the soldiers continued shooting at them.

"I killed him!" yelled Pelón, as they ran. "I killed him and he looked me in the eyes and knew who I was before he died! Oh, it was wonderful!"

Some of the soldiers got on their horses and tried to give chase, but the two boys knew these mountains like the back of their hands and cut through the breaks, leaping from boulder to boulder, leaving the armed men far behind. Finally, they were down in the deep canyons where the wild orchids grew, and they were going to start back up the mountainside when they came upon the doe and her little fawn once again. The deer had been bedded down.

"Wait," said Juan. "Maybe this is a good place for us to hole up for the day. We don't want to get up on top and run into the soldiers or someone who might turn us in to them."

"Who'd turn us in?" asked Pelón. He was so excited that he was ready to pop. "I killed him! I killed him! Oh, my God, it was wonderful! Seeing him squirm around, I put a bullet into his fat belly for every one of my brothers! We did it, Juan! We really did it!"

"Yes, we did. But now we got to keep calm so we don't get killed, too. Come, let's get up on that ridge and bed down like the deer do and keep very quiet 'til nighttime."

And they'd no more than hidden themselves when here came five mounted soldiers down into the bottom of the canyon with an old Indian leading them on foot. The two boys held their breath, watching them pass by down below in the trees. Once, the Indian stopped and glanced up in their direction, but then he just went on down the canyon bottom, leading the soldiers away.

"Did you see how *el indio* looked up towards us?" asked Pelón.

"Yes," said Juan. "He knows we're up here. We better go before they circle above us and come in from behind."

The two boys took off up the ridge as fast as they could go, startling the doe and her fawn, who'd bedded down above them.

"You better run, too!" said Juan to the deer as they went racing by them.

But the deer didn't run with them. Instead, they ran downhill. Juan and Pelón were coming off the top of the ridge when they heard the shooting down below.

Juan stopped "They shot the deer," he said.

"How do you know?" asked Pelón.

"I just know," said Juan, tears coming to his eyes.

And he took off racing for home as fast as he could go. He had to see if his beloved dear old mother was all right.

Two days later, Pelón disappeared. It was rumored that he'd joined Francisco Villa's army and had been given the rank of Captain, making him the youngest officer Villa had ever welcomed into his armed forces.

Writings

Novels: *Macho!* Bantam, 1973; Arte Público Press, 1992. *Rain of Gold,* Arte Público Press, 1991; *Lluvia de Oro,* Delta, 1996. *Wild Steps of Heaven,* Delacorte, 1996. **Nonfiction:** *Jury: The People vs. Juan Corona,* Little, Brown, 1977. **Short Stories:** *Walking Stars: Stories of Magic and Power,* Arte Público Press, 1994. Also in *Short Fiction by Hispanic Writers of the United States, Hispanic American Literature,* and elsewhere. **Screenplay:** *The Ballad of Gregorio Cortez* 1983.

Helena María Viramontes

Helena María Viramontes is one of Hispanic literature's most distin-guished craftspersons of short fiction. Her writing career began while she was still young and was affiliated with the avant garde Chicano magazine ChismeArte. She was the literary editor of that streetwise mag-azine, the whole of which was emblematic of her own writing style—in touch with her upbringing on the streets of East Los Angeles and very hip, but polished owing to her creative writing and film studies.

Viramontes was born on February 26, 1954, in East Los Angeles, one of eight siblings in a working-class family. She graduated from East L.A.'s Garfield High School and, in 1975, graduated from Immaculate Heart College with a B.A. in English. Her love of literature led her to study English and creative writing over the next two decades. Her work as a writer was put on hiatus when she married and became the mother of two children, to whom she devoted most of her time. In 1994, almost a decade after the publication of her first book, she finished her Masters of Fine Arts in creative writing. By the time she had her M.F.A. degree in hand, Viramontes was already a force on the Hispanic literary scene, and her works had been canonized in some of the most important textbooks and anthologies, includ-ing those used by academia.

Viramontes creates highly crafted tales of women struggling to make their lives in the barrios. However, her imagery, as in "The Moths," is often classically based and her command of language reveals years of hard study and her works are the result of numerous drafts. Viramontes's powerful writing is based in politics and are ground in the sociological reality of working-class Latinas. In her conscious effort to give voice to women through her stories, she is personally battling and subverting patriarchal practices. Sonia Saldívar-Hull wrote, "Her groundbreaking narrative strategies, combined with her sociopolitical focus, situate her at the forefront of an emerging Chicana literary tradition that redefines Chicano literature and feminist theory." The feminist journal, *Belles Lettres,* added:

> Viramontes's stories convey the impact of repression on women's lives and graph-
> ically depict the price paid by women who dare to challenge a misogynist social system
> that moves rapidly to squelch their every attempt toward self-definition . . .The result is
> a rich, challenging narrative that rewards the reader with insight to the passions and
> torments that drive the characters.

Under the Feet of Jesus, Viramontes's first and only novel, is an apparently simple and direct narrative that follows the life of a thirteen-year-old migrant worker girl, but soon becomes an indictment of corporate agriculture in California and its practices of child labor and pesticide poisoning. The book is narrated from the point of view of the young girl, Estrella, who also questions the limitations placed on her as a female. Reviewers see Viramontes as working in the social realist vein of John Steinbeck and Upton Sinclair. But despite the brutal disregard for life by agricultural companies which she portrays in *Under the Feet of Jesus, The Bloomsbury Review* said that, "Her lush, precise prose lends beauty to this world and shows us that the struggle for dignity is as vital a struggle as survival."

Personal Stats

Chicana writer, professor. Born: February 26, 1954, in East Los Angeles. *Education:* B.A., Fine Arts and English, Immaculate Heart College, 1975; attended University of California, Los Angeles, 1975; M.F.A. in Creative Writing, University of California, Irvine, 1994. *Career:* Assistant professor, Creative Writing Program, Cornell University, 1994 to present. *Awards/Honors:* First Prize for fiction, *Statement Magazine,* California State University, Los Angeles, 1977; First Prize for fiction, University of California, Irvine Chicano Literary Contest, 1979; National Endowment for the Arts Fellowship, 1989; Sundance Institute Storytelling Award, 1989; Robert McKee Story Structure Award, National Latino Communications Center, 1991; finalist, Women Script Writing Project, Paul Robeson Fund Exchange, 1991; finalist, Chesterfield Film Company, Universal Studios, 1991; National Association of Chicano Studies Certificate of Distinguished Recognition, 1993. *Address:* English Department, Cornell University, Ithaca, NY 14853

"Her groundbreaking narrative strategies, combined with her sociopolitical focus, situate her at the forefront of an emerging Chicana literary tradition that redefines Chicano literature and feminist theory."

Sonia Saldívar-Hull

The Moths

from *The Moths and Other Stories,* Arte Público Press, 1995, pp. 26–32

I was fourteen years old when Abuelita requested my help. And it seemed only fair. Abuelita had pulled me through the rages of scarlet fever by placing, removing and replacing potato slices on the temples of my forehead; she had seen me through several whippings, an arm broken by a dare-jump off Tío Enrique's toolshed, puberty, and my first lie. Really, I told Amá, it was only fair.

Not that I was her favorite granddaughter or anything special. I wasn't even pretty or nice like my older sisters and I just couldn't do the girl things they could do. My hands were too big to handle the fineries of crocheting or embroidery and I always pricked my fingers or knotted my colored threads time and time again while my sisters laughed and called me bull hands with their cute waterlike voices. So I began keeping a piece of jagged brick in my sock to bash my sisters or anyone who called me bull hands. Once, while we all sat in the bedroom, I hit Teresa on the forehead, right above her eyebrow, and she ran to Amá with her mouth open, her hand over her eye while blood seeped between her fingers. I was used to the whippings by then.

I wasn't respectful either. I even went so far as to doubt the power of Abuelita's slices, the slices she said absorbed my fever. "You're still alive, aren't you?" Abuelita snapped back, her pasty gray eye beaming at me and burning holes in my suspicions. Regretful that I had let secret questions drop out of my mouth, I couldn't look into her eyes. My hands began to fan out, grow like a liar's nose until they hung by my side like low weights. Abuelita made a balm out of dried moth wings and Vicks and rubbed my hands, shaping them back to size. It was the strangest feeling. Like bones melting. Like sun shining through the darkness of your eyelids. I didn't mind helping Abuelita after that, so Amá would always send me over to her.

In the early afternoon Amá would push her hair back, hand me my sweater and shoes, and tell me to go to Mama Luna's. This was to avoid another fight and another whipping, I knew. I would deliver one last direct shot on Marisela's arm and jump out of our house, the slam of the screen door burying her cries of anger, and I'd gladly go help Abuelita plant her wild lilies or jasmine or heliotrope or cilantro or hierbabuena in red Hills Brothers coffee cans. Abuelita would wait for me at the top step of her porch holding a hammer and nail and empty coffee cans. And although we hardly spoke, hardly looked at each other as we worked over root transplants, I always felt her gray eye on me. It made me feel, in a strange sort of way, safe and guarded and not alone. Like God was supposed to make you feel.

On Abuelita's porch, I would puncture holes in the bottom of the coffee cans with a nail and a precise hit of a hammer. This completed, my job was to fill them with red clay mud from beneath her rose bushes, packing it softly, then making a perfect hole, four fingers round, to nest a sprouting avocado pit, or the spidery sweet potatoes that Abuelita rooted in mayonnaise jars with toothpicks and daily water, or prickly chayotes that produced vines that twisted and wound all over her porch pillars, crawling to the roof, up and over the roof, and down the other side, making her small brick house look like it was cradled within the vines that grew pear-shaped squashes ready for the pick, ready to be steamed with onions and cheese and butter. The roots would burst out of the rusted coffee cans and search for a place to connect. I would then feed the seedlings with water.

But this was a different kind of help, Amá said, because Abuelita was dying. Looking into her gray eye, then into her brown one, the doctor said it was just a matter of days. And so it seemed only fair that these hands she had melted and formed found use in rubbing her caving body with alcohol and marihuana, rubbing her arms and legs, turning her face to the window so that she could watch the Bird of Paradise blooming or smell the scent of clove in the air. I toweled her face frequently and held her hand for hours. Her gray wiry hair hung over the mattress. Since I could remember, she'd kept her long hair in braids. Her mouth was vacant and when she slept, her eyelids never closed all the way. Up close, you could see her gray eye beaming out the window, staring hard as if to remember everything. I never kissed her. I left the window open when I went to the market.

Across the street from Jay's Market there was a chapel. I never knew its denomination, but I went in just the same to search for candles. I sat down on one of the pews because there were none. After I cleaned my fingernails, I looked up at the high ceiling. I had forgotten the vastness of these places, the coolness of the marble pillars and the frozen statues with blank eyes. I was alone. I knew why I had never returned.

That was one of Apá's biggest complaints. He would pound his hands on the table, rocking the sugar dish or spilling a cup of coffee and scream that if I didn't go to Mass every Sunday to save my goddamn sinning soul, then I had no reason to go out of the house, period. Punto final. He would grab my arm and dig his nails into me to make sure I understood the importance of catechism. Did he make himself clear? Then he strategically directed his anger at Amá for her lousy ways of bringing up daughters, being disrespectful and unbelieving, and my older sisters would pull me aside and tell me if I didn't get to Mass right this minute, they were all going to kick the holy shit out of me. Why am I so selfish? Can't you see what it's doing to Amá, you idiot? So I would wash my feet and stuff them in my black Easter shoes that shone with Vaseline, grab a missal and veil, and wave goodbye to Amá.

I would walk slowly down Lorena to First to Evergreen, counting the cracks on the cement. On Evergreen I would turn left and walk to Abuelita's. I liked her porch because it was shielded by the vines of the chayotes and I could get a good look at the people and car traffic on Evergreen without them knowing. I would jump up the porch steps, knock on the screen door as I wiped my feet and call Abuelita, mi Abuelita? As I opened the door and stuck my head in, I would catch the gagging scent of toasting chile on the place. When I entered the sale, she would greet me from the kitchen, wringing her hands in her apron. I'd sit at the corner of the table to keep from being in her way. The chiles made my eyes water. Am I crying? No, Mama Luna, I'm sure not crying. I don't like going to mass, but my eyes watered anyway, the tears dropping on the table-cloth like candle wax. Abuelita lifted the burnt chiles from the fire and sprinkled water on them until the skins began to separate. Placing them in front of me, she turned to check the menudo. I peeled the skins off and put the flimsy, limp-looking green and yellow chiles in the molcajete and began to crush and crush and twist and crush the heart out of the tomato, the clove of garlic, the stupid chiles that made me cry, crushed them until they turned into liquid under my bull hand. With a wooden spoon, I scraped hard to destroy the guilt, and my tears were gone. I put the bowl of chile next to a vase filled with freshly cut roses. Abuelita touched my hand and pointed to the bowl of menudo that steamed in front of me. I spooned some chile into the menudo and rolled a corn tortilla thin with the palms of my hands. As I ate, a fine Sunday breeze entered the kitchen and a rose petal calmly feathered down to the table.

I left the chapel without blessing myself and walked to Jay's. Most of the time Jay did-n't have much of anything. The tomatoes were always soft and the cans of Campbell soups had rusted spots on them. There was dust on the tops of cereal boxes. I picked up what I needed: rub-bing alcohol, five cans of chicken broth, a big bottle of Pine Sol. At first Jay got mad because I thought I had forgotten the money. But it was there all the time, in my back pocket.

When I returned from the market, I heard Amá crying in Abuelita's kitchen. She looked up at me with puffy eyes. I placed the bags of groceries on the table and began putting the cans of soup away. Amá sobbed quietly. I never kissed her. After a while, I patted her on the back for com-fort. Finally: "¿Y mi Amá?" she asked in a whisper, then choked again and cried into her apron.

Abuelita fell off the bed twice yesterday, I said, knowing that I shouldn't have said it and wondering why I wanted to say it because it only made Amá cry harder. I guess I became angry and just so tired of the quarrels and beatings and unanswered prayers and my hands just there hanging helplessly by my side. Amá looked at me again, confused, angry, and her eyes were filled with sorrow. I went outside and sat on the porch swing and watched the people pass. I sat there until she left. I dozed off repeating the words to myself like rosary prayers: when do you stop giv-ing when do you start giving when do you . . . and when my hands fell from my lap, I awoke to catch them. The sun was setting, an orange glow, and I knew Abuelita was hungry.

There comes a time when the sun is defiant. Just about the time when moods change, inevitable seasons of a day, transitions from one color to another, that hour or minute or second when the sun is finally defeated, finally sinks into the realization that it cannot with all its power to heal or burn, exist forever, there comes an illumination where the sun and earth meet, a final burst of burning red orange fury reminding us that although endings are inevitable, they are necessary for rebirths, and when that time came, just when I switched on the light in the kitchen to open Abuelita's can of soup, it was probably then that she died.

The room smelled of Pine Sol and vomit, and Abuelita had defecated the remains of her cancerous stomach. She had turned to the window and tried to speak, but her mouth remained open and speechless. I heard you, Abuelita, I said, stroking her cheek, I heard you. I opened the win-dows of the house and let the soup simmer and overboil on the stove. I turned the stove off and poured the soup down the sink. From the cabinet I got a tin basin, filled it with lukewarm water and carried it carefully to the room. I went to the linen closet and took out some modest bleached white towels. With the sacredness of a priest preparing his vestments, I unfolded the towels one by one on my shoulders. I removed the sheets and blankets from her bed and peeled off her thick flannel nightgown. I toweled her puzzled face, stretching out the wrinkles, removing the coils of her neck, toweled her shoulders and breasts. Then I changed the water. I returned to towel the creases of her stretch-marked stomach, her sporadic vaginal hairs, and her sagging thighs. I removed the lint from between her toes and noticed a mapped birthmark on the fold of her buttock. The scars on her back, which were as thin as the life lines on the palms of her hands, made me realize how little I really knew of Abuelita. I covered her with a thin blanket and went into the bathroom. I washed my hands, turned on the tub faucets and watched the water pour into the tub with vitality and steam. When it was full, I turned off the water and undressed. Then I went to get Abuelita.

She was not as heavy as I thought and when I carried her in my arms, her body fell into a V. And yet my legs were tired, shaky, and I felt as if the distance between the bedroom and bathroom was miles and years away. Amá, where are you?

I stepped into the bathtub one leg first, then the other. I bent my knees slowly to descend into the water slowly so I wouldn't scald her skin. There, there, Abuelita, I said, cradling her, smoothing her as we descended, I heard you. Her hair fell back and spread across the water like eagles' wings. The water in the tub overflowed and poured onto the tile of the floor. Then the moths came. Small gray ones that came from her soul and out through her mouth fluttering to light, circling the single dull light bulb of the bathroom. Dying is lonely and I wanted to go to where the moths were, stay with her and plant chayotes whose vines would crawl up her fingers and into the clouds; I wanted to rest my head on her chest with her stroking my hair, telling me about the moths that lay within the soul and slowly eat the spirit up; I wanted to return to the waters of the womb with her so that we would never be alone again. I wanted. I wanted my Amá. I removed a few strands of hair from Abuelita's face and held her small light head within the hollow of my neck. The bathroom was filled with moths, and for the first time in a long time I cried, rocking us, crying for her, for me, for Amá, the sobs emerging from the depths of anguish, the misery of feeling half-born, sobbing until finally the sobs rippled into circles and circles of sadness and relief. There, there, I said to Abuelita, rocking us gently, there, there.

Writings

Book of Short Stories: *The Moths and Other Stories,* Arte Público Press, 1985; 1995. **Novel:** *Under the Feet of Jesus,* Dutton, 1995. **Anthologies:** *Chicana Creativity & Criticism: Charting New Frontiers in American Literature,* co-edited with María Herrera-Sobek, Arte Público Press, 1987; University of New Mexico, 1995. *Chicana Writes: On Word & Film,* co-edited with María Herrera-Sobek, Third Woman Press, 1995. **Films:** *Champ,* American Film Institute, 1991. **Stories:** In *The Americas Review, Third Woman, Cuentos: Stories by Latinas, Woman of Her Word: Hispanic Women Write, L.A. Weekly, The Harper Anthology of Fiction, An Anthology of Multicultural American Writings, Imagining America: Stories of the Promised Land, Growing Up Latino, New Worlds of Literature, The Heath Anthology of American Literature,* and other magazines, anthologies, and textbooks.

Jose Yglesias

One of the pioneers of English-language Hispanic literature, it can also be said that Yglesias was the first writer with a Cuban American consciousness. For more than thirty years, he wrote novels and stories based on Hispanic life in the United States, and he saw them published by some of the largest and most respected publishing houses in the country.

Jose Yglesias was born in the cigar-making community of Ybor City, a section of Tampa, Florida, on November 29, 1919. He was the child of a Cuban mother and a Spanish father who returned home to Galicia when Yglesias was only a child. Among the cigar rollers, a proud and intellectual lot of workers if ever there was one, he learned about Hispanic literature, history, and politics—interests that would inform his fiction and non-fiction. And like the tobacco workers, Yglesias was largely self-educated. Two days after graduating from high school, he went to New York City; after serving in the Navy (1942–45) during World War II, he attended Black Mountain College for one year (1946–47). He returned to New York City in 1948, married, and began a family while he worked for a pharmaceutical company, where he eventually became an executive.

During the 1950s, Yglesias began writing reviews and articles for magazines and, in 1963, saw his first novel published: *A Wake in Ybor City,* which, like most first novels, is highly autobiographical. Yglesias soon became a full-time writer—of stories for such magazines as *The New Yorker, Esquire, The Atlantic, The Nation,* and *The Sunday Times Magazine*; of novels that deal mostly with

Hispanics in the U.S.; and of journalistic, non-fiction books about such topics as Franco's Spain and Castro's Cuba. Two of his stories are included in *Best American Stories* and form a part of his posthumous collection, *The Guns in the Closet* (1996), the title story of which originally appeared in *The New Yorker* (and is included in this anthology as well). In all, he wrote ten books of fiction, three of which were published posthumously. Yglesias died of cancer in December, 1995. Aside from his literary legacy, he also left behind a son, Rafael Yglesias, who is a distinguished novelist and screenwriter/director.

Jose Yglesias's first book, the novel *A Wake in Ybor City,* stands out as groundbreaking and will have its third reprint edition in 1997. It covers three days in the life of a Cuban American family in Ybor City in 1958; a series of crises threatens to rocks the foundation of this close-knit family. In addition to concentrating on the texture of family life, Yglesias also focuses on the male role in the Hispanic matriarchal family. If *A Wake in Ybor City* (1963) harkens back to Yglesias's upbringing in Tampa, *An Orderly Life* (1968) presents his alter-ego Rafael Sabas narrating (in first person) his pursuit of the American Dream and his climb up the ladder at a pharmaceutical company in New York. The novel criticizes the corporate life and the Latino male's pursuit of manhood (*machismo*). In *The Truth about Them* Yglesias's focus returns to the Cuban-American family, but this time the story goes back to 1890 in the cigar factories of Ybor City. The narrator, another Yglesias alter-ego, is a left-wing journalist who, in search of his Latin roots, visits Castro's Cuba. *The Truth about Them* is one of the first novels about the search for roots, a theme that occupied Hispanic literature in this country during the 1970s and 1980s.

In 1964, Yglesias traveled with his wife Helen and their eleven-year-old son Rafael to Galicia, Spain, where Yglesias retraced the derails of his father's birth and death there. The result of this trip was *The Goodbye Land* (1967). A reviewer in the *Times Literary Supplement* described the book as "a son's journey to the village where his father's last years were spent . . . . It has its own quiet suspense and the discovery of facts; more important, it has the very delicately registered sense of self discovery."

Double Double is Yglesias's first novel without a Hispanic setting or protagonist. It represents his attempt to understand the turbulent 1960s in American life. However serious the intent may have been, the novel tends to satirize and indict the hypocrisy as well as the idealism of its protagonist and first-person narrator, Seth Evergood. In *The Kill Price,* which is set against César Chávez's farm worker movement, Yglesias takes up death and dying. Death manifests itself in many ways here, but its most potent manifestation is metaphorical: the rejection of self-knowledge, denial. The theme of death and dying reappears in Yglesias' last novel, *The Old Gents* (1996), which was written during his last days when he was terminally ill with cancer. This time, the story is a bittersweet take on an aged nov-

elist's renewed instinct for living, even to the extent that he becomes infatuated with a young actress.

In *Break-In,* also published posthumously in 1996, Yglesias created a retired, Cuban American fire chief who, despite his latent racism, grapples with his sense of social responsibility in deciding to take an African American teenager under his wing. Yglesias provided a warm, humorous, and humane response to the problem of racism in our society; it was a parting gesture from one of America's most candid and kind observers of the human comedy.

Personal Stats

Cuban American writer, businessman. **Born:** November 29, 1919, in Tampa, Florida. **Died:** December, 1995, in New York City. **Education:** Attended Black

Mountain College, 1946–47. **Career:** Dishwasher, stock clerk, assembly line worker, and typist-correspondent, 1937–42; film critic, *Daily Worker,* New York, New York, 1948–50; Merck, Sharpe & Dohme International (pharmaceutical company), 1953–63. **Memberships:** PEN, Writers Guild, American Writers Union. **Awards/Honors:** Guggenheim Fellowships, 1970 and 1976; National Endowment for the Arts Creative Writing Fellowship, 1974.

The Guns in the Closet

from *The Guns in the Closet,* Arte Público Press, 1997

Until now, Tony believed he had been liberated by his Venezuelan grandfather's name—freed to be the special person that for years he unthinkingly felt himself to be. Ybarra. "Basque, you know," he would say when the subject came up. He was an editor in a New York publishing house, and author of an occasional essay, and it was understood, especially by European editors visiting his office, that his name set him apart from—well, whatever American foolishness or provinciality or philistinism infected the scene at the moment. He was aware that there was more than a trace of snobbery in this; aware, too, of the defensive residue, for he never forgot the discrimination that his name had subjected him to—mild, he admitted—during his adolescence in New York public schools and even at Harvard, though never in publishing, he liked to believe. Motel desk clerks in New England and the Midwest still took a second look at him when they noticed the name on the charge card, and allowed his appearance and his speech to convince them that he was all right. Those tiny encounters when he stood for inspection kept him, he thought, open to the world of the ghettos—the blacks, Puerto Ricans, and Chicanos—and it pleased him that his son Bill, who he had made sure learned Spanish fluently, should have lately come alive to the name. It amused him when Bill referred to himself in company—so as not, perhaps, to be challenged by his parents—as a Third World person. Today, Tony was uneasy.

Bill had come down from the apartment near Columbia University that he shared with other students—like him, activists who had been suspended after the campus strike—to have Sunday brunch at home. A surprise, for these were not family brunches, and Tony knew that Bill could no longer bear the two or three writers and editors, all West Side liberal neighbors, who would be there. "It's the Third World that's important, not the American moral conscience!" he had yelled one Sunday three months earlier. "Up the NLF!" And he had not been back since. Today, Bill sat out the two pitchers of Bloody Marys, the quiche, the fruit salad, the French loaves and cheeses from Zabar's, and tension grew between him and Tony as suppressed as Bill's opinions were today.

Tony thought about his old friend Clifford, who would have been here if he were not in Algiers on a writing assignment. "Dear chaps, you're luckier with Bill than others are with their children," he'd said the last time Tony ant his wife, Gale, had discussed Bill with him. *"They deal* with their kids as if they were a declining power negotiating with a newly emerged nation. The new diplomacy, right?"

Right. Tony saw that Gale had caught him studying Bill, and he smiled thinly, as if to say *Don't ask me*. And Bill of course intercepted all this and, unseen by the guests, winked at his parents, as if he in turn were replying *I'm here, that's all*. But later, when the others had left, he offered to go down with his father to walk the dog, and Gale exclaimed triumphantly, "Aha!" Bill laughed helplessly as in the days when he was a boy and they had uncovered one of his ruses.

"Shall I take money with me?" Tony asked as if asking an audience.

"No money," Gale said.

Bill shook his head and threw up his arms. A routine family charade, and Tony decided that his anxiety was baseless. But when Bill was saying good-bye, Gale took the boy's head between her hands, as she had begun to do during the strike at Columbia, and kissed him. Trouble, Tony thought; she always knows.

Going down in the elevator, both quiet in the presence of other tenants, Tony noticed that Bill wore a J. Press jacket he had not seen in a long time. No army fatigue jacket. His hair was almost short, his pants were not jeans, his shoes were not work boots, and there were no Panther buttons on his chest. He seemed to have abandoned the new life-style, and it surprised Tony that his son's appearance did not please him; he looked ordinary.

Ordinary? Then he must not be a Weatherman. Thinking about Bill afflicted Tony with non sequiturs. "Bill, you don't have money to keep your apartment, do you?" he said. "You're not there anymore. We haven't been able to reach you for two weeks."

Bill shook his head. "No," he said, "but I don't want to be up there anymore."

So he was downtown. "Are you in a commune?"

Bill pulled the dog toward Riverside Drive. "Too many people on Broadway," he explained, and crossed the Drive to the park. When Tony caught up with him, he was bending down to unleash the dog and let him run.

"Well, are you in a commune?" Tony asked, and smiled to appear casual.

From his bent position, Bill looked up and smiled a mocking smile; he shook his head. Tony was not reassured—not even when Bill straightened, threw out his arms, and took a deep breath, as if that was what he had come out for. Bill began to jog down the path to the esplanade and motioned his father on. "Good for you!" he called, and again he went through the motions of inhaling and exhaling with vigor.

When Tony got to him, he said, "Listen Dad, I'd like to bring some stuff down tonight from my place. For you to keep for me. Just for a couple of days."

There were people brushing by. "Sure," Tony said, thinking it was books or clothes. "We're not going out. Anyway, you have a key." Bill looked at him so seriously that Tony stopped, suspicious again. "What stuff?"

Bill turned his head away. They were alone on the path now. "Guns," he said quietly.

Later, Tony wished he could have seen his son's face when he said that, but only the back of his neck was in view. There were wet leaves on the ground, and everything was still. Then a burst of laughter from a group of young people who appeared in the path on their way out of the park. They crowded Tony to one side and gave him time to think. I must not show my fear, he thought, especially my fear for him. But the questions burst out of him like exclamations. "They're not yours, are they? Whose are they?"

"No questions like that," Bill said. In a moment, he added, "Of course they don't belong to *me*."

"I see," Tony said, subdued. They had come onto the esplanade and there were people everywhere, walking their dogs, sitting on the benches, or simply strolling. Tony did not know whether it was their presence that forced him to speak casually, that created a new equality between him and Bill, or the boundaries that Bill had set up. I do not own this part of him, he thought; I can say yes or no, but that is all. He had liked being a father and it shamed him now that he was elated, as he walked alongside him, to find that Bill had his own mysterious corners, his own densities.

Finally, he said, "I shall have to talk to Gale first. It's her decision, too." He had never, with Bill, called Gale anything but "your mother," and he knew he was being mean in his new equality. Both to Bill and to his wife. Bill could walk away from their lives—perhaps even should—but parentage cannot be removed. He reached out and touched Bill's shoulder.

"O.K.," Bill said. "You tell me when I phone you later."

But he had come to me—*me*—and in the wind that blew from the river Tony's eyes teared. "You said they were at your place," he said. "Is that uptown?"

Bill nodded.

"And your friends living there—do they know?"

Bill exhaled and began his explanations. "They were away last weekend and the FBI broke in. The kids next door told them about it. The agents went through their apartment to get to the fire escape—it's kind of hard to get into ours with the locks I have on the door—and the kids came home while the agents were there. The super had let the two of them in, but the kids told them to get out. So the pieces have to be removed right away. They were just lying under the bed in duffel bags—they must have seen them. My friends have been trying to get to me all week."

"And the apartment is in your name!"

Bill did not answer.

"You can bring them," Tony said. "It will be all right with your mother, I'm sure."

"O.K.," Bill said. "I have to go now." He handed his father the leash. "I'll call you tonight." The dog followed him, and he turned back after a few paces. "Listen, when I call I'll ask if I can sleep over and tell you how soon I'll be there. You be down on the street when I arrive."

"All right," Tony said, and the sound of his voice was so strange to him that he leaned down to hold the dog to hide his sensation. Bill's legs did not move away, so Tony looked up and saw him bring a hand up to his waist and make it into a fist quickly, casually.

"All power to the people," Bill said in a conversational voice. Then he smiled, in order, as they said in their family, to take the curse off it. "See you."

Alone, Tony felt cool and light-headed. He wanted to run and did, and the dog ran after him. Nothing unusual—the kind of sprint that men walking dogs in the park will often break into. During the war, he had reacted this way when, as pilot on a scout observation plane, he climbed to the catwalk and into his plane to be catapulted from the ship: his hands checked the canopy, the stick between his legs—all concentration while his emotions unreeled without control and unrelated images flitted in and out of his mind. He knew only that he was being observed and that he must be true to some unconfessed vision of himself.

He walked back to the apartment slowly. How to tell Gale. Dinner guests would have to be put off. Last summer, the caretaker of the Maine estate they rented had asked him what kind of name his was, and when he replied that it was Spanish—no use saying Basque—the old man had said, "Spanish! Now, there's nothing wrong with that, is there?" The guns must go in the closet in his study—that was one place their thirteen-year-old daughter, who now should be back from her friend's apartment, never looked.

In the elevator, he thought, But if *they* didn't come back to the apartment with warrants, then they must have a reason to wait. Do they hope to catch Bill? Do they have a watch on the place and if Bill walks out in a few hours with . . . He would not say this to Gale. She was lying on the living room couch with the Sunday Times, and he got a pad and pen and sat next to her and wrote out the conversation—the gist of it—he had had with Bill.

Gale smiled when he handed it to her but when she had read it she sat up. "But—" she began. Behind her came the wail of a Beatles record from their daughter's room.

Tony put a finger to his lips. "Not here," he said.

The color went out of her face. "I've got to go out for a cup of coffee," she said. "Right now!"

They walked up and down Broadway and sat in a coffee shop and talked. She wanted to be angry at someone. "Couldn't you have brought him back to the apartment?" she said.

Tony felt like putting his head in his hands. "I didn't think . . ."

She waved a hand defeatedly, in understanding. "And there's no way of getting in touch with him?"

By the time they returned to the apartment, the exhilaration he had first felt was gone. They were no sooner inside than Gale had to take up the pad and write on it a warning about their daughter. She must not know unless it is absolutely necessary. He nodded, noticing the misspelling. And the cleaning woman who came three times a week, she wrote. She must be kept out of his study. He nodded again and took the sheet from the pad and went into the small bath off the study and tore it into small pieces and flushed them down the toilet. Thank God, Gale had not thought of the danger to Bill when he removed the guns from the apartment uptown.

Tony sat in the study and knew that Gale was restlessly tidying the apartment. Later, he heard her on the phone calling off the evening's appointment, arguing with their daughter to keep her from having friends in. Then silence. He could not read or write. He kept visualizing the walkup near Columbia, which he had visited only three or four times. So many of the tenants were young people moving in and out that surely duffel bags would attract no attention. He thought of the solution: a decoy. Someone must first leave with the duffel bags that had been under the bed but with something else in them. Of course. He got up from his chair to tell Gale. No. It was Bill he should get to. Run up to the apartment? Ten minutes by taxi. Gale wouldn't notice.

He had taken his jacket out of the hall closet when he realized that he dare not be seen up there today. Which of Bill's friends could he call? Which of them had gone this far with him in his politics? He did not know. He told Gale, who was lying on the couch again, that he was going down for cigarettes. She looked blank, then questioning, and Tony smiled and shook his head. From a street booth, he called a friend of Bill's who had been with him in the Columbia strike. The operator came on and asked what number he was calling. He told her—safe enough in a public booth, he thought. In a moment, she came back on to say the number had been disconnected. When he got back to the apartment, Gale did not look up from the couch. As he put his jacket back in the closet he saw that she would not look up. She had thought of the danger.

He went to his study and tried not to think. There was a manuscript in his briefcase that one of the young editors liked. Another book on Vietnam. They already had one for the winter list. It was foolish not to talk aloud to Gale in the apartment. He could not believe the FBI had time to listen to his phone, to the hours of his daughter's, his wife's, and his own conversations, just because of Bill. He remembered a manuscript on surveillance that his house had turned down. To cover the whole apartment, the sound would have to be transmitted to a nearby station no more than two or three blocks away, to be either recorded or monitored. Thank God, he was not a paranoid left-winger.

Yet when the phone rang at eleven forty-five and he heard Bill say, "Dad?" he gave way to the fear that had made him write on the pad. He had to clear his throat before he could answer.

"Listen, Dad, I'm in the neighborhood." His voice was easy—he was a good actor. "I'm at a party and I don't want to go all the way downtown when I leave, so I'm going to do you and Mom the honor of staying with you overnight. O.K.?"

"O.K.," he said and knew he was not playing his part well. He tried to ask the question. "Bill . . ."

"I'll be there in an hour," Bill said with that touch of highhanded misuse of parents that had once been genuinely his. "Thanks," he added, out of character.

"Bill . . ." Tony began again and then did not risk it.

After a pause Bill said, "See you then," and hung up.

The next hour would tell. Tony went to the bedroom where Gale was watching a talk show and said with the casualness he had not managed on the phone that Bill was coming by in an hour to spend the night. She looked at him with the kind of reproach that women transmit with a glance when they think their men are acting like boys. He shrugged, went to the kitchen, heated some coffee, and drank it in his study. Once *this* was over, he told himself, he would make Bill have a long talk with him. There had been no battles during his adolescence—none of the rows that are usual with fathers and sons—and he did not want Bill's activities now, whatever they were, to be surrogates for them. He had been proud when Bill so suddenly, at Columbia, had become political; he had alerted everyone at the office when Bill was scheduled to appear on a program last year of the show Gale was now watching. He had not used parental concern as an excuse for trying to keep him at school or to deflect him—not even when, after Dean Rusk had spoken at the new Hilton, Bill came home battered from a fight with the cops on Sixth Avenue.

Ten minutes before the hour was up, Tony went downstairs. Between midnight and one, the doorman was always in the basement helping the janitor wheel the garbage cans onto the street by the side entrance. A police car was parked at the corner, its lights on; one cop stood at the back entrance of the bakery two doors down, waiting for the pastry they cadged each night, and the other was at the all-night diner for coffee. Tony lit a cigarette and stood at the door of the building as if he had come out for a breath of air. There were still many people on Broadway, but fewer, and the prostitutes were more visible. The cops went back to their car to drink the coffee and eat the Danish. He raised a hand in greeting when one looked his way, and both of them grinned. Nothing suspicious about me, he thought; I'm a respectable, middle-aged West Sider.

The cops pulled out as soon as they were finished, having lit cigarettes and set their faces into the withdrawn, contemptuous expressions that signified they were back on the job. A Volks station wagon turned into the street, paused, and then parked where the patrol car had been. Bill sat next to the driver; the friend Tony had tried to call earlier was behind the wheel. Tony walked over as Bill got out; his friend stayed inside and did not turn off the engine.

"Everything all right?" Tony asked.

"Great!" Bill said. He walked to the back of the car, opened the window, and beckoned with his head. There were two long leather cases lying in the car; they looked handsome and rich. "Golf clubs," Bill said, and picked up one and handed it to Tony. He took the other, fitted an arm through its strap, and carried it over one shoulder. With his free hand he waved to his friend, and the car drove off.

"Thank God, you didn't bring them in the duffel bags," Tony said, almost gaily. "I wanted to call and tell you that you should first have left the house with the duffel bags and then . . ."

"That's what we did," he said. "Sent a decoy out first."

Tony put his arm through the strap of the second case and walked alongside Bill to the entrance of the apartment building. We are the perfect picture of the middle-class father and son, he thought. I would say, seeing the two of us, that we belong to a country club in Westchester, play tennis from spring to late fall, swim, golf, of course, and keep a boat at the Seventy-ninth Street Basin. During the winter, we get together at the Athletic Club for handball, followed by a short swim in the heated pool. The son dashes out immediately after, but the father gets a rubdown and later joins two or three others his age for lunch upstairs by the wide, tall windows looking down on Central Park. Ah, yes. His Venezuelan grandfather's name and his childhood in the Spanish section of Chelsea would keep him always on a circular stage slowly revolving to the view: you never cease to act the role that the eyes of others create.

Tony said, "You're going to find your mother very upset."

"About this?" Bill said. "I'll talk to her."

"Well, not inside," Tony advised. "We've been careful to say nothing that we wouldn't want overheard."

Bill looked down, but Tony saw he was amused. "Well, Dad, it's not very likely," he said in the lobby. "Their tapping equipment must be overtaxed these days. Too many groups into heavy stuff, you know." And in the elevator he explained, in such detail that it alarmed Tony that he should know the subject so well, how you can detect with the use of an FM radio whether there is a bug in the apartment.

"We have to talk about you," Tony said. "I don't know what *you* are into, and it worries me."

"Sure, O.K.," Bill said. They were on their floor, about to turn to the door of their apartment. "Look, you know I'm grateful to you that I learned Spanish and something about the culture. I got you to thank for that." He stopped, and Tony thought there must be many things Bill did not thank him for. "But I'm a Third World person, you know, and that's how I'm going to live."

Gale was not at the front of the apartment. Tony led Bill through the dining room and kitchen to the study. They leaned the cases against the back wall of the closet, and when they closed the door on them Bill said, "It'll only be for a couple of days. We'll let you know when."

"Remember I stay home Tuesdays to read manuscripts," Tony said.

"O.K.," Bill said, nodding, and on the way to the living room turned and added, "It won't be me."

Gale was standing in the living room in her robe. She held one hand up in a fist and shook it at Bill in pretended anger. He laughed. Well, for Christ's sake, Tony thought.

She asked, "Can I make you something to eat?"

"No time, Mom," Bill said. "I've got to go."

"But you said—" Tony began.

Gale completed it: "You were staying overnight!"

Bill's expression reminded them of his old joke that his parents talked like an orchestra. "I can't. My friend is waiting for me."

"But he drove away," Tony said.

"I saw him from my window," Gale added.

"He's two blocks farther down, waiting." Bill walked over to his mother to say good-bye. "I'll be in touch."

Tony watched her hug him but could not hear what she whispered in his ear. When she let him go, she was pale and ready to cry. Tony, said, "I'm coming down with you."

In the hall, he tried to tell Bill some of the things he had thought that day. They came out badly. "I have to tell you that I don't agree with what you're doing. They're the wrong tactics. They won't work here. You don't know what real Americans are. You'll bring down the most—"

"Christ, Dad, you're not on the Susskind program." That special hardness was in his voice; Tony did not know where he got it. "You know all the arguments as well as I do. Remember the time you came off his talk show and said there's just no way to make radical change palatable to liberals like that?"

"You're not going to compare me to him!"

"Not unless you force me," Bill said, and stopped because people had got on the elevator.

In the lobby, Tony let them go ahead. He said quietly, as if making a new start, "I'm worried about what's going to happen to you."

"Don't worry, I'm learning karate," Bill said seriously; "No pig is going to run me down and twist my arm behind my back. From now on we're doing the bogarting. Twice a week I go to Connecticut to the rifle ranges and practice shooting." He laughed. "I need a lot of practice."

"What's that for!"

"I've got a very simple test for radicals," Bill said. "When I read about some radical movement, I ask, did they arm themselves, did they pick up the gun? If they didn't, they aren't serious."

On Broadway, Tony flinched when he saw a middle-aged writer coming toward them with his young wife—his third. They had the giggly look of people who have been turning on. And an after-the-party boredom with one another. Tony introduced them to Bill, and the writer made an effort to focus on him. "Pretty quiet at Columbia this year," he said. "Anything happening?"

"I wouldn't know," Bill said.

Quickly, Tony asked the writer how his new novel was doing. He began to talk about the reviews. Tony saw Bill edge away, and the writer tried to hold him by saying, "Say, you ought to take a look at it. It's a revolutionary book."

"We have to go," Tony said. "I'll call you tomorrow."

Bill was down the block and the writer called, "Read the book, kid. It'll blow your mind!"

Tony was breathless with the need to say something to his son that would somehow get to—what? He didn't know; he simply exhaled when he reached his side.

Bill shook his head. "Don't worry," he said, as if he understood. The Volks station wagon was at the corner waiting, and Bill paused. "You know, I've been down to Fourteenth Street several times, eating at the Spanish restaurants and sitting at the bars. A couple of old Republicans like Fidel, but none speak well about the Puerto Ricans." He shook his head again.

"Well . . ."

"You say your grandfather was an anarchist—right?" Bill asked. "Did you talk to him much? I got to talk to you about him. Sometime. O.K.?"

"Yes, yes," Tony said. He wondered what that old man wearing a beret while he fixes the windows and doors in the worn-out apartment and built cages for the pigeons on the roof—had thought of him and his books.

When he got back home, he found Gale lying in bed reading. He felt sure she had been to the closet in his study. She looked up when he took out his robe and began to undress. "I don't want to talk about it until they're gone," she said, "and that had better be soon or I shall go out of my mind." He didn't answer, and after a moment she asked, "When is that going to be?"

"Two days," he said, but he did not really know. He lay next to her, his arms folded over his chest, and went over everything Bill had said. He could not quite remember what was to happen. Someone would get in touch with him. There were the facts of Bill's day-to-day life to piece together. And all that rhetoric. He was going to live like a Third World person. What the hell did that mean? This is the real generation gap, he thought—you can't grab hold of these kids; they sum up your life and their own in a phrase and leave you gasping. They wrench you out of the dense element that is your daily life and there you are—on the shore, on the shore, on the shore.

At breakfast next morning, Gale announced that she was going to do volunteer work at the public school all week. Penance for sending their own to private schools, but also this week, he suspected, to be out of the way.

Tony went to the office late. There had been no call at the apartment, and there was no call here, either. He returned early with three manuscripts to read the next day. Again, no call. Gale was not home and he took the dog and headed for the Drive, as if that would help him recall his talk with Bill. He let the dog loose and stood at the parapet at the esplanade and smoked and stared at the river.

A short dark man who looked to Tony like a typical Puerto Rican came over with an unlit cigarette, asking for a light. Tony handed him his cigarette and he held it delicately and took a light from it. He looked Tony directly in the eye when he thanked him. He did not walk away but turned to study the river, too, and it was then Tony realized that the man had spoken to him in Spanish. "If you are home tomorrow morning," he said now, still in Spanish, "someone will come to pick up the packages you have been so kind to hold for us."

Tony smiled in a kind of reflex and found that he could not turn on his fake smile. He thought, This is a trap; I must get away. Instead, he replied in Spanish, "For us?"

"Your son did not tell you whose they are?" He had the sweet accent of Puerto Ricans.

Tony shook his head.

The man said, "MIRA. Have you heard of us?"

Tony nodded. The bombings in the Bronx. An underground terrorist group operating in New York. A bad manuscript called "Colonies in the Mother Country" had mentioned them. Crazily, he wondered if he had been right to reject it.

The man seemed to watch all this going on in his head, and as if to help him added, "We are madmen."

"Talk to me," Tony said and pointed to a bench. "What about my son?"

"Your son?" The man waited for him to sit first, bowing a little and standing to one side. "But you must know better than we do—if he trusted you with packages. What can I tell you?"

"We are very worried about his activities," Tony replied. "I do not want you to divulge anything that is confidential but if you can tell me something . . ."

"Oh, there do not have to be any mysteries between us," the man said, and looked around at a man going by with a dog. He waited until he had passed. "Your son is very much of an Hispano. He is closer in feeling to us, he says, than to any of the others."

"Others?"

"The other revolutionary groups," he explained. "American ones. We are all in touch. He is a liaison man with us. There are certain things that a Puerto Rican cannot do. It looks funny for us to be in certain places or buy certain things. Too conspicuous. You understand?"

Tony nodded and looked at the river, trying to place Bill in all this. His dog came back to the bench and the man leaned down and patted him. "What a friendly little dog he is," he said. "My younger brother was killed in the independence uprising after the war. Just one of the many killed in Puerto Rican towns all over the island . . . One of our problems is getting guns to comrades on the island," he said inconsequentially, talking as if this might help Tony. "What better proof that we are an oppressed colony than the fact that guns, which are so easy to come by in these states, are almost impossible for Puerto Ricans to obtain."

"The laws are not the same?" Tony said.

"Jesus Christ himself could not qualify to own a gun there."

Tony took out a pack of cigarettes and offered it. The Puerto Rican accepted with the grace that only a Latin seems able to put into such a gesture. "I admired your article on the Latin-

American revolutionaries very much," he said, and Tony was startled—could this man have read the quarterly where he had published two essays in the last five years? "The one on their situation after the death of Che. I had not known that wonderful saying of Marti's: 'El arbor que mas crece es el que tiene un muerto por debajo.'" ("The tree that grows tallest has a dead man buried beneath it.")

"That is what I fear," Tony said.

The man squinted and then struck himself on the forehead. "What a fool I am! You ask me about your son, you are worried like a good father, and all I talk about is dying and killing. Forgive me, compañero." They were quiet a moment. The Puerto Rican looked at his cigarette and flicked the ash off it carefully. "It is true that for us it is especially necessary to think about the possibility of death, to get used to it even. But that is not what interests us—that does not interest us one bit."

"Forgive me if I tell you that I do not think you have a chance," Tony said.

"That, too, does not interest us," the Puerto Rican replied very gently, in a tone that seemed solely concerned with Tony's feelings.

Tony got up, and because he was suddenly ashamed at the abruptness with which he was ending their talk extended his hand.

The man took it in both of his. "I know what it is you are too polite to say," he said. "That your son is not a Puerto Rican. But do you not find that wonderful? Is not that the best guarantee that we will win this time? Look, those Young Lords in the barrio want to free Puerto Rico, too, but almost none of them can really speak Spanish. Some of the older nationalists cannot believe in them, but I say it is what is here"—he stopped to place a hand on his own heart—"that matters."

"I wish you success," Tony said.

The man nodded slowly, solemnly. Then he smiled. "Perhaps we shall see one another again. If you go to the island to write one of your studies, there are people we would like you to meet. See what Yankees we have become—we know the value of publicity now, even if only among the professors who read the magazines where you publish." He laughed and added, "At ten tomorrow morning then, a girl will ask you one more favor—to help her take the packages to her car."

It was Gale's custom to look at him carefully when she greeted him—her way of asking for news—but today she began a story about a Taiwanese child at school, so pointedly, Tony felt, that it was a rebuff. When she stopped, he said, "Tomorrow."

She stepped over to him and pecked him on the cheek. "How do you know?" she whispered.

He lied. "Bill called."

The phone rang, and Gale picked it up. "Cliff!" she exclaimed.

"Tell him to come over," Tony called. Back from Algiers, thank God—the one person he could talk to about all this.

"He heard you," Gale said, "but he hasn't unpacked."

Tony insisted, as eager as when they had been undergraduates, "Tell him to come over and we'll open cans for dinner—I want to discuss business."

Clifford had spent a month in Algiers talking to Eldridge Cleaver. The last time they had spent an old-fashioned evening together, Tony had come up with the idea of the trip, and he did want to know if Clifford was going to get a book out of it. He wanted to talk about simultaneous hardcover and paperback publication, but it was really the chance to spend the evening with something in mind other than the guns in the closet that attracted him. And the possibility that Clifford could help with Bill.

Clifford had got a bottle of Cuban añejo through customs and he held it out in greeting. "Limes and Seven-Up!" he called. "I feel like my comic-strip name—Clifford Moon!"

Gale said, "You don't look it!"

He was wearing a Pierre Cardin vest suit and a flowered silk shirt with wide sleeves. In the month he had been away his sideburns had grown long and bushy; his mustache curved over the corners of his lips. He stretched out on a chair and showed his Moroccan slippers—sheepskin with embroidery.

"In Algiers everyone is stoned all the time," Clifford said, beginning on his first Mojito—a Cuban drink he had brought back from trips made to cover the Cuban revolution. "You really should have fresh mint for this, but it'll do. They just don't know what the joys of drinking are in Algiers. I think I shall have to take a stand against hash, pot, grass—what inelegant names! It turns everyone into lobotomized types."

"Never mind all that," Tony said. "Have you got a book?"

"Dear chaps, I've scarcely been allowed to turn the experience over in my mind," he replied, and he let his arms droop down the sides of his chair. "I haven't even called my agent."

Tony waved a hand. "Oh, your agent—we've already discussed it."

"Did he say there won't be any minimum royalty on the paperback?" Clifford asked, sitting forward.

"Well . . ."

"I want more than the five per cent for my share," Clifford said. He laughed. "I'm getting myself a fur coat this winter."

"Well!" Tony said, and he didn't know if it was envy that made him decide then that he could not discuss Bill.

Gale said, "Let's drive down to Washington together for the Kent State demonstration. Or do you have to work?"

"Yes, no—yes!" Clifford said. "Dear me, I mean yes. There'll be beautiful young people there from all over the country. They're bound to get stoned and disrobe—like Woodstock. And I can work that into the book." He picked up his drink from the floor and looked slyly at Tony over the rim of his glass. "How the revolution sells nowadays. Though I don't know to whom. The young don't read. I daresay it's the anxious middle-aged who want to know what their children are doing. In the fifties they would've gone to their analysts. This is better for us." He looked sly again. "Right, chaps?"

Promptly at ten the next morning, the downstairs buzzer sounded. Alone in the apartment, Tony opened the door, and a few minutes later watched the girl walk from the elevator toward him. She wore a maxi raincoat unbuttoned over a mini skirt. Her legs were stunning. "Is everything all right?" he asked.

"Oh, hi!" she said, delighted. "I'm parked just across from you."

He had thought that if she was alone he would have to make two trips with the cases, but she touched her right biceps and said, "Muscles," and took one of them. Tony watched the doorman study her legs when he held the door open for them. Damn. The writer whose new novel was just out was on the sidewalk—alone this time.

"Hey!" the writer said. "You didn't call."

"Stay right there," Tony said, following the girl. "I'll be right back." She opened the trunk of a Mercedes Benz at the opposite curb, and while he placed his case in it Tony was aware that the writer watched them.

She brushed her long hair back when she straightened, and said, "Thanks."

"O.K.?" Tony said, wondering if he should shake hands.

"A message from Bill—he won't be in touch for a while," she said with a smile.

"What!" he said.

"Your friend is waiting," she said, and turned away.

He hovered as she got in behind the wheel. "Tell him we want to see him, please," he said, and watched her smile in that nonwavering, idiotic way.

When he got back to the writer, they watched her drive off. Without looking at him, the writer said, "You play golf?"

"Me?" Tony asked. "Oh no, just helping a neighbor."

"Wow!" he replied. "You got that in your building!"

When Tony walked into the apartment, it felt eerie, like the time they returned from the theater to find that someone had broken in. He went straight to the study and closed the door to the closet. He could not concentrate on the manuscripts he had brought home. He made a cup of coffee and tried to think of what Bill's message meant. He would not tell Gale. On the radio in the study, the news commentators said that the national revulsion against the Kent State killings was escalating. The third time he heard the same news on the hour break, he turned the radio off and remembered Bill's instructions about how to find a tapping bug. He flicked the radio on again and dialed to the low end of the band and slowly moved up. On the third try, he caught a faint beep. He held the dial there; it built in volume. With both hands he picked up the radio and moved it in the direction of the wall phone. The beep became steadier and louder: the tap was there. With shaking hands Tony put the radio back on its shelf and turned it off. Something else to keep to himself.

Later in the week, he and Gale went to Washington with Clifford and walked among the young people on the green. He looked for Bill, letting Gale and Clifford sit through the speeches while he roamed. He came back exhausted, and when Gale said, "Aren't they beautiful?" he could only nod, because his eyes were full of tears and his throat was tight. He felt better for being there, but on the way home anxiety returned; and each time a bomb exploded that winter he fought back the desire to call the police and find out, before the *Times* got to the stands, who was involved. He went to all the demonstrations. They were dear to him. He looked at the young people, no longer searching for his son, who had never called, and said inwardly, over and over, without irony, accepting his country at last while he repeated Bill's name in Spanish—Guillermo Ybarra—*I commend my son, fellow Americans, to your care.*

Writings

Novels: A Wake in Ybor City, Holt, Rinehart and Winston, 1963; Arno Press, 1980. *An Orderly Life,* Pantheon Books, 1968. *The Truth about Them,* World Publishers, 1971. *Double, Double,* Viking Press, 1974. *The Kill Price,* Bobbs-Merrill, 1976. *Home Again,* Arbor House, 1987. *Tristan and the Hispanics,* Simon & Schuster, 1989. *Break-In,* Arte Público Press, 1996. *The Old Gents,* Arte Público Press, 1997. **Short Fiction:** *Guns in the Closet,* Arte Público Press, 1997. **Nonfiction:** *The Goodbye Land,* Pantheon Books, 1967. *Down There,* World Publishing Company, 1970. *In the Fist of the Revolution: Life in a Cuban Country Town,* Pantheon Books, 1968. *The Franco Years,* Bobbs-Merrill, 1977. **Short Stories:** In *The New Yorker, The Nation, Esquire,* and *The New York Times Magazine.*

Sources

Algarín, Miguel, and Miguel Piñero, eds. *Nuyorican Poetry: An Anthology of Puerto Rican Words and Feelings.* Morrow, 1975.

Candelaria, Cordelia. *Chicano Poetry: A Critical Introduction.* Greenwood, 1986.

Dictionary of Hispanic Biography. Gale Research, 1996.

Dictionary of Literary Biography: Chicano Writers. Vols. 82 and 122, 1989 and 1992, Gale Research.

Fernández, José, and Roberto Fernández. *Bibliographical Index of Cuban Authors.* Universal, 1983.

Flores, Juan. *Divided Borders: Essays on Puerto Rican Identity.* Arte Público Press, 1993.

Francisco, Lomelí. *Chicano Literature.* Greenwood Press, 1984.

Herrera-Sobek, María. *Beyond Stereotypes: The Critical Analysis of Chicana Literature.* Bilingual Press, 1985.

Hispanic Writers. Gale Research, 1991. *(Note: Most of the author quotes appearing in the margins of* The Hispanic Literary Companion *were found in this source.)*

Horno-Delgado, Asunción, et al, eds. *Latina Writings and Critical Readings.* University of Massachusetts, 1989.

Kanellos, Nicolás. *Dictionary of Hispanic Literature of the United States.* Greenwood Press.

———*Hispanic Almanac: From Columbus to Corporate America.* Visible Ink Press, 1994.

———, ed. *Short Fiction by Hispanic Writers of the United States.* Arte Público Press, 1993.

———, and Claudio Esteva-Fabregat, *Handbook of Hispanic Culture in the United States,* 4 vols. Arte Público Press, 1994–1995.

————, with Cristelia Perez. *Chronology of Hispanic American History.* Gale Research, 1995.

Roberta Fernández, ed. *In Other Words: Literature by Latinas.* Arte Público Press, 1995.

Hospital, Carolina, ed. *Los Atrevidos: Cuban American Writers.* Linden Lane Press, 1989.

Rodríguez de Laguna, Asela, ed. *Images and Identities: The Puerto Rican in Two World contexts.* Transaction Books, 1987.

Tatum, Charles. *Chicano Literature.* Twayne, 1983.

Valdez, Luis, and Stan Steiner. *Aztlán: An Anthology of Mexican American Literature.* Random House, 1972.

Who's Who Among Hispanic Americans, 1994–95. Gale Research, 1994.

Index